China, the European Union and Global Governance

LEUVEN GLOBAL GOVERNANCE

Series Editor: Jan Wouters, *University of Leuven, Belgium*

The *Leuven Global Governance* series comprises high-quality monographs and edited volumes dedicated to innovative research on global governance. The series focuses particularly on the following themes: European Union and global multilateral governance; trade and sustainable development; peace and security studies; human rights, democracy and the rule of law; space governance and comparative federalism. In full recognition of the complex issues involved, the series favours studies approaching global governance from a multidisciplinary, multi-level and multi-actor perspective.

Titles in the series include:

Private Standards and Global Governance: Economic, Legal and Political Perspectives
Edited by Axel Marx, Miet Maertens, Johan Swinnen and Jan Wouters

China, the European Union and Global Governance
Edited by Jan Wouters, Tanguy de Wilde d'Estmael, Pierre Defraigne and Jean-Christophe Defraigne

China, the European Union and Global Governance

Edited by

Jan Wouters

University of Leuven (KU Leuven), Belgium

Tanguy de Wilde d'Estmael

Université catholique de Louvain, Belgium

Pierre Defraigne

Madariaga – College of Europe Foundation, Belgium

Jean-Christophe Defraigne

University Faculties of St Louis, Belgium

LEUVEN GLOBAL GOVERNANCE

Edward Elgar

Cheltenham, UK • Northampton, MA, USA

Published by
Edward Elgar Publishing Limited
The Lypiatts
15 Lansdown Road
Cheltenham
Glos GL50 2JA
UK

Edward Elgar Publishing, Inc.
William Pratt House
9 Dewey Court
Northampton
Massachusetts 01060
USA

A catalogue record for this book
is available from the British Library

Library of Congress Control Number: 2012930623

MIX
Paper from responsible sources
FSC® C018575

ISBN 978 1 78100 426 5

Printed and bound by MPG Books Group, UK

Contents

PART 3 THE WORLD FINANCIAL AND MONETARY SYSTEM

PART 4 CLIMATE CHANGE AND ENERGY

PART 5 SECURITY AND POLITICS

Contributors

ABOUT THE EDITORS

Prof. Dr ***Jan Wouters***, Director, Leuven Centre for Global Governance Studies, at the University of Leuven (KU Leuven) and InBev-Baillet Latour EU-China Chair. Jan Wouters is Professor of International Law and International Organizations, Jean Monnet Chair *Ad Personam* EU and Global Governance and Director of the Leuven Centre for Global Governance Studies and Institute for International Law, KU Leuven. He is Visiting Professor at Sciences Po and the College of Europe, President of the Flemish Foreign Affairs Council and *Of Counsel* at Linklaters. He is a Member of the Royal Flemish Academy of Belgium for Sciences and Arts. He studied law and philosophy in Antwerp and Yale University (LLM 1990), was a Visiting Researcher at Harvard Law School and obtained his PhD at KU Leuven (1996). He taught at the Universities of Antwerp and Maastricht, was Visiting Professor at Liège and Kyushu University and *Référendaire* at the European Court of Justice (1991–94).

Prof. Dr ***Tanguy de Wilde d'Estmael***, Institute for European Studies and InBev-Baillet Latour EU–China Chair, Université catholique de Louvain (UCL). Tanguy de Wilde is Professor of International Relations and European Politics at the UCL. He is President of the Louvain School of Political and Social Sciences and Director of the InBev-Baillet Latour EU–Russia and EU–China Chairs. A Member of the European Studies Institutes (UCL-FUSL), he is a Visiting Professor at the College of Europe in Bruges (Department of EU International Relations and Diplomacy Studies). Tanguy de Wilde has been Director of the Centre d'études des crises et des conflits internationaux (CECRI-UCL from 2001 to 2007) and a Visiting Professor in Paris, Tunis, Geneva, Beirut and Toulouse.

Mr ***Pierre Defraigne***, Executive Director, Madariaga – College of Europe Foundation. Pierre Defraigne has been Executive Director of the Madariaga – College of Europe Foundation since April 2008. An economist and European civil servant from 1970 to 2005, he retired as Deputy Director-General in DG Trade in March 2005 after having been Head of Cabinet for Pascal Lamy, European Commissioner for Trade

(1999–2002). Previously, he was Director for North–South Relations and Head of Cabinet for Etienne Davignon, Vice-President of the European Commission (1977–83). He set up the Brussels branch of the French Institute for International Relations (Eur-Ifri), which he managed from 2005 to 2008. Pierre Defraigne is a lecturer in economics at the College of Europe (Bruges) and at the Institute for European Studies (UCL and FUSL). He is also a Visiting Professor at Zhejiang University (China). His interests focus on international economic policies, political economy and relations with developing countries.

Prof. Dr ***Jean-Christophe Defraigne***, Institute for European Studies, University Faculties of St Louis, Brussels. Jean-Christophe Defraigne holds a PhD in Economics from the University of Brussels. In 2003–4, he was research fellow at the University of International Business and Economics of Beijing (Jing Mao Da Xue, formerly known as the University of MOFCOM/MOFTEC) on EU–China economic relations and on the comparison of regional integration processes in Europe and Asia. He has also been a research expert for China's Zhejiang government, the *JETRO* and *Notre Europe*. He is currently Professor in Economics at the Institute for European Studies of St Louis-Brussels University and Visiting Professor at Zhejiang University and at the Louvain School of Management. His research focuses on the comparative analysis of technological changes and industrial and trade policies in Europe, the USA and East Asia.

ABOUT THE CONTRIBUTORS

Prof. Dr ***Michel Aglietta***, Université de Nanterre, Paris X and Counsellor at CEPII. Professor Aglietta is Emeritus Professor at the University of Paris-X Nanterre and scientific advisor for the Center of International Studies and Forecasting (CEPII), and for Groupama-am. He is a former member of the French Council of Economic Advisors attached to the Prime Minister and former senior member of the Institut Universitaire de France. His most recent books are: *Corporate Governance Adrift*, with A. Rebérioux (Edward Elgar, 2005); *Désordres dans le capitalisme mondial*, with A. Berrebi (Odile Jacob, 2007); *Macroéconomie Financière* (5th edn entirely revised), Collection Grands Repères, La Découverte, 2008); *La Crise* (Michalon, November 2008); *Crise et rénovation de la Finance*, with Sandra Rigot (Odile Jacob, 2009); *Les hedge funds: entrepreneurs ou requins de la finance?*, with Sabrina Khanniche and Sandra Rigot (Perrin, 2010).

Dr ***Elena Atanassova-Cornelis***, Research Fellow and Lecturer, KU Leuven, UCL and Antwerp University. Elena Atanassova-Cornelis holds a PhD in Japanese Studies (2007) from KU Leuven where she is at present a Research Fellow. She teaches courses on 'Geopolitical and Strategic Issues of Northeast Asia' at the Université Catholique de Louvain (UCL) and 'East Asian International Relations' at the University of Antwerp (UA), Belgium. She has also lectured at Ghent University, Belgium, and the Brussels School of International Studies (BSIS) of the University of Kent, UK. Her research interests include contemporary Japanese foreign policy and East Asian international relations with a special focus on security. She currently focuses on Japan's national security transformation, Japan–China–US security relations, and the evolution of a new security order in East Asia. She also examines non-traditional security issues in Asia, especially in the context of EU–Asia relations.

David Belis, Research Consultant – Taishindo Services, HIVA Research Institute for Work and Society, KU Leuven. David Belis is research consultant at Taishindo Services and at HIVA Research Institute for Work and Society, KU Leuven. Prior to this he was research fellow and project coordinator at the Institute for International and European Policy and junior member of the Leuven Centre for Global Governance Studies at KU Leuven. His main research areas are global climate governance and EU–Asia climate relations. Previously, he was project manager of the InBev-Baillet Latour EU–China Chair at the Leuven Centre for Global Governance Studies. He obtained a masters degree in Chinese Studies and Comparative and International Politics at KU Leuven.

Prof. Dr ***Qu Bo***, China Foreign Affairs University. Qu Bo is a post-doctoral research associate at Princeton University under the programme of Oxford-Princeton Global Economic Governance, and assistant professor of China Foreign Affairs University (Beijing). He holds a PhD in political science from Peking University. His research interests focus on international monetary and financial cooperation, China's participation in international institutions and international political economy. He has published on IPE, IMF lending conditionality and case study research methods.

Prof. Dr ***Hans Bruyninckx***, Director of HIVA Research Institute for Work and Society and Senior Member of the Leuven Centre for Global Governance Studies, KU Leuven. Hans Bruyninckx is Professor in Global and European Environmental Governance at the Faculty of Political Sciences and Senior Member of the Leuven Centre for Global Governance

Studies at KU Leuven. His research emphasises the influence of the various globalisation processes on the global governance of environmental problems and sustainable development. The translation and testing of innovative and critical social theories (such as network and flows perspectives) to multi-level governance arrangements of global environmental and sustainable development issues are at the core of this team's research efforts. His recent research includes specific expertise for the role of China in environmental governance.

*Mr **Bram Buijs***, Clingendael International Energy Programme (CIEP), Clingendael Asia Studies, Clingendael Institute. Bram Buijs joined the Clingendael International Energy Programme (CIEP) in January 2009. After taking a Master's degree in Mathematics he specialised in energy and geopolitics in a second Masters on Contemporary Asian Studies, writing his thesis on the future challenges facing China's energy system. In between these studies he spent six months in Shanghai, China, studying Mandarin and returned to Shanghai in 2006 to set up a representative office for a Dutch high-tech industrial design company. For one and a half years he combined work in China with an intensive Chinese language programme at the Shanghai International Studies University. He will continue with research on energy and Asia at CIEP, initially focusing on the challenges to a sustainable energy system in China and its stance in post-Kyoto climate treaty negotiations.

*Mr **Matthieu Burnay***, Project Manager of the Inbev-Baillet Latour EU–China Chair, Leuven Centre for Global Governance Studies, KU Leuven. Matthieu Burnay studied Law and Political Science at the Facultés universitaires Saint Louis in Brussels and the Katholieke Universiteit Brussel. He obtained a Master of Laws in International Relations from Peking University and a Master of Science in International Affairs from the London School of Economics. Since November 2010, he has served as Project Manager of the InBev-Baillet Latour EU–China Chair at KU Leuven. He is also a Junior Member of the Leuven Centre for Global Governance Studies.

Pei-fei Chang, doctoral student, Political Science Department and Institute for International and European Policy (IIEP), KU Leuven. Pei-Fei Chang obtained a Masters degree in European Politics and Policy (MEPP) at the Political Science Department, KU Leuven. Since 2008, she has been a doctoral student under Prof. Bruyninckx and a member of the IIEP.

Dr ***Jingquan Chen***, Second Secretary, Mission of the People's Republic of China to the EU. Jingquan Chen holds a doctoral degree in Management Science from Wuhan University. He currently serves as Second Secretary in the Chinese Mission to the EU, responsible for EU–China bilateral coordination on research cooperation in energy, environment and climate change areas. Prior to his current position, he worked in the National Natural Science Foundation of China as Deputy Director of the Division of Development Strategy.

Prof. Dr ***Richard N. Cooper***, Weatherhead Center for International Affairs, Harvard University (USA). Richard N. Cooper is Maurits C. Boas Professor of International Economics at Harvard University. He is a member of the Trilateral Commission, the Council on Foreign Relations, the Executive Panel of the US Chief of Naval Operations and the Brookings Panel on Economic Activity. He has served on several occasions in the US government, as Chairman of the National Intelligence Council (1995–97), Under-Secretary of State for Economic Affairs (1977–81), Deputy Assistant Secretary of State for International Monetary Affairs (1965–66) and senior staff economist at the Council of Economic Advisers (1961–63). He was also chairman of the Federal Reserve Bank of Boston (1990–92) and Vice-Chairman of the Global Development Network (2001–7). As a Marshall Scholar, he studied at the London School of Economics and earned his PhD at Harvard University. His most recent books include *Boom, Crisis, and Adjustment* (with others), *Macroeconomic Management in Korea, 1970–1990* (with others), *Environment and Resource Policies for the World Economy* and *What the Future Holds* (with others).

Hanne Cuyckens, PhD Candidate, Institute for International Law and Leuven Centre for Global Governance Studies, KU Leuven. Hanne Cuyckens studied law at the Université Catholique de Louvain (UCL). She obtained a Masters in pluridisciplinary analysis of the European Construction from the Université Libre de Bruxelles (ULB) and a Master of Arts in EU International Relations and Diplomacy Studies from the College of Europe (Bruges). Since September 2009, she has been assistant and PhD candidate at the Institute for International Law and a Junior Member of the Leuven Centre for Global Governance Studies, KU Leuven.

Mr ***Stewart Fleming***, Associate Fellow at Chatham House (The Royal Institute of International Affairs). Formerly Senior Associate Member at St Antony's College (Oxford), a Research Visitor at the London School of

Economics (LSE) and an economics columnist for *European Voice*. He was formerly correspondent from New York and Frankfurt and US Editor of the *Financial Times*. Mr Fleming studied at Wallasey Grammar School (1954–62), Horace Mann School, New York (1959–60) and Emmanuel College, Cambridge (1963–66), where he obtained a BA in Economics.

Dr ***Jagannath P. Panda***, Associate Fellow, Institute for Defense Studies and Analyses (IDSA), New Delhi. He is also the Managing Editor of *Peace and Development Digest* of the Foundation for Peace and Sustainable Development, New Delhi. Prior to joining IDSA, Dr Panda worked as Centrally Administered Fellow at the Indian Council for Social Science Research (ICSSR), Ministry of HRD, New Delhi. He is a recipient of the V. K. KrishnaMenon Memorial Medal for his excellent academic record in international law and diplomacy from the Indian Society of International Law (ISIL), New Delhi. His writings have been published in various peer-reviewed journals such as: *Strategic Analyses* (Routledge), *China and Eurasia Forum Quarterly* (Silk Road Studies, Sweden), *China Report* (Sage), *Asian Politics and Policy* (Wiley-Blackwell), *Asian Ethnicity* (Routledge), etc. He has also published in other international and national journals/newspapers such as: *China Brief* (Jamestown Foundation), *Taiwan Journal* (Taipei), *World Focus*, *Mainstream*, *The Pioneer*, *The Hindu*, etc. Dr Panda was an institutional fellow at the SIIS, Shanghai from June to September 2009. He has worked as a lead member on various Task-Force projects from DRDO and the Government of India on issues related to China and Tibet and conducted projects for the National Bureau of Asian Research (NBR), Washington, DC. His forthcoming book titled *China's Path to Power: Politics of Party, Military, and State* is currently in publication.

Prof. Emer. Dr ***Sylvain Plasschaert***, University of Antwerp (UFSIA) and KU Leuven. Prof. Plasschaert was a fiscal economist and a frequent consultant to the World Bank. Over a long period at Leuven he taught a course on 'Economic Developments in China', and published extensively on China's developmental path, such as: *China: inzicht in zijn doorbraak* (Davidsfonds, 2007).

Dr ***Simon Schunz***, European Commission, at the time of writing, Post-doctoral Researcher, Leuven Centre for Global Governance Studies, KU Leuven. He holds degrees in European Studies from the College of Europe (Bruges) and in Political Science from the Free University in Berlin. He was a Visiting Scholar at the Elliott School of International Affairs

(George Washington University, Washington, DC) and at the German Institute for International and Security Affairs (SWP, Berlin/Brussels). His research interests include EU foreign and environmental policies and global environmental governance. He has published, *inter alia*, in the *Journal of Common Market Studies*, the *Journal for Contemporary European Research* and *WeltTrends*.

*Dr **Bernard Snoy***, Visiting Professor, Institute of European Studies, Université catholique de Louvain (UCL), former Executive Director of the World Bank. Bernard Snoy is currently Visiting Professor at the Institute of European Studies of the Université catholique de Louvain, where he teaches among other courses on the EU enlargement process and on EU energy policy. Previously, Bernard Snoy has been, among other roles, Economic Advisor at the European Commission, Chief of Staff of the Belgian Minister of Finance, Executive Director of the World Bank, Member of the Board of Directors of the European Bank for Reconstruction and Development (EBRD), Director of the Economic Working Table of the Stability Pact for South Eastern Europe and Coordinator of the economic and environmental activities of the Organisation for Security and Cooperation in Europe (OSCE).

Lucia van Geuns, Clingendael International Energy Programme (CIEP), Clingendael Asia Studies, Clingendael Institute. Lucia van Geuns joined the Clingendael International Energy Programme (CIEP) in 2003 after a career with Royal Dutch Shell (1980–2002). She has a strong background in all aspects of exploration and production of oil and gas. She studied Earth Sciences at Leiden University and focuses her research on the global oil industry, Asian security of supply issues and innovative technology. She coordinates the research theme 'Energy and Sustainable Development' with particular attention to transition issues. She is a member of the board of the World Energy Council Netherlands (WEC NL) and a member of the Earth and Lifesciences Council (RAL) of the Royal Netherlands Academy of Arts and Sciences (KNAW).

*Mr **Xiaodong Wang***, Counsellor, Office of the Director-General, World Trade Organization (WTO), Cabinet Member and Advisor to H.E. Mr Pascal Lamy, Director-General of the WTO. He graduated from the International Studies Department, Nanjing University in 1995 with a BA, and was assigned to the Ministry of Foreign Trade and Economic Cooperation (then MOFTEC) responsible for China's accession to the WTO. From 1997 to 1998 he studied at the University of Adelaide, Australia and obtained a Masters degree in Economics. From 1998 to early 2003 he was posted at the Chinese Mission to the United Nations and then the Chinese Mission to the WTO in Geneva, Switzerland. In August 2004, he joined the American Chamber of Commerce (AmCham-China, Beijing) as the Director of Policy and Government Affairs. He has been working with the WTO Secretariat since September 2005.

Prof. Dr ***Yiwei Wang***, Distinguished Professor, Executive Dean of the Institute of International and Public Affairs, Director of the China–EU Academic Network, Tongji University. He was formerly scholar-in-residence at the Chinese Mission to the EU (political analyst) and associate professor on leave at the Center for American Studies at Fudan University. He was formerly assistant Dean of the Institute of International Studies at Fudan University (2004–7), adjunct deputy director of the Department of American Studies of the Shanghai Institute for International Studies (SIIS, 2004), and Fox Fellow at the Yale Center for International and Area Studies (2000–1) and Korea Foundation-Yonsei Distinguished Visiting Professor at the Graduate School of International Studies of Yonsei University (2005). He obtained his PhD in 2001 from the Department of International Politics, Fudan University and his BA in 1995 from the Department of Environmental Science and Technology, East China University of Science and Technology. He has published widely in *The Annals of the American Academy of Political and Social Science*, the *Japanese Journal of Political Science*, *International Studies* and the *Journal of Interdisciplinary Studies*.

Dr ***Chien-Huei Wu***, Assistant Research Fellow, Academia Sinica, Taipei, Taiwan. He received his PhD at the European University Institute, Florence in 2009. Since then, he worked as Assistant Professor in National Chung Cheng University, Chiayi, Taiwan for a short period. Before pursuing his doctoral degree in Florence, he worked for the Ministry of Justice in Taiwan as a district attorney. His research interests cover international economic law and EU external relations law. He pays particular attention to Asian regionalism and the WTO–IMF linkage and he also follows closely EU–China and EU–ASEAN relations.

Abbreviations

3G	Grouping of dissenters to the G20 process
ABC	Agricultural Bank of China
ACP	African, Caribbean and Pacific countries
ACU	Asian Currency Unit
AIDS	Acquired Immune Deficiency Syndrome
APT	ASEAN +3
ARF	ASEAN Regional Forum
ASEAN	Association of Southeast Asian Nations
AU	African Union
AWG-KP	Ad Hoc Working Group on the Future of the Kyoto Protocol
AWG-LCA	Ad Hoc Working Group on Long-Term Cooperative Action
BASIC	Brazil – South Africa – India – China
BAU	Business-as-usual
BIS	Bank for International Settlements
BMD	Ballistic Missile Defence (BIS)
BRIC	Brazil–Russia–India–China
BRICS	Brazil–Russia–India–China–South Africa
BWI	Bretton Woods I
BWII	Bretton Woods II
CASS	Chinese Academy of Social Sciences
CBC	People's Construction Bank of China
CBD	Convention on Biological Diversity
CCCPC	Central Committee of the Communist Party of China
CCP	Chinese Communist Party
CCS	Carbon capture and storage
CDM	Clean Development Mechanism
CDM Rules	Measures for the Operation and Management of Clean Development Mechanism Projects
CERs	Certified Emission Reductions
CFSP	Common Foreign and Security Policy (EU)
CNCCP	China's National Climate Change Programme
CNH	Exchange rate of the Yuan in offshore currency markets (primarily Hong Kong)

CNOOC	China National Offshore Oil Corporation
CNP	Comprehensive national power
CO_2eq	Carbon dioxide equivalent
COACH	Cooperation Action within CCS China–EU
COD	Chemical oxygen demand
COP	Conference of the Parties
CPC	Communist Party of China
CREIA	China Renewable Energy Industries Association
CSDP	Common Security and Defence Policy (EU)
CSIS	Center for Strategic and International Studies
DDA	Doha Development Agenda
DNA	Designated National Authority
DOE	Designated Operational Entity
DPJ	Democratic Party of Japan
DPRK	Democratic People's Republic of Korea
DR-CAFTA	Dominican Republic – Central America – United States Free Trade Agreement
DSB	Dispute Settlement Body
EB	Executive Board
EBA	Everything But Arms
EC	European Commission/European Community
ECB	European Central Bank
ECU	European Currency Unit
EEC	European Economic Community
EIA	US Energy Information Administration
EMS	European Monetary System
ENP	European Neighbourhood Policy
EPA	Economic Partnership Agreements
EPC	European Political Cooperation
ERUs	European Emission Reduction Units
ESDP	European Security and Defence Policy
ESS	European Security Strategy
EU	European Union
EU ETS	European Union Emissions Trading System
FCL	Flexible Credit Line
FDI	Foreign Direct Investment
Fed	US Federal Reserve
FIEs	Foreign Invested Enterprises
FOCAC	Forum on China–Africa Cooperation
FSB	Financial Stability Board
FTA	Free trade Agreement
FX	Foreign exchange

G2	Group of Two
G4	Group of Four
G5	Group of Five
G7	Group of Seven
G8	Group of Eight
G20	Group of Twenty
GATT	General Agreement on Tariffs and Trade
GDP	Gross Domestic Product
GHG	Greenhouse gas
GI	Geographical Indications
GPA	Agreement on Government Procurement
GSP	Generalised System of Preferences
GW	Gigawatts
GWEC	Global Wind Energy Council
HFCs	Hydrofluorocarbons
HK	Hong Kong
HKMA	Hong Kong Monetary Authority
ICCPR	International Covenant on Civil and Political Rights
ICT	Information and communications technology
IEA	International Energy Agency
IFI	International Financial Institutions
IGCC	Integrated gasification combined cycle
IMF	International Monetary Fund
IMF FCL	International Monetary Fund Flexible Credit Line
IMF PCL	International Monetary Fund Precautionary Credit Line
IMFC	International Monetary and Financial Committee
IMS	International Monetary System
IP	Intellectual Property
IPCC	Intergovernmental Panel on Climate Change
IPN	International Production Networks
IPR	Intellectual Property Rights
ISDP	Institute for Security and Development Policy
IT	Information Technology
KMT	Kuomintang
LDC	Least Developed Country
LDP	Liberal Democratic Party
mb/d	Millions of barrels per day
MDGs	Millennium Development Goals
MEF	Major Economies Forum
MIT	Massachusetts Institute of Technology
MNE	Multinational enterprise
MoU	Memorandum of Understanding

Mtoe	Million tonnes of oil equivalent
MW	Megawatts
NAFTA	North American Free Trade Agreement
NAMA	Non-Agricultural Market Access
NDRC	National Development and Reform Commission
NEPAD	New Partnership for African Development
NGO	Non-governmental organisation
NLGCC	National Leading Group on Climate Change
NZEC	Near Zero Emissions Coal initiative
OAU	Organisation of African Unity
ODI	Outward Direct Investment
OECD	Organisation for Economic Cooperation and Development
OECD DAC	OECD – Development Assistance Committee
OPEC	Organisation of the Petroleum Exporting Countries
P5	Permanent Member of the Security Council
PBC/PBoC	People's Bank of China
PCA	Partnership and Cooperation Agreement
PCL	Precautionary Credit Line
PFCs	Perfluorocarbons
PLA	People's Liberation Army
PP	Project participant
PPP	Purchasing Power Parity
PR	Public relations
PRC	People's Republic of China
QUAD	Group formed by the United States, Canada, the European Union and Japan in the WTO
R&D	Research and development
RE	Renewable energy
RIC	Russia–India–China
RMB	Renminbi
ROI	Return on investment
ROK	Republic of Korea
RPS	Renewable Portfolio Standard
RTAs	Regional Trade Agreements
SAARC	South Asian Association of Regional Cooperation
SACU	Southern African Customs Union
SDF	Self-Defence Forces
SDR	Special Drawing Rights
SOE	State-Owned Enterprise
SPS	Sanitary and Phytosanitary Measures
SPT	Six-party talks

STRACO$_2$	Support to Regulatory Activities for Carbon Capture and Storage
TBT	Technical Barriers to Trade
TFEU	Treaty on the Functioning of the European Union
toe	Tonnes of oil equivalent
TRIPs	Trade-Related Aspects of Intellectual Property Rights
UK	United Kingdom
UN	United Nations
UNCTAD	United Nations Conference on Trade and Development
UNDP	United Nations Development Programme
UNEP	United Nations Environment Programme
UNFCCC	United Nations Framework Convention on Climate Change
UNSC	United Nations Security Council
US	United States
USCC	The US–China Economic Security Commission
USSR	Union of Soviet Socialist Republics
VERs	Voluntary Export Restraints
WTO	World Trade Organization

Acknowledgements

The editors of this book would like to express their gratitude to the InBev-Baillet Latour EU–China Chairs at the University of Leuven (KU Leuven) and the Université catholique de Louvain (UCL), the Leuven Centre for Global Governance Studies (KU Leuven), the Institute for European Studies at the Facultés Universitaires Saint Louis (FUSL), the Institute for European Studies at UCL, the Madariaga – College of Europe Foundation and the InBev-Baillet Latour Chair at the College of Europe for their involvement in and support for the project. Special thanks should go to the Fonds Wetenschappelijk Onderzoek – Vlaanderen (FWO) for supporting part of the costs for the publication.

The editors would also like to thank all the contributors, David Belis from Taishindo Services for his work on Part 4 on 'China–EU and the Challenge of Global Climate Change and Energy', Matthieu Burnay from the Leuven Centre for Global Governance Studies (KU Leuven) and Maddalena Malgarini from the Madariaga – College of Europe Foundation for the editing and coordination, and Derek McGlynn for the linguistic editing of the papers.

This book stems from the international conference 'China, the EU and the Restructuring of Global Governance' held on 6 and 7 May 2010 in Brussels, with the kind support, besides the partners quoted above, of the European Economic and Social Committee, the Fonds de la Recherche Scientifique (FNRS), the European Union and the Belgian Chinese Chamber of Commerce.

Introduction: China's rise as a global actor, its consequences for global governance and how Europe copes with it

Jean-Christophe Defraigne, Jan Wouters, Tanguy de Wilde d'Estmael and Pierre Defraigne

After four centuries of isolation, followed by one century of colonisation and three decades of inward-looking industrialisation after its return to unity, China has now fully reinserted itself into the world economy as a sovereign power. The Chinese empire had been the largest economy in the world until the early nineteenth century when capitalist industrialisation allowed the Western powers to overtake the Middle Kingdom. However, in the pre-modern world China's hugeness was not appreciated as the global economy was fragmented into highly insulated and inward-looking economic blocs within which international trade was quite marginal compared to local trade. Between the sixteenth and twentieth centuries, European powers, driven by capitalism, made the world economy less fragmented through economic and colonial expansion. At a daunting human cost, they built a globalised economy by the early twentieth century. During that century the Western powers – Europe and successively the US – naturally shaped the governance structure of the global system that they had dominated for centuries.

In the aftermath of the Second World War the US and Western Europe (except for defeated Germany) set up the multilateral institutions in charge of global governance. The trading system was progressively liberalised within the framework of the General Agreement on Tariffs and Trade (GATT). The new monetary system designed at Bretton Woods secured fixed exchange rates that gave the dollar the role of international reserve currency under the supervision of a US-dominated International Monetary Fund (IMF). Post-war reconstruction and economic development of the countries in the South would be facilitated by the

World Bank. The maintenance of peace and security was entrusted to the United Nations (UN), in particular its Security Council.

Despite the proclaimed multilateralism, the design and the functioning of the new institutions in charge of global governance reflected the strength of the great powers, notably the US. At Bretton Woods, the US government rejected Keynes' proposal of a supranational currency, the 'bancor', to impose an international monetary system based on the dollar. By the end of 1950, President Truman renounced the fight to gain Senate consent for the Havana Charter (1947), which would have created an International Trade Organization based on one country-one vote. Instead, the US used the GATT as a negotiation forum with little formal institutionalised powers and managed to impose its agenda of trade liberalisation during the first decades of its functioning. The US and Western European powers clearly dominated these multilateral institutions, reflecting their economic and strategic weight in the global system.

The Western European powers gained more influence thanks to their economic integration. The establishment of the European Economic Community (1957), with the creation of a customs union, a common commercial policy with representation in the GATT (Article 113, later 133 of the Treaty of Rome), the common market project, followed by the move towards the single market by 1993 and the setting up of the Eurozone in 1999, enabled Western Europe to strengthen its bargaining position vis-à-vis the US hegemon. The US and Europe dominated the governance system of the global economy organised under the market capitalism system.

After 1949, China became part of the group of developing economies which followed the Stalinist model of economic development based on state-led import-substitution industrialisation. They insulated themselves from the capitalist world and attempted to build a socialist economy in a rural country which was lagging behind in terms of technology and industrialisation. China built up a heavy industrial base and strengthened its infrastructure, enabling the country to reduce substantially extreme poverty and to improve considerably education and health standards, albeit at a terrible human cost during the tragedies of the Great Leap Forward and the Cultural Revolution. After having pursued an extensive growth path based on Soviet technology, the economic development of China was slowed down by its isolation, especially in terms of access to technology. A turn in US foreign policy taken by the Nixon administration enabled China to join the global capitalist economy. The Chinese government opened the economy, giving up its state monopoly on foreign trade and enabling multinational enterprises to invest in China. The Chinese leadership managed the transition towards a less centralised and more market-oriented economy, but at the same time took a hands-on stance using macroeconomic (currency and international capital flow control) and industrial policy tools both to provide for relative macroeconomic stability and the emergence of large Chinese firms. Access to world markets and better technology enabled the Chinese economy to experience an exceptional growth rate for three decades. Forecasts suggest that the Chinese economy will overtake the US and Europe by the 2040s.

In the 1970s, the Chinese leadership gave up confronting Western powers directly. It no longer challenged the global capitalist order and decided to compete economically rather than politically within the economic and political governance framework designed by the Western powers. The Chinese leadership started by securing its role in global governance and by making the necessary internal adaptations to do so. It progressively learned about the functioning of the global economy, especially after having joined the World Trade Organization (WTO) in 2001. During this adaptation and learning process, China adopted a low profile based on Deng Xiao Ping's '24-character principle', which was to 'observe calmly; secure our position; cope with affairs calmly; hide our capacities; bide our time; be good at maintaining a low profile; and never claim leadership'. European and US officials and commentators complained sometimes about the lack of visible strategy and action in different fields. However, from 2000 the Chinese leadership became more confident and more able to express China's views on global affairs. The sheer size of the Chinese economy, its trade surplus and financial reserves, its pollution emissions and the modernisation of its armed forces meant that China could no longer maintain its low profile on global governance.

The financial crisis of 2008 accelerated this change, as it challenged the existing global governance structures designed by the Western powers and the latter's traditional hegemonic position. The G7 made way for the G20 as a 'premier forum of international cooperation' between the main industrialised and emerging economies. The European Union (EU), US and Japan are no longer able to impose their agenda in the WTO's Doha Development Agenda (DDA), whose success is nowadays in the hands of the emerging economies. A 'new Bretton Woods' is required to adapt the evolving needs of the international monetary system. The US is suffering from a legitimacy crisis in terms of economic governance due to its incapacity to correct its macroeconomic imbalances and the destabilisation generated by the deregulated US financial system. The neo-liberal model of economic governance, enshrined in the so-called 'Washington Consensus' and triumphant in the early 1990s following the collapse of the Soviet Union, is now openly contested by most emerging economies. These favour a model characterised by more state intervention (exchange rate policy, industrial and trade policies, social and education policies), a model that has been hastily labelled the 'Beijing Consensus'. China reacted more swiftly to the crisis than Europe, which was confronted with severe tensions within the Eurozone.

These developments highlight that the Western-designed global governance rules and institutions will have to adapt to give way to the new emerging powers – most notably China. This book aims to explore the different fields of global governance that are likely to be affected by the recent rise of China, as well as analysing Europe's attitude to this phenomenon. Since opening its country to the world in the late 1970s, the Chinese leadership has promoted its vision of a multipolar world in trying to counter the US hegemonic position and avoid unilateralism. For decades, the EU has been a strong supporter of a universal rules-based multilateral system in the different domains of global governance. To what extent are these two visions compatible? The Chinese leadership has often stated that there is no great conflict of interest between China and Europe. The EU and the People's Republic of China (PRC) managed to engage in a strategic partnership in 2003. Nevertheless trade, monetary policy, environment, energy, security and human rights have been a source of tension throughout the past decade. This book delves into these different key areas and examines the Chinese and European perspectives on global governance in these fields.

SHIFTS IN THE GLOBAL ORDER

The first part of the book focuses on the rise of China in the world, a comparison of Chinese and European points of view on global governance and a look at how global governance has already been reshaped by China's rise in world affairs. Jean-Christophe Defraigne takes a long-term perspective to analyse the origins of and prospects for China's re-emergence as a global power and the implications for the US, Europe and the global governance system. Yiwei Wang outlines the problems of perception and identity between China and Europe which are at the root of tensions in Sino-European relations. Stewart Fleming shows how the rise of China and other emerging powers has created a new geopolitical context. He analyses how this new configuration and the financial crisis of 2008 generated the need for a new forum on global governance which became the G20. He assesses the prospects for this new global governance body and the roles China and the EU could play in it.

THE WORLD TRADING SYSTEM

In the second part of the book 'The World Trading System', the contributors analyse the impact of China–EU relations on world trade as well as on the institutionalisation and reform of its regulatory mechanisms.

In Chapter 4, Jan Wouters and Matthieu Burnay examine the interactions between China and the EU within the WTO. In contexts where bilateral negotiations do not prove successful in tackling trade concerns, the WTO has become an important venue for the EU and China to discuss their trade disputes. Both have increasingly brought cases before the WTO's Dispute Settlement System. The authors argue that mutual misperceptions prevent China and the EU from developing a constructive collaboration aimed at restructuring the WTO.

In Chapter 5, Xiaodong Wang explains the root causes of the current stalemate in the negotiations in the WTO's DDA. After having emphasised the specificities of the Doha Round with regard to the former Rounds, he argues that the current leadership vacuum, the extensive use of Free Trade Agreements as well as the difficulties in finding trade-offs, strongly impede the ability to conclude the Round and pursue the necessary reform of the institution. In this context, he insists on the positive role China and the EU can play in negotiating the future agenda and fighting against protectionism.

In Chapter 6, Chien-Huei Wu draws a detailed comparison of European and Chinese policies towards Africa. In this respect, he puts forward the differences between the main European and Chinese policy instruments, namely the Cotonou agreement and the Forum on China–Africa Cooperation (FOCAC), as well as current practices. He argues that a middle way exists between the European conditional engagement and the Chinese non-interference principle. In this respect, he supports the development of a trilateral cooperation that would decrease the confrontation between both actors to the benefit of the African continent.

THE WORLD FINANCIAL AND MONETARY SYSTEM

The third part of the book focuses on the Chinese and European positions on the changing international monetary system. In Chapter 7, Pierre Defraigne explains the origin of the global macroeconomic imbalances by analysing US and Chinese macroeconomic policies. He shows how the US and Chinese models of growth have been complementary since 2000 and how the savings of the world – and notably of China – contributed to the

US rising trade deficit and to a speculative bubble, generating unsustainable growth for the world economy. He identifies three key issues which have to be addressed: pragmatic macroeconomic cooperation to cope with current account imbalances; the taming of global finance through strict domestic and regional regulation, supervision and taxation; and ultimately a new Bretton Woods based on a basket of currencies of Special Drawing Rights (SDR) type.

In Chapter 8, Michel Aglietta outlines the nature of the international monetary system since Bretton Woods, emphasising the contradictions of a key currency system in which the dollar is only a semi-standard and the imbalances are generated by US monetary policy. He explains how the international monetary system should be restructured and proposes a new governance system for the IMF, notably advocating more regulation of the financial markets, the strengthening of a regional monetary zone in East Asia with a limited convertibility of the renminbi (RMB) and a political role for the Eurozone in the IMF.

In Chapter 9, Sylvain Plasschaert looks into the issue of the valuation of the Chinese currency, the RMB, and the frictions it generates between China and its Western partners. He assesses to what extent the RMB is really undervalued. His analysis indicates that the value of the RMB over the past decade has not been the main reason behind China's important trade surplus; instead, structural domestic characteristics of the Chinese economy have been more significant. Plasschaert concludes from this analysis that the Western demands for an appreciation of the RMB do not constitute an adequate means to correct the trade imbalances between China, Europe and the United States.

In Chapter 10, Qu Bo considers China's management of its insertion into the global financial and monetary system and the Chinese approach to the restructuring of this system. He shows how China's position in this domain was driven by necessities imposed by domestic reform of the Chinese economy. He explains to what extent the Asian financial crisis in 1997, China's entry to the WTO in 2001 and the financial crisis of 2008 influenced China's engagement in international monetary cooperation. He concludes by examining China's propositions to regulate the global financial system, including the views of the Chinese government on key issues such as the internationalisation of the RMB and the Asian Monetary Cooperation Mechanism.

CLIMATE CHANGE AND ENERGY

Part 4 of the book is dedicated to two interrelated areas of global governance that are very much influenced by the changing international world order: global climate change, the most serious ecological crisis of our time, and the energy challenge, referring to the difficult task of transforming and finding sustainable and reliable energy production and consumption pathways.

In Chapter 11, David Belis and Simon Schunz investigate the material realities and policy responses in China and Europe and the evolution – driven by China's rise – in the global governance of climate change and energy policy. It is especially since the Copenhagen Conference in 2009 that China's changing position has become obvious in the climate regime. Due to massive growth in domestic energy consumption and demand, China has become the largest greenhouse gas emitter and energy consumer in the world. Its leverage, therefore, in both international climate as well as energy fora, has increased exponentially. In Chapter 12, Richard Cooper argues for an action-based multilateralism to cope with the challenges arising from Chinese and American passivity in climate and energy governance. Challenges are embodied in the 'pledge and review approach' adopted by the Copenhagen Accord and Cancun Agreements, which focus on concrete policy actions rather than on binding targets.

Under the 'pledge and review approach', China translated a number of its domestic policy actions into international – but voluntary – pledges. In Chapter 13, Jingquan Chen elaborates on China's domestic climate and energy actions through the lens of the Chinese government. One consequence of China's swift rise has been Europe's loss of leverage in international climate negotiations. An interesting issue in this context, linking the EU to China, is the future of the Clean Development Mechanism (CDM). In Chapter 14, Pei-fei Chang, David Belis and Hans Bruyninckx elaborate on the use, role and validity of the CDM for EU–China cooperation in the renewable energy sector, with a particular focus on the wind power industry.

Bernard Snoy's contribution in Chaper 15, as well as Chapter 16 by Bram Buijs and Lucia van Geuns, elaborates specifically on an intersecting issue for climate and energy policy: renewable energy and low-carbon technology cooperation and competition. Snoy focuses primarily on the emergence of European, Chinese and EU–China energy policies while Buijs and van Geuns scrutinise EU–China bilateral energy competition, but also highlight instances of cooperation in the field of renewable energy in the broader context of existing international, bilateral and domestic regulatory frameworks.

SECURITY AND POLITICS

The fifth part of the book focuses on global security and starts with a closer look at how China's rise and the consolidation of its status as a major power in East Asia challenge the US hegemonic position in the region. In Chaper 17, Elena Atanassova-Cornelis analyses the manifestation of strategic mistrust and security dilemmas between Tokyo and Washington, and Beijing, and then moves on to explore recent trends of engagement and cooperation between the three powers. Subsequently, she examines the primary components of the evolving regional security order and looks at the EU's policy towards East Asia. She concludes by arguing that while the US-led security system continues to be the main provider of East Asian stability and hence ensures America's regional primacy, it is increasingly complemented by regional multilateralism in non-traditional security areas. In turn, this opens the way for Europe's strengthened engagement with the region, including with China, and hence for the EU's implementation of a more multilateral approach to global governance.

In Chaper 18, Tanguy de Wilde d'Estmael begins with the assumption that the EU and China share at least two common points in international relations: in the latter part of the twentieth century, they embodied, each in their own very different manner, a kind of third way in the then bipolar world; and in the twentieth-first century, they leave some doubt about the kind of power they are developing. It is this unique facet of these two atypical powers that the author intends to clarify before moving on to a more controversial aspect of their relationship, coercion by the EU through the continuing 1989 arms embargo against Beijing. The latter situation is quite paradoxical: this use of coercion remains a stain on the otherwise carefully woven fabric of multifaceted cooperation.

In Chapter 19, Hanne Cuyckens elaborates on the extent to which the EU and China, who are both emerging global actors, are capable of balancing US hegemony and shaping a new world order characterised by multipolarity. She provides a brief overview of the legal framework of EU–China relations. She then analyses both actors' views on multipolarity and the relationship between the EU, the US and China. She shows that, even though the US remains the most important global actor, the world order is evolving towards a more multipolar balance of powers and emerging actors such as the EU and China will definitely (even if to different extents) have a role to play in the redefinition of this new world order.

In Chapter 20, Jagannath P. Panda concludes this fifth part by analysing the practice and pledge of China's new advocacy of multipolarism in the context of the BRIC (Brazil–Russia–India–China). She outlines the extent of Chinese support for a 'developing world' dialogue that remains the crux of the Chinese global strategy. While the focus is on analysing the scope of the BRIC in China's multilateral dialogue, the chapter also delves into the rationale behind China's formulation and support of ad hoc settings like the BRIC. Panda sees the Chinese course of multilateralism with multi-polarism as a well-constructed 'dual-mode' strategy to handle rising Western opposition and to encourage constructively its desired future structure of global politics.

CHINA–EU RELATIONS IN TURBULENT TIMES: WHICH WAY FORWARD?

Finally, building on the analysis outlined in these five parts, Jan Wouters and Matthieu Burnay provide general conclusions and propose some policy recommendations on how to enhance the relationship between China and the EU in a way that reconciles their strategic agenda and contributes to tackle the changing global governance system.

PART 1

Shifts in the global order

1. China shakes the world: challenges arising from shifts in the global balance of power

Jean-Christophe Defraigne

INTRODUCTION

This chapter adopts a long-term analysis to put the recent emergence of China in the world economy into a broader perspective. This will show that since its reopening in the 1980s, China is progressively reclaiming the place it enjoyed in the world economy prior to the industrial revolution. However the re-emerging Chinese economy is now expanding in a globalised world economy characterised by a high degree of interdependence rather than relatively independent, inward-looking 'world economies' as Braudel described the economic world system prior to the sixteenth century. This contribution will outline how the recovery of China's relative size in today's world economy is generating a profound shift in the global balance of power. It will attempt to assess to what degree the rise of China will erode the current US hegemony and will generate increasing tension. Finally, this contribution will determine to what extent this rebalancing of the world economy is comparable to the erosion of the British hegemony in the world economy during the late nineteenth century, which generated a multipolar capitalist global economy characterised by major conflicts and crises until a clear hegemonic position was established by the end of the First World War.

THE RISE OF CHINA IN THE GLOBAL ECONOMY

China, an Ancient Economic Power Prior to the Integration of the Global Economy

Historians generally consider China as the most advanced civilisation in terms of size, GDP and technology until the early modern times and for some even until the Industrial Revolution (Jacques, 2009: 80; Bairoch, 1997: 530). The largest European cities of the Renaissance were still dwarfed by the capital cities of the Chinese Empires (Bairoch, 1997: 529). The Chinese Empires benefited from a market which had no equivalent in the Western world in terms of size and integration. The importance of intra-Chinese trade and the existence of some advanced public goods with a centralised administration account for the size of Chinese markets and cities. These developments also meant that China was more than three centuries ahead of Europe regarding the process of monetisation of the economy.

Before the Industrial Revolution, Chinese merchants had developed ties across South East Asia and by the fifteenth century Chinese explorations had reached the Persian Gulf and the Eastern coast of Africa. In terms of transport, seafaring and military technology, the Chinese were far more advanced than their Western counterparts but it had no direct consequences on the economic development of Europe. The world economy was still fragmented into separate world-systems with little interdependency (Braudel, 1985: 43–7). In the fifteenth century, China certainly enjoyed the technological and military capacity to achieve a worldwide colonisation and expansion process like those launched by the Western European states in the sixteenth century (Mote, 2003: 616). However, by the end of the fifteenth century, China had renounced its military expedition, had drastically reduced overseas long-distance trade and had chosen a path of relative isolation. The reasons advanced by Chinese and Western historians to explain this abrupt change highlight the social and economic domestic disturbance generated by overseas trade and contacts (Mote, 2003: 617; Jacques, 2009: 78). The imperial system was anxious that the importation of cultural, religious and philosophical concepts could undermine the authority of the state. The fast economic rise of the long-distance merchants gave them a new influence in Chinese society which could have jeopardised the Mandarin hierarchical system. The imperial system suppressed this potential threat to its stability, which it did not need to survive. By having checked the rise of a merchant bourgeoisie, the imperial system gained three centuries of stability. However, this choice resulted in a considerable slowdown in technological innovation and entrepreneurship.

In Europe, on the contrary, long-distance trade was strongly supported by the European monarchs (Wallerstein, 1974). Western European monarchs helped to set up colonial expeditions and chartered companies. In their mercantilist view, controlling long-distance trade was a way to keep bullion inside their national economy and to finance the costs of their continuous wars with other competing European powers. Although the rise of merchants progressively challenged the monarchs' absolute authority, ensuring financial resources through long-distance trade and colonisation was perceived as a necessity for Western powers maintaining increasing costly standing armies (Defraigne, 2004). From the end of the Middle Ages to the Napoleonic wars, military spending and long-distance trade continued to increase. The share of GDP devoted to military expenditures increased from 1 per cent in the late Middle Ages to between 6 and 12 per cent in the late eighteenth century (Bean, 1973). These developments generated, albeit at a terrible human cost for Europe and its colonies, an exceptional military capacity, technological progress and the rise of a powerful class of entrepreneurs and bankers that prepared the conditions for the industrialisation of Western Europe and its future global hegemony.

China's Decline as an Economic Power: 1820–1950

Favoured by these developments and by its rich endowment in key raw materials (coal and iron), the industrialisation of Western Europe in the nineteenth century dramatically widened the gap with the rest of the world, notably China. According to Maddison's estimates, China's GDP ranked first, ahead of India, France and the UK, as late as 1820, but afterwards China's weight in the global economy would constantly decrease until the 1950s, reflecting its incapacity to industrialise comprehensively (Maddison, 1995: 28). The Western colonisation process durably affected the pattern of East Asian trade which became primarily turned towards Europe in the nineteenth century, reducing intra-regional trade between China and its neighbours (Petri, 1993: 19; Yoshihara, 1988). The imperial system, which had already been weakened by centrifugal forces since the eighteenth century, would not be able to prevent Western commercial penetration and partial colonisation in the nineteenth century. The de facto colonisation of China's coastal cities by Western powers, followed by Russia and Japan, accelerated the collapse of the imperial system which was replaced by a weak republican China, fragmented between different warlords during the 1910s and 1920s (Gray, 1994: 170; Isaacs, 1961).

The absence of a strong and modern independent state prevented the rise of an autonomous class of industrial entrepreneurs as well as an industrial policy for the fledgling Chinese industry. By the time of the Japanese invasion of the 1930s, Chinese merchants and entrepreneurs still did not possess the ownership-specific advantages to create multinational enterprises that could compete with their global competitors in high-tech or capital-intensive industries and services. The domestic market growth was far from impressive: GDP per capita only increased by 14 per cent between 1913 (two years after the birth of the Republic) and 1930 (before the depression of the 1930s and the Japanese invasion) (Maddison, 1995). After the rule of the warlords and the civil war, the weak and corrupted state that emerged under the Kuomintang (KMT) military dictatorship of Jiang Jieshi could not be considered as providing the necessary institutions for modern large-scale industrialisation driven by private entrepreneurs (Bergère, 1986). Militarily, the KMT proved unable to resist the Japanese aggression efficiently (Kolko, 1994). Even a substantial part of the Chinese urban bourgeoisie and petite bourgeoisie was willing to support the rise of the People's Liberation Army (PLA) and the Chinese Communist Party (CCP) against the KMT in the late 1940s because of the mass corruption and the insecurity generated by the KMT officials and criminal triads (Bianco, 1997; Belden, 2003).

The Creation of a Modern State and the Economic Usolation of China: 1950–71

The programme and strategy of the CCP in 1949 was quite different from the experience of the Bolshevik Party in 1917 (Lew, 1980). It was more nationalist and Jacobin than orthodox Marxist. Its major goal was to build a national, sovereign, modern state apparatus for China. The Mao doctrine insisted on the alliance of four classes: the working class, the peasantry, the petite bourgeoisie and the nationalist bourgeoisie against the pro-imperialist bourgeoisie led by the KMT (Teiwes, 1989: 77; Gray, 1994: 288). The CCP irreversibly weakened what was left of the feudal structure in Chinese society and laid the foundation of a centralised and modern state. China became more politically and economically integrated, although the very low level of infrastructure development meant that the level of economic integration in the 1950s was extremely low. For example, in the late 1940s, the railway network of the whole of mainland China was no greater than Taiwan's (Clough, 1989).

The anti-imperialist foreign policy of China and the Cold War clashed with US interests in the region. The Western powers continued to recognise the KMT in Taiwan as China's only legitimate government, preventing mainland China from joining multilateral institutions. Economically, the US and some European countries imposed an embargo on China after the Korean War which meant that the Chinese economy suffered from very restricted access to Western and Japanese technology until the 1970s. The few foreign firms present in China in 1949 were completely expropriated by 1956 (Bergère, 1986: 298). In the 1950s China became technologically dependent on the USSR to launch its import substitution industrialisation plans. However, the CCP contested the hegemonic position of the USSR in the so-called 'socialist' bloc (Fontaine,

1983). The de-Stalinisation process and the improvement of relations between the USSR and the West engaged by Khrushchev generated a clash with the CCP who wanted to widen the anti-imperialist front, especially in East Asia where communist parties or armed forces were quite strong and the US administration was committed to containing communist expansion through military means. By 1958, economic cooperation between the USSR and China virtually ground to a halt. China was completely isolated economically, technologically and militarily.

Throughout the 1960s, the CCP clung to power in this period of economic and political isolation. The Great Leap Forward was a disastrous attempt to accelerate industrialisation without proper technology and a qualified labour force and management. It was a criminal mistake by the Chinese leadership which caused millions of casualties in probably the greatest famine of the twentieth century and generated the biggest fall in Chinese output since the end of the Japanese invasion (Lardy, 1989). Internally, the combination of the dramatic consequences of the failure of the Great Leap Forward and the bureaucratisation of the CCP generated the fear of an emerging 'bourgeois revisionism' within the party (Harding, 1989). Externally, rising tensions with the USSR, as well as with the US due to their massive military interventions in East Asia led to a militarisation of Chinese society. This dramatic combination of internal and external factors helps to explain the launch of the Cultural Revolution and the further isolation of the Chinese economy. In the late 1960s and early 1970s, China's economy was almost in a state of autarchy and China's share of world trade reached its twentieth century nadir, falling from 1.5 per cent in 1953 to 0.6 per cent in the 1970s (Lardy, 2002: 31). Mao and Zhou must have been aware that this situation was unsustainable in the long run. Chinese growth was much slower than its pro-US East Asian neighbours. Thanks to the strategy of containment of communism in East Asia, Japan, South Korea and Taiwan were given special economic support by the US (Lanzarotti, 1992; Friedman and Samuels, 1993; Samuels, 1994). The US provided them with substantial aid plans and offered free technology transfers (Samuels, 1994; Lanzarotti, 1992). The US also helped these countries to integrate into the economic multilateral institutions (GATT, IMF, World Bank, OECD) and to benefit from the vast wave of trade liberalisation in the capitalist world economy in the 1960s and 1970s (Komiya and Itoh, 1988; Jones, 1997; Bouissou, 2007). This helped East Asian economies to adopt export-led growth and attract foreign direct investment (FDI) flows which generated some technological spillover. The CCP leadership could watch their pro-US capitalist neighbours move into the electronic age and develop advanced technological capacities at a much faster pace than mainland China. In terms of military technology, China had developed nuclear and spatial capacities with Soviet help (Whiting, 1989: 483). However, apart from these very specific military fields, civilian technology was decades behind that of Western countries and Japan. Even if the CCP leadership was able to protect most of the top Chinese scientists, the brutal and long disruption provoked by the Cultural Revolution in the universities and scientific community was not helping China to catch up.

As soon as the opportunity to break its isolation arose, Mao and Zhou took it, even if it meant for Mao a cynical U-turn in internal politics. In 1969, at the height of the Cultural Revolution, while official CCP propaganda targeted US imperialism as one of the main threats against 'socialism', the Chinese leadership was secretly negotiating their rapprochement with the US through Pakistan (Pollack, 1989). To facilitate the building of a relationship with the US, Mao made his position very clear describing his own anti-imperialist rhetoric to the US as 'empty cannons' (Kissinger, 1994: 728). Because of the strong and radical domestic opposition to the Vietnam War which threatened to destabilise the US, because of the loss of geopolitical credibility due to the stalemate in Vietnam (which was perceived in Washington as one of the reasons that emboldened the USSR to intervene so roughly in the crushing of the Prague Spring in Czechoslovakia in 1968) and because of the dramatic macroeconomic consequences of the military spending on the US economy and the dollar, Nixon and Kissinger were determined to extricate the US from Vietnam without giving the Soviet Union a stronger geopolitical position. Recreating links with mainland China to isolate Vietnam and weaken the USSR could fulfil this objective. The coincidence of different motives by Washington and Beijing was at the root of Kissinger and Nixon's trips to China in 1971–72 which opened an era of cooperation between the capitalist industrialised powers and China (Kissinger, 1994).

The Reintegration of China into the Global Capitalist Economy: 1972–2001

The opposition within the CCP to this radical change of foreign policy was quickly isolated and silenced by Mao and Zhou Enlai. Lin Piao, the head of the People's Liberation Army who had been praised as one of the great figures of the Cultural Revolution, suddenly became a 'national traitor' and died in unclear circumstances (MacFarquhar, 1989: 333). The Gang of Four was openly undermined by Mao himself (MacFarquhar, 1989: 349). Deng Xiaoping soon came back from his forced isolation. After the Nixon–Mao meeting, China actively pursued policies to reintegrate into the world capitalist economy and to gain the trust of the US and its allies. China quickly ceased to use its anti-imperialist rhetoric and began to depoliticise its diplomacy, accepting discussion with governments that the CCP had labelled 'fascist' and 'imperialist' a few years before. China continued to try to block Soviet expansion in Asia (notably against Vietnam) and in the Third World (in Africa and the Middle East) which made it an objective ally in the eyes of Washington (Pollack, 1989: 448).

The US broke China's isolation. After lifting its veto on giving the People's Republic of China (PRC) its seat in the United Nations, the US supported China's accession to multilateral institutions like the IMF and the World Bank. Thanks to US support and China's strong opposition to the USSR and Vietnam, China created new political and economic links with its pro-US East Asian neighbours. The Japanese premier Tanaka visited China in the same year as Kissinger. By the late 1970s, China had normalised diplomatic relations with the US and most of their East Asian allies (Joyaux, 1988).

The PRC leaders seized the opportunity to break China's isolation, offered to them by the US. It gave China the possibility to open up economically and resume trade, investment flow and import of technology with the most advanced economies in the world.

The opening of the PRC that started in the 1970s was very different to the one experienced by the imperial China of the nineteenth century. The opening was not directly imposed through military means, as in the Opium Wars. The CCP had built a modern, sovereign and relatively centralised state structure and it controlled the pace of the economic and political opening more effectively than the weakening imperial system of the late nineteenth century. It also provided China with an industrial presence, including a limited but not negligible heavy industry, transport and energy infrastructure. Despite the tragic failure of the Great Leap Forward and the economic disturbances generated by the Cultural Revolution, the Chinese economy experienced solid growth between 1950 and 1978. China's GDP increased by 385 per cent in these three decades, which was a better performance than India (with 294 per cent) or Argentina, but far less than Thailand, Brazil or South Korea. GDP per capita was doubled, a far better performance than India but still not as good as Brazil and far behind South Korea (own calculations from Maddison, 1995). At the end of this period, the famines and the large pockets of extreme misery that characterised the first half of the twentieth century were eventually eradicated (Gray, 1994). Finally, it also provided elementary public goods in terms of education, security and health coverage that made China so attractive for foreign investors compared with other economies with similar levels of economic development.

The PRC adopted a cautious and gradual policy to attract FDI in order to accelerate industrialisation, generate exports and benefit from technology and management know-how transfers. At the beginning, in 1980, the open-door policy targeted FDI from the Chinese entrepreneurs in Hong Kong, Macao and Taiwan and only a very limited number of strictly defined geographic zones could host these investments. Progressively the PRC authorities extended this opening to other investors and widened its geographical scope. In less than three decades, China became the largest recipient of FDI flows among developing countries. In relative terms, the current share of FDI to GDP of the Chinese economy is among the highest of the large developing economies (UNCTAD, 2010).

The PRC also gave a greater economic autonomy and credit access to small and medium rural enterprises. Some specialised in the light and labour-intensive industries, notably in textiles, where the vast pool of cheap labour force gave China a comparative advantage. China managed to secure access to Western markets by applying to join the GATT in the mid-1980s and then by accessing the WTO before the phasing out of the agreement on textile and clothing that was due in 2005 (so that it was not to be disadvantaged compared to the WTO member states that were competing against Chinese textile and clothing exports in international markets).

Finally the Chinese authorities pursued active industrial policies in the capital-intensive and high-tech industries, organising mergers and acquisitions to benefit from economies of scale. The Chinese state was clearly inspired by the Japanese and South Korean experience. They supported their overseas expansion with the adoption of a 'going global' strategy, provided 'window-guidance' for the first Chinese multinational enterprises (MNEs) and tied aid programmes to commitments to facilitate their penetration of developing countries just as Japan did in East Asia in the 1980s (Defraigne, 2008).

In 30 years China became one of the most open among the largest economies in the world and its share in world trade rose from 0.6 per cent in the early 1970s to over 4.4 per cent in 2010 (Lardy, 2002: 31; WTO, 2010). From the late 1970s to the end of the Cold War, the US accepted that their allies sold technology and invested in capital and R&D-intensive production facilities in the PRC. Internal reforms to improve productivity in the countryside, the lifting of the technological and investment embargo, access to the largest share of the world economy (the OECD economies) combined with the modern public goods created by the CCP in their three first decades of power were the conditions behind the exceptionally high growth of China. The acceleration of economic development transformed China into one of the leading players in the global trading system.

Because of its integration into the international production networks of MNEs and its role as provider of components and low-tech manufactured products, the Chinese economy has become one of the biggest workshops in the world. It provides the majority of the world's production of some household appliances (DVD players, microwave ovens, photocopiers) and became the biggest car producer in the world in 2009 (Jacques, 2009: 162; *Financial Times*, 21 October 2010). As the share of the manufacturing sector was responsible for 48.6 per cent of China's GDP in 2008 compared with 22.4 per cent for the US or 30 per cent for the Japanese economies, it is not surprising that China already has had a tremendous impact on the global markets for raw materials and energy products and on the environment (UNPD, 2010).

CHINA CHANGES THE BALANCE OF POWER IN THE GLOBAL ECONOMY

China, and to a lesser extent India, Brazil and Russia, have all experienced an acceleration of growth this last decade that has changed the balance of power in the world's trading and financial systems. During the Uruguay Round, in the course of which many emerging economies were experiencing the severe effects of the debt crisis and its capital shortages, their weak bargaining positions forced them to give in to the US and European demands on liberalisation of services, intellectual property and trade-related investment measures. On the contrary, the Doha Round witnessed fierce resistance from the large emerging economies against the so-called 'Singapore issues' and other liberalisation demands, notably in services (Blustein, 2009; Laborde, 2007). The BRICs have been able to maintain their protectionist tools in pursuit of their industrial policies to strengthen their national champions.

The G8 was transformed into the G20 which has become far less Western-centred. Debates about the reforms of the IMF with propositions by some Western member states to give a greater weight to emerging economies (in the current system, China with an economy larger than that of Germany and 1.3 billion people has less weight than Belgium and the Netherlands combined – with a GDP almost five times smaller and less than 30 million citizens) (IMF, 2010). The recent global financial crisis has highlighted the new strength of the emerging economies and notably of China. The US now considers it vital to have a bilateral dialogue with China on a series of global issues such as trade, global warming or the reform of the financial system, generating the possibility of an emergent G2.

Many analysts consider that the growth prospects of the European, US and Japanese economies are likely to remain modest for the coming decade. With the explosion of the real estate market bubble, the continued fragility of the financial sector which blocks the expansion of credit and rising public and household debt, domestic demand is likely to stay weak for years to come. The greatest part of world growth is expected to come from the large emerging economies (McKinsey, 2009). In 2003, Goldman Sachs analysts had made a projection of the comparative growth of the OECD and BRIC economies (Wilson and Purushothaman, 2003). Their estimates showed that before 2050, China's GDP will have caught up with that of the US, dwarfing the Japanese and the larger European Union member states.

The shrinking of the US, Japanese and EU economies in the global world economy is likely to be one of the most striking features of the twenty-first century. It will certainly affect the balance of power in the global economy but will it generate a multipolar world in which the West has lost its hegemonic position in the international trading and financial systems and in which China is on an equal footing with the US and Europe?

CHINA: A POOR ECONOMIC GIANT DEPENDENT ON FOREIGN TECHNOLOGY? THE OBSTACLES CHINA FACES IN CATCHING UP ECONOMICALLY WITH THE US, EUROPE AND JAPAN

The Limits of China's Extensive Growth and the Difficult Acquisition of Technological Capability

Even if China should become the largest economy in the world by around 2040, it does not mean that it will be the most influential economic power. In the early nineteenth century, China was already the second largest economy because of the sheer size of its population but had little or no influence on world markets, the international financial system of the gold standard and the trading system. At that time, China was a big economy that was closed, mostly rural and with a population getting relatively poorer compared to Western economies. China's current growth is certainly different in that respect. China is now one of the most outward-looking among the largest economies of the world and it is narrowing its standard of living gap with developed economies. Nevertheless, the gap is still huge. Chinese consumers with standards-of-living comparable to those in developed economies probably amount to less than 60 million people in the late 2000s (Rocca, 2010). There are 800 million Chinese who are still rural poor and who can dedicate only a tiny fraction of their income to non-local production. Even taking Goldman Sachs' forecast that the Chinese economy will match the US GDP by the 2040s, the GDP per capita of the PRC will only have reached the level of Portugal, the least advanced economy of Western Europe (Wilson and Purushothaman, 2003).

Global technological standards and branding have generally been imposed by large economies with relatively high standards of living. Some analysts like Martin Jacques consider that the size and cultural weight of China will provide it with the ability to impose new technological and marketing standards around the globe (Jacques, 2009). However, there are still only a handful of cases where Chinese products have imposed a new global standard, rather, they have been only able to create local standards as a way to resist penetration by foreign firms of Chinese markets (Cao et al., 2006).

Over the last two decades, MNEs have reorganised their production processes regionally or globally in what some authors have called the 'wintelist' production system (Zysman and Schwartz 1998: 6; Lafay, 2004: 72). MNEs outsource many segments of their production processes to focus on branding and innovation capacities in order to keep an edge over competitors from emerging countries and impose the new technological and branding standards on markets. MNEs create international production networks that include many firms from emerging economies but they segment the stages of production so as to try to keep control of upstream (innovation) and downstream (marketing and branding) activities and to check the possible expansion of subcontractors. Controlling international R&D and marketing networks has become essential for MNEs to preserve their market power and to extract rents from consumers and subcontractors. Chinese firms still have to overcome these entry barriers and gain these ownership-specific advantages in terms of branding, innovation and international management in order to play among the global incumbents.

China's technological base has been strengthening rapidly this last decade. The share of the GDP allocated to R&D spending increased from 0.73 per cent of the GDP in 1991 to 1.4 per cent in 2010 (OECD, 2010). The number of Chinese holding a science degree and a PhD has grown steadily these last two decades (Naughton, 2007; UNDP, 2009) and every year more Chinese study abroad. However, some Chinese degrees cannot be compared to those of the rich OECD countries. In 2005, McKinsey estimated that only 10 per cent of Chinese engineers had sufficient knowledge to be directly employed by MNEs in China (De Joncquières, 2005). Furthermore, a quarter of the Chinese students that graduate overseas do not come back to China and among those who do, the majority choose to work for foreign MNEs based in China (Naughton, 2007). In terms of patents and scientific articles, China does not compare with South Korea and is still very far behind Japan (OECD, 2010). Many of the Chinese patents are specific to the Chinese market and are not used elsewhere as indicated by the limited level of royalties paid to China, which are only about 7 per cent of those received by South Korea (own calculation from UNDP, 2008). More MNEs built R&D facilities in China (over 1,200 in 2010), but many of these laboratories are doing simple and specific scientific tasks as part of an international production network controlled by a foreign-based MNE while others are involved in product development rather than fundamental research (Naughton, 2007: 370; Hua, 2005: 13). The share of China's R&D spending devoted to fundamental research is much lower than that of the US, Japan and South Korea (Sachwald, 2007). There is a difference between creating the new standard for the next generation of a particular product and adapting an existing standard to the specific needs of the Chinese market. While China's R&D capacities are clearly developing fast, Chinese firms still do not possess strong innovative capacities.

Some Chinese firms managed to create brands that have gained international recognition such as Lenovo, Huawei or Haier but even the most famous Chinese brands do not compare in terms of visibility with Japanese, Western or even Korean brands (such as Samsung or Hyundai). Chinese firms have tried to improve their branding and access to international distribution networks by acquiring foreign firms. This was the case for the attempted acquisition of the US Maytag by Haier, of the IBM PC division by Lenovo in 2005, of Thomson television and Schneider by the Chinese TV producer TCL, of South Korea's Ssanyong by the Shanghai automotive industrial corporation or of Volvo by Geely in 2010 (Defraigne, 2012). These acquisitions show the new financial strength and the new will of Chinese firms to meet international branding, innovation and management standards but this also highlights their current weaknesses. Empirical studies show that Chinese MNEs also encounter serious difficulties in managing and coordinating their subsidiaries overseas (Defraigne, 2008).

To help the Chinese enterprises gain these ownership-specific advantages and transform themselves into global competitors, the Chinese state is pursuing an industrial policy, inspired in part from the previous Korean and Japanese experience of business internationalisation

(Defraigne, 2008). China provides low-cost loans to the national champions that it has selected in its 'going global' strategy aimed at creating large Chinese MNEs. The Chinese state has favoured mergers in order to rationalise production capacities (USCC, 2007). The Chinese often use diplomatic tools and tied aid programmes to favour the penetration of Chinese MNEs in developing economies, as Japan did in the 1980s with neighbouring countries such as Thailand (Hatch and Yamamura, 1997). Cheap loans make Chinese firms able to compete for procurement bids not only in developing economies but even in the EU, with construction contracts granted by Eastern European member states to Chinese MNEs. This considerable support has been widely criticised by Western governments and firms as a distortion of fair competition. It explains the refusal by Western economies to grant China 'market economy status' in the WTO framework, which makes it easier for them to raise protectionist tariffs against Chinese imports.

This state support has helped Chinese MNEs to grow rapidly these last 15 years. In the 1990s, there were only three Chinese firms in the global 500 largest firms in terms of sales, but in 2009 the number has risen to 46 (Fortune, 2010). Even if Chinese outward direct investment (ODI) stock remains much smaller than that of the large economies of the OECD, Chinese ODI has grown exponentially since 2000 to reach US$229.6 billion in 2010 (UNCTAD, 2010).

Nevertheless, despite this strong support by the Chinese state and impressive growth in terms of assets and sales, the rising Chinese MNEs still remain fragile when compared to their global competitors. The largest Chinese firms are still far more labour-intensive and less profitable than their OECD counterparts. Their current performance is weak even when compared to the largest Japanese and Korean firms during their first phase of internationalisation (in the 1960s for Japanese firms and in the 1980s for Korean) (Defraigne, 2008). Most of these Chinese champions, even those in the global 500, benefit from a protected dominant position in their large domestic market and it is unlikely that most of them would survive international competition without Chinese state protection (Defraigne, 2012).

The largest Korean firms, the *chaebols*, in the 1970s and early 1980s experienced such weaknesses and benefited from state nurturing to help them to adapt to international competition (Jones, 1997; Hobday, 1995). Brazil also nurtured large champions like Embraer, Vale, Gerdau, Odebrecht or Oi for decades before they gained enough experience through the learning-by-doing effect and scale to compete on global markets, and even today they remain domestic-oriented (Brainard and Martinez-Diaz, 2009). However, apart from Japan, none of the emerging economies have yet managed to generate global competitors in rising high-tech industries that are technologically autonomous. Even Korea's Samsung, probably the most advanced firm in terms of R&D from the emerging economies, still depends, like many of its Korean counterparts, upon Japanese technology.

Compared to Japan and Korea, China will face more serious obstacles in its pursuit of a successful industrial policy. As mentioned earlier, Japan and South Korea both benefited from the free transfer of technology from the US thanks to the context of the Cold War. They enjoyed, for more than two decades, easy access to the US market and a benevolent attitude of the US regarding their industrial and protectionist policies. China has not been provided with such opportunities. It still faces an embargo on key dual technologies (those that can be applied to both the civilian and military sectors) which the US maintains with its allies (Casarini, 2009). Numerous Chinese firms violate the intellectual property of Western and Japanese firms but since it joined the WTO, the pressures are mounting on China to honour its multilateral commitment in terms of trade-related intellectual property aspects (Sutter, 2008: 99; Ash, 2008: 212). Japan and Korea's domestic markets were highly protected for decades before their largest firms could compete with their Western competitors. Until the 1980s, their domestic markets were not a priority for Western firms. East Asia was in the periphery and the centre of the world economy was still the North Atlantic. Until the late 1970s, East Asia was not even considered by Western MNEs as a completely secure location to invest given the tense regional geopolitical situation due to the Vietnam War and the anti-imperialist Chinese foreign policy (Jones, 1997). Western MNEs were not particularly present in the region which facilitated the penetration of the East Asian neighbouring economies by Japanese MNEs at the start of their international expansion.

The situation is much more complicated for Chinese firms. East Asia and especially China have become much more central to the world economy. China's domestic market with its high growth rate and its great development potential attract Western MNEs and the crisis of 2008 will strengthen their will to widen their access to Chinese consumers. The Chinese domestic market is already far more open today than Japan's was until the 1980s and Korea's until 1997. Compared to the GDP, inward FDI flows are much more important than was the case for Japan and Korea at the time of the internationalisation of their largest firms (Defraigne, 2009). Foreign competitors are much more established today in China than they ever were in Japan and South Korea.

China is resisting penetration by gaining time in the implementation of its multilateral commitments and by providing its national champions with privileged access to its procurements. The Chinese government also encourages R&D spending which has increased dramatically these last 15 years. However, accounting for less than 1.5 per cent of their GDP, the absolute level of China's total R&D expenditure remains far below that of Japan and Germany (OECD, 2010). Given this combination of great opportunities and challenges, it is extremely difficult to assess the capacity of China's largest firms to catch up technologically, to establish globally recognised brands in high-tech industries and to resist Western and Japanese competitors.

The Risks for the Chinese Economy if Technological Progress is Too Slow

China's technological development is not only crucial for catching up technologically with the most advanced economies and to transform some of its national firms into global competitors but it is also needed to reduce serious imbalances in the development of its economy.

During these last two decades, China's growth has become more extensive than intensive. Growth can be roughly attributed to three factors: labour, capital and technology. In the case of China's growth, it enjoyed labour productivity gains generated by the better use of manpower in the countryside, transferring the labour surplus from the agricultural to the manufacturing sectors driven by the progress in agricultural productivity and the industrialisation of the 1980s and 1990s. The largest part of these transfers has now been completed and demography analysts expect a slowdown in the population growth after 2015 (Naughton, 2007). This means that labour productivity gains will play a decreasing role in future Chinese economic growth. China's growth has also been generated by the adoption and diffusion of new technologies and/or new management know-how through imports of machine tools, Chinese gaining management and engineering skills abroad or spillover by FDI flows from foreign-based MNEs. Although this factor is likely to remain a large contributor to future Chinese growth, the share of total factor productivity (a proxy used by macroeconomists for technological and management know-how development) in Chinese growth has been gradually decreasing since the 1990s and early 2000s (Banque Mondiale, 2004). However, compared to labour and technology, capital investment has been a much more decisive factor in the high growth rate that the Chinese economy enjoyed these three last decades (Aglietta, 2007). Chinese growth has been driven by an exceptionally high level of investment without any comparison in modern history. With investment accounting for more than 40 per cent of the GDP, China has overtaken the highest level of investment experienced in the twentieth century by economies such as Japan, South Korea and the USSR. This exceptional level of investment is made possible by the exceptionally high savings rate in China, both by households and enterprises (above 50 per cent of the GDP in 2008), and by cheap access to capital due to the state-backed financial system (Rocca, 2010; Defraigne, 2009).

Such fast, investment-led growth generates a serious imbalance in the Chinese economy. The high savings level is the corollary of low domestic consumption which encourages export-led growth and a high dependency on overseas markets to which access can never be fully secured. The large investment is also the result of industrial policies by both the local and central authorities which aim to increase the size of their local or national champions to benefit from more economies of scale and better resist competition. These sometime conflicting industrial policies pursued at different levels of government have generated overcapacities in many of the manufacturing industries (Gipouloux, 2006; European Commission – DG Relex, 2007). The competing industrial policies of local authorities have sometime prevented the rationalisation of production capacities at the national level. Inefficient local champions using obsolete and polluting technologies continue to operate thanks to government financial support and intra-Chinese technical barriers to trade which continue to fragment the Chinese domestic market (Defraigne, 2012). This explains why the production units of the less advanced provinces are the most polluting and energy-consuming (Jun, 2010). If these trends are not corrected, the pollution and energy costs will generate an increasing burden on the Chinese economy, slowing down its growth substantially (Naughton, 2007: 493). The Chinese government is trying to curb these overcapacities by encouraging rationalisation, by trying to discourage new entrants into overcrowded industries (like the automotive industry) and by increasing state-owned company payout to the government in order to reduce their capacity to invest (*Financial Times*, 30 December 2010). These policies have limited the phenomenon but have certainly not eradicated it.

Low interest rates and high investment rates have also contributed to a speculative bubble in the real estate market in the major Chinese cities. Despite attempts by government to cut down on these speculative investments, the Chinese real estate sector is still considered as being unstable, generating fear of a crisis such as was experienced by Japan in 1990 and East Asia in 1997 (Chancellor, 2011).

Without continued technological progress, serious macroeconomic imbalances such as an aging demographic, overcapacities, real estate bubbles, a high degree of dependency on foreign market access due to a limited domestic market, pollution and energy costs could seriously affect the growth path of the Chinese economy in the short and medium run and delay its catch-up for decades.

THE IMPACT OF CHINA'S FUTURE GROWTH ON GLOBAL GOVERNANCE AND MULTILATERAL INSTITUTIONS

If the Chinese economy can avoid these pitfalls, it can surely hope to become the largest economy, albeit not the most developed one, in the world by the mid-twenty-first century. This will generate a major change in the global balance of power. Many analysts point out the possibility of rising rivalry between China and the West. China's increasing demand for raw materials and energy is already generating a reaction. *The Economist* magazine published a special issue in December 2010 about China's military build-up and the potential for confrontation between the US and China in East Asia. Western concerns over China's economic and strategic rise are mounting, especially since the 2008 economic crisis (*The Economist*, 4 December 2010).

The current global order and its multilateral institutions have been set up by the US and its Western allies in the aftermath of the Second World War. The context of the Cold War and the size of the US economy in the global capitalist system meant that developing countries could not really challenge the domination of Western industrialised nations in the multilateral institutions. Given the historical political weight of Europe, its economic weight and geostrategic position in confronting the USSR, the US had to share control of these institutions with its Western European allies.

As for the global trading system, when the GATT was created in 1947, the GDP of the US accounted for two-thirds of the combined GDP of all its contracting parties. Britain with the Commonwealth was still a major player due to its size in world trade but this was mainly because of the Commonwealth system and Britain's share in the world trade and economy continue to decline with the decolonisation process. Until the creation of the WTO in 1995, the GATT agenda was de facto determined by the US and Europe (Narlikar, 2005: 17).

For the international monetary and financial system, a tacit agreement between Europe and the US was to give the chair of the IMF to a European and that of the World Bank to an American. The European countries joined together and with the US both enjoyed the capacity to block decisions unilaterally at the IMF (Lenain, 1993).

The only contender was the so-called Soviet bloc but this constituted an inward-looking group of economies that were not part of the multilateral system dominated by capitalist economies. When some of its members decided to join the GATT, such as Poland, Romania and Hungary in the 1960s and 1970s, they adapted to the existing set of rules. Some attempts were made during the 1970s by developing economies to improve their bargaining power vis-à-vis the US and Europe with the creation of the Group of 77 in the GATT or the demand for a 'new world order' by Algeria at the UN in 1974 (Bairoch, 1997: Vol. III: 675; Vanderwee, 1990: 351).

However, these attempts were short-lived and did not resist the shock of the debt crisis of the 1980s. Throughout the Uruguay Round and the management of the debt crisis in the 1980s and early 1990s, the agenda of the multilateral institutions continued to be largely dominated by the US and Western Europe.

The end of the Cold War and the rise of the Eastern Asian and other large emerging economies began to change this balance of power. During the 1980s and 1990s, China and India began to accelerate the opening of their economies, attracting FDI and inserting themselves into the global division of labour. The rise of the large emerging economies gave them the possibility to exert a greater influence on the multilateral system. They even managed to block the agenda of the US, Europe and Japan on the issue of intellectual property and investment liberalisation with the rejection of the so-called Singapore issues during the Doha Development Agenda negotiations. The handling by the IMF of the East Asian crisis in 1997–98 was another benchmark in the erosion of the consensus on economic global governance that had been imposed by the US hegemony. The IMF bail-out plan with its conditionality (notably the relaxation of foreign direct investment control, the opening of capital markets and the opening of the financial sector) was clearly perceived by the East Asian economic and political elites as an attempt to impose the Western model of economic governance and to enable Western companies to penetrate the emerging East Asian economies. Jeffrey Garten who was the US Undersecretary of Commerce dared to declare that the 'worsening financial flu will lower the Asian immunity to US business' (Higgott, 2000: 259) while some East Asian officials talked of 'robbery' by 'a new imperialism', a vocabulary seldom used by the East Asian elites during the Cold War era. One of the results of this was that East Asian countries and other merging economies began to adopt macroeconomic policies and mechanisms (joint financial stabilisation funds such as the Chiang Mai initiative, undervaluation of their currencies to generate trade surpluses and foreign exchange reserves) to avoid depending on the IMF bail-outs (Aglietta, 2007; Sapir, 2008).

There are clear signs that the multilateral system and its governance model that emerged from the hegemonic position of the US in the aftermath of the Second World War has not adapted itself to the change in the balance of economic power that has occurred during the last two decades. In 2010, China still had the same weight in the decision-making process of the IMF as a small economy like Belgium. India, Brazil, Japan and Germany are still not permanent members of the Security Council. If multilateral institutions cannot adapt to a changing balance of power, they are likely to lose credibility and be replaced by alternative decision forums, either multilateral (G20), bilateral or regional. The rise of China and other large emerging powers will weaken the grip of the US and Europe in the current multilateral institutions or force a reshaping of these institutions. The US and the European powers will have to share the global governance driving seat with China.

COULD CHINA BECOME THE MAIN CONTENDER TO REPLACE THE US'S ERODING HEGEMONIC POWER? A COMPARISON BETWEEN THE DECLINE OF THE US AND THE RISE OF CHINA IN THE TWENTY-FIRST CENTURY AND THAT OF THE UK AND GERMANY IN THE LATE NINETEENTH CENTURY

If the US hegemonic position is progressively eroding, could this change in the global balance of power be compared with the decline of Great Britain in the nineteenth century when other large industrialised economies like the US, Germany, France or Japan emerged and began to challenge British economic leadership?

The End of the 'Pax Britannica': the Erosion of British Hegemonic Power in the Late Nineteenth Century

After the Napoleonic wars, Britain dominated world trade in manufactured goods. Progressively, the lobby of industrialists grew in the UK and they imposed the abolition of the protectionist 'corn laws' so as to promote international free trade. On the liberalisation of international trade, many Western countries followed Britain, such as France, the US, Germany and smaller European countries (Benichi, 2008: 23). Many countries or empires outside the Western world faced gunboat diplomacy and had to open their borders to British trade, notably China. Britain dominated a relatively liberalised global trading system from the 1840s to the 1870s. The international monetary system was based on the gold standard and the dominant currency was the pound sterling. Militarily, after their victory at Trafalgar against Napoleon, the Royal Navy did not face any serious competitors for the control of sea lanes. For more than six decades, the world was dominated by the *Pax Britannia* in terms of trade and industry, finance and military means.

Progressively, other major countries began to industrialise. Both the US – after the civil war of 1861–65 – and Germany – through the Zollverein and Prussia's alliance with Western German entrepreneurs – became more integrated and industrialised. With new technologies characterised by more important economies of scale, ensuring access to larger markets became more important (Chandler, 1994; Defraigne, 2004). The relative British decline in terms of trade and industrial production extended over decades but one benchmark was certainly the crisis of 1873. This financial crisis was the start of the so-called 'Great Depression', a long deflationary period characterised by overcapacities which lasted from 1873 to 1895 (Beaud, 1990: 175; Gildea, 1996: 274). Caused by a massive speculation in real estate and on the stock markets, this crisis affected industrialised countries on both sides of the Atlantic (Hauser et al., 1952: 398). It triggered a wave of protectionist measures across the US and European countries, such as the German tariff of 1879, the French Loi Méline in 1892 and the US McKinley tariff of 1890 (Benichi, 2008: 25). US industry could rely on a fast-developing domestic market. For Germany, the domestic market was not sufficient. To benefit from economies of scale and jump the tariff barriers of its trading partners, German industry organised a complex, vertically integrated system of dumping, supported by national government-backed cartels (Maschke, 1969: 248). German export manufacturers began to catch up with the British. After three decades of mounting protectionism and German dumping, the British progressively abandoned their free-trade approach. By the first decade of the twentieth century, they adopted a preferential system that gave products made in Britain a privileged access to Commonwealth countries. 'Buy British' campaigns were being developed and non-tariff barriers (technical barriers to trade) were erected from the 1880s until 1914 (Wilkins, 1970: 101; Hagen, 1999: 50). Chamberlain defended the notion of an 'imperial contract' with the possibility of enacting a tariff for the Commonwealth in 1907 (Defraigne, 2004: 79).

As commercial frictions increased and free trade gave way to blatant protectionism, the large industrialised countries began to secure access to additional markets and sources of raw materials. The imperialist race for colonies started again. For Great Britain, after the 1840s, colonies had been seen as a waste of resources in a free-trade world by many British economists and politicians until the 1870s. Some prominent figures in British politics, including Disraeli, were seriously considering relinquishing the colonial possessions. By the last decade of the nineteenth century, the situation was completely reversed with a dramatic extension of the

British Empire as far as Tibet, a jingoist imperialist ideology and the Commonwealth perceived as the main secure outlet for British manufacturing. This radical change is best illustrated by the evolution of Disraeli's approach to the colonial question. In the 1860s, Disraeli considered the colonies as a dead weight and favoured 'self-government' for most of the British colonies (Hauser et al., 1952: 352) but by the late 1870s, Disraeli had become one of the strongest supporters of British imperialism and the extension of the Empire (Hauser et al., 1952: 355).

For the French government, colonies were perceived as a way to secure the development of the French economy when European markets were considered saturated. This position is described without ambiguity by Jules Ferry, the head of the French government: 'Europe can be considered like a trading company that has seen its turnover shrink over the years. European consumption is saturated. We need to create new layers of consumer from the other parts of the globe if we want to avoid the bankruptcy of European society' (translated from Ferry, 1890: 406).

Until 1890, German foreign policy had been characterised by a prudent and skilful use of the balance of power in a multipolar Europe. Chancellor Bismarck focused on consolidating the position of the newly unified Germany through a complex web of alliances (Milza, 1990: 15). After Bismarck, the German Reich's foreign policy became more bold and aggressive, trying to catch up with Britain and France in terms of colonial possession (Hauser et al., 1952). Germany began an intensive naval military build-up that led to an arms race with Britain symbolised by the opposition between German Admiral Von Tirpitz and British Admiral Fisher and widely publicised to the public opinions by the media of the time (Gildea, 1996: 403). German foreign policy supported the Boers' uprising in South Africa against the British and tried to contain French influence in Morocco through diplomatic and military interventions. The German government and industry developed the *Bagdadbahn* project, the construction of a railway network that could connect Germany with the Ottoman Empire and provide an access through Bassorah to the Indian Ocean. It also provided Germany with an easier access to the oilfields of the Middle East at a time when oil was becoming an increasingly important source of energy, especially for military purposes (Engdahl, 2004: 23).

For the British government and industry, the rise of Germany became the most important economic and military threat in the first decade of the twentieth century. That might be paradoxical as the United States had overtaken the UK as the largest economy in the world and the most technologically advanced with the largest 'prime movers' establishing subsidiaries in Europe. Nevertheless, the fast growth of the US economy and the continued inflow of migrants meant that US manufacturing was still mainly directed towards the domestic market. At the margins, Germany's expansion was colliding with British interests more than those of the US. Furthermore, important transatlantic financial links between the UK and its former colony generated a different attitude in the City, the financial centre, and from British investors (Benichi, 2008).

The UK developed an alliance with France and Russia to contain the rising influence of Germany and its allies. After Morocco, the Balkans became another manifestation of the conflict of interests between the UK and Germany and their respective allies. Many contemporary commentators expected that the Balkan wars of 1912 and 1913 would degenerate into a full-scale European war (Gildea, 1996: 410). Eventually, the assassination of the Austrian Archduke at Sarajevo in the summer of 1914 became the spark that ignited the calamitous fire of the First World War.

The overall result of this global bloody confrontation was to accelerate the decline of the UK and create a period without a clear hegemony until the disaster of the Second World War which let the US emerge as the superpower of the capitalist camp. The UK won what proved to be a pyrrhic victory as the First World War did not prevent Germany from continuing to rise and overtake Britain as an economic power.

Limitations of Comparisons with the Late Nineteenth Century in Understanding Twenty-first Century Changes to the Balance of Power

From this retrospective view of the decline of the UK in the late nineteenth century, it is easy to draw analogies with the current situation. Is the 2008 financial crisis a benchmark similar to that of 1873? Will this crisis generate a wave of protectionism and a new race for privileged market access through the establishment of zones of influence by the great economic powers like the US, Europe and China? Could this lead to a new arms race? What potential web of alliances will emerge from the Western decline and the rise of China? Despite obvious similarities, important differences remain.

Trade, Investment Flows, Protectionism and Economic Interdependency

Like Great Britain in the late nineteenth century, the US moved from a trade surplus after the Second World War to a trade deficit in the 1960s. The difference was that the British deficit was more than covered by the export of services and the repatriation of the returns of British investments abroad (Benichi, 2008). Unlike the British trade deficit, the US deficit was compensated by the selling of US financial assets to the rest of the world (Benichi, 2008).

Following their rising trade deficit in the late 1960s, the US turned to mild protectionism, using mechanisms like Voluntary Export Restraints (VERs) and Technical Barriers to Trade (TBT) or enacting protectionist laws like the Omnibus Foreign Trade and Competitiveness Act of 1974, strengthened in 1988 (Barton et al., 2006). There were some temporary and sporadic outbursts of protectionism (such as the US steel safeguards in 2001–2) (Hoekman and Kostecki, 2010: 429). However, generally, the US economy continued to open itself to the rest of the world – except for agriculture – until the eruption of the 2008 crisis. Even the recent protectionist moves by the US government (like Obama's 'Buy American' provisions) remain limited and cannot compare to those it took in 1930–31, such as the Smoot-Hawley initiative that imposed tariffs of more than 60 per cent (Ashbee, 2010: 148).

Since the 1980s, the US and Europe focused on the liberalisation of services and FDI flows and on intellectual property. This came as little surprise as US, European and Japanese MNEs internationalised their production processes. The share of the manufacturing sector has continued to shrink in the US economy – from 35.2 per cent in 1970 to 22.4 per cent of GDP in 2010 (United Nations, 2010). This is a new phenomenon that did not exist in the nineteenth century.

Just before the First World War, trade and FDI already accounted for a significant part of GDP in the European and US economies, almost at comparable levels to the 1990s. Siemens and AEG had already established affiliates in the UK and the US while companies like Singer and GE were already present in Europe (Wilkins, 1974; Hagen, 1999; Feldenkirchen, 1997). However, a major difference is the current share of intra-industrial vertical trade in the global economy that reflects the internationalisation of the production processes of MNEs which are producing or outsourcing different segments of their production in various countries according to their respective location-specific advantages. The international production networks that began to emerge in the 1960s but really took off in the 1990s generated a level of interdependency between the countries involved in these networks that had never been experienced before. Since the inception of its open-door policy and even more since 1992, China has been involved in these networks and this has generated an increased interdependency with the Western economies that did not exist between Germany, the UK and the US at the beginning of the twentieth century. This phenomenon also helps to avoid, despite the seriousness of the current crisis, a return to the disastrous protectionist policies of the late nineteenth century and the 1930s and to maintain what the WTO called 'a low-intensity' protectionism (WTO, 2009).

Nevertheless, one has to consider the limited resilience of these international production networks (IPN). Some US firms that outsourced or created subsidiaries in clusters of Mexican *maquiladoras* have since decided to relocate their activities to China, especially after China joined the WTO, generating the closure of 3,000 companies in the border region (*Le Monde*, 8 April 2003). Ireland created a business cluster in the assembly of computers in the early 1980s but lost major players like Dell and HP in the 2000s when they decided to relocate to new member states of the EU, like Poland, which offered better location-specific advantages (cheaper labour and land and closer proximity to continental Europe) (Cunningham-Sabot, 2009: 233). Business clusters that are not focused on high-tech can be replicated by other emerging countries, giving new options for MNEs to adapt their IPN according to new location-specific advantages. To what extent could the Chinese economy suffer the diversion of FDI toward competing emerging economies, thereby weakening China's insertion in the IPN of Western MNEs?

The first elements that can weaken China's interdependency with Western economies arise from the consequences of China's successful growth. The productivity gains of the industries located in the coastal areas generates demand for wage increases and more humane working conditions, as the cases of Honda and Foxconn have shown. Chinese workers begin to organise and some of their demands are backed by the central government which hopes that increasing wages will stimulate domestic consumption and reduce both their dependency on overseas markets and commercial frictions with their main trading partners. The CCP is also worried that inflation can reduce the purchasing power of the Chinese working class and, combined with the high level of social inequality, generate serious social tensions. Wages are therefore increasing fast in the developed regions. Land cost rise considerably because of economic development but also because of speculation bubbles. The central government is also progressively increasing the tax burden on MNEs by aligning them towards the standard corporate tax rate. These factors reduce the location-specific advantages of the coastal areas. Some MNEs have decided to move further inland but geography and infrastructure bottlenecks put serious limitations on the possibility of MNEs to 'go west'.

Some other less developed East Asian economies have already attracted companies involved in labour-intensive activities creating FDI flows away from China. Some European companies have also repatriated activities back from China. Furthermore, the US and Japanese authorities have strategic concerns over a too high level of dependency on China, notably in electronics, semiconductors and raw materials. They are trying to promote FDI and outsourcing to alternative locations such as the ASEAN or India. It is very difficult to assess the extent to which business will respond to such foreign policy incentives and lower the attractiveness of China for FDI. If strategic tensions between the US, Japan and China were to increase significantly, it is probable that it would generate some FDI diversion out of China.

Another crucial element is that many MNEs regionalise their production processes more than they globalise it. MNEs like VW, Danone and Xerox have set up semi-autonomous production processes in different regions (e.g. East Asia, Europe, North America and Latin America). Many of the largest parts of the IPN are organised at the regional level rather than at the global level (Dicken, 2007; Oman, 1994; UNCTAD, 1998). Geographic proximity is still an essential element in a world that is far from flat. Furthermore, institutional arrangements like customs unions, free-trade areas and webs of bilateral trade agreements or economic partnership agreements are still mainly intra-regional and they strengthen the regionalisation of production by MNEs. If this trend is dominant, Western MNEs could have subsidiaries in East Asia that operate on a regional rather than a global basis. In that case the degree of interdependency would lower over time. It is true that two-thirds of the foreign investors in China originate from East Asia and this share has been rising this last decade. Intra-regional East Asian trade is developing faster than inter-regional trade, a trend that is likely to continue as the Chinese market continues to grow faster than its Western counterparts.

The high level of interdependency between China and the West may have reached its zenith in the first decade of the twenty-first century. The sudden opening of China to FDI in the 1980s after decades of isolation, the enormous wage and real-estate price differential, China's critical size and the existence of some public goods that favoured FDI are the main factors that explain the massive insertion of China into the IPN of Western MNEs and the emergence of this economic interdependency. In the mid-run, as the wage and real-estate price differential lowers, China could also suffer from FDI diversion, a phenomenon observed in the advanced economies of the ASEAN in the 1990s, in Mexico in the 2000s or in Ireland after the EU enlargement of 2004 (Nesadurai, 2003; Cunningham-Sabot, 2009). China will certainly continue to attract FDI flows from Western MNEs but it might be more market-seeking than efficiency-seeking. If this is so, arguments for a degree of economic interdependency that would prevent the emergence of serious geopolitical conflicts between China and the West are seriously weakened. Market-seeking FDI do not create the same level of interdependency as efficiency-seeking ones. One should not forget that the US MNEs were the most important market-seeking investors in Germany and Japan prior to the Second World War (Wilkins, 1974; Chandler, 1994; Francks, 1992).

Interdependency is certainly one of the key factors that account for the limited outbursts of protectionism so far despite the seriousness of the global crisis, but it does not mean that the multilateral system is not under intense pressure. During the last Doha Development Agenda (DDA) WTO round, the US and the EU did not manage to get most of their agenda through, as they did in the Uruguay Round. More than a decade after Seattle, the current negotiation process has stalled. Since the failure of Cancun in 2003, the US has developed the concept of 'competitive liberalisation' trying to develop numerous bilateral preferential trade arrangements (Blustein, 2009: 174). Since then, the main trading partners have engaged in competition to secure bilateral or regional trade arrangements. Through bilateral deals the largest trading economies manage to gain preferential access to some markets and impose some of their agenda on their smaller trading partners, as is true of agreements like DR-CAFTA,[1] Cotonou's EU EPA[2] projects or Japan's EPAs with some of its ASEAN partners. This process has generated a proliferation of regional trade agreements (RTAs) that have generated overlapping agreements with different timetables, making the trade system less transparent and weakening the WTO.

In the context of the current economic slowdown and increased pressure for protectionism, preferential trade agreements are a way to secure market access that could be compared to the post-1873 competition for overseas markets. Of course, the vast majority of these agreements are WTO compatible and the potential regional trading blocs in East Asia, Europe-Mediterranean-ACP and NAFTA-DR-CAFTA are based upon the principle of an 'open regionalism'. This was not the case for the colonies but one should not forget that commercial competition in the late nineteenth and early twentieth centuries also occurred in markets that were not formal colonies like South America, Russia, the Balkans, the Ottoman Empire and China. Even the colonies, prior to 1914, were not completely closed to foreign trade and investments. The British-Dutch MNE Unilever operated in Belgian and French colonial Africa and the subsidiary of Siemens in Great Britain could supply British colonies (Feldenkirchen, 1997; Mandel, 1973).

Formal multilateral institutions focused on global economic governance did not exist in the 1873–1914 period, but neither was it a period characterised by hermetic imperial commercial fortresses.

The Scramble for Raw Materials and Energy

Furthermore, the rising demand of emerging economies, most notably of China, for raw materials and energy products has generated an atmosphere of competition between China, Europe and the US. Chinese penetration in Africa is perceived with increasing anxiety by the former European colonial powers, especially by France. In terms of FDI stocks and trade, the European Union continues to be the dominant economic power in Africa. Nevertheless, Chinese ODI flows and trade to Africa have increased dramatically since 2003. Chinese projects are developing fast and the amounts of Chinese official aid for development programmes in Africa are now comparable to those of the EU and the multilateral institutions, but without much of the conditional elements in respect of environment and good governance standards. A moralistic discourse is rooting itself in the EU institutions and European chancelleries claiming that Chinese development programmes to Africa provide an alternative access to capital that enables African ruling elites to avoid tackling human rights, governance and environment standards. However, one could argue that the main source of Western aid to Africa comes through bilateral programmes that impose far less constraints on the recipients about these specific issues. It would be difficult to claim that bilateral French or Belgian aid programmes to Congo, the Democratic Republic of Congo, Togo or Gabon have always been very binding as regards such issues for the benefiting governments (Defraigne and Belligoli, 2010). The same phenomenon can be observed in the Middle East, notably with Iran. To the eyes of the Chinese leadership, the moralistic rhetoric put forward by Western nations and the Western-dominated multilateral institutions like the IMF or the World Bank can be perceived as a way to protect their dominant economic and strategic positions in Africa and the Middle East.

The Chinese government only uses economic power (trade, FDI and aid programmes) to secure access to key raw materials but this is likely to generate rising friction with the EU and the US. Indeed, some Western analysts claim that the Chinese government is bending market competition rules by using an active industrial policy and that China should rely on global market mechanisms to import its key raw materials. However, this would be the first time since the late nineteenth century that a major power would rely on simple market mechanisms to secure its strategic sources of energy and raw materials. English and US interventions in the Middle East, from the creation of the Anglo-Persian Oil Company in the early twentieth century to the recent wars in Afghanistan and Iraq, have shown that to establish their leadership, the so-called 'seven sisters' that dominated the global oil industry relied heavily on diplomacy and military intervention. The French and Italians, who were latecomers, also relied on strong government intervention when building energy MNEs and securing supply (Defraigne, 2004). Furthermore, when the China National Offshore Oil Corporation (CNOOC) attempted to use market mechanisms (even with probable Chinese state financial support) to take over the US oil producer Unocal, it faced a veto by the US Congress on national security grounds (*Financial Times*, 23 May 2005; Sutter, 2008: 181). In a global oligopolistic energy market where the US and Europe remain key players, it is quite improbable that China would not take the same road as its predecessors.

Strategic Tensions

Just as with Great Britain in the late nineteenth century, the US government has decided both to contain and to engage with China. The US containment strategy is quite obvious. The US have tried to build a network of strategic and military cooperation agreements with China's neighbours from the traditional Cold War alliance networks which include Japan, South Korea, Taiwan and Thailand to newcomers like Mongolia, Uzbekistan, India (under the Bush administration) and Vietnam. Despite some reservations from Germany and France, the US has managed to persuade its Western European allies to uphold the arms embargo against China (Casarini, 2009; Sutter, 2008: 347). To a certain extent, China today does not enjoy strong and reliable allies like Germany in the late nineteenth century, although one could argue that even if Germany had many allies on paper, a lot of the treaties in the complex alliance system set up by Bismarck were not fulfilled. Germany faced the defection of Russia (linked through the *Dreikaiserbund* alliance treaty) and of Italy (part of the *Triplice*) in 1914. However, China does not currently enjoy a similar web of alliances with *major* global players (despite strong ties with some regional powers like Iran or Venezuela, which have difficult relations with Western countries). Even China's partnership-building with Russia since the end of the Cold War and especially after the US invasion of Iraq in 2003 could be reversed by the recent warming of US–Russian relations (Shirk, 2007). The main response of China is to use its trading power to break this containment strategy. However, as some of the following chapters will show, China is engaged in a rapid modernisation of its army and is building a regional military projection capacity (although it is still far from having a global one). Chinese military spending is still way behind the US, both in relative and absolute terms, but the respective growth rates and public debt of those two giants could generate a less asymmetrical situation in the decades to come.

A greater technological gap

A major difference between the situation prevailing after the 1873 crisis and that after the 2008 crisis is probably the technological gap between the hegemonic power and its potential contender. By the late nineteenth century German firms quickly became 'prime movers' in key new industries such as electrical products and chemistry and in many aspects Great Britain was caught-up with by both the US and Germany. The UK still maintained advantages in international services (banking, insurance, finance and transport) and in some strategic technologies (such as military shipbuilding) but was matched or surpassed in some advanced industries (Chandler, 1990). This is clearly not yet the case for the United States. The international flow of technological rents, number of patents, scientific articles with international quotations, absolute R&D spending and number of researchers per inhabitant shows that no economy can yet match the advanced technological level of the US, even Japan and Europe (OECD, 2010; UNCTAD, 2008). Despite impressive progress China still lags behind, especially in fundamental research, internationally used patents, scientific articles with international quotations and absolute R&D spending (Sachwald, 2007; UNCTAD 2008). Because of the different geopolitical context and the new multilateral trading system that includes TRIPs (Trade-Related Aspects of Intellectual Property Rights) aspects, it will be more difficult for China to acquire technology than it was for the most advanced economies in East Asia like Japan, South Korea and Taiwan (Defraigne, 2008). Over what period of time the effects of size, learning by doing and massively funded industrial policies by the Chinese authorities can fill the technological gap with Europe, Japan and then the US is impossible to assess. It will depend eventually on exogenous factors (major technological breakthrough, pandemics, new substantial global and regional crises or new patterns in demographics and environment) and also of the capacity of the Chinese government to tackle the current challenges that could jeopardise sustainable growth of its economy. Given the current gap, it cannot be reasonably expected for China to catch up with the most advanced economies in the next two decades. In that respect, the current configuration is different from the period of 1873–1914 and the US hegemonic position seems less directly challenged in the mid-run than that of the UK in the late nineteenth century.

EUROPE: A PERIPHERAL ROLE AS THE BALANCE OF POWER SHIFTS BETWEEN THE US AND CHINA

What could be the role of the European Union in this configuration? In its current state, it is difficult to see the EU playing a decisive role because it is far from being a full global power. Its inability to present a united front has always weakened its global influence and placed it in the limited role of soft power. Some analysts have pointed out that in the 1980s, the Chinese leadership expected the EU to transform itself into an autonomous global power, challenging the hegemony of the US and helping to create the multi-polar world wished for by the CCP leadership. Progressively, China and other developing powers became disillusioned by the weaknesses of the emerging EU foreign policy and the incapacity to reach consensus on important security and global governance issues (Sutter, 2008; Casarini, 2009). There were renewed expectations by the Chinese after the second war in Iraq because of the stand taken by Germany and France against the US-led unilateralist military invasion. Because of the division between EU member states on this issue, Germany, France, Belgium and Luxemburg openly mentioned the possibility of building a core of EU members having a common defence force with a common foreign policy (*Financial Times*, 9 December 2003). Chirac and Schroeder contemplated Franco-German mergers in the defence industry to establish a common industrial military base (*The Economist*, 22 May 2004). At the same time, they were discussing the possibility of lifting the arms embargo against China which implied the possibility of transferring more high-tech to China (Casarini, 2009). However, this strategy which was defiant of US policy, was soon abandoned, mergers were not completed and the arms embargo was not lifted.

In terms of foreign policy, the institutional changes generated by the Lisbon Treaty have yet to prove that EU credibility has been significantly improved. Confusion remains on the precise hierarchy and division of power between the three highest supranational offices. Europe continues to be dominated by the triumvirate or *directoire* of the three largest economies. The Lisbon institutional framework continues to offer Germany, France and the UK blocking minorities against the other EU members.

In the different fields of economic governance, trade policy is where the EU influence is the greatest because it negotiates as a single entity. But even in matters of trade, the member states' agenda can seriously clash with the Commission's. This was quite visible when the French government openly opposed Commissioner Peter Mandelson's deal during the DDA negotiation on the agricultural question, seriously undermining Europe's bargaining position (*Le Monde*, 25 October 2005). Because of the limited European supranational financial transfers that could compensate the member states that will be the most affected by a trade agreement, those in charge of the EU trade policy need to negotiate a carefully balanced package which seriously limits their room for manoeuvre vis-à-vis their international trading partners.

Regarding the global trading system, there is clearly a convergence with many of the positions held by the US. The US and European Union authorities, having the most advanced economies with Japan, share common concerns about the Singapore issues and labour standards and would like to impose them through a multilateral rule-based system. At the same time, as the multilateral trade system is blocked due to the better bargaining position of some of the large emerging economies, both the US and the EU are engaged in competitive bilateralism and multiple Regional Trade Arrangements (RTAs) with emerging economies. The EU will naturally be closer to the US than China because of its degree of economic maturity. China's industrial policy of nurturing potential Chinese global competitors in capital-intensive and high-tech industries constitutes a common threat for the dominant position of the MNEs from the US, Europe and Japan. Most aspects of Chinese industrial policy will continue to be opposed by the most developed economies in the mid-run, such as China's: limiting international access to public sector procurement; subsidising of state-owned enterprises (SOEs) through cheap credit by state-owned banks; controlling the value of the Chinese currency; leniency on intellectual property (IP) violations by Chinese firms; and using development programmes to ensure access to raw materials and procurements overseas.

Regarding the international monetary system and financial global governance, Europe does not have a common position. Substantial differences remain among member states on their respective views about how to manage the global monetary and financial system. The development of the euro has certainly considerably increased the weight of the EU in the international monetary system. Despite the current crisis of the eurozone, the euro has become an international hard currency, reducing the US *seignorage* obtained since the establishment of the Bretton Woods institutions which gave the dollar the official status of world currency. Since the recent crisis, some member states are pushing for a higher degree of financial regulation but there is no consensus on these issues, notably between the three biggest European economies. Again, disunity considerably weakens Europe's bargaining position in this field of global governance.

The handling of the financial crisis has again shown the weakness of the EU as an actor. There was no European equivalent of the Paulson plan as fiscal policy remains the prerogative of member states. The coordinated fiscal rescue package was again organised by the *directoire* comprised of Brown, Sarkozy and Merkel. European Commission President Barroso tried vainly to present it some days later as a European plan. The financial crisis and its destabilising effects on the eurozone could generate more devolution of power at the supranational level of terms of financial transfers and financial regulation but the changes have been timid ad hoc responses to the turmoil of the financial markets rather than a visible coherent long-term strategy on global and European financial governance.

On the matter of access to energy and raw materials, the EU has a position of historical incumbency with major MNEs already enjoying a dominant position on the global market. Again, this is a situation that should bring it closer to the US position than that of China. The EU might feel threatened by the rise of Chinese MNEs in these sectors, notably in its traditional 'backyard' of Africa and the Mediterranean.

Apart from trade aspects in which the supranational powers of the EU are the strongest, the EU is not likely to exert a great influence in a global environment characterised by the rise of China and the erosion of US policy. Lacking strong supranational institutions with well defined powers, the EU external policies can only have a limited impact. The common economic interest with the US is likely to be stronger than with China as the former together with Europe is an established economic power. As long as the EU lacks a common defence policy, it will remain dependent on the US in terms of military technology and engagement capacity. This absence of hard power will severely constrain the EU in its strategic choices for a new model of global economic governance that could adapt to the rise of China and other large emerging economies. Furthermore, despite important inter-regional trade and investment flows, the EU's economic and strategic diplomacy in East Asia remains timid and is not well defined. East Asia is not the most dynamic region in the world and it is where the rise of China and the containment and engagement strategies of the US will be decisive in any shift in the balance of power in the first half of the twenty-first century. Most economic forecasts suggest that the centre of the world economy will shift from the Atlantic to the Pacific. If Europe cannot stop its relative economic decline and continues to be divided by the contradictions of its three economic powers, it is most likely to play a peripheral role as power shifts between the US, as the declining hegemony, and China, as the rising contender.

NOTES

1. Dominican Republic-Central America-United States Free Trade Agreement.
2. Economic partnership agreements.

REFERENCES

Aglietta, Michel L. Y. (2007) *La Chine vers la Superpuissance*. Paris: Economica.

Ash, Robert (2008) 'Europe's commercial relation with China', in D. Shambaugh, E. Sandschneider and H. Zhou (eds), *China–Europe Relations: Perceptions, Policies and Prospects*. London: Routledge, pp. 189–230.

Ashbee, Edward (2010) *The US Economy Today*. Manchester: Manchester University Press.

Bairoch, Paul (1997) *Victoires et déboires*, Vols I, II, III. Paris: Gallimard.

Banque Mondiale (2004) *La Chine et l'OMC: Adhésion, Politique de Réforme et Stratégie de Réduction de Pauvreté*. Washington: Banque Mondiale.

Barton, John H., Goldstein, Judith, Josling, Timothy and Steinberg, Richard (2006) *The Evolution of the Trade Regime: Politics, Law and Economics of the GATT and the WTO*. Princeton, NJ: University Press.

Bean, Richard (1973) 'War and the birth of the nation state', *Journal of Economic History*, 33: 203–21.

Beaud, Michel (1990) *Histoire du Capitalisme de 1500 à nos Jours*. Paris: Seuil.

Belden, Jack (2003) *China Shakes the World*. Beijing: Foreign Languages Press.

Benichi, Régis (2008) *Histoire de la Mondialisation*. Paris: Vuibert.

Bergère, Marie-Claire (1986) *L'Age d'Or de la Bourgeoisie Chinoise*. Paris: Flammarion.

Bianco, Lucien (1997) *Les origines de la Révolution Chinoise*. Paris: Folio.

Blustein, Paul (2009) *Misadventures of the Most Favored Nations*. New York: Public Affairs.

Bouissou, Jean-Marie (2007) *Le Japon Contemporain*. Paris: Fayard-CERI.

Brainard, Lael and Martinez-Diaz, Leonardo (2009) *Brazil as an Economic Superpower?* Washington, DC: Brookings Institution Press.

Braudel, Fernand (1985) *La Dynamique du Capitalisme*. Paris: Flammarion.

Cao, Cong, Suttmeier, Richard P. and Simon, Denis Fred (2006) 'China's 15 Years Science and Technology Plan', *Physics Today*, December. Available at: http://www.levininstitute.org/pdf/Physics%20Today-2006.pdf (accessed 17 February 2011).

Casarini, Nicola (2009) *Remaking Global Order: The Evolution of Europe–China Relations and Its Implications for East Asia and the United States*. Oxford: Oxford University Press.

Chancellor, E. (2011) 'Entranced by China's bubbling economy', *Financial Times*, 6 February. Available at: http://www.ft.com/cms/s/0/13604674-3092-11e0-9de3-00144feabdc0.html#axzz1EEjIVguO (accessed 17 Febraury 2011).

Chandler, Alfred D. (1990) *Scale and Scope, the Dynamic of Industrial Capitalism*. Cambridge, MA: Harvard University Press.

Clough, Ralph (1989) 'Taiwan under nationalist rule, 1949–1982', in *Cambridge History of China*, Vol. 15. Cambridge, MA: Cambridge University Press.

Cunningham-Sabot, E. (2009) 'L'Irlande, victime idéale de la crise mondiale', in *Images Economiques du Monde 2010*. Paris: Armand Colin.

De Joncquières, G. (2005) 'Not patently obvious', *Financial Times*, 24 October 2005.

Defraigne, Jean-Christophe (2004) *De l'Intégration Nationale à l'Intégration Continentale*. Paris: L'Harmattan.

Defraigne, Jean-Christophe (2005) 'The prospects of Chinese firms in an opening economy: breaking away from the "flying geese" pattern or turning into another case of East Asian ersatz capitalism?', *Belgian Review of Geography (BELGEO)*, III: 275–307.

Defraigne, Jean-Christophe (2008) *Sleeping Giants or Global Competitors? Assessing the Possibilities of the Largest Chinese Firms to Evolve from State-Nurtured National Champions into Global Competitors*, Working Paper. Brussels: CEREC-FUSL.

Defraigne, Jean-Christophe (2009) 'La Chine: perspectives economiques et sociales', *Revue Economique et Sociale*, 67 (1): 156–73.

Defraigne, Jean-Christophe (2012) 'The limits of the sustainability of China's growth', in Eric Florence and Pierre Defraigne (eds), *Economy, Society and Politics in Twenty-First Century China*. London: Routledge.

Defraigne, Jean-Christophe and Belligoli, Serena (2010) *Ties Between Business and Aid Programs in Africa: A Comparative Analysis between the European and Chinese Cases*. Glasgow: EBHA Annual Conference 2010, 26–28 August.

Dicken, Peter (2007) *Global Shift: Reshaping the Global Economic Map in the 21st Century*. London: Sage.

Economist, The (2010) 'Friend or foe? A special report on China's place in the world', 4 December.

Engdahl, William (2004) *A Century of War: Anglo-American Oil Politics and the New World Order*. London: Pluto Press.

European Commission – DG Relex (2007) *EU–China Economic Observatory: A Report for the European Commission*, Draft Report, Issue 6. Brussels: European Commission.

Feldenkirchen, Wilfried (1997) 'Competition and cooperation in the German Electrical industry in the home and world markets', in H. Pohl (ed.), *Competition and Cooperation of Enterprises on National and International Markets*. Stuggart: Franz Steiner Verlag.

Ferry, Jules (1890) *Le Tonkin et la Mère Patrie*. Paris: Havard.

Fontaine, André (1983) *Histoire de la guerre froide*. Paris: Fayard.

Fortune (1995) 'Fortune Global 500 – 1995', in *Fortune*. New York: Times Warner.

Fortune (2010) 'Fortune Global 500 – 2010', in *Fortune*. New York: Times Warner.

Francks, Penelope (1992) *Japanese Economic Development*. London: Routledge.

Friedman, D. and Samuels, R. (1993) 'The Japanese aircraft industry and Japan's technology ideology', in J. Frankel and M. Kahler (eds), *Regionalism and Rivalry: Japan and the United States in Pacific Asia*. Chigago: NBER and University of Chicago Press.

Gildea, Robert (1996) *Barricades and Borders: Europe 1800–1914*. Oxford: Oxford University Press.

Gipouloux, François (2006) *La Chine du 21ème siècle: Une Nouvelle Superpuissance?* Paris: Armand Colin.

Gray, John (1994) *Rebellions and Revolutions: China from the 1800s to the 1980s*. Oxford: Oxford University Press.

Hagen, Antje (1999) 'German direct investment in the United Kingdom, 1871–1918', *Business History*, 41 (2): 37–68.

Harding, Harry (1989) 'The Chinese state in crisis', in *Cambridge History of China*, Vol. 15. Cambridge: Cambridge University Press, pp. 107–89.

Hatch, W. and Yamamura, K. (1997) *Asia in Japan's Embrace: Building a Regional Production Alliance*. Cambridge, MA: Cambridge University Press.

Hauser, Henri, Benaerts, Pierre, Maurain, Jean and L'Huilier, Fernand (1952) *Du Libéralisme à l'Impérialisme 1860–1878, Peuples et Civilisations*. Paris: PUF.

Higgott, Richard (2000) 'Regionalism in the Asia Pacific: two steps forward, one step back', in R. Stubbs and G. Underhill (eds), *Political Economy and the Changing Global Order*, 2nd edn. Oxford: Oxford University Press, pp. 254–63.

Hobday, Mike (1995) *Innovation in East Asia: The Challenge to Japan*. Aldershot, UK and Brookfield, US: Edward Elgar.

Hoekman, Bernard and Kostecki, Michel (2010) *The Political Economy of the World Trading System*. Oxford: Oxford University Press.

Hua, Chen (2005) 'China outward FDI meets challenges', *China Business Weekly*, 24 April.

Huang, Yasheng (2003) *Selling China: Foreign Direct Investment During the Reform Era*. Cambridge: Cambridge University Press.

Huang, Yasheng (2008) *Capitalism with Chinese Characteristics: Foreign Direct Investment during the Reform Era*. Cambridge: Cambridge University Press.

Huang, Yasheng (2010) 'China's unbalanced growth has served it well', *Financial Times*, 7 October.

IMF (2010) Official IMF website: http://www.imf.org.

Isaacs, Harold (1961) *The Tragedy of the Chinese Revolution*. Stanford, CA: Stanford University Press.

Jacques, Martin (2009) *When China Rules the World*. London: Allen Lane.

Jones, David Martin (1997) *Political Development in Pacific Asia Polity*. Cambridge: Cambridge University Press.

Joyaux, François (1988) *La Nouvelle Question d'Extrême-Orient 2: l'Ere du Conflit Sino-Soviétique 1959–1978*. Paris: Payot.

Jun, Li (2010) *China's Climate Policy for a Low-Carbon Development Pathway*. Paper presented at the International Conference 'Tearing Down the Great Wall of Ignorance between China and the EU', European Economic and Social Committee, 19 November, Brussels.

Kissinger, Henry (1994) *Diplomacy*. New York: Simon & Schuster.

Kolko, Gabriel (1994) *A Century of War*. New York: New Press.

Komiya, Ryutaro and Itoh, Motoshige (1988) 'Japan's international trade and trade policy 1955–1984', in I. Takashi and D. Okimoto (eds), *The Political Economy of Japan*, Vol. 2, *The Changing International Context*. Stanford, CA: Stanford University Press, pp. 173–224.

Kroeber, Arthur (2005) 'China's century is still a long march away', *Financial Times*, 22 June.

Laborde, David (2007) 'Doha, un cycle en développement', in CEPII, *L'Economie Mondiale 2008*. Paris: La Découverte.

Lafay, Gérard (2004) *Initiation à l'Economie Internationale*. Paris: Economica.

Lanzarotti, Mario (1992) *La Corée du Sud: une Sortie du Sous-développement*. Paris: IEDES & PUF.

Lardy, Nicolas (1989) 'The Chinese economy under stress 1958–1965', in *Cambridge History of China*, Vol. 14. Cambridge: Cambridge University Press.

Lardy, Nicholas R. (2002) *Integrating China in the Global Economy*. Washington, DC: Brookings Institution Press.

Lardy, Nicholas R. (2006) *Toward a Consumption-Driven Growth Path*. Policy Brief, Institute for International Economics. Available at: http://www.iie.com/publications/pb/pb06-6.pdf (accessed 18 February 2011).

Lenain, Patrick (1993) *Le FMI*. Paris: La Découverte.

Lew, Roland (1980) *1949: Mao prend le pouvoir*. Bruxelles: Editions Complexe.

MacFarquar, Roderick (1989) 'The sucession to Mao and the end of Maoism', in

The Cambridge History of China, Vol. 15. Cambridge: Cambridge University Press.
McKinsey Global Institute (2009) *Global capital market: entering a new era*. Available at: http://www.mckinsey.com/Insights/MGI/Research/Financial_Markets/Global_capital_markets_entering_a_new_era (accessed 27 January 2012).
Maddison, Angus (1995) *L'Economie Mondiale 1820–1992: Analyse et Statistiques*. Paris: OCDE.
Mandel, Ernest (1973) *Traité d'Economie Marxiste*. Paris: 10/18 Bourgois.
Maschke, E. (1969) 'Outline of the history of German cartels from 1873 to 1914', in François Crouzet (ed.), *Essays in European Economic History: 1798–1914*. London: Hodder & Stoughton Educational, pp. 226–58.
Milza, Pierre (1990) *Les Relations Internationales de 1871 à 1914*. Paris: Armand Colin.
Mote, Frederick W. (2003) *Imperial China 900–1800*. Cambrige, MA: Harvard University Press.
Narlikar, Amrita (2005) *The World Trade Organization*. Oxford: Oxford University Press.
Naughton, Barry (2007) *The Chinese Economy: Transition and Growth*. Cambridge, MA: MIT Press.
Nesadurai, Helen S. (2003) *Globalization, Domestic Politics and Regionalism: The ASEAN Free Trade Area*. London: Routledge.
OECD (2010) *Science, Technology and Industry Outlook 2010*. Paris: OECD.
Oman, Charles (1994) 'Globalisation and regionalization', OCDE, Paris.
Perkins, D. H. (1989) 'China's economic policy and performance', in *Cambridge History of China*, Vol. 15. Cambridge: Cambridge University Press.
Petri, Peter (1993) 'The East Asian trading bloc: an analytical history', in Jeffrey Frankel and Miles Kahler (eds), *Regionalism and Rivalry: Japan and the United States in Pacific Asia*. Chicago: University of Chicago Press.
Pollack, J. D. (1989) 'The opening to America', in *the Cambridge History of China*, Vol. 15. Cambridge: Cambridge University Press.
Rocca, Jean Louis (2010) *Une Sociologie de la Chine*. Paris: La Découverte.
Sachwald, Frédérique (2007) *La Chine Puissance Technologique Emergente*. Paris: IFRI.
Samuels, Richard J. (1994) *Rich Nation Strong Army: National Security and the Technological Transformation of Japan*. New York: Cornell University Press.
Sapir, Jacques (2008) *Le nouveau 21ème siècle: du siècle américain au retour des nations*. Paris: Seuil.
Shirk, Susan (2007) *China: Fragile Superpower*. Oxford: Oxford University Press.
Sutter, Robert G. (2008) *Chinese Foreign Relations*. Lanham, MD: Rowman & Littlefield.
Teiwes, Frederick C. (1989) 'Establishment and consolidation of the Regime', in *Cambridge History of China*, Vol. 14. Cambridge, MA: Cambridge University Press.
UNCTAD (1993) *1993 World Investment Report*. Geneva: UNCTAD.
UNCTAD (1998) *1998 World Investment Report*. Geneva: UNCTAD.
UNCTAD (2003) *China: An Emerging FDI Outward Investor*, e-brief. Geneva: UNCTAD.
UNCTAD (2006) *2006 World Investment Report*. Geneva: UNCTAD.
UNCTAD (2008) *2008 World Investment Report*. Geneva: UNCTAD.

UNCTAD (2010) *2010 World Investment Report*. Geneva: UNCTAD.
UNDP (2008) *Human Development Report 2008*. New York: UNDP.
UNDP (2009) *Human Development Report 2009*. New York: UNDP.
UNPD (2010) Available at http://data.un.org. (Accessed 2011).
USCC (2007) *United States–China Economic and Security Review Commission Hearings*. Washington, DC: USCC.
Vanderwee, Herman (1990) *Histoire Economique Mondiale: 1945–1990*. Paris: Academia Duculot.
Wallerstein, Immanuel (1974) *The Modern World-System*, Vol. 1. San Diego, CA: Academic Press.
Wedeman, Andrew H. (2003) *From Mao to Market*. Cambridge, MA: Cambridge University Press.
Whiting, Allen (1989) 'The Sino-Soviet split', in *Cambridge History of China*, Vol. 14. Cambridge, MA: Cambridge University Press.
Wilkins, Mira (1970) *The Emergence of the Multinational Enterprise: American Business Abroad from the Colonial Era to 1914*. Cambridge, MA: Harvard University Press.
Wilkins, Mira (1974) *The Maturing of the Multinational Enterprise: American Business Abroad from 1914 to 1970*. Cambridge MA: Harvard University Press.
Wilson, Dominic and Purushothaman, Roopa (2003) *Dreaming with the BRICs*, Global Economic Paper No. 99. New York: Goldman Sachs.
World Trade Organization (WTO) (2009) LAMY, Pascal: Opening Speech, WTO Public Forum, 2009, www.wto.org/english/forums.../dg_speech_e.pdf
World Trade Organization (WTO) (2010) statistics. Available at: http://stat.wto.org/CountryProfile.
Yoshihara, Kunio (1988) *The Rise of Ersatz Capitalism in Southeast Asia*. Oxford: Oxford University Press.
Zysman, John and Schwartz, Andrew (1998) *Enlarging Europe: The Industrial Foundations of a New Political Reality*. Berkeley, CA: International and Area Studies, University of California.

2. China and the EU in global governance: seeking harmony in identities[1]

Yiwei Wang

Taking a historical perspective, the current state of China–US relations could hardly be worse and China–EU relations could not be better since the former have overlapping geopolitical interests, for instance in the Taiwan Strait, while the latter have not. But even China and the EU are not cooperating well in Africa where they have increasingly overlapping geopolitical interests. This is a reminder that to grasp the true essence of China–EU relations, it is necessary to go beyond traditional realist or liberalist perspectives.

As both an old and new country, China shares more similarities with the EU than with the US. Such a conclusion can be drawn by reference to the shared diverse cultures, hierarchical traditions and secular societies of China and the EU, or from American exceptionalism based on Protestantism and its anti-communism gene. China is an old civilisation but a new player in world affairs, and so is the EU. China is a cultural community instead of a nation-state[2] and so is the EU. China enjoys dynamic and diverse identities, as does the EU, which cause both clashes and collaborations between the two.

CHINA'S DYNAMIC IDENTITIES IN TODAY'S WORLD

Liang Qichao, a great scholar at the end of the Qin Dynasty, has classified Chinese history as 'China's China', 'Asia's China' and 'the world's China' which also embodied China's three identities (Liang, 1901: 11–12). In today's world, China's China refers to socialism with Chinese characteristics. Asia's China refers to eastern civilisation (East Asian civilisation). The world's China refers to a developing country and emerging power.

China lost its traditional identity following the Opium Wars (I: 1840–42, II: 1856–60) and has witnessed the Long March to seek its new identity. The traditional Chinese world outlook 'all-under-heaven' (or China's China, in which China equals the world) collapsed fundamentally when China lost the war with Japan in 1895. Not until 1912, when the Republic of China was founded as the first democratic nation in Asia, did China finally accept a new identity of Asia's China and partly the world's China,[3] with the integration of a Western system based on sovereignty and nation-state, combined with a traditional Chinese political structure. When the People's Republic of China was founded in 1949, China got a new identity: socialist state. At the same time, China identified itself as the big brother of the Third World during Mao's era. After it began to open and reform, China became an emerging power by integrating with Asia and the world through the embrace of regionalisation and globalisation, and through which Chinese identities such as Asia's China and the world's China are fully coming into being. Since China is seeking 'win-win' development and integration with the world instead of independent development as in the past, its identity as pure 'China's China' is being replaced more and more by 'Asia's China' and 'the world's China'. China joined the WTO in 2001, which is usually considered as the milestone on the way to China's full membership in 'the world's China'.

Until now, China has adopted a 'peaceful rise/peace development' strategy and 'harmonious world' outlook. But with the rise of economic China, political China follows and cultural China comes thereafter. The relations between China and the world have reached the stage of 'the world's China' vs. 'China's world', i.e. between China's place in the world and the Chinese world perspective. And today's Chinese aggressive diplomacy and public opinion indicates that China's focus has shifted more and more from 'the world's China' to 'China's world'.

No doubt, the world's China, i.e. China's identity as a developing country and emerging power, is more discussed and recognised in today's world. China's China and Asia's China are working under domestic constraints in shaping China's international behaviour.

Of course, China's identity is changing not just because China is undertaking transition during a period of openness and reform but partly because the world's identity is also changing, i.e. a new world identity is being shaped. After the Second World War, a new international order emerged. The Western/American version of globalisation is giving way to diverse globalisation. China is adjusting itself to prepare for the future and the world should also adjust itself to match the rise of the emerging powers.

In all, there are four identities for China: China's China as a socialist state, Asia's China as an Eastern civilisation, the world's China as an emerging power and China as a developing country. How does one make China's four identities coexist harmoniously? Chinese historian Zhang Baijia described the interface between China and the world as 'the world impacts China through China's self-changing' (Zhang, 2002: 4–19). Such logic has been tested by Chinese modern semi-colonial and semi-feudal history and continues to be tested by the practice of 'socialism with Chinese characteristics'.

Also, because of that, China always claims that foreign policy is the extension of domestic politics and highlights the guideline of non-interference in the internal affairs of others, considering it as one of the five principles of peaceful coexistence. Chinese low-profile diplomacy *tao guang yang hui* can also be grasped using such logic, which means that the Chinese government always focuses on domestic politics first. China has hesitated to take diplomatic initiatives in former times.

Has the logic changed now? Has China reached the stage of 'Changing Itself through Changing the World'? (Zhang, 2002). Partly yes. After all, the world is on the eve of dramatic changes needed to cope with global challenges and to meet the demands of the emerging powers. But such changes fall far behind China's changes. Whatever changes China has made, some countries remain unsatisfied with the quite new but not totally new China.

Partly no. We should not exaggerate or over-explain China's rise which is mainly benefiting from the process of globalisation. Rising Chinese power is not just an independent power which China can use freely, but a structural power dependent on the world. And most importantly, China is still a developing country. Chinese Premier Wen Jiabao often makes a multiplication-division comparison:

> As premier of China, my responsibility is heavy, the job is demanding, and there is endless work to do. 1.3 billion is a very big number. So if we use multiplication, any small problem multiplied by 1.3 billion will end up being a very big problem. For a very big aggregate divided by 1.3 billion, it will come to a very tiny figure. This is something that is quite difficult for foreign visitors to understand and appreciate (Downie *et al.*, 2003).

The future balance between China's world and the world's China will be determined by the interaction between China and the world and it will be tested by a China–EU clash of identities.

THE EU'S IDENTITY CRISIS OR IDENTITY DILEMMA?

Unlike China's enduring dynamic identities, 'Europe, as a whole, is going through a clear identity crisis at both national and individual levels.' (Radu, 2010: preface). As George Weigel has pointed out:

> Europe, and especially Western Europe, is in the midst of a crisis of civilizational morale. The most dramatic manifestation of that crisis is not to be found in Europe's fondness for governmental bureaucracy or its devotion to fiscally shaky health care schemes and pension plans, in Europe's lagging economic productivity or in the appeasement mentality that some European leaders display toward Islamist terrorism. No, the most dramatic manifestation of Europe's crisis of civilizational morale is the brute fact that Europe is depopulating itself. (Weigel, 2005: 1)

The European sovereign debt crisis makes the retirement age a controversial issue among EU member states, which not only reveals the above-mentioned European morale problem as 'European society has lost its moral and cultural bearings' (Weigel, 2005: 2) but also reveals a European identity crisis for its postmodern model and for European capitalism(s).

More importantly, the EU is facing identity dilemmas also. In general, the EU can be described as a normative power. However, the EU's self-identification as such has both advantages and disadvantages.

In Europe's eyes, the EU is a *sui generis* normative power which distinguishes it from others and from history as discovered by Ian Manners:

> [...] the EU is a normative power: it changes the norms, standards and prescriptions of world politics away from the bounded expectations of state-centricity. However, it is one thing to say that the EU *is* a normative power by virtue of its hybrid polity consisting of supranational and international forms of governance; it is another to argue that the EU *acts* in a normative (i.e. ethically good) way. (Manners, 2008: 65)

Ian Manners also outlined 'sustainable peace' as a prime normative principle of the EU. However, an international survey seriously questions the EU's role in the world:

> Europe should be a force for stability in the world. But an EU without an effective foreign policy mechanism, without the ability to shoulder its share of the military burden associated with keeping the world safe, with a faltering Euro and with too many new members is a big void where the world needs strength. Sometimes the greatest threat comes from those who could take action to preserve stability but who do not. (Rothkopf, 2009)

In today's world, mutual learning and tolerance among different civilisations is an inexhaustible source of strength for social progress. The European Union is a rising power in a declining continent (Germany is the only exception), which reveals the dilemmas of representativeness, integration and words and deeds concerning the EU's identification as a normative power (Wang, 2009: 69–70).

Besides normative power, Robert Cooper inclined to identify the EU as a 'postmodern' model when compared with other countries still living in a 'modern' stage, like China, or 'pre-modern' stage, like Afghanistan (Cooper, 2000: 1–55). However, other countries are not simply retracing Europe's history. Such an argument is full of European superiority and Euro-centricity, based as it is on a strong mentality of linear evolution.

However, when the EU inclines to identify China as a modern country while percieving itself as having reached the postmodern stage, China actually considers that Europe is taking a modern-day version of the 'all-under-heaven' approach which China gave up on a century ago. In this regard, the EU is also repeating Chinese historical mistakes.

China's rise as a result of the global power shift is redefining Europe's mentality/identity from universalism to post-universalism and vice versa. Europe is also shaping China's new identity by turning 'China's China' into 'the world's China'.

CLASH OF IDENTITIES BETWEEN CHINA AND THE EU

Similarly to China, the EU holds four identities in the eyes of the Chinese: the largest developed economic bloc, a postmodern model, Western civilisation and European capitalism(s). So, according to the multiplication principle, there should be $4 \times 4 = 16$ combinations for China–EU relations.

However, only reciprocal combinations make sense; in other words, there are four kinds of identity clashes in China–EU relations:

1. *Socialism vs. capitalism.* China's China vs the EU's EU, or why China still feels the ideological gap with the EU. Some Eastern European countries even consider China as a communist country like the old Soviet Union, which leads to less flexible EU positions towards China regarding democracy or human rights. However, China highlights the 'people's heart', i.e. the essence and goal of democracy and human rights and not just the means and procedures that are particularly espoused by the European green and liberal parties.
2. *Eastern civilisation vs. Western civilisation.* Asia's China vs Europe's EU, or why China still feels a cultural gap with the EU. China is one of the few ancient civilisations that has not been colonised by Europe at some point, which leads to today's confrontation over universalism.

China considers European universalism as Europeanism especially as 'the silent majority' wakes up with the rise of the middle class in BRIC countries.

3. *Developing country vs. developed countries bloc.* The world's China I vs. the world's EU I, which invites controversial debate over China's international responsibilities. China defines itself as a developing country since China's per capita GDP ranks only around 100 in the world, while Europeans consider China as being irresponsible and hiding behind the curtain of being a developing bloc.
4. *Emerging power vs. postmodern model.* The world's China II vs. the world's EU II, which causes a possible zero-sum game between China and the EU in the eyes of conservative Europeans. The World Bank sharply increasing China's weighting and the reduction of that of Europe and Japan provides evidence for such a mentality. Unlike the European image of a postmodern model as having surpassed the modern stage, Chinese realists simply treat Europe as a defensive or declining power.

The China–EU identity gaps, for instance Europe identifying China as a hierarchical state without a dynamic/diverse society and vice versa, creates a lot of misperceptions between Chinese and Europeans.

It would be much more productive if the EU accepted the Chinese model as an alternative to its own, considered China as a different civilisation, and did not attempt to tailor the model according to a modern EU mentality, including with regard to such issues as human rights and democracy. As one of the most topical global issues, climate change reveals these lessons more clearly.

CASE STUDY: WHY CHINA AND THE EU ARE INHARMONIOUS IN COPING WITH CLIMATE CHANGE

Identity follows responsibility and responsibility reflects identity. Multilateral and dynamic identities draw multilateral and dynamic responsibilities. For both China and the EU appropriate responsibilities should follow their respective four identities.

Climate change is a good case. China's position on climate change should keep the following three dimensions in balance with its four identities since the third dimension can be divided further in two.

1. *'China's China'*. For the Chinese, basic human rights mean the right to live and develop. Facing global climate change, feeding up 1.3 billion people and providing a comfortable environment for them are the basic responsibilities of the Chinese government. In doing so, Chinese emission rights have not been used up when compared with other countries. Chinese per person emission is less than one-third that of developed countries.
2. *'Asia's China'*. Asian countries suffer the most from climate change due to population density and rapid modernisation. As the biggest country in Asia and the most populous country in the world, China will take an increasingly leading role in building up an Asian regional mechanism to cope with climate change on the basis of the economic frameworks.
3. *'World's China'*.
   (a) *Developing country*. As a permanent member of the UN Security Council representing the developing countries, China should protect their rights by highlighting the principle of 'common but differentiated responsibility' under the Kyoto Protocol, preserving sovereignty by not accepting international inspection or deep quantified emission cuts, but volunteering to reduce emissions in their own way besides the emissions necessary for survival. For developing countries, development is key.
   (b) *Emerging power*. China is one of the emerging powers in the process of rapid development. One-third of Chinese greenhouse gas emissions are internationally transferred emissions. In other words, China exports products but inputs pollution at the same time. 'Made in China' is not just made for Chinese people, but is largely consumed by foreigners, especially Westerners who do not pay a tax on such international transfers of emissions.

As a special developing country and emerging power, China plays a leading role beyond its national interests in coping with climate change in the developing world and among emerging powers. Climate change is not just a challenge but also an opportunity to change the Chinese development model. Having realised this – even if the Chinese per person emission level is quite low – and considering climate change trends and the need for future international comparative advantage, China is voluntarily cutting its greenhouse gas emissions intensity per unit of GDP by 40–45 per cent below 2005 levels by 2020.

Of course, the order and level for the previously mentioned identities/responsibilities change over time, but the identity of 'China's China' is always the fundamental core.

At the same time, the EU plays a leading role in climate change being the largest developed economic bloc, a postmodern model, a Western civilisation, and as the representative of European capitalism(s).

The climate change issue, then, entails four paradigms for China–EU relations:

1. Relations between the biggest developing country and the biggest developed bloc mean that China–EU climate change relations lead to a convergence of the main contradictions between the two blocs, which holds the key for negotiation.
2. Relations between an emerging power and postmodern model, which result in a potential zero-sum game between China and the EU over the historical, legal and moral responsibilities for climate change, since the origins of today's climate change can be traced back to the European Industrial Revolution.
3. Relations between Eastern and Western civilisations, which lead to different approaches in dealing with climate change: adaptation or mitigation? The EU favours proactive options, for instance enforced reduction of CO_2 (mitigation) on the basis of dominant civilisation, while China favours living with the consequences (adaptation) of climate change on the base of a civilisation based on harmony between man and nature.
4. Relations between socialism and capitalism, which bring together different mentalities in negotiating: justice or efficiency? Although in domestic aspects socialism with Chinese characteristics has many similarities with the European social market economy, in international aspects China prefers democratisation in international relations by seeking to build a just and equal international order while the EU prefers global governance based on European style norms and efficiency.

China plays the key role in bridging the gap between the developing world and developed world and between emerging powers and developed countries in particular. So, to deal with China in climate change and other issues is to deal with the developing world and BASIC (emerging powers) countries.

Again, lack of China–EU harmony regarding climate change can be traced back to China's identity dilemma in Europeans' eyes and to the EU's identity dilemmas in Chinese eyes. On the one hand, the Chinese identity dilemma would come from the difficulty of hiding behind the developing country curtain, the expectation that China would take more responsibility as an emerging global power and, finally, the confusion and competition arising from China's reserved and efficient way in dealing with global issues as an Eastern civilization and socialist state. On the other hand, the EU's identity dilemmas in Chinese eyes can be embodied in the contradictions between Europe's failure to represent developed countries, the post-modern model, the unity of the Western bloc, and the sustainability of capitalism.

As Europeans are more and more concerned about living standards instead of national ranking, they easily make China the scapegoat of globalisation as happened following the Copenhagen climate change conference, which, in the eyes of the Chinese, had been hijacked by the Europeans. Europeans are concerned with the world's China while China still focuses more on China's China. Chinese–European perception gaps are still increasing as opposed to decreasing.

China's complex identities and stage of development indicates that soft conflict with the EU is unavoidable over international responsibilities in global affairs. It will be part of the relations between China and the EU during a transition period. China's identities will shift from history-oriented and present-oriented to future-oriented sooner or later. As a consequence, China will have more and more common understanding and shared responsibilities with the EU on global affairs. The EU should be patient in waiting for a new China; at the same time it should dispel its illusion of westernising China and its anxiety of being 'Sinised'. Harmonious coexistence and intensive cooperation between China and the EU will not only offer more hopes for global security, but will also reduce global insecurity.

The climate change issue reminds us again that China–EU relations should move beyond the bilateral dimension to reaching the true essence of the relations of the above-mentioned four paradigms. The difficulties and complexities can also provide great hope for a relationship that pursues a humanitarian mission.

As the UK House of Lords, European Union Committee – Seventh Report argued after three months of introspection:

> As was shown at the Copenhagen climate change conference in 2009, the balance of global power is moving strongly eastwards and southwards. Without resolving its relationship with China, the EU cannot achieve its aims. The role which China and the EU can play in shaping 21st century global affairs will be crucial to solving the world's problems. (UK House of Lords, 2010: 6)

LOOKING AHEAD: SEEKING CHINA–EU HARMONY IN GLOBAL GOVERNANCE

Identity not only means self-identification but also means being identified by others. The mission for China and the EU is to bridge their identity and perception gaps.

Around 2,500 years ago, Confucius argued: 'The gentleman aims at harmony, and not at uniformity. The mean man aims at uniformity and not at harmony.' How can China and the EU handle the new paradigm in their relationship to avoid the 'mean man' outcome? This is a true challenge for future leaders both in China and in the EU.

Given their diverse and dynamic identities, both China and the European Union share ambitions to shape the international order according to their own values. The only way to avoid a clash of ideas and identities is to look for and to stress the elements of agreement and consensus. Putting domestic and ideological disputes to one side, China and Europe increasingly share common international values, such as effective multilateralism and global governance. But even in the domestic field, China shares common social values with Europe, such as secularity in the societal sphere and cultural diversity.

With four identities for both, China and the EU are the most important pillars in the world hardware and software (cultural 'G2'), not only in traditional international regimes such as the UN Security Council but also in newer platforms such as the G20, to bridge the gaps between developing countries and developed countries, to get the win-win result for emerging powers and the developed world, to create a harmonious relationship between Eastern and Western civilisations and to reach the same goal by different means through the coordination of socialism with Chinese characteristics (Chinese model) and European capitalism (EU model). In short, the dynamic identities of both China and the EU lead to a natural partnership for the two key players in the construction of a multipolar world and for the ushering in of effective multilateralism, while at the same time rising above the clash of identities in dealing with global challenges and seeking China–EU harmony in global governance. This is the mission for both China and the EU, which are possibly the only two consistent and ancient civilisations with dynamic identities in the world.

In times of uncertainty, China–EU relations need to take a leap forward from common interests and common challenges to common values (consensus), to work on a new global consensus and to build a harmonious world with long-lasting peace and common prosperity.

NOTES

1 This paper originated in and was updated from the author's presentation paper on 'Clash of Identities: Why China and the EU are Inharmonious in Global Governance' at the international conference 'China, the European Union and the Restructuring of Global Governance', Brussels, 6–7 May 2010. The author appreciates the comments from the conference and especially appreciates Stanley Crossick for his editing help and comments.

2 China has 56 nations (ethic groups). Although the development of nations in China has a long history, they were usually called race, tribe, etc., but not 'nation', a word translated from the Japanese language. See Wang (2006).

3 For instance, one of the two founding fathers of the Chinese Communist Party, Chen Duxiu, only discovered in his twenties that China is just 'one country' in the world.

REFERENCES

Cooper, Robert (2000) *Post-Modern State and the World Order*. Demos. Available at: http://www.demos.co.uk/files/postmodernstate.pdf?1240939425 (accessed 11 January 2011).

Downie, Leonard Jr, Bennett, P., Pomfret, J., Philip, P. Pan and Goodman, Peter S. (2003) 'Interview with Wen Jiabao: a complete transcript from Chinese Premier's meeting', *Washington Post*, 21 November.

Liang, Qichao (1901) 'Introduction to Chinese history', in *Yinbinshi Heji* [*Complete Works of Liang Qichao*]. Beijing: Beijing Press, Vol. 1, No. 6.

Manners, Ian (2008) 'The normative ethics of the European Union', *International Affairs*, 84 (1): 45–60.

Rothkopf, David (2009) 'The world's 10 most dangerous countries', *Foreign Policy*, 7 August.

UK House of Lords, European Union Committee – Seventh Report (2010) *Stars and Dragons: The EU and China*, 23 March. Available at: http://www.parliament.the-stationery-office.co.uk/pa/ld200910/ldselect/ldeucom/76/76i.pdf (accessed 11 January 2011).

Wang, Yiwei (2006) 'Seeking Chinese new identity: the myth of Chinese nationalism', *World Economy and Politics* (Beijing), 2: 14–21.

Wang, Yiwei (2009) 'The identity dilemmas of EU normative power: observations from Chinese traditional culture', in André Gerrits (ed), *Normative Power Europe in Global Politics: A Discussion*, Clingendael European Papers No. 5. The Hague: Netherlands Institute of International Relations (Clingendael), pp. 67–76. Available at: http://www.clingendael.nl/publications/2009/20091200_cesp_paper_gerrits.pdf (accessed 11 January 2011).

Weigel, George (2005) *Is Europe Dying? Notes on a Crisis of Civilizational Morale*, AEI Outlook Series. Washington, DC: American Enterprise Institute for Public Policy Research. Available at: http://www.aei.org/outlook/22139 (accessed 11 January 2011).

Zhang, Baijia (2002) 'Gaibian ziji yingxiang shijie' ['Changing thyself, influencing thy world'], *Zhongguo Shehui Kexue* [*Social Sciences in China*], 1 (1): 4–19.

FURTHER READING

Callahan, William A. (2009) *China: The Pessoptimist Nation*. Oxford: Oxford University Press.
Curtin, Deirdre M. (1997) *Postnational Democracy: The European Union in Search of a Political Philosophy*. The Hague: Kluwer Law.
Deflem, M. and Pampel, F. (1996) 'The myth of postnational identity: popular support for European identification', *Social Forces*, 75 (2): 119–43.
Delanty, Gerard (1995) *Inventing Europe – Idea, Identity, Reality*. London: Macmillan.
Fuchs, D., Gerhards, J. and Roller, E. (1995) 'Nationalism versus Eurocentrism? The construction of collective identities in Western Europe', in M. Martiniello (eds), *Migration, Citizenship and Ethno-National Identities in the European Union*. Aldershot: Avebury, pp. 212–47.
Fuchs, D. and Schlenker, A. (2006) *European Identity and the Legitimacy of the EU*. Available at: http://www.eu-consent.net/library/brx061012/Klingemann_-Lodz0603.pdf (accessed 11 January 2011).
Habermas, J. (1996) 'Struggles for recognition in the democratic constitutional state', in C. Taylor and A. Gutmann (eds), *Multiculturalism*. Princeton, NJ: Princeton University Press, pp. 107–48.
Jacobs, D. and Maier, R. (1998) 'European identity: construct, fact and fiction', in M. Gastelaars and A. De Ruijter (eds), *United Europe: The Quest for a Multifaceted Identity*. Maastricht: Shaker Publishing, pp. 13–34.
Mallab, Sebastian (2010) 'For rising China, an identity crisis', *Washington Post*, 26 March.
Smith, Anthony D. (1991) *National Identity*. London: Penguin.
Wang, Yiwei (2011) 'Is Chinese-European Cultural G2 possible? A comparison of the concepts of "harmonious world" and "global governance"', *Acque e Terre* (*Marco Polo Magazine*), No. 1. Available at: http://marcopolomagazine.wordpress.com/2011/02/17/is-chinese-european-cultural-g-2-possible-by-wang-yi-wei/.
Zhu, Liqun (2008) 'Chinese perceptions of the EU and the China–Europe relationship', in D. Shambaugh, E. Sandschneider and Zhou Hong (eds), *China–Europe Relations*. London: Routledge, pp. 148–73.

3. Europe, China and the Group of Twenty

Stewart Fleming

At the annual meeting of the International Monetary Fund in Istanbul in 2009, Managing Director Dominique Strauss-Kahn dismissed as irrelevant the regular meetings of the finance ministers of the Group of Seven (G7) advanced industrial economies. He described the body, which has been one of the most important venues for international economic policy cooperation and coordination efforts since the early 1970s, as effectively dead. 'The old G7, I was about to say the late G7', he remarked, adding, in an interview with television channel France 24, that its meetings were 'a bit without substance' and 'floating in the clouds with communiqués which no longer interest anyone'.[1] Instead, he suggested, the international economic policy diplomacy which the G7 had engaged in would in future be focused on the new Group of Twenty (G20), which includes leading emerging market economies such as China, India and Brazil, as well as the G7 members.

Strauss-Kahn was not alone in 2009 in playing down the significance of the G7. Professor Barry Eichengreen, a leading authority on international economic policy, has described as a *coup d'état* the way in which the 'G20 has seized power from the G7/8 as the steering committee for the world economy' (Eichengreen, 2009).

But are the high hopes for the future of the upgraded G20 forum justified? Has it really become the key international venue for international economic policy cooperation, a place where China, now the world's second-largest economy, can, and believes it should, bring its increasing economic weight to bear? And should it also be the venue of choice for the European Union and its bigger members to engage in international economic policy coordination efforts, including its policy discussions with China? Or could the EU seek to replicate America's approach by putting most of the emphasis on bilateral meetings with China in its strategic economic dialogue?

The European Union has been in the vanguard of those who believe that China, given its fast-expanding geopolitical weight, should be integrated as rapidly as possible into multilateral global governance structures. Seeking to exclude or sideline it, the EU decided, would not accommodate what China has dubbed its 'peaceful rise' to the status of world power. Hence, for example, the enthusiasm with which the EU facilitated and welcomed China into the World Trade Organization a decade ago and its decision, in 2008, to launch with American President George W. Bush the new G20 leaders' summit.

Today, however, the Union is finding dealing with China to be as big a challenge as some feared it might be. It is over four years since then EU Trade Commissioner, Peter Mandelson, in a speech in Beijing on 7 November 2006, signalled the Union's growing frustration with what he viewed as China's failure 'to fulfil its WTO obligations, open its markets further and commit to trading fairly' (Mandelson, 2006). Mandelson also highlighted the problem Europe faces in structuring its diplomatic relations with China. 'China needs a continental partner in Europe; Europe needs a continental policy on China,' he said. This was an implicit swipe at the way the bigger EU countries plough their own furrow with Beijing, allowing China to employ a 'divide and rule' approach when it wants to, just as the United States has done in Europe for decades.

Today it is difficult to argue that the EU has made much progress in either presenting China with the continental negotiating partner Mandelson called for, or in opening China's markets to a wider range of European exports and trading fairly. As the world's largest importer of Chinese goods, purchasing around a fifth of Chinese exports, and as an increasingly important focus for Chinese foreign direct investment, the EU should have a strong negotiating position. But, as Charles Grant, Director of the Centre for European Reform, a London think tank, put it in a report published in July 2010, 'China's strategy is to exploit foreigners' desire for access to its markets as a means of gaining their technology.' In spite of their vociferous complaints, 'neither Western business leaders nor governments are likely to get significantly tougher with China,' he added (Grant, 2010). No wonder then that François Godement, in a searing (and controversial) indictment of the EU's approach to China for the European Council on Foreign Relations, accused Europe in 2009 of 'ignoring reality' in its dealings with an increasingly assertive China. He claimed that while China 'now takes centre stage on all big global issues [. . .] the EU's leverage has weakened to the point where China feels it can largely ignore it' (Fox and Godement, 2009).

Before the transatlantic financial crisis erupted in 2007, the EU had launched a somewhat more organised process of economic policy engagement with China. It was not, even then, acting with the same degree of discipline which Washington has brought to the task, although the challenges it faces are similar, whether you look at trade, currency relationships or global economic stability. Then, during the transatlantic crisis, the EU became distracted from its engagement with China by fears that the 'Great Recession', triggered by American financial market excesses, could undermine its banking system and turn into a rerun of the 'Great Depression' of the 1930s.

Now, renewed diplomatic efforts are underway. But looking at the ill-coordinated list of European Union level meetings for the autumn of 2010, the first of which was Commission Vice President Catherine Ashton's trip to Beijing for a mere *tour d'horizon*, they still do not seem to be as well focused as Washington's. So, if the EU is finding it hard to replicate the American bilateral 'G2' model for organising its economic diplomacy with China, should it try to relaunch the mooted 'G4' talks which would have brought together China, the US, Japan, and the eurozone, the world's leading currency blocs?

Alternatively, should it put most of the emphasis on the new G20 as a venue for international economic policy coordination? Perhaps in the G20, backed by a broader coalition of emerging market countries, the EU could better pursue the objective of encouraging China to adjust its economic policies to take account of their impact on the world economy and so demonstrate its willingness to take on the global responsibilities which its increasing economic weight calls for. After all, together, G20 members account for around 80 per cent of world gross domestic product, hence the claims by its supporters and members that it is a more representative and legitimate venue for debates about how to manage a globalised economy more effectively in future.

ORIGINS

The G20 of today has its origins in a meeting of finance ministers at the Willard Hotel in Washington in 1998 in the midst of the Asia debt crisis. A decade later, however, in November 2008, in the wake of the global financial disaster triggered by the collapse of the American investment bank Lehman Brothers two months earlier, the G20's profile was transformed. Then US President George W. Bush with EU agreement, raised the G20's status by inviting the leaders (rather than finance ministers and central bank governors) of the G20 governments to Washington to try and agree upon steps to counter the threat of a collapse of the global economy.

Strauss-Kahn's warm words for the new G20 in Istanbul a year later will have been strongly influenced by the effort he has been making since taking office to polish up the reputation and legitimacy of the International Monetary Fund (IMF) in the developing world, particularly in Asia. There, its credibility had been badly damaged in the late 1990s by its heavy-handed and misguided dealings with the countries that were caught up in the Asian debt crisis. Strauss-Kahn will also have been aware that the United States had long been unhappy with the G7 as a forum because it judged that it includes too many European members. The big emerging market countries have also been pressing, justifiably, for a bigger say in the governance of both the global economy and the IMF. Accommodating them would diminish the over-representation of European countries at international economic policy meetings and at the IMF, a US foreign policy goal. Such a move could also, many claim, paradoxically, increase, not reduce, Europe's influence by pressuring it to speak with a single voice.

Only hours after Strauss-Kahn's comments in Istanbul about the diminishing significance of the G7, he was rebuffed, however. Several EU officials rallied to the defence of the G7. Publicly, Jean-Claude Juncker, President of the Eurogroup, which brings together finance ministers whose countries are members of the euro, remarked, 'We do not want the G7 brought to an end' (Fleming, 2009). Privately, one top EU official added, pointedly, 'we [the members of the G7] can scarcely talk about international currency issues with Argentina [a G20 member which defaulted on its debts in December 2001] in the room.' This official was highlighting the fact that the advanced industrial economies grouped in the G7 have certain common interests and problems which they can discuss frankly only among themselves and not in a big forum in the presence of, for example, economically unstable, default-prone borrowers such as Argentina. Professor John Kirton of the University of Toronto has supported this view. G7 leaders, he says, 'value the small cohesive club for the enhanced opportunities it gives them to speak freely and frankly and learn seriously [. . .] that is why some G7 finance ministers still speak far more fondly of their own October 2008 action in combating the current financial crisis than they do of their simultaneous G20 gathering' (Kirton, 2009). Significantly G7 finance ministers conferred on the telephone during both the Greek and Irish sovereign debt crises in 2010. There can be no doubt that G7 members are happier to be now conducting their business in private, free from the media scrum which follows the G20 around and which had previously attached itself to their sessions. This is one reason they chose the remote Canadian arctic town of Iqaluit for a mid-winter meeting in February 2010.

History, however, suggests that hopes the G20 could become, like the G7 has been, a vital forum for international economic policy cooperation among the world's biggest economies are unlikely to be fulfilled, certainly not in the next decade. The G20 is unlikely, for example, to make much progress in bringing about a coordinated reduction in international economic imbalances, notably the huge trade surpluses of China, Germany and Japan and the offsetting deficits in the United States. As Mervyn King, the Governor of the Bank of England presciently remarked in a speech in January of 2010, '[...] so far the only specific agreement [amongst the G20] is to talk to each other. Concrete steps to reduce the scale of global imbalances have, to date, been notable by their absence.' The G20 Summit in Seoul, South Korea, in November 2010, served to underscore the depth of divisions within the group on this issue rather than to narrow the differences. Even the European Central Bank has expressed doubts. 'It remains to be seen whether significant progress will be made in the main deficit and surplus economies in terms of living up to the commitments made at the Pittsburgh G20 Summit,' an ECB assessment says (European Central Bank, 2010: 99).

Similarly, neither history nor recent developments suggest that the G20's goal of standardising financial market regulation around the world in order to promote financial market stability is likely to be blessed with swift results. Asian countries such as Japan, China or India, which escaped the worst of the 2007–10 financial crisis, see no reason for a rapid root-and-branch reform of their financial systems or the rules, regulations and supervision of their banks. As was clear from the Seoul summit statement, however, emerging market economies in the group will support in principle G20-endorsed efforts to improve international financial regulation. But, understandably, they see no reason to adopt recommendations for reform designed primarily by advanced economy countries which have demonstrably failed so disastrously to deliver financial stability to their own economies.

Rather, the emerging market economies will decide, on a 'pick-and-mix' basis which elements of the international regulatory reform regime they will adopt and how and when they will implement them. They will do so partly in order that regulatory innovations fit with their own economic priorities and legal and cultural traditions. But also, as a senior Indian government official made clear privately at the time of the Seoul summit, they will do so because they have a vested interest in fostering the creation of global financial markets in which they and their banks expect to play an increasing role. They will also seek to make the most of the competitive advantage they have been gifted by the damage which the transatlantic sub-prime-triggered financial crisis has wreaked on their American and European bank and financial market competitors. Many Western banks – Barclays, JP Morgan Chase and Deutsche Bank, for example – are already operating on a global scale. Their problems in the crisis have presented emerging market competitors with a catching-up opportunity. This competitive advantage would be eroded by, for example, hastily imposing on their banks what some emerging market policymakers see as unnecessarily onerous new liquidity or capital requirements.

Even within the transatlantic community, cooperative action on financial market reform has been patchy. Certainly, as Howard Davies, former head of the British Financial Services Authority, has pointed out, America's 2010 reform package, the Dodd-Frank Wall Street Reform and Consumer Protection Act, was not designed with anything other than US interests in mind (Davies, 2010).

On trade issues too, the results of the G20's discussions have been, at best, mixed. It is widely accepted that, although not fully observed, the G20 members' commitment at the first summit in Washington, in November 2008, to avoid responding to the collapse in global trade by erecting new barriers bore fruit. This helped to prevent a rush to impose 'beggar-thy-neighbour' protectionist rules in the heat of the financial crisis. Such a trade war was one of the factors which helped to trigger the Great Depression of the 1930s.

But the G20's commitments to bringing the Doha Round of multilateral trade negotiations to a successful conclusion remain just warm words. In spite of the five summits so far, worries about a descent into protectionism remain. Jeffrey Schott, a trade expert at the Peterson Institute for International Economics in Washington, says: '[...] unless the leaders devote attention and political capital to the trade agenda, the Doha Round may go into deep hibernation, risking substantial damage to the multilateral trading system [...]' (Schott, 2010: 1).

MISREADING HISTORY

Since the end of the Second World War there has been a long history of multilateral economic policy *cooperation* and *coordination* within formal, statutory, institutional structures such as the International Monetary Fund, the World Bank and the World Trade Organization and its predecessors. But, after the breakdown of the Bretton Woods fixed exchange rate regime in August 1971, in the more informal venues which then sprang up, such as the Group of Five (G5), Group of Seven (G7) and Group of Eight (G8), non-statutory bodies which most closely resemble the G20, results have been, to say the least, more mixed. Indeed, if you define the economic policy *coordination* efforts by these bodies ambitiously, i.e. agreements negotiated by governments to change their economic policies in ways they would not have done independently, the 'successes' have been few. Even then the value of their claimed longer-term benefits has been questionable.

The G5 has its origins in the so-called 'Library Group' of finance ministers from the United Kingdom, France and West Germany, invited by the United States' Treasury Secretary, George Schultz, in the spring of 1973 to an informal meeting to discuss pressing international economic issues as the Bretton Woods fixed exchange rate regime imploded.

Later that year, Japan began to participate and central bankers were invited to join their finance ministers' discussions. The first session took place, discreetly, in the library of the White House in Washington and it was some time before the designation 'G5' was applied to the meetings. Then in November 1975, with the economies of the industrial countries facing the aftermath of the oil price shock, rising inflation and recession, French President Valéry Giscard d'Estaing raised the status of the group by inviting the leaders rather than finance ministers and central bankers of the five countries which then made up the Library Group to a heads of government level 'summit' meeting in the Château de Rambouillet.

It was not until the fourth economic summit in Bonn in July 1978, however, by which time first Italy and then Canada had joined what was by then the Group of Seven, that participants agreed to take specific, coordinated, economic policy decisions to try and boost economic growth. The United States agreed to lift domestic oil price controls. In return, the so-called *locomotives* who were charged with dragging the world economy forward, Japan and West Germany, agreed to, and implemented, steps to inject fiscal stimuli into their economies.

For some the Bonn Summit was a rare example of fully fledged international economic policy coordination. 'It is widely believed that the 1978 Bonn summit accord represented a rare, perhaps even unique, case of comprehensive policy coordination among the industrial democracies,' wrote Robert D. Putnam and Randall Henning (Putnam et al., 1989). At the Bonn Summit in 1978 (economic) policy coordination reached its greatest level of ambition, according to Professor Peter Kenen (Kenen et al., 2004).

But many, especially German, officials still see the 1978 Bonn Summit as a disaster. The fiscal stimulus was ill-timed, they argue. The agreement focused on accelerating growth in the G7 when it was already becoming clear that, particularly in the United States, inflation was the looming danger. 'The package [. . .] continues to be debated, especially in Germany where it was widely seen as the cause of a pick-up of inflation in 1979,' says Kenen (Kenen et al., 2004).

By 1979 inflation in the US had reached double digit levels and was threatening to destabilise both the US economy and the dollar.

Washington was forced to reverse course. In order to curb resurgent inflation and restore economic stability, Paul Volcker, the newly appointed chairman of the Federal Reserve Bank, America's central bank, courageously drove short-term market interest rates up to over 20 per cent, inducing a double-dip US recession, in order to curb inflation and restore economic stability. By 1980, the West German government, too, found itself battling inflation and rapidly eroding confidence in its economic policies. It, too, had to resort to a stiff dose of monetary austerity and an induced recession to bring inflation down and restore confidence. Then, beginning in 1982, Washington's ferocious economic adjustment triggered a debt crisis in Latin America which, because of the damage inflicted on American banks which had loaned huge sums to the region, itself threatened to metamorphose into a global financial crash. Seen in the light of these repercussions, the Bonn G7 Summit scarcely looks like the triumph of economic policy coordination some claim.

Many experts also have a jaundiced view of the international economic policy coordination initiative launched at the Plaza Hotel in 1985. This was widely seen at the time as another 'success' for international economic policy coordination. A meeting of (what was still) the G5 finance ministers and central bank governors at the Plaza Hotel in New York agreed to try to manage, in a coordinated way, foreign exchange market interventions and monetary policies. The goal was to try and bring about a further, orderly, devaluation of the US dollar. The dollar had already begun to decline six months earlier. But US Treasury Secretary, James A. Baker, judged that the US might not be able to resist rising protectionist pressures from the US Congress without such an accord.

Even before a follow-up meeting at the Louvre in Paris in February 1987, it was clear that this coordination exercise was also running out of steam. Although new commitments were agreed at the Louvre, fiscal policy actions promised by the United States and Germany were not implemented and intensifying policy divisions, notably between the US and West Germany, triggered the Wall Street crash in October later that year.

So, like the Bonn Summit, the Plaza Accord, which led Japan to stimulate its economy to offset the rise in the yen, subsequently ran into fierce criticism. Sceptics have argued that, far from being a success, it helped to lay the foundations for Japan's financial market bubble of the late 1980s and the property and stock market bust of the early 1990s and two decades of economic stagnation. 'Many observers of the Japanese economy have subsequently criticised the Japanese stimulus as having begun the bubble economy,' says Kenen (Kenen et al., 2004).

EUROPE

Europe's own experience of economic policy cooperation and coordination also exposes the challenges such diplomatic activity faces, even when more formal institutional structures underpin it.

In one shape or another the European Union has close to forty years of intergovernmental macroeconomic policy cooperation and coordination behind it, ranging from initially unsuccessful efforts to stabilise exchange rates in the 1970s to the successful launch in 1999 of the single currency. Including Estonia which joined in 2011, 17 EU countries are now members of the single currency club. It is presided over by a strongly independent central bank tasked with running a monetary policy for all of them. A bolder experiment in the field of economic policy coordination amongst sovereign states is hard to imagine.

But events of the past few years have demonstrated that, in spite of this history and this depth of commitment, founded as it is on a treaty between states which are quite politically and culturally homogeneous, economic policy coordination has been hard to achieve. Both the European Union and the Eurogroup of eurozone finance ministers have struggled in this period to spread economic stability across the region, and they failed to prevent the 2007–10 financial crisis threatening the survival of the single currency.

In 2010 it was only after several months of difficult negotiations, and with the threat that Greece's sovereign debt crisis would infect both other eurozone countries and an already weakened transatlantic banking sector, that the single currency's members took effective coordinated action. So, early in May, one week after having put together (with IMF involvement) a 110 billion euro Greek sovereign debt bail-out plan, euro area governments and the IMF agreed on a massive 750 billion euro sovereign debt support package which could be used if financial contagion from Greece spread to Ireland, Portugal or Spain.

In spite of these initiatives, by November 2010 Ireland's parlous economic and financial condition gave rise to renewed fears that the single currency, and even the Union itself, could begin to fall apart. By 19 November, a team of advisers from the European Commission, the European Central Bank and the International Monetary Fund was ensconced in Dublin negotiating the terms of a Greek-style bail-out for the Emerald Isle. Confirmation that Ireland would also need an official bail-out quickly followed on 21 November.

HEGEMONY

Beyond these lessons of history there are other factors which suggest that too much hope should not be invested in the G20 as a venue in which far-reaching economic policy agreements can be nailed down.

What successes there have been in the field of economic policy cooperation, including those achieved with robust institutional backing from the International Monetary Fund, the World Bank and the World Trade Organization and its predecessor, the General Agreement on Tariffs and Trade (GATT), have occurred during a period when the United States occupied a hegemonic position in the world, militarily and economically.

At the alleged high points for economic policy cooperation and coordination, the Bonn Summit in 1978 and the Plaza Accord of 1985, Europe and Japan were sheltering under America's protective nuclear umbrella, aware how vulnerable they were with a nuclear armed Soviet Union on their doorsteps. This provided a powerful incentive to accept Washington's leadership, albeit often reluctantly.

The vibrancy of the US economy, its innovative capacity and its extraordinary ability to commercialise breakthroughs in its (and other nations') scientific laboratories have helped to underpin America's global economic influence, especially with the other G7 members who enjoyed the benefits of rapid US growth and shared similar levels of economic prosperity. America's economic vigour also helped to legitimise the economic theories and policies which it embraced and which, certainly in the years since President Ronald Reagan took office in 1981, it encouraged and pressured its friends and allies around the world to adopt.

The financial disasters of 2007–10 have triggered a backlash against what could be seen as America's intellectual hegemony in the field of economic policy and theory, just as its misguided and mismanaged unilateralist-inspired adventures into Iraq and Afghanistan have weakened it militarily. So, today, the US is not well positioned to dominate economic policy debates amongst its allies as it did in the heydays of the G5 and G7. 'Fiscal, economic and political failures at home [. . .] are threatening the ability of the United States to exert the global influence that it could and should [. . .] it is not reckless American activity in the world that jeopardizes American solvency but American profligacy at home,' concluded Roger C. Altman and Richard N. Haas, two of their nation's pre-eminent foreign policy thinkers, in an article in *Foreign Affairs* in November 2010 (Altman and Haas, 2010). Equally, however, no other emerging power is in a position to wield the economic, military or intellectual influence which Washington has enjoyed during the past sixty years and which gave America such a powerful voice in global economic policy debates and decisions.

NEW CONTEXT

So assessments of the role which the G20 might play, and the role China or Europe might play within the G20, need to be made in this new geopolitical context. Unsurprisingly, influential observers are questioning not just the capacity, but also the legitimacy of the G20 as a venue for economic diplomacy. This new forum is seen variously as too unrepresentative and too big, unwieldy and diverse, both in membership and interests, for it to be an effective venue for economic policy cooperation, never mind for coordination. Its members do not share a common view of how economic policy should work. It also has a membership whose interests clash too powerfully (China, India and the United States most obviously) for coordination to be undertaken. As Mervyn King's remarks quoted earlier suggest, the already protracted debate about the rebalancing of the global economy is demonstrating the limits of economic policy cooperation in a world in which leadership is lacking, economies are closely integrated but interests clash.

There are all too obvious examples of the rivalries in the G20 which will make it a fractious forum for economic policy debates compared with, say, the G7 which itself was at times fractious enough for all but the toughest negotiators. As India, for example, looks across the Himalayas or across the G20 table, it sees in China a strategic rival and threat as well as a trading partner. The *New York Times* reported recently that Pakistan is 'handing de facto control of the strategic Gilgit-Baltistan region in the northwest corner of disputed Kashmir to China' (Harrison, 26 August 2010). This is just one development viewed anxiously by India which has tense relations with Pakistan, rumbling border disputes with China and is watching nervously as China extends its naval presence in the Indian Ocean through the construction of port facilities in Pakistan.

OUTSIDERS

One group which has been giving the rise of the G20 a distinctly cool reception has been the outsiders. Earlier last year, Svein Gjedrem, Governor of the Central Bank of Norway, launched a comprehensive attack on the new forum. Fair-mindedly, he paid tribute in a speech in Washington on 25 February 2010 to the early G20 initiatives, saying: 'I fully recognise the important role played by the G20 at the time of the crisis'. He noted in particular the agreement reached at the April 2009 London Summit to boost dramatically the resources of the IMF. But, Governor Gjedrem went on,

> The G20 lacks the legitimacy that historically has been associated with a truly multilateral framework [. . .] it is a weakness that the members of the G20 represent only themselves [. . .] it includes only the countries that established it [. . .] membership seems to have been somewhat arbitrarily determined and not solely on the basis of relative size or importance in the global economy [. . .] entire groups of countries and regions are left out. (Gjedrem, 2010).

Some of the excluded in the developing world, particularly in South East Asia, have also made their dissatisfaction plain. George Yeo, the Foreign Minister of Singapore (a city-state which seems determined to become a focus of both G20 dissent and new ideas) was instrumental in the formation of a new 'Global Governance Group', dubbed '3G', with the objective of trying to ensure that 'the decisions of the G20 take into account the interests of other countries and are supported by them'.[2]

The 3G grouping of dissenters at the G20 process now boasts (including Singapore) 28 participants, smaller countries ranging from Malaysia to New Zealand, Qatar, Senegal and Sweden. Its members talk about the 3G's role as in part aimed at strengthening the legitimacy of the G20, not least by ensuring that when their interests are at stake they are included, formally, in discussions. The G20 should be a 'variable geometry' venue they argue, meaning that participation should vary according to whom might be most affected by any decisions that are made.

Governor Gjedrem of Norway goes further. He believes that international economic policy cooperation should take place in statutory multilateral institutions. 'The IMF is the logical choice,' he says. The 3G members also want closer links with the United Nations, especially as the G20 shows signs of widening the range of issues it addresses.

CONCLUSION

The early successes of the G20 seem to have been a function of the extraordinary crisis which the world faced in late 2008 and early 2009. 'This sudden new enthusiasm for G20 summitry has been sustained by the speed, scope and severity of the global financial and economic crisis,' wrote Professor John Kirton (Kirton, 2009).

So it is hard to be optimistic about the G20's immediate future if the world economy recovers smoothly. In these circumstances, suggestions that the G20 can become the dominant new forum for international economic policy debates look overblown. Its most important role is more likely to be as a venue where key players among the advanced and emerging market economies of the world can meet, debate and so gain a better understanding of each other's motivations.

On critical issues, the major powers, particularly China and the United States, but also Brazil and the European Union, will deal bilaterally with each other. In the case of the EU, or at least its biggest members, they will still, with the US, operate in the G7 format, as they did in mid-May and November 2010 in response to the burgeoning threat from the European sovereign debt crisis. So, the G20 will be just one of many venues for international economic policy discussions. Professor Kirton argues that a period of coexistence, cooperation and competition lies ahead for the G7/8 and G20. 'Both [are] bound to succeed, existing alongside one another, complementing each other's activities and engaging in healthy competition', he says (Kirton, 2009).

If global economic recovery continues smoothly even this may prove to be an optimistic view. It will be interesting to see whether, in this case, future G20 meetings are going to be as well attended as those that have taken place so far. Will they produce the sort of short-term outcomes which will be greeted in the global media as indicative of 'successes', or 'marred' by public disputes which will begin to erode the G20's credibility?

For G20 members are not bound together in the way that the G7 members were, and still are, in terms of their common interests and values. Because of these ties the G7 will endure. Indeed, as mentioned earlier, one purpose the G20 serves is to take the G7 out of the limelight of media attention and allow it to go back more to its roots as a somewhat secretive, and so more effective, conclave. This is actually enhancing the G7's importance.

For Europe, however, this poses one particular problem. With France, Germany and Britain clinging limpet-like to their membership of the G7 and, certainly in the case of France and Britain, their illusions of continued 'great power' status, Peter Mandelson's dream of Europe providing a 'continental partner' for China remains just that, a dream. This is a weak position for such an important trading bloc with a single currency to occupy. This weakness is all the greater since the European Union is still failing to understand that, in a tumultuous world, it needs to be in a stronger position to defend, militarily as well as diplomatically, its global interests, rather than focus merely on a narrowly defined 'neighbourhood'.

Already China accords greater weight and status to its dealings with the United States than to a disparate European Union which finds itself dealing with this Asian tiger from a position of increasing inferiority, not least in the minds of its Chinese interlocutors. It would, however, be unwise to conclude too definitely from the lack of concrete results out of the Pittsburgh Summit in September 2009, or Toronto or Seoul in 2010 – where glossing over differences was the order of the day – that the G20's best days are certainly already behind it.

If, as many expect, China hits severe economic turbulence and Europe's sovereign debt crisis and a slowing American recovery contribute to a another downturn in the fragile world economic recovery, then the search for global solutions to global economic crises will, in the absence of a more effective forum, again have to centre on the G20, in spite of its inadequacies.

NOTES

1 Strauss-Kahn (2009).
2 Quoted in George Yeo, Minister of Foreign Affairs, 'Speech given in Parliament during Committee of Supply Debate, 5 March 2010', in Chowdhury (2010: 7).

REFERENCES

Altman, R. C. and Haass, R. N. (November/December 2010) 'American profligacy and American power', *Foreign Affairs*, 89 (6). New York: Council on Foreign Relations.
Chowdhury, Iftekhar A. (May 2010) *The Global Governance Group ('3G') and Singaporean Leadership: Can Small be Significant?*, ISAS Working Paper No. 108. Singapore: Institute of South Asian Studies.
Davies, Howard (2010) 'Focus on the meat and two veg of reform', *Financial Times*, 31 August.
Eichengreen, Barry (2009) 'The G20 and the crisis', *East Asia Forum*, 10 March. Available at: http://www.eastasiaforum.org/2009/03/10/the-g20-and-the- crisis/ (accessed 13 January 2011).
European Central Bank (2010) *Monthly Bulletin April 2010*. Available at: http://www.ecb.int/pub/pdf/mobu/mb201004en.pdf (accessed 13 January 2011).
Fleming, Stewart (2009) 'Juncker: G7 is best place for currency issues', *European Voice*, 6 October. Available at: http://www.europeanvoice.com/article/2009/10/juncker-g7-is-best-place-for-currency-issues/66048.aspx (accessed 13 January 2011).
Fox, James and Godement, François (2009) *A Power Audit of EU–China Relations*, April. European Council on Foreign Relations. Available at: http://ecfr.3cdn.net/532cd91d0b5c9699ad_ozm6b9bz4.pdf (accessed 13 January 2011).
Gjedrem, Svein (25 February 2010) *Multilateral Approaches to Global Challenges*. Speech at the Peterson Institute for International Economics, Washington, DC. Available at: http://www.norges-bank.no/templates/article____76222.aspx (accessed 13 January 2011).
Grant, Charles (July 2010) *Is China Being Beastly to Foreign Investors?* Centre for European Reform. Available at: http://centreforeuropeanreform.blogspot.com/2010_07_01_archive.html (accessed 13 January 2011).
Harrison, Selig S. (2010) 'China's discreet hold on Pakistan's northern borderlands', *New York Times*, 26 August.
Kenen, Peter B., Shafter, Jeffrey R., Wicks, Nigel and Wyplosz, Charles (2004)

International Economic and Financial Cooperation, Geneva Reports on the World Economy No. 6. Geneva: Centre for Economic Policy Research.

Kirton, John (2009) *Coexistence, Cooperation, Competition. G Summits*. Available at: http://www.g20.utoronto.ca/biblio/kirton-aspenia-2009.pdf (accessed 13 January 2011).

Mandelson, Peter (2006) *Europe and China: Partnership, Competition and Leadership*. Speech, 7 November, Beijing.

Putnam, Robert D., Henning, Randall C., Cooper Richard N., Eichengreen, Bary, Henning, C., Randall, Holtam Gerald and Putnam, Robert D. (1989) *Can Nations Agree*? Washington, DC: Brookings Institution.

Radu, Michael (2010) *Europe's Ghost. Tolerance, Jihadism, and the Crisis of the West*. New York: Encounter Books.

Schott, Jeffrey J. (May 2010) *A Trade Agenda for the G20*, Policy Brief PB 10–11. Washington, DC: Peterson Institute for International Economics. Available at: https://www.iie.com/publications/pb/pb10-11.pdf (accessed 13 January 2011).

Strauss-Kahn, Dominique (2009) Interview at *France 24*, 3 October.

PART 2

The world trading system

4. China and the European Union in the World Trade Organization: living apart together?

Jan Wouters and Matthieu Burnay

INTRODUCTION

Following the optimism associated with the first intergovernmental organisation to govern international trade in its early days – from 1995 onwards – the World Trade Organization (WTO) has since increasingly encountered challenges and difficulties in adapting to the needs of its membership. The long-standing failure to conclude the Doha Development Agenda (DDA), launched in the aftermath of 9/11 in November 2001, is particularly obvious in this respect. These negotiations mirror the strongly diverging interests and the lack of leadership and trust among WTO members, as well as the complexity of agreeing further liberalisation in sensitive areas, such as trade in agricultural goods and services, among others.[1]

With the shift in the global balance of economic power, the dynamics of multilateral negotiations have undergone important changes. A comparison of the evolving share of global GDP between G7 and BRICS countries illustrates this. Whereas in 1992 the G7's share of global GDP was 51.3 per cent, in 2012 it stands at 37.8 per cent. In comparison, the BRICS share increased from 15.2 per cent to 27.4 per cent (estimation for 2012), mainly thanks to a Chinese share increase of 10.7 per cent over this period (IMF, 2012). In the words of the Warwick Commission, the former dominance of the US, Japan and the EU, 'is giving way to a dispersal of economic power in a southerly and easterly direction' (Warwick Commission Report, 2007: 13).[2] Whereas during the GATT era, transatlantic deals or consensus among members of the QUAD[3] were often sufficient to conclude agreements (Schott, 2010: 355) – which explains to a large extent the success of the Uruguay Round – the multipolar economy now requires the backing of both emerging and developed countries to secure major agreements. In spite of their diverging development paths, emerging countries have indeed been increasingly effective in building strong coalitions to secure their interests. The successful blocking of a joint American and European proposal on agriculture during the 2003 Cancún Ministerial Conference illustrated developing countries' capacity and willingness to remain united when their interests as developing countries are at stake (Srivastava, 2008: 32).

The WTO bodies have failed to a large extent to adapt to the greater multipolarisation of the world economy and the rise of emerging powers, particularly in Asia.[4] Emerging countries are still strongly under-represented in the WTO Secretariat. For instance, only five of the 629 WTO officials come from China, despite the country's status as the second largest economy (Hsieh, 2010: 1027). The appointment of the first Chinese member of the Appellate Body in 2008 nevertheless signals its growing stake in the system and China is equally pushing to increase the number of Chinese WTO officials in the Secretariat.

In addition, the growing multipolarisation makes it more difficult to conclude negotiations in an institution where the 'Single Undertaking' rule is applied. Single Undertaking implies that 'nothing is agreed until everything is agreed' and that 'all members subscribe to all parts of a negotiated package without option for opting in or out' (Capling and Higgott, 2009: 322). This condition complicates the securing of substantial deals among members with such diverging strategies and competing interests.

Finally, the world trade system has failed to translate the development component of the DDA into real policies aimed at anchoring the interests of the weaker members of the WTO. The disappointment of the developing countries is understandable: it is indeed not the first time that 'development friendly language' was used at the beginning of a round and was not transposed into clear commitments (Drahos, 2003: 80).

The legislative inertia generated by a stalled DDA creates strong incentives for WTO members to use preferential trade agreements (including free trade agreements and regional trade agreements) to secure their trade interests. This is more than a challenge to further liberalisation; this tendency threatens the workability of the multilateral trading system. It can indeed turn WTO members from 'building blocks into stumbling blocks on the road towards a stronger multilateral trading system' (Defraigne, 2011: 1).

The present chapter analyses the interactions between China and the EU in the WTO. It is submitted that both actors are vital pillars of the organisation, thanks to their historical participation and their respective economic power, but also because of the growing frictions in their bilateral relations. As will be shown, their interactions have multiple impacts on the WTO. On the one hand, their increasing use of the dispute settlement system vis-à-vis each other in order to address major trade disputes strengthens this unique part of the WTO's functioning and contributes to the rule of law in international trade. On the other hand, their strongly diverging interests in the DDA – which will not be the main focus of this chapter – and primarily mutual misperceptions constitute major obstacles to the development of a potentially useful mutual engagement to conclude the DDA and reform the WTO.

CHINA AND THE EU: TWO ECONOMIC GIANTS WITH COMPETING INTERESTS?

China and the EU are two pillars in the multilateral trading system and within its main multilateral institution, the WTO. Their particular experience in the WTO, their respective economic weight and the growing trade disagreements between them explain this importance.

Two Actors with a Different History in the WTO

As a founding member of the WTO, the EU (formerly European Communities) has been, to a large extent, a rule-making agent that has successfully set the agenda of the organisation. The European Communities along with other developed economies were indeed part of the QUAD, which has often been considered as assuming the role of an 'informal steering committee for the WTO system' (Das, 2001: 39; Wouters and De Meester, 2007: 163), or as being 'the most powerful blocking coalition of all the coalitions in the [Uruguay] round' (Drahos, 2003: 90). Furthermore, the EU has strongly lobbied to set the boundaries of the World Trade Organization according to its own trade interests. The vigorous – but in the end unsuccessful – pressure to include the 'Singapore issues' in the negotiations of the Doha round is particularly obvious in this regard.[5, 6] Being a founding member of the WTO, the EU still benefits today from a particular credit and strength in the various dynamics that are at play in the multilateral trading system.

In contrast with the long-standing European participation in the multilateral trading system, China entered the WTO in 2001, following a long and complex set of bilateral and multilateral negotiations with the main WTO members, including the European Communities.[7] The Chinese accession constitutes a major accomplishment in the process of integrating China into the global economic order. China nevertheless paid a high price for it and made deeper concessions than other developing countries.[8] In addition to the commitment to respect the WTO *acquis* and translate it into Chinese law, China has been bound to so-called 'WTO plus' obligations. Those 'China-specific' obligations include a transitional safeguard clause available to other members when confronted with increased Chinese imports as well as the possibility for other members to treat China as a non-market economy for anti-dumping calculation until 2016.[9] During the accession process, many were sceptical regarding the Chinese ability and willingness to implement all its commitments.[10] Ten years later, a balanced assessment can be drawn recognising both the huge positive evolutions that have taken place in the Chinese legal system and trade practices as well as the remaining shortcomings in the implementation of WTO disciplines and rules. In contrast with the EU, which has been a real rule-maker and agenda-setter, China still has a very limited experience in the WTO and has not taken on the opportunity to shape the institution. Nevertheless, Chinese participation in the WTO in its own right has been a major turning point in the history of the world trade system, which needs to take into account both the actions and expectations of this economic giant.

Two Pillars of the International Trading System

Both China and the EU are deeply integrated in the global economy. On the one hand, the Chinese policy of opening itself and instituting reforms has opened the gates to spectacular development and growth of its economy accompanied by deep social changes. With the second biggest GDP and an average annual growth of 9.7 per cent per annum since the late 1970s, China has become one of the world's top manufacturers and a highly attractive destination for foreign direct investment (FDI).[11] These linkages with the outside world have therefore strongly contributed to Chinese economic growth.[12] On the other hand, EU economic integration has been at the core of the European project. Even if the European share of global GDP has constantly decreased since 1995 (IMF, 2010) and the economic recovery after the recent financial crisis has proved to be particularly difficult, the EU is still the largest free economic zone and enjoys one of the highest GDP per capita (IMF, 2010). This status is notably strengthened by a common currency in the eurozone.

The 'complementarity' between the Chinese, cheap labour-based, export-market economy and the European 'knowledge-based' economy has been translated into a growing interdependence between both actors. Economic issues have therefore always been central in the relationship between China and the European Union. Instead of strategic and political shared interests, the main areas of cooperation between China and the EU remain related to trade.[13] Two decades ago, business between both regions accounted for nearly nothing, yet China has now become the main producer of manufactured goods entering the European market (European Commission, 2010:1). In 2010, total EU imported goods amounted to €281.9 billion. Furthermore, China is Europe's fastest growing export market. EU exports to China reached €78.4 billion, which shows the major European trade deficit in its bilateral relations with China. Concerning the services market, EU service exports to China total €18 billion and imports from China amount to €13 billion.[14]

All these data show how interdependent and significant the ties have become. On the one hand, China has effectively gained access to the huge European internal market and its inherent knowledge and technologies. On the other hand, the EU has benefited from cheap Chinese manufactured goods and a huge emerging market. The practice nevertheless shows that growing disagreements and trade practices challenge the maximisation of possible benefits which accrue from the bilateral trade exchange, and this topic is addressed in the next section.

An Increasingly Difficult Relationship

In spite of the regularity of the dialogue between the two players – during the annual EU–China Summit, EU–China High Level Economic and Trade Dialogue and in the various sectoral dialogues – growing divergences and competing interests have become apparent. The European side is therefore becoming more and more concerned about the massive trade deficit it has with China. This concern is moreover strengthened by the lack of proper revaluation of the Chinese renminbi. Since the transition from an export-driven economy to the development of a strong internal market will take time, it is likely that China will not start a shock therapy in amending its trade policy.[15] In the words of François Godement in his very critical but pragmatic *Power Audit of EU–China Relations* 'there are troubling indications that, in spite of the hopes pinned on China's public domestic spending package and its new accent on social policies, China is still wedded to an all out export policy' (Fox and Godement, 2009a: 50). Partly caused by decreasing European industrial strength, the European trade deficit vis-à-vis China also implies that China is not respecting its WTO commitments. In this respect, some spheres of the Chinese economy remain closed to foreign investment or attempts to enter the market, for instance in the services sector. Non-tariff barriers are regularly used in order to limit the access of business enterprises into the Chinese market. Non-respect of intellectual property rights, cash subsidies to Chinese companies, unachievable demands and a restrictive bureaucracy constitute very strong obstacles to European business opportunities in the Chinese market (Grant and Barysch, 2008: 37).

For its part, the Chinese government has been increasingly concerned about the rise of protectionism and lack of trust of its European partners. The EU is subjected to growing public pressure to protect its key industries. In this respect, countries from Southern and Central Europe whose competitiveness is directly threatened by inexpensive Chinese goods (Feng, 2007, in Gill and Murphy, 2008: 9) are not the only EU member states willing to protect some of their industries. Other member states are becoming keen to defend their high-technology businesses, for instance in the green energy sector.[16] The extensive use of anti-dumping and non-tariff barriers by the EU is therefore often considered a protectionist practice by the Chinese government. Furthermore, Chinese leaders have also shown increasing disappointment regarding the non-recognition of China as a market economy. Since the market economy status was one of the main incentives for China to enter the WTO,[17] the issue has proved to be highly sensitive in the bilateral dialogues and constitutes a strong – misused – bargaining tool for the EU.

Since 2005–6, trade disagreements have furthermore coincided with a general degradation of the bilateral relationship. Several authors consider that this period saw the end of the 'honeymoon' between both entities.[18] On the one hand, China has become increasingly self-confident in its development and is less likely to accept foreign intervention that may disturb domestic tensions or threaten the fragile political and social stability of the country.[19] On the other hand, the EU has become increasingly frustrated by the non-responsiveness of the Chinese government to the European so-called 'conditional engagement'.[20] In this respect, it is arguable that the partnership between China and the EU has failed to become really strategic even if it has turned out to be more comprehensive.[21]

In this difficult context, it appears that bilateral dialogue as well as the use of soft law – which is extensively used in EU–China relations (Snyder, 2010: 265) – has had mixed results. The cancellation of the 11th EU–China summit that was to take place in Lyon in December 2008 mirrors this uncertainty. Following the announcement of a meeting between Nicolas Sarkozy – who held the double mandate of French President and head of the Council of the EU – and the Dalai Lama on 6 December 2008 in Gdansk (Poland), China did not hesitate to bring its domestic security agenda to the forefront. It retaliated in order to punish France and the EU.[22] This cancellation of a top-level summit during the height of the economic crisis that required strong cooperation and coordination among interdependent partners could have various meanings. Some analysts understood the incident as a proof of growing Chinese disinterest in the

European economy and market.[23] In the authors' view, it shows the importance of international institutions, like the WTO, in framing the dialogue and solving trade disputes between actors.

To summarise, after having shown that China and the EU are major actors in the multilateral trading system thanks to their respective economic powers and strong ties, this chapter has found that China and the EU do face increasing difficulties in solving their growing trade disputes through bilateral dialogue. Since the WTO constitutes the main multilateral framework to regulate international trade and an important source of hard law, it is relevant to analyse the interactions between both actors in this framework. We will argue that the actions and perspectives of China and the EU both reinforce and challenge the institution.

CHINA–EU INTERACTION: FOR A REINFORCEMENT OF THE WORLD TRADE ORGANIZATION

The use of the assets provided by the WTO to discuss trade issues inherent to China–European relations is per se an important source of legitimacy for the multilateral trading system. In this respect, the growing recourse to the WTO's dispute settlement system as a way to settle bilateral trade disputes strongly reinforces the legitimacy of the WTO. This being said, the use of the dispute settlement system is not a means to replace bilateral dialogue. Rather, it is an additional framework to settle the disputes mainly when bilateral dialogue does not lead to acceptable outcomes. The attraction of the WTO's dispute settlement system can be explained by different factors. First, and contrary to the bilateral economic dialogue, decisions of the Dispute Settlement Body (DSB) based upon panel or Appellate Body reports are legally binding for WTO members. Second, as legal and economic arguments prevail over political ones, it becomes much more difficult for China to use political retaliation when a dispute is being resolved in the context of the dispute settlement system. Third, the WTO is also an efficient forum to guarantee a common European approach. Free-riding by EU member states is much more difficult in this multilateral context where the EU takes the lead over its member states.[24] In order to assess EU–China interaction in front of the WTO dispute settlement system, it is important to evaluate the number, timing and content of those disputes.

Since China acceded to the WTO, eight cases involving China and the EU have been brought before the WTO's dispute settlement organs. The EU was the complainant in six cases[25] and China in two cases.[26] It is important to specify that these do not include cases where the EU or China were third parties to cases involving other actors. The number of direct cases appears to be limited in comparison to the 17 trade disputes China has so far had with the United States.[27] Generally speaking and contrary to some fears expressed at the time of Chinese entry in the WTO,[28] the accession of China has not led to a flood of cases that would have strongly challenged the efficiency of the WTO's dispute settlement system. The number of cases the EU has brought against China does not depart strongly from the former's policy and strategy regarding disputes with other rapidly emerging countries. In this respect, the EU has acted as a complainant four times against India and once against Brazil since 2001.[29]

Concerning the timing of the disputes, it appears that the dispute settlement system was not used in the strict sense by China and the EU during the first years following Chinese accession. During this period, they nevertheless used the threat of litigation which allowed the parties to find agreement without proceeding to start up the WTO's dispute settlement machinery. For instance, the European Communities threatened to bring a case that concerned restrictions imposed by the Chinese government on coke used for the production of steel. Both actors finally succeeded in finding an agreement before the launch of a dispute at the WTO level.[30] The use of formal litigation started in 2006 with the *Auto Parts* case, which was the first WTO case (launched by the EU, together with the US and Canada) brought against China. Only in 2009 was the first case brought by China against the EU under the WTO framework. This division into three phases (China as a reluctant litigant, China as a respondent, China as a complainant) tallies with the common analysis made of the Chinese participation in the WTO's dispute settlement system.[31] The following elements explain this evolution of the two actors' behaviour.

First, enhancement of Chinese capacity building has been a necessary step for the country to pursue a formal dispute at the WTO level. Its lack of expertise has long prevented China from bringing cases before the WTO. China's participation as a third party to many disputes has proved to be an efficient and affordable way to increase its legal capacity. The great incentives to carry out research and education on the WTO and international economic law have been an efficient process to broaden and deepen Chinese expertise (Hsieh, 2010: 1008).

Second, bilateral relations were stable and relatively constructive in the years following the accession of China to the WTO. No one will nevertheless forget the major trade disputes on textiles around 2005. China had made very significant efforts to enter the WTO and the EU, like the other members, left the country time to transpose its new commitments into its legal system.[32] Furthermore, the launch of the Comprehensive Strategic Partnership in 2003 between both actors meant that they prioritised the use of bilateral fora over multilateral arenas. With the growing discontent over bilateral trade (see above), the use of multilateral fora and the WTO's dispute settlement system has then become a gateway to express and shape the assertiveness of both actors.

Third, the Chinese socialisation in the international system and in the WTO explains to a certain extent China's growing legal assertiveness.[33] Litigation (*song*) is not the preferred tool to solve disputes in the traditional Chinese legal culture. 'Reason, compassion and norms higher than law' (Chang, 2010: 217) have indeed historically been considered as the most valued and legitimate methods of solving disagreements. The greater involvement of China in the WTO has nevertheless enhanced the Chinese understanding of the utility, effectiveness and legitimacy of a system ruled by law.

If the substance of their trade disputes is examined, it is obvious that some of the cases recently brought before the dispute settlement system are of critical importance for both bilateral trade and the regulation of international trade. In particular the cases *EC – Anti-Dumping Measures on Iron or Steel Fasteners* and *China – Measures Related to the Exportation of Various Raw Materials* are significant in this respect.

On 23 June 2009, the European Communities requested consultation with China regarding restrictions on the export of some raw materials from China including coke, magnesium and zinc.[34, 35] In addition to quantitative restrictions on some of those materials, China was accused of imposing further restrictions on the right to export, with the whole process being monitored by public institutions including ministries and chambers of commerce.[36] Because the consultations failed to solve the dispute, a panel was formed on 29 March 2010 resulting from a request by the EU along with the US and Mexico.[37] The panel provided its conclusions on 5 July 2011 and concluded that the Chinese export duties were inconsistent with China's Protocol of Accession. It held that China had failed to demonstrate that the trade restrictions contributed to the improvement of its citizens' health and to the protection of limited resources.[38] As expected, China appealed this decision. The Appellate Body nevertheless confirmed the findings made by the Panel on 30 January 2012.[39] In the words of Ji and Huang, this case has 'the potential to fundamentally impact the framework of China's export regulatory system' (Ji and Huang, 2011: 3). Resource scarcity and the needs of a fast-growing economy have led China to pursue a complex internal and external strategy which aims to preserve and extend its stocks of available raw materials. In this respect, the 12th Five Year Plan mentions energy security and access to raw materials as two top priorities. Obviously, the condemnation of China's restrictive export practices in this field will be highly influential.

On 31 July 2009, China requested consultations for the case that would become well-known as *EC – Anti-Dumping Measures on Iron or Steel Fasteners*. The Chinese action was initiated following the EU decision to impose anti-dumping measures on Chinese companies exporting iron or steel fasteners.[40] This is a practice that is extensively used against the world's largest exporter. Because of the failure to settle the disagreement through consultations, China finally called for the formation of a panel on 13 October 2009.[41] It considers the measures imposed by the EU protectionist and contrary to WTO rules 'in the process starting from anti-dumping initiation, investigation to final determination' (Ji and Huang, 2011: 9). More particularly, China contests the European use of the individual treatment regime. The Panel published its report on 3 December 2010 and gave China one of its greatest victories in the WTO dispute settlement system to date. In its conclusions, the Panel declared the contested measures contrary to the WTO Agreement, the GATT 1994 and the Anti-Dumping Agreement in a number of respects.[42] This decision is susceptible to challenge, especially on the anti-dumping policy of the EU against China. The EU therefore decided to appeal the decision.[43] The Appellate Body upheld the findings of the Panel on 15 July 2011.[44]

At a time when the Doha Round is in a deadlock, the significance of the use of the WTO dispute settlement system must not be downgraded since 'panels and the Appellate Body are increasingly being asked to fill in the grey areas and in doing so, often take on the role of legislator' (Shaffer, 2003, in Don Harpaz, 2010: 1156). The active participation of China and the EU in this framework confirms the utility and effectiveness of the system. At the same time, strong reliance on the WTO dispute settlement system in times of a paralysed WTO legislator could carry the risk of unwarranted 'judicial activism'.

CHINA–EU INTERACTION: WHEN MISPERCEPTION LIMITS THE SCOPE FOR COLLABORATION

Since the launch of the Doha Round in 2001, the positions defended by the EU and China have strongly diverged. China has supported to a large extent G20 viewpoints (Lim and Wang, 2010) that strongly depart from European identified interests. It supports differentiated treatment in function of the level of development, the suppression of export subsidies for agricultural goods as well as the differentiation in the coefficients aimed at reducing high tariffs for non-agricultural market access (NAMA).[45]

Beyond this problem lies another challenge, which is much more problematic, since it affects the expectations each actor has regarding the strategy of the other. China and the EU do not share the same expectations as to the responsibility they should take in the negotiations of the Doha Round and the reform of the multilateral trading system. Contrary to the efficient use of the dispute settlement system, which enhances the legitimacy of the WTO as the main framework to regulate international trade, this misperception constitutes a major challenge.

On the one hand, the European side has for a while called upon China to become a 'responsible stakeholder' within the WTO. This implies that China should become much more active in the negotiations of the Doha Round and in the process of WTO reform. Contrary to this expectation, the activity of China in the WTO has been described as being a 'listening and learning exercise' (Warwick Commission's Report, 2007: 17) and as corresponding to the behaviour of a 'developing country' (Harbinson, 2009: 12). As was often expected at the time of Chinese accession, China has been acting so far as a 'good citizen' (Jackson, in Cass, et al., 2003: 28). This stance appears to be insufficient and unsatisfactory for the EU. The latter wishes to see China joining India and Brazil as engines of the developing world in order to successfully conclude the Round. Furthermore, the Chinese low profile contradicts the European affirmed normative power that implies a will to activate the main stakeholders in international organisations as well as to push them to assume their responsibilities. The EU has affirmed this expectation regularly during the Trade Policy Review of China. In the Trade Policy Reviews of 2006 and 2010 it asked diplomatically but clearly for 'an active role by China'[46] and 'courageous leadership in the DDA negotiations [. . .] reflecting its weight as a leading trading nation'.[47]

On the other hand, while recognising the 'irreplaceable role' of the multilateral trading system and a commitment to 'pushing forward the Doha Round negotiations to an early and successful conclusion',[48] China has kept a rather low profile in the negotiations of the Doha Round and WTO reform. A number of interconnected dimensions of Chinese strategy and agenda are involved here: China's relative interests in the current round, relations with other developing countries and the growing use of preferential trade agreements.

China's interests in the current round of negotiations are relatively limited in comparison with the other main emerging economies, namely Brazil and India. On the one hand, the Doha Round does not cover *stricto sensu* China's main trade concerns. The Chinese economy is indeed strongly centred on manufactured goods. By contrast, India's reliance for growth on services which represents 13.1 per cent of its GDP[49] explains to a large extent the country's activism and constraining stances in the DDA negotiations. On the other hand, China has already given up a lot during its process of accession by agreeing, for instance, to stringent tariff cuts compared to the ones agreed by other developing countries. As an indication, China's average bound level of tariffs is 10 per cent, whereas that of India is 48.5 per cent. In this respect some authors point to an erosion of Chinese enthusiasm following the substantial commitments made in the process of acceding to the WTO (Lim and Wang, 2010: 1320). Because of this lack of interest, China is keen to avoid hurting or challenging the position of other developing countries. Assuming the role of a leader would indeed imply a stronger visibility and vulnerability of China regarding a developing world which is very often strongly suspicious of Chinese intentions. Finally, preferential trade agreements have become a major means to secure Chinese trade interests and to bypass the blockade of the multilateral trading system. In the words of Zeng, these agreements can create a framework 'consistent with Chinese interests, but also by advancing Chinese interests in areas where multilateral cooperation seems to have delivered suboptimal outcomes' (Zeng, 2010: 642). Preferential agreements are, for example, very useful to obtain recognition as a market economy. In spite of its unwillingness to claim a leadership role and to challenge its domestic interests, China is nevertheless likely to remain a committed stakeholder in the WTO.

Mutual misperception strongly challenges the likelihood of China–EU interaction contributing positively to a favourable outcome in the Doha Round and in WTO reform. On the one hand, these misperceptions inhibit the trust necessary in building strong and strategic engagement and cooperation. They also make it highly difficult to develop a constructive coalition of interests between the two actors.

CONCLUSION

In an address to the Annual Session of the WTO Parliamentary Conference on 22 March 2011, Director General Pascal Lamy alleged that 'a WTO in crisis is not what is expected of responsible members of the international community' (Lamy, 2011). This strong statement can be related to two main dynamics studied in this chapter. First, it puts forward the mounting challenge faced by the WTO – an institution that has failed to adapt to a changing world and whose structures do not really fit the new balance of economic power. Second, it underscores the need for major world powers to be responsible stakeholders in order to ensure the sustainability of the WTO.

In this respect, the authors have submitted that China and the EU are main actors in the WTO and necessary partners to any reform. Their economic weight as two major markets of consumption and production as well as their particular historical experiences in the WTO largely explain their status. In a situation where EU–China bilateral trade relations have become increasingly difficult, this multilateral forum appears to be a relevant and useful venue to discuss and solve bilateral and international trade concerns.

It has been demonstrated that the EU and China increasingly use the WTO dispute settlement system for cases of primary importance for both bilateral and multilateral trade issues. In a time when the Doha Round is in a stalemate, this practice confirms the WTO as a main forum for interpretative decisions regarding trade regulations and enhances its legislative *acquis* as a guarantee of economic progress and legal certainty. This chapter has nevertheless shown that mutual misperception and disagreements over the role each actor should play render it difficult to upgrade EU–China interaction sufficiently to become a major lever which would help break the current impasse in the Round. Obviously, the frequent use of the WTO's dispute settlement system does not suffice in pushing forward the necessary reforms of the organisation as a whole.

This mirrors the failure to develop a real bilateral engagement as well as partnership at the multilateral level. On the one hand, China continues to develop a rather instrumental use of the multilateral arena. China envisages it mostly as a means to promote and achieve its domestic interests. This explains to a certain extent the country's reluctance to become an affirmed and exposed leader. On the other hand, the EU has failed to effectively engage China in the years following its accession to the WTO. It has, for instance, not used one of its remaining bargaining tools, namely the possible recognition of China as a market economy before 2016.

Both China and the EU benefit strongly from the multilateral trading system. Since a failure of the Doha Round would strongly hurt the WTO, China and the EU share a common interest and responsibility in seeing the organisation being confirmed and reinforced as the premier forum for the regulation and liberalisation of international trade.

NOTES

1 This issue is addressed by Xiaodong Wang in Chapter 5 on 'What lessons can be learned from the Doha Round?'

2 The Warwick Commission brought together leading WTO experts and issued a major report in 2007, *The Multilateral Trade Regime: Which Way Forward?* It identified the main challenges confronting the WTO and made policy recommendations to overcome them.

3 For difficult negotiations, an agreement among influential countries is often a necessary prerequisite to push for a final consensus. In the Uruguay Round, the Quadrilaterals or

the QUAD was the informal group that played the most influential blocking and pushing role. It comprised Canada, the United States, Japan and the European Union.

4 The need to take into account the shift in the balance of power has been recognised regularly by high-ranking officials. John Lipsky, First Deputy Managing Director of the IMF, stated in 2009: 'The resilience of Asian economies in this crisis, their substantial contributions to global growth in recent years and the region's importance in international capital flows are underpinning the transformation of international fora' (Lipsky, 2009).

5 See Young (2007: 803–4).

6 Disagreements on the boundaries of the WTO are one of the main obstacles to the conclusion of the Doha Round. The opposition between more comprehensive or exclusive interpretations of the limits within which the WTO should concentrate constitutes indeed a constraining divergence on one fundamental aspect of the agenda. See the Warwick Commission's Report (2007: 25–7).

7 To understand the negotiation strategy of the EU during the Chinese accession process, see Zimmerman (2008). In his view, it appears that the concept of 'normative power Europe' did not really apply to the European trade strategy in those two cases in which human rights did not play a central role in the bilateral dialogue contrary to the one carried on with the United States. See also Depayre (2009).

8 See Tang (2009) and Lardy (2002).

9 The non-recognition of market economy status has clear implications since it makes it possible for trade partners to evaluate the prices of a product as a function of the prices applied in another country with which the market shares some similarities with the Chinese.

10 For a good assessment of the expectations and fears expressed at the time of the Chinese accession to the WTO, see Cass et al. (2003).

11 http://www.worldbank.org (last consulted 6 July 2011).

12 See Arora and Vamvakidis (2010: 11–12).

13 See Gill and Murphy (2008: 9).

14 European Commission, 'Bilateral Trade Relations: China'. Available at: http://ec.europa.eu/trade/issues/bilateral/countries/china/index_en.htm (last consulted 7 July 2011).

15 Although inflation might put internal pressure on China to revaluate its currency more rapidly.

16 See, for instance, Holslag (2007: 11).

17 See Tang (2009: 2).

18 See Shambaugh (2007).

19 See Godement (2010: 2–3).

20 See Holslag and Geraerts (2007: 5).

21 On the EU–China Strategic Partnership see Renard (2011).

22 The ambiguities inherent in the system of rotating the Council presidency appeared to be the main source of the leverage China had when reacting to the meeting. This had two main consequences. On the one hand, EU member states capitalised on the French misfortune and did not maximise the strong political risk taken by Nicolas Sarkozy. On the other hand, China used European disunity to its advantage. It demonstrated its full dissatisfaction to France prompted by several disagreements preceding the Olympic Games. Furthermore, it cancelled the EU–China summit, which was an important means of warning the next presidencies, and the EU as a whole, not to consider this meeting as a precedent.

23 See Fox (2008). This perspective confirms to a certain extent the radical views of some Chinese academics like Professor Pan Wei (Peking University) who argues that the 'EU is weak, politically divided and militarily non-influential. Economically, it is a giant, but we no longer fear it because we know that the EU needs China more than China needs the EU': Pan, in Fox and Godement (2009b).

24 The common commercial policy is an exclusive EU competence: see article 3(1)(e) and article 207 of the Treaty in the Functioning of the European Union.

25 DS339: Measures affecting imports of automobile parts (30 March 2006); DS372: Measures affecting financial information services and foreign financial information suppliers (3 March 2008); DS395: Measures related to the exportation of various raw materials (23 June 2009); DS407: Provisional anti-dumping duties on certain iron and steel fasteners from the European Union (7 May 2010).
26 DS397: Definitive anti-dumping measures on certain iron or steel fasteners from China (31 July 2009) and DS407: Provisional anti-dumping duties on certain iron and steel fasteners from the European Union (7 May 2010).
27 It is interesting to note that all the cases brought by China as a complainant have been directed against the EU or the United States. This shows the great importance of these two markets for the Chinese economy. In the words of Ji and Huang, it is 'normal for a member to address the bigger issues first, especially when it has limited human and financial resources' (2011: 32).
28 See Cass et al. (2003: 37).
29 http://www.wto.org (last consulted 7 July 2011).
30 For an extensive presentation of this case, see Gao (2007: 380–4).
31 See Kennedy (2009: 3) and Wouters (2009).
32 See Kennedy (2009: 3).
33 In this sense, see Don Harpaz (2010).
34 World Trade Organization (2009) *China – Measures Related to the Exportation of Various Raw Materials*, Request for consultations by the European Communities, WT/DS395/1 G/L/889, 25 June, p. 1.
35 For a detailed explanation of the incentives to apply export restrictions on raw materials, see Korinek and Kim (2011: 255–81).
36 World Trade Organization (2009) *China – Measures Related to the Exportation of Various Raw Materials*, Request for consultations by the European Communities, WT/DS395/1 G/L/889, 25 June, p. 2.
37 See World Trade Organization (2010) *China – Measures Related to the Exportation of Various Raw Materials*, Constitution of the Panel Established at the Requests of the United States, the European Communities and Mexico, WT/DS394/8, WT/DS395/8, WT/DS398/7, 30 March.
38 World Trade Organization (2011) *China – Measures Related to the Exportation of Various Raw Materials*, Reports of the panel, WT/DS394/R, WT/DS/395/R, WT/DS398/R, 5 July.
39 See World Trade Organization (2012) *China – Measures Related to the Exportation of Various Raw Materials*, Reports of the Appellate Body, WT/D5394/AB/R, WT/D5395/AB/R, WT/D5398/AB/R, 30 January.
40 See Council Regulation (EC) No. 91/2009 of 26 January 2009 imposing a definitive anti-dumping duty on imports of certain iron or steel fasteners originating in the People's Republic of China.
41 *European Communities – Definitive Anti-Dumping Measures on Certain Iron or Steel Fasteners from China: Request on Certain Iron or Steel Fasteners from China*, Request for the Establishment of a Panel by China, 13 October 2009, WT/DS/397/3.
42 *European Communities – Definitive Anti-Dumping Measures on Certain Iron or Steel Fasteners from China: Request on Certain Iron or Steel Fasteners from China*, Report of the Panel, 3 December 2010, WT/DS397/R.
43 *European Communities – Definitive Anti-Dumping Measures on Certain Iron or Steel Fasteners from China: Request on Certain Iron or Steel Fasteners from China*, Notification of an appeal by the European Union, 29 March 2011, WT/DS397/7.
44 See World Trade Organization (2011) *European Community – Definitive Anti-Dumping Measures on Certain Iron or Steel Fasteners from China*, Report of the Apellatte Body, WT/D5394/AB/R, WT/D5395/AB/R, WT/D5398/AB/R, 30 January.
45 WTO Trade Policy Review Body (2006) *Trade Policy Review of the People's Republic of China*, Report by the People's Republic of China, 17 March, WT/TPR/G/161.
46 WTO Trade Policy Review Body (2006) *Trade Policy Review People's Republic of China*, Minutes of meeting, WT/TPR/M/161, § 93.

47 WTO Trade Policy Review Body (2010) *Trade Policy Review People's Republic of China*, Record of the Meeting, 2010, WT/TPR/M/230, § 134.
48 WTO Trade Policy Review Body (2008) *Trade Policy Review: Report by China*, 7 May, WT/TPR/G/199.
49 http://www.worldbank.org

REFERENCES

Books and Articles

Arora, V. and Vamvakidis, A. (2010) 'Gauging China's influence', *Finance and Development*, 47 (4): 11–13.

Capling, A. and Higgott, R. (2009) 'Introduction: the future of the multilateral trade system – what role for the World Trade Organization?', *Global Governance*, 15 (3): 313–25.

Cass, Deborah Z., Williams, Brett G. and Barker, George (eds) (2003) *China and the World Trading System*. Cambridge: Cambridge University Press.

Chang, W. (2010) 'Classical Chinese jurisprudence and the development of the Chinese legal system', *Tsinghua China Law Review*, 2 (2): 207–72.

Das, Dilip K. (2001) *Global Trading System at the Crossroads: A Post-Seattle Perspective*. London: Routledge.

Defraigne, P. (2011) 'Back to trade multilateralism', *Madariaga Paper*, 4 (2). Available at: http://www.madariaga.org/madariaga-papers/420-back-to-trade-multilateralism (last consulted 1 June 2011).

Depayre, G. (2009) *How Did the EU View China's Accession to the WTO*. Paper presented in the context of the Seminar Series on 'China in the WTO: An Early Harvest', 19 October, Leuven.

Don Harpaz, M. (2010) 'Sense and sensibilities of China and WTO Dispute Settlement', *Journal of World Trade*, 44 (6): 1155–86.

Drahos, P. (2003) 'When the weak bargain with the strong: negotiations in the WTO', *International Negotiations*, 8 (1): 79–109.

Dür, A. and Zimmerman, H. (2007) 'Introduction: the EU in international trade negotiations', *Journal of Common Market Studies*, 45 (4): 771–87.

Feng, Zhongping (2007) 'Promoting the deeper development of China–EU relations', in David Kerr and Liu Fei (eds), *The International Politics of EU–China Relations*. Oxford: Oxford University Press, pp. 267–79.

Fox, J. (2008) 'It's Tibet, not the economy, stupid', *European Council on Foreign Relations*, 28 November. Available at: http://www.europeanvoice.com/article/2008/11/it-s-tibet-not-the-economy-stupid/63257.aspx (last consulted 12 April 2011).

Fox, J. and Godement, F. (2009a) *A Power Audit of EU–China Relations: Policy Paper*. European Council on Foreign Relations. Available at: http://ecfr.3cdn.net/532cd91d0b5c9699ad_ozm6b9bz4.pdf (last consulted 1 June 2011).

Fox, J. and Godement, F. (2009b) 'Running rings around the E.U.', *New York Times*, 22 April. Available at: http://ecfr.eu/content/entry/commentary_iht_fox_godement_eu_china/ (last consulted 29 March 2011).

Gao, H. (2007) 'Taming the dragon: China's experience in the WTO dispute settlement system', *Legal Issues of Economic Integration*, 34 (4): 369–92.

Gill, B. and Murphy, M. (2008) *China Europe Relations, Implications and Policy Responses for the United States*, Report of the CSIS Freeman Chair in Asian Studies, CSIS. Available at: http://csis.org/files/media/csis/pubs/080507-gill-chinaeuroperelations-web.pdf (last consulted 1 June 2011).

Godement, F. (2010) *A Global China Policy*, ECFR Policy Brief, June. Available at http://ecfr.eu/page/-/documents/A-global-China-policy.pdf (last consulted 1 June 2011).

Grant, C. and Barysch, K. (2008) *Can Europe and China Shape a New World Order?*, Centre for European Reforms. Available at: http://www.cer.org.uk/pdf/p_837.pdf (last consulted 1 June 2011).

Harbinson, S. (2009) *How Did China View Its Accession to the WTO?* Paper presented in the context of the Seminar Series on 'China in the WTO: An Early Harvest', 12 October, Leuven.

Holslag, J. (2007) *Clouds Ahead: China's Energy Policy in the Light of Climate Change: Options for Cooperation with the EU*. Brussels: BICCS.

Holslag, J. and Geraerts, G. (2007) *China and Europe: The Myth of a Post-Modern World*, BICCS Background Paper, 2 (7).

Hsieh, P. L. (2010) 'China's development of international economic law and WTO legal capacity building', *Journal of International Economic Law*, 13 (4): 997–1036.

Ji, W. and Huang, C. (2011) 'China's experience in dealing with WTO dispute settlement: a Chinese perspective', *Journal of World Trade*, 45 (1): 1–37.

Kennedy, M. (2009) *China in the WTO Dispute Settlement System*. Paper presented in the Context of the Seminar Series on 'China in the WTO: An Early Harvest', 9 November.

Korinek, J. and Kim, J. (2011) 'Export restrictions on strategic raw materials and their impact on trade and global supply', *Journal of World Trade*, 45 (2): 255–81.

Lamy, P. (2011) Speech at the Annual Session of the Parliamentary Conference on the WTO at the WTO Headquarters, 22 March . Available at: http://www.wto.org/english/news_e/sppl_e/sppl189_e.htm (last consulted 12 April 2011).

Lardy, Nicholas (2002) *Integrating China into the Global Economy*. Washington, DC: Brookings Institution Press.

Lim, C. L. and Wang, J. Y. (2010) 'China and the Doha Round Development Agenda', *Journal of World Trade*, 44 (6): 1309–31.

Lipsky, J. (2009) *Asia, the Financial Crisis and Global Economic Governance*. Speech at the Federal Reserve Bank of San Francisco Conference, 20 October. Available at: http://www.imf.org/external/np/speeches/2009/102009.htm (last consulted 12 April 2011).

Renard, T. (ed.) (2011) *Conference Report on EU–China Building upon a Dialogue among Strategic Partners*. Brussels: Egmont Royal Institute for International Relations.

Schott, J. J. (2010) 'Does the WTO need to change', *Current History*, 109 (730): 355–7.

Shaffer, Greg (2003) *Defending Interests: Public Private Partnerships in WTO Litigation*. Washington, DC: Brookings Institution Press.

Shambaugh, D. (2007) 'The "China honeymoon" is over', *International Herald Tribune*, 26 November. Available at: http://www.nytimes.com/2007/11/26/opinion/26iht-edshambaugh.1.8482459.html (last consulted 12 April 2011).

Snyder, Francis (2010) *The EU, the WTO and China: Legal Pluralism and International Trade Regulations*, China and International Economic Law Series.

Oxford: Hart.
Srivastava, S. (2008) 'Negotiating analysis: the Cancun Ministerial of the WTO', *International Studies*, 45 (1): 23–43.
Tang, X. (2009) *How Did China View Its Accession to the WTO? Some Observations Regarding China's Return to the Multilateral Trading System*. Paper presented in the context of the Seminar Series on 'China in the WTO: An Early Harvest', 12 October, Leuven.
Warwick Commission's Report (2007) *The Multilateral Trade Regime: Which Way Forward?* Launched on 6 December at the World Trade Organization, Geneva.
Wouters, J. (2009) *China in the WTO Dispute Settlement System – The Best Is Yet to Come: A Commentary on Matthew Kennedy*. Paper presented in the context of the Seminar Series on 'China in the WTO: An Early Harvest', 9 November, Leuven.
Wouters, Jan and De Meester, Bart (2007) *The World Trade Organization: A Legal and Institutional Analysis*. Antwerp and Oxford: Intersentia.
Young, A. R. (2007) 'Trade politics ain't what it used to be: the European Union in the Doha Round', *Journal of Common Market Studies*, 45 (4): 789–811.
Zeng, K. (2010) 'Multilateral versus bilateral and regional trade liberalization: explaining China's pursuit of free trade agreements', *Journal of Contemporary China*, 19 (66): 635–52.
Zimmerman, H. (2008) 'How the EU negotiates trade and democracy: the cases of China's accession to the WTO and the Doha Round?' *European Foreign Affairs Review*, 13 (2): 255–80.

Official Publications

Agreement Establishing the World Trade Organization, signed in Marrakesh, Morocco, 15 April 1994.
Council Regulation (EC) No. 91/2009 of 26 January 2009 imposing a definitive anti-dumping duty on imports of certain iron or steel fasteners originating in the People's Republic of China.
European Commission (2010) 'EU–China Trade in Facts and Figures', June. Available at: http://trade.ec.europa.eu/doclib/docs/2009/september/tradoc_144591.pdf (last consulted 7 July 2011).
European Commission, 'Bilateral Trade Relations: China'. Available at: http://ec.europa.eu/trade/issues/bilateral/countries/china/index_en.htm (last consulted 7 July 2011).
International Monetary Fund (2012) 'World Economic Outlook Database', April. Available at: http://www.imf.org/external/pubs/ft/weo/2012/01/weodata/index.aspx (last consulted 12 June 2012).
Treaty on the Functioning of the European Union, *OJ* 2010, C 83/47, 30 March 2010.
World Trade Organization (2009) *China – Measures Related to the Exportation of Various Raw Materials*, Request for Consultations by the European Communities, 25 June, WT/DS395/1 G/L/889.
World Trade Organization (2009) *European Communities – Definitive Anti-Dumping Measures on Certain Iron or Steel Fasteners from China: Request on Certain Iron or Steel Fasteners from China*, Request for the Establishment of a Panel by China, 13 October, WT/DS/397/3.

World Trade Organization (2010) *China – Measures Related to the Exportation of Various Raw Materials*, Constitution of the Panel Established at the Requests of the United States, the European Communities and Mexico, 30 March, WT/DS394/8, WT/DS395/8, WT/DS398/7.

World Trade Organization (2010) *China – Measures Related to the Exportation of Various Raw Materials*, Communication from the Chairman to the Panel, 21 October, WT/DS394/10, WT/DS395/10, WT/DS398/9.

World Trade Organization (2010) *European Communities – Definitive Anti-Dumping Measures on Certain Iron or Steel Fasteners from China: Request on Certain Iron or Steel Fasteners from China*, Report of the Panel, 3 December, WT/DS397/R.

World Trade Organization (2011) *China – Measures Related to the Exportation of Various Raw Materials*, Reports of the Panel, 5 July, WT/DS394/R, WT/DS/395/R, WT/DS398/R.

World Trade Organization (2011) *European Communities – Definitive Anti-Dumping Measures on Certain Iron and Steel Fasteners from China*, Report of the Appellate Body, WT/D5397/AB/R, 15 July.

World Trade Organization (2011) *European Communities – Definitive Anti-Dumping Measures on Certain Iron or Steel Fasteners from China: Request on Certain Iron or Steel Fasteners from China*, Notification of an Appeal by the European Union, 29 March, WT/DS397/7.

World Trade Organization (2012) *China – Measures Related to the Exportations of Various Raw Materials*, Reports of the Appellate Body, WT/D5394/AB/R, WT/D5395/AB/R, WT/D5398/AB/R, 30 January.

World Trade Organization Trade Policy Review Body (2006) *Trade Policy Review of the People's Republic of China*, Report by the People's Republic of China, 17 March, WT/TPR/G/161.

World Trade Organization Trade Policy Review Body (2006), *Trade Policy Review People's Republic of China*, Minutes of Meeting, 6 June, WT/TPR/M/161 (06-2701).

World Trade Organization Trade Policy Review Body (2008) *Trade Policy Review: Report by China*, 7 May, WT/TPR/G/199.

World Trade Organization Trade Policy Review Body (2010) *Trade Policy Review People's Republic of China*, Record of the Meeting, WT/TPR/M/230.

Websites

World Bank: http://www.worldbank.org
World Trade Organization: http://www.wto.org

5. What lessons can be learned from the Doha Round?

Xiaodong Wang[1]

The Doha Development Agenda (the Doha Round) was launched in 2001 in the capital of Qatar. It is the ninth round of multilateral trade negotiations and it has the largest ever participation. All 153 members of the World Trade Organization are taking part in the negotiations, covering around 20 topics. The Doha Round has set a record as the longest trade negotiation round ever, surpassing its predecessor, the Uruguay Round, which lasted eight years, from 1986 to 1994.

Why is it taking so long to conclude? What makes the Doha Round different from previous rounds? What can we learn from the negotiations so far? All these questions are extremely relevant and deserve thorough reflection and research.

There have been studies which explore the underlying reasons behind the Doha stalemate. Different authors have reached different conclusions. Some attribute it to the fact that the Round can only bring limited market access opportunities and thus fails to attract sufficient business support. Some argue that hard-line positions taken by emerging countries and the lack of leadership by the US and EU have led to the current deadlock. Others note that the political cycles in some key players and frequent changes of chief negotiators are the main barrier to the conclusion of the Round. For example, it is difficult for US negotiators to offer concessions before a Presidential election or mid-term elections, for obvious reasons. Likewise, it is sensitive for Japanese negotiators to show flexibility before the Japanese Diet session. This also applies to China, Brazil or India.

These are all thoughtful ideas. At the outset, it might be interesting to compare the Doha Round with previous rounds, on a factual basis, to see what has changed and what has not changed throughout GATT/WTO history.

The most obvious change is the number of participants in the negotiations. In 1947, when the first round (Geneva Round) was concluded, there were only 23 contracting parties. In the Dillon Round, there were 39 negotiating parties, which expanded to 74 in the Kennedy

Round. When the Uruguay Round started in 1986, there were 103 participants, which had increased to 128 by its conclusion in 1994. Today, we have a much larger membership than 60 years ago. When the Doha Round was launched in 2001, we had 144 WTO members; now, nine years later, we have 153. A larger membership proves the legitimacy and comprehensive representation of the WTO, but it is also true that it adds to the complexity of the negotiations.

With regard to the negotiating issues, during the first five rounds of GATT negotiations, industrial tariffs were the only topic (see Table 5.1). In the Kennedy Round, anti-dumping and were included for negotiation. New codes such as that on Government Procurement were included in the Tokyo Round and a big step forward was achieved in the Uruguay Round in which Agriculture, Textiles and Clothing and Services and Intellectual Property Rights were brought into the negotiation agenda for the first time in history. In the Doha Round, we have around 20 negotiating topics. New disciplines such as Trade Facilitation, Fishery Subsidies, Geographical Indications (GI), the Convention on Biological Diversity (CBD), and Environmental Goods and Services are now under discussion, among which a new agreement on Trade Facilitation is now in good shape.

From Table 5.1 we can clearly see that, with the expansion of the institution, there are more and more participants in the trade negotiations and the issues for negotiation have also increased. Empirical evidence seems to suggest a correlation between the number of participants, issues for discussion and the years needed to complete the round. Another new development in the Doha Round is the methodology used for tariff reductions, i.e. the Swiss Formula in the non-agricultural market access (NAMA) negotiations. For the first time in the tariff negotiations, participants have agreed to use a formula to undertake tariff reductions. It is automatic and the tariff reduction will be on a line-by-line basis with no prior exclusion. By design, the higher the tariff, the more it will be cut. The objective of the Swiss Formula is to reduce tariff peaks and harmonise tariff structures. As compared to the 'average tariff cut' approach used in previous rounds, the Swiss Formula is more straightforward and transparent. However, on the other hand, it is so rigid that it gives no room to developed members to shelter those lines sensitive to their domestic industries, i.e. high tariffs on shoes, textiles and clothing or automobiles. Due to the above-mentioned complexities, it took much longer for negotiators to agree on the formula, the coefficients or the flexibility terms for developing countries so as to reach a balance of obligations among members at different levels of development.

It is true that to reach a concluding deal among 153 members on 20 topics under the single undertaking approach poses a huge challenge for

Table 5.1 Rounds of GATT/WTO trade negotiations

Year	Place/name	Subjects covered	Countries (participants)
1947	Geneva	Tariffs	23
1949	Annecy	Tariffs	13
1951	Torquay	Tariffs	38
1956	Geneva	Tariffs	26
1960–61	Geneva *Dillon Round*	Tariffs	26
1964–67	Geneva *Kennedy Round*	Tariffs and anti-dumping measures	62
1973–79	Geneva *Tokyo Round*	Tariffs, non-tariff measures, 'framework' agreements	102
1986–94	Geneva *Uruguay Round*	Tariffs, non-tariff measures, rules, services, intellectual property, dispute settlement, textiles, agriculture, creation of WTO, etc.	123
2001–	Doha *Doha Round*	Tariffs, non-tariff measures, services, rules, intellectual property, dispute settlement, trade facilitation, cotton, LDC, etc.	153

Source: Based on WTO Secretariat website.

the system. It is also true that members need more time to establish and agree upon a new methodology for tariff reduction. However, these are not fundamental factors that have delayed the conclusion of the Doha Round. The real difficulties lie a lot deeper beneath the surface. The following developments are more decisive in explaining the current Doha stalemate.

First, the rise of emerging countries, especially China, India and Brazil, has altered the demand and supply curve in international trade and the balance of power in the multilateral trading system. The impact of this rise can be witnessed from various perspectives. The symbolic feature of emerging countries' influence is their economic weight. In 1990, developed countries, as a whole, accounted for 75 per cent of world merchandise imports; in 2000, this share went down to 71 per cent. In 2008, the figure was around 63 per cent and it went down further to 59 per cent in 2010. On the other hand, the share of developing economies in global imports increased from 23 per cent in 1990 to 34 per cent in 2008 and reached 38 per cent in 2010. China, as an emerging country, has become the leading global trading power. While overtaking Germany as the world's top exporter in 2009, China also became the second largest single importer in the world, right after the US. When China first opened up in 1978, its share of the world's imports was only 1 per cent. Thirty years later, its share has increased eightfold (World Trade Organization, 2010). Influence and negotiating power come with economic weight and this was reflected in the WTO negotiations. Brazil took the initiative in establishing the G20 group in agricultural negotiations. India, China and Indonesia formed the backbone of the G33 group. India, Brazil and South Africa are key players in NAMA 11, a group formed by developing countries in industrial tariff negotiations. As a result of the change in the balance of power, the Quad, a leading group composed of the US, the EU, Japan and Canada in the Uruguay Round, has been replaced by a new G5, namely the US, the EU, China, India and Brazil, since July 2008. However, the new composition of the leading group in the system has failed to produce more coordinated and efficient solutions to difficult issues. For the moment, this new vehicle is still in its start-up period and it can only function well once consensus is reached on respective roles and responsibilities. Unfortunately, the Doha Round was launched in a period of transition with a leadership vacuum.

Secondly, the proliferation of free trade agreements (FTAs) undermined the role of the WTO in achieving multilateral market opening. In theory, countries can achieve market opening through three main channels, namely unilateral/autonomous trade liberalisation, bilateral/regional FTAs and multilateral trade negotiations (GATT/WTO Rounds). Conventional wisdom is that FTAs are complementary to multilateral trade opening, as both share the same ultimate objective: to achieve the reduction of trade barriers. However, in reality, in the eyes of many WTO members, FTA negotiations can provide a much quicker and more convenient channel delivering market access opportunities with targeted trading partners with minimum political pain at home. Negotiating bilateral FTAs has become a trade policy priority for some WTO members. The number of FTA notifications proves that this trend has been accelerating over the last ten years. In 1979, there were 71 FTAs. The number of Regional Trade Agreements (RTA) notifications under the WTO increased to 129 in 1994, when the Uruguay Round was concluded. The number rose sharply to 277 in 2001 and by 2009, there were 462 RTA notifications to the WTO (representing about 240 FTAs in operation, as agreements in Goods and Services are counted separately in WTO terminology) (World Trade Organization, 2010). Today, two-thirds of the

EU's merchandise exports are intra-regional trade, 32 per cent of US merchandise exports are to Canada and Mexico, its NAFTA trading partners, and 25 per cent of ASEAN exports are carried out within ASEAN countries. With the US–Korea and the Korea–EU FTAs in place, around 25 per cent of Korea's exports will be covered (World Trade Organization, 2010).

It might be true that bilateral FTA negotiations are quicker to conclude and the trade-offs are easier to manage for national governments, as compared to trade talks involving 153 negotiating partners. It might also be more politically attractive to bring targeted market access to business communities at home. In some cases, FTAs can also enter into policy areas, such as investment, the environment or competition policy, for which the WTO has failed to negotiate global disciplines. However, some of these have materialised at the expense of the WTO negotiations. Like it or not, FTAs have partially replaced the WTO function in achieving market access. In addition, FTA negotiations have diverted the focus of some governments and many trade negotiators, a scarce resource in most developing countries, have been relocated from Geneva to carry out FTA negotiations in their respective capitals. Furthermore, the existence of FTA margins has created new issues for the process of multilateral trade negotiations. A good example is the 'preference erosion' issue in the Doha industrial tariff negotiations. To ensure they continue to enjoy preferential margins under bilateral FTA agreements, some least-developed countries have tried to slow down the multilateral tariff reduction process. This new phenomenon has shown how FTA preferences and most-favoured nation principles can contradict each other at a certain point.

Thirdly, the single undertaking process deserves to be looked at again, should no sufficient trade-offs be found across the board among key players. The single undertaking has been one of the key pillars of multilateral trade negotiations, ensuring that the diverse interests of members can be incorporated in a final package. 'Nothing is agreed until everything is agreed' is the precondition and guarantee for horizontal trade-offs across the board. The Uruguay Round was a proven success, in which the single undertaking process not only brought Agriculture, Textiles and Clothing under the WTO disciplines, but it also established new disciplines on intellectual property rights and services. In the author's view, the success of the Uruguay Round lies in the fact that it achieved trade-offs between market access issues and new agreements. In the Doha Round, when investment, competition policy and transparency in GPA, the so-called 'Singapore Issues', were taken off the table in 2001, the weight of the negotiations was mostly put on the market access front and the possibility of a trade-off between market access and new disciplines diminished. In addition, the various kinds of country-specific flexibility for developing countries further reduced the scope of new market access opportunities, as well as room for a final horizontal trade-off. Among the G5 countries, the new core group, a final trade-off on market access concessions is yet to be found, which is a critical precondition for the final package.

The lack of common objectives and coordinated moves in the new leading group, the proliferation of FTAs and a single undertaking process with limited trade-off options have together formed the key barriers to concluding the Doha Round.

Despite all these challenges, the WTO remains the prime forum for trade negotiations and the sole trade dispute settlement body. The GATT/WTO has served the world economy well for the past 60 years. It successfully contained high-intensity trade protectionism in the recent financial crisis and its role is irreplaceable in establishing global trade disciplines on issues such as agricultural subsidies, anti-dumping, trade facilitation or fishery subsidies.

But the WTO needs to improve itself if it is to remain the key venue for market opening. It should find ways to increase the efficiency and effectiveness of its decision-making process so that agreements can be reached in a timely manner. Secondly, the WTO should continue to be the frontrunner in new discipline-making. On top of tariffs and agricultural subsidies, WTO discussions and negotiations should come closer to the needs of the business community. Issues such as technical barriers to trade, Sanitary and Phytosanitary measures (SPS) measures, government procurement disciplines, trade remedies, competition policies, environmental goods and services, and standards should be at the centre of future discussions. In addition, the system could further strengthen the sense of ownership of its members, especially that of developing-country members, to make them more responsible for the future of the system.

EU AND CHINA COOPERATION IN STRENGTHENING THE MULTILATERAL TRADING SYSTEM

Both the European Union and China are key players in the world economy in terms of GDP, trade and influence. The EU is the world's largest economic bloc, China is the world's second largest single economy. According to 2009 figures, the EU remains the world top trader, its exports and imports of merchandise accounting for respectively 16 per cent and 17 per cent of world trade (excluding intra-EU trade). China is the second largest exporter and the world's third largest importer, accounting for 13 per cent and 11 per cent of the world's total exports and imports. In other words, the EU and China together already account for almost 30 per cent of global trade.

In terms of influence in the multilateral trading system, along with the US, the European Union has long played a leadership role in GATT/WTO history. The EU was not only a key Quad member in the Uruguay Round, but is also an indispensable member of today's decision-making process. China has been playing an active and constructive role in WTO activities and in the Doha negotiations since 2001, and has joined India and Brazil in the G5.

Although the EU and China are different in many respects, i.e. level of development, culture, history and policy priorities, the two have a lot in common as well. As two leading world economic and trade powers, the EU and China share a collective responsibility in ensuring the credibility of the multilateral trading system and a successful conclusion of the Doha Round. A failure of the Round would be a big blow to the multilateral system and it is something that both sides should try to avoid. Europe and China should work closer together with other major trading partners to find a compromise acceptable to all. The Doha Round is a real test of the legitimacy and effectiveness of the multilateral trading system and it simply cannot fail. As two major trading powers in the WTO, both sides may find it useful to undertake a dialogue on the future agenda of the WTO and global economic governance in a broader context. Dialogue on the basis of mutual understanding is necessary to strengthen the political trust between China and Europe, and it is also vital for the future of the organisation.

Fighting against trade protectionism is another area where the EU and China can work closely together. For example, the EU and China could set a good example for the world on how to handle bilateral trade disputes in a spirit of dialogue and compromise.

In addition, together with other major players in the multilateral trading system, the EU and China should explore the future agenda of the WTO and discuss how to ensure a more efficient and effective global governance structure for global trade. The European Union and China are big enough and important enough to take such responsibility for the future of the system. This can be done, and it should be done as soon as possible.

NOTE

1. Office of the Director General, World Trade Organization. All views expressed in this article are the author's and do not represent the official position of the WTO.

REFERENCE

World Trade Organization (2010) *International Trade Statistics, 2010*. Geneva: WTO.

6. Beyond European conditionality and Chinese non-interference: articulating EU–China–Africa trilateral relations

Chien-Huei Wu

INTRODUCTION

In 2006, China published its first White Paper on African policy. This signalled China's ambition to play a greater role in Africa, with influence based on its great volume of foreign aid to African countries and extensive trade and investment activities. The European Union (EU), traditionally a major actor through a variety of policy instruments, including preferential trade, economic partnership agreements and official development aid, has gradually realised that China is to be a competitor, if not a threat, in exercising influence in Africa. The competition for influence and conflicts of interest between the EU and China in Africa seem inevitable, not only over geopolitics, but also regarding human rights protection, environmental concerns and energy security issues. The worries of European politicians, academics and civil society centre on China's appetite for African resources, its human rights violations and environmental impacts. A widespread, albeit incomplete, perception is that as a result of fundamentally different values, there is a difference in approach between the EU and China: European conditionality versus Chinese non-interference. In this context, this chapter aims to compare the approaches of the EU and China toward African development policies, and to explore the feasibility of an EU–China–Africa trilateral relationship. It starts with a survey and critique of the existent regulatory frameworks and policy documents on African development policies, with an emphasis on trade preferences, economic partnership agreements and foreign aid, and looks to highlight the differences between the European and Chinese approaches. The chapter then examines the Commission communication entitled *The EU, China and Africa: Towards Trilateral Dialogue and Cooperation*, and explores the potential value and challenges of such a trilateral approach. A short conclusion summarising the main findings and arguments of this chapter will be provided at the end.

THE EU'S REGULATORY FRAMEWORK ON AFRICAN DEVELOPMENT POLICY

The EU–Africa Summit represents the most important forum for political dialogue on EU–Africa relations. Since its inception and institutionalisation in 2000, it has gradually gained weight and influence over EU development policy, with the high-tide mark coming with the 2007 Lisbon EU–Africa Summit. The EU and Africa endorsed the Joint Africa–EU Strategy (2007) that aimed to set forth an overarching framework for EU–Africa relations (Joint Africa–EU Strategy, 2007: 5); both subscribed to the guiding fundamental principles of 'the unity of Africa, the interdependence between Africa and Europe, ownership and joint responsibility, and respect for human rights, democratic principles and the rule of law, as well as the right to development' (Joint Africa–EU Strategy, 2007: 6).

The Joint Africa–EU Strategy puts forward four main objectives, namely:

- to reinforce and elevate the Africa–EU political partnership;
- to strengthen and promote peace, security, democratic governance and human rights, fundamental freedoms, gender equality, sustainable economic development [. . .] and to ensure that all the Millennium Development Goals (MDGs) are met in all African countries by the year 2015;
- to jointly promote and sustain a system of effective multilateralism;
- to facilitate and promote a broad-based and wide-ranging people-centred partnership.

(Joint Africa–EU Strategy, para. 8)

The Joint Africa–EU Strategy further prioritises four strategic aspects: peace and security; governance and human rights; trade and regional integration; and key development issues. In 2005, the European Commission, European Parliament, European Council and representatives of the member states adopted the European Consensus on Development (2006), which articulates the European vision for development and spells out EU development policy. The European Consensus on Development acknowledges common objectives and principles on which to formulate a road map for the renewed EU development policy, and sets forth the eradication of poverty in the context of sustainable development as the chief EU objective (European Consensus on Development, 2006: 5). It further speaks of development as a central goal in itself, and defines sustainable development as being comprised of good governance, human rights and political, economic, social and environmental aspects (European Consensus on Development, 2006: 7).

In terms of legal instruments governing EU–Africa cooperation and partnership, the Cotonou Agreements, signed by the EU on the one side, and the African, Caribbean and Pacific (ACP) countries on the other, is pertinent. This agreement finds its predecessors in the Lomé and Yaoundé Conventions, which date back to the early days of when the European Economic Community was conceived. The Cotonou Agreement (2000) marked a new era of EU–Africa (ACP) relations and is indicative of shifts in the essence and nature of these relations. The reduction and eventual eradication of poverty – which should be realised in a way which is consistent with sustainable development and gradual integration of the African (ACP) countries into the world economy – is prioritised in the Cotonou Agreement (2000: art. 1). The Cotonou Agreement also touches upon essential elements such as respect for human rights, democratic principles and rule of law (2000: art. 9(2)) and identifies good governance as a fundamental element (2000: art. 9(3)).

In relation to trade, one of the principal provisions of all four Lomé Conventions was non-reciprocal trade preferences (Babarinde and Faber, 2005: 4). By contrast, the Cotonou Agreement envisages reciprocal trade relations negotiated and implemented through economic partnership agreements at a later stage. The negotiation of the Cotonou Agreement took place in the framework of the WTO, at which the EU's banana trade regime has been repeatedly challenged by Latin American countries. Furthermore, the EU–Africa (ACP) waiver obtained in the Doha Ministerial Conference expired on 31 December 2007, and a WTO-compatible EU–Africa (ACP) trade regime is of great concern to the EU. The EU thus aimed to pursue a WTO-compatible economic partnership agreement with ACP countries.

The Cotonou Agreement instructed the EU and corresponding African groupings to start negotiating a new trade agreement in September 2002, with the aim of bringing those agreements into effect when the preparatory period closed on 31 December 2007 (Cotonou Agreement, 2000: art. 37(1)). Under that agreement, since 2005, least developed countries (LDCs) were to be allowed 'duty-free access for essentially all products' building on the level of existing trade arrangements (Cotonou Agreement, 2000: art. 37(9)); other possibilities for equivalent trade preferences are provided for non-LDCs that are not in a position to enter into economic partnership agreements (Cotonou Agreement, 2000, art. 37(6)). Consequently, African countries may well seek WTO-compatible economic partnership agreements which necessitate reciprocal market access and trade liberalisation and may be potentially detrimental to the economic interests of African countries. Alternatively, African LDCs may opt for the Everything But Arms (EBA) initiative for non-reciprocal preferences. The African countries not enlisted as LDCs may refer to the reformed Generalised System of Preferences (GSP) (Babarinde and Faber, 2005: 18) for preferential access to the EU market.

In addition to trade preferences, development aid, debt relief and aid for trade also play a significant role in EU development policy, which is also largely governed by the Lomé Conventions and Cotonou Agreement. A major objective in reforming the Lomé development aid regime is to simplify the aid procedures and rationalise the financial aspect of cooperation by allowing partner countries to concentrate their aid in specific sectors (Hoelbink, 2005: 148). This emphasises flexibility, the performance of recipient countries and the possibility of adjustment to changing situations (Hoelbink, 2005: 153). A similar idea is reflected in the European Consensus on Development (2006). The EU commits to the principle of ownership under which responsibility for strategies and programmes should belong to partner countries, thereby allowing the policy space to be shaped by the specific needs and circumstances of beneficiaries (European Consensus on Development, 2006: para. 1.4).

The Cotonou Agreement highlights the debt burden and balance of payments problems facing African countries and directs the EU to contribute to debt relief initiatives at the international level and explore possibilities to mobilise resources other than the European Development Fund for internationally agreed debt relief initiatives (Cotonou Agreement, 2000: art. 66(1)). The European Consensus on Development makes clear that debt reduction is comparable to indirect budget support and thus calls for coordination between donors and reductions in transaction costs with the aim of helping African countries shield themselves from external shocks (European Consensus on Development, 2006: para. 117).

CHINA'S REGULATORY FRAMEWORK ON AFRICAN DEVELOPMENT POLICY

Since its inauguration in 2000, the Forum on China–Africa Cooperation (FOCAC) has become the major institutional framework governing political exchange, economic and trade cooperation, and cultural exchange between China and African countries. The FOCAC is 'a framework for collective dialogue between China and African countries on the basis of equality and mutual benefit' (FOCAC, 2000: 2nd preamble). Ministerial level meetings take place every three years while summits, where the heads of states participate, are to be convened every six years. After each ministerial conference, a three-year action plan accompanied by a number of follow-up actions is launched. The FOCAC is multilateral in the sense that its members comprise China and most African countries, with the exception of those that maintain diplomatic relations with Taiwan. However, the essence of the FOCAC remains bilateral because China usually settles foreign aid and economic cooperation deals with individual African countries prior to the meetings of the FOCAC. The FOCAC functions, mainly, as a Chinese public relations platform rather than a negotiating forum. The FOCAC is part of Chinese efforts that operate under the umbrella of a South–South cooperation framework, whereas EU–African (ACP) relations under the Lomé Conventions and Cotonou Agreement are generally referred to as a North–South cooperation initiative (FOCAC, 2000: para. 9).

In 2006, China published its first white paper on African policy: *China's African Policy* (China's Ministry of Foreign Affairs, 2006). Although it does not provide much detail, it has attracted much political attention and academic interest. *China's African Policy* firstly states that China is the biggest developing country, while Africa is the continent with the greatest number of developing countries. *China's African Policy* puts forward four groups of general principles and objectives guiding China's foreign policy toward Africa: sincerity, friendship and equality; mutual benefit, reciprocity and common prosperity; mutual support and close coordination; learning from each other and seeking common development (*China's African Policy*, part III). In this respect, China adheres to its 'Five Principles of Peaceful Coexistence' and reiterates that the One China principle is the foundation of relations between China and African countries (*China's African Policy*, part III).

In terms of trade relations, *China's African Policy* underlines facilitation for the entry of African commodities into the Chinese market and the implementation of China's promise to provide African LDCs with duty-free access for certain products (China's African Policy, part IV, para. 2(1)). Preferential trading policy, especially towards African LDCs, is generally decided by policymakers and announced by the highest-ranking political leaders. The FOCAC is one of China's best arenas for presenting its preferential trade offers. At the 2006 Beijing Summit, Chinese President Hu Jintao offered to further open up its duty-free market to 29 African LDCs having diplomatic relations with China by increasing from 190 to over 440 the number of exempted items (Hu Jintao, 2006). Moreover, according to the FOCAC Sharm el-Shelkh Action Plan, adopted at the 4th FOCAC Ministerial Conference on 12 November 2009, China promised to further open up its market to African LDCs with the aim of exempting from tariffs 95 per cent of their exported goods. The first step of that plan was to grant zero-tariff treatment to 60 per cent of products originating from African LDCs in 2010 (FOCAC, 2009: para. 4.4.3).

According to the White Paper on China–Africa Economic and Trade Cooperation (China's Information Office, 2010), progress has been made faster than the action plan envisaged. As of July 2010, African products enjoying the zero-tariff treatment had increased to 4,700 items (China's Information Office, 2010: part I). The White Paper also expects that the 95 per cent exemption from tariffs objective would be achieved by the end of 2010 (China's Information Office, 2010: part I).

China's official development aid is governed by a complicated and compartmentalised system. China has employed a unilateral approach and tends to announce its foreign aid to African countries in the FOCAC. For example, at the 2006 Beijing Summit, Hu Jintao announced that China would double its 2006 assistance to Africa by 2009; provide US$3 billion in preferential loans and US$2 billion in preferential buyer's credits to Africa during the period 2006–9; set up a China–Africa Development Fund; and build a conference centre for the African Union (AU). China, in its African policy paper, declares its willingness to increase assistance to African countries with no political strings attached (*China's African Policy*, part IV, para. 2(9)).

In terms of debt reduction and relief, China maintains that it will enter into consultations with African countries with a view to resolving the debt owed by African countries to China (*China's African Policy*, part IV, para. 2(8)). The FOCAC is thus again providing a good opportunity for China to announce decisions to cancel the debts of African countries. For example, at the 2006 Summit, Hu Jintao cancelled the debts of heavily indebted poor countries and LDCs which had diplomatic relations with China for interest-free government loans which matured at the end of 2005 (Hu Jintao, 2006). Similarly, as set out in the FOCAC Sharm el-Sheikh Action Plan adopted at the 2009 FOCAC Ministerial Conference, China offered to cancel interest-free government loans set to mature at the end of 2009 (FOCAC, 2009: para. 5.1.3). Clearly, the pattern is that maturing government zero-interest loans will be periodically cancelled or forgiven.

CONTRASTING EUROPEAN AND CHINESE APPROACHES TOWARD AFRICAN DEVELOPMENT POLICIES

A Values-based Premises

The Joint Africa–EU Strategy underlines the central role of democratic governance and human rights promotion in the EU–Africa dialogue and partnership. In accordance with the spirit of this document, the EU and Africa would work together to enhance the effectiveness of multilateral frameworks and promote the values of democracy, human rights and the rule of law (Joint Africa–EU Strategy, 2007: para. 27). The European Consensus on Development reiterates the common values of EU partnerships and dialogues with non-member countries: 'respect for human rights, fundamental freedoms, peace, democracy, good governance, gender equality, the rule of law, solidarity and justice' (European Consensus on Development, 2006: para. 13). It is claimed that development policy is a part of EU efforts intended to enhance its international profile, and that the inclusion of political objectives and political conditions in EU development policy is reflective of the Union's value-based identity (Bretherton and Vogler, 2006: 132–3).

Nonetheless, the EU's insistence on political conditionality has encountered resistance from African countries and required adjustment. The Joint Africa–EU Strategy points to the limits of the EU value-based conditions in order to ensure the predictability of development aid (Joint Africa–EU Strategy, 2007: para. 27). Similar concerns are addressed in the European Consensus on Development, which instructs the EU to define clearly the value of additional conditions, if any, when selecting modalities for implementing development aid and to disburse its development aid based on results and performance indicators. Imposed conditionality should evolve into something nearer a negotiated contract based on mutual commitments (European Consensus on Development, 2006: paras 113 and 115).

By contrast, the main spirit underpinning the FOCAC, the main forum for China–Africa cooperation, as indicated by the 2000 Beijing Declaration, lies in the purposes and principles of the UN Charter and the Charter of the Organisation of African Unity (the OAU). China and African countries place equal, if not more, weight on the 'Five Principles of Peaceful Coexistence' as advanced by Zhou Enlai (FOCAC, 2000: para. 1). With a stronger tone, contributors to the 2000 Beijing Declaration added that 'no country or group of countries has the right to impose its will on others, to interfere, under whatever pretext, in other countries' internal affairs, or to impose unilateral coercive economic measures on others' (FOCAC, 2000: para. 1). They further declare, in accordance with its own course of development, that a country has the right to choose its own social system, development model and way of life, and to choose its own approaches and models to promote and protect human rights (FOCAC, 2000: para. 4). '[T]he politicisation of human rights and the imposition of human rights conditionalities on economic assistance should be vigorously opposed as they constitute a violation of human rights' (FOCAC, 2000: para. 4).

The FOCAC thus presents itself as a forum in which the operative values and norms differ from those of Western countries. In contrast to the lengthy preaching of the European Consensus on Development, the Beijing Declaration of the Forum on China–Africa Cooperation is straightforward, powerful and arguably more appealing. The axiom of Western countries, namely the improvement of human rights and reduction of violations through the imposition of conditionality, is here condemned. Similar ideas were expressed in the 2006 Beijing Summit of the FOCAC. The Declaration of the Beijing Summit of the FOCAC firstly stated that China–African relations and cooperation would be founded on the 'Five Principles of Peaceful Coexistence' and 'international principles that promote multilateralism and democracy in international relations'. It also called for South–South cooperation, with China being recognised as the biggest of the developing countries and Africa being the continent with the biggest number of developing countries (FOCAC, 2006).[1]

In terms of values-based premises, political objectives including democracy, the rule of law, and respect for human rights and fundamental freedoms are of great importance to EU–African relations. In this respect, conditionality has been imposed in order to ensure their effective implementation. Nonetheless, because of the increasing resistance from the African side and responding to challenges posed by China, there has been a trend towards more limited conditions in the EU's development policy. In contrast, although China expressly clings to the non-interference approach, it may exercise influence, politically or diplomatically, formally or informally, to induce changes in the behaviour of African countries. This may contribute to support or counteract pressure from the international community, bolster China's efforts to represent itself as a responsible actor, or secure its economic interests. Therefore there exists some middle ground in the spectrum between European conditionality and Chinese non-interference. In examining European and Chinese approaches toward African development policies, special regard should be paid to the substantial content of policy instruments and implementation measures. The devil is always in the detail.

TRADE PREFERENCES AND ECONOMIC PARTNERSHIP AGREEMENTS

In accordance with the EU's values-based identity, political conditionality is one of the major characteristics of EU external preferential trade instruments. As the preamble of the Cotonou Agreement declares, '[...] a political environment guaranteeing peace, security and stability, respect for human rights, democratic principles and the rule of law, and good governance is part and parcel of long-term development', and '[...] responsibility for establishing such an environment rests primarily with the countries concerned' (Cotonou Agreement, 2000: fifth preamble). The political dimension of the Cotonou Agreement attaches great importance to essential and/or fundamental elements of sustainable development. Serious violation would trigger sanctions against the offending African (ACP) countries (Babarinde, 2005: 29–30). The inclusion of conditions means that the Cotonou Agreement differs significantly from its predecessor. Under the Lomé Conventions, EU attempts to influence the behaviour of African (ACP) countries consistently failed. The EU's success in persuading the African (ACP) countries to accept conditions can be attributed to the end of the Cold War, expansion of the EU to include less-developed eastern European states, and the realisation of African (ACP) countries that they will have to compete for aid (Babarinde, 2005: 20).

According to Article 96 of the Cotonou Agreement, whenever the EU, its member states or any African (ACP) country consider that the other party has failed to fulfil an obligation stemming from 'respect for human rights, democratic principles and the rule of law' as referred to in Article 9(2) of the Cotonou Agreement, a consultation procedure should be initiated and relevant information supplied to the other party and the Council of Ministers with a view to reaching a mutually acceptable solution (Cotonou Agreement, 2000: art. 96(2)(a)). If a mutually acceptable solution is not possible after consultation procedures, or the consultation is refused, measures in accordance with international law and proportional to the violation may be taken. Those punitive measures should be revoked as soon as the reasons for implementing them are addressed. In deciding on the measures to be taken, priority should be given to those least disruptive of the application of the Cotonou Agreement. The suspension of the Cotonou Agreement is understood to be the last resort (Cotonou Agreement, 2000: art. 96(2)(c)).

Regarding the fundamental element, namely good governance, the Cotonou Agreement qualifies the application of consultation procedures and appropriate measures to serious cases of corruption. In other words, only serious cases of corruption are taken to constitute a violation of the fundamental element (Cotonou Agreement, 2000: art. 9(3)). Article 97 of the Cotonou Agreement regulates the consultation procedures and redress measures and dictates 'it is above all incumbent on the party where the serious cases of corruption have occurred to take the measures necessary to remedy the situation immediately' (Cotonou Agreement, 2000: art. 9(3)). Nonetheless, when a mutually agreed upon solution is not possible, or the consultation is refused, measures proportional to the seriousness of the situation may be taken. The Cotonou Agreement also instructs the parties, in deciding on the measures to be taken, to select those which least disrupt the agreement's application, with suspension being the last resort (Cotonou Agreement, 2000: art. 97(3)).

In contrast to the EU's preferential trade policy, which is normally regulated by legal instruments, either through international conventions or agreements – as in the case of the Lomé Conventions or the Cotonou Agreement – or through the EU's autonomous instruments – as in the case of the Generalised System of Preferences (GSP) – China has not adopted or maintained a clearly defined legal instrument and thus suffers from having less legal certainty and decision-making transparency. Nevertheless, China's offer of preferential trade is unconditional in terms of positive and negative conditions. Further, the benefits that come with China's trade preferential status are significant. For example, trade preferences cut tariffs by an average of 10.4 per cent in 2006. Nevertheless, sensitive goods, for instance cotton, remained subject to high tariffs (Minson, 2008: 2–3). Underlining the tenuous nature of China's approach, only limited progress has been reported in free-trade agreement negotiations with African countries. Negotiations between China and the Southern African Customs Union (SACU) have been initiated, but there has been no significant progress. This is in part due to the industrial composition of South Africa whose textile industry is against the FTA talks and, in part, due to political considerations, given that Swaziland maintains official diplomatic relations with Taiwan.

DEVELOPMENT AID AND DEVELOPMENT COOPERATION

The European Consensus on Development states that the preferred means of supporting African economic and fiscal reforms and poverty reduction is through budgetary support enabling recipient countries to 'cope with growing operating budgets, promote harmonisation and alignment on national policies, contribute to lower transaction costs and encourage results-based approaches' (European Consensus on Development, 2006:

para. 113). The European Consensus on Development emphasises that such an approach will normally require the support of international financial institutions, and thus instructs the EU to coordinate with them in order to ensure that their efforts are complementary. In providing budgetary support, the European Consensus on Development underlines the importance of the multilateral frameworks and thus directs the EU to respect the recommendations of the OECD Development Assistance Committee (DAC) and to abide by the Good Practice Guidelines on budget support, in particular in terms of alignment, coordination and conditions (European Consensus on Development, 2006: para. 114). Closer cooperation with international actors, including emerging donors, through a tripartite dialogue so as to ensure the coherence and complementarities of development aid is encouraged (Joint Africa–EU Strategy, 2007: para. 54). In that regard, the Paris Declaration on Aid Effectiveness (OECD, 2005) is pertinent (Joint Africa–EU Strategy, 2007: para. 51).

In order to strengthen further the ownership and robust participation of civil society in development aid, the Cotonou Agreement includes non-state actors in development financing (Cotonou Agreement, 2000: art. 77(3)). In the context of EU–African development aid, the following agents may be eligible for EU financial support, subject to the consent of the African state(s) concerned: African national and/or regional public or semi-public agencies, departments or local authorities; private organisations and private operators; community enterprises; EU or African financial intermediaries; and agents of decentralised cooperation and other African or EU non-state actors (Cotonou Agreement, 2000: art. 58(2)). At the same time, the Cotonou Agreement also pays due regard to co-financing and encourages coordinated co-financing, which may lessen the burden of procedures and enhance the effectiveness of aid (Cotonou Agreement, 2000: art. 65).

Contrary to the EU's preference for budgetary support, Chinese aid to African countries often takes the form of support for the construction of infrastructure, which is generally coupled with economic cooperation and trade activities. This practice blurs the line between official development aid, as defined by the OECD DAC, and other forms of development assistance. The resulting construction programmes are generally implemented by Chinese enterprises funded by Chinese banks, notably the Export-Import Bank of China. Under the FOCAC Sharm el-Sheikh Action Plan, China promised to play a greater role in the development of African infrastructure by providing loans and free assistance to African countries. Preferential loans of up to US$10 billion during the period 2010–12 are to be offered to African countries, mainly for infrastructural and social development projects (FOCAC, 2009: para. 4.3.3).

As far as development cooperation is concerned, while the EU aims to strengthen African ownership by including African civil society organisations in development aid, there seems to be no space for such civil society organisations in China's development aid to Africa. Whereas coherence and complementarity are emphasised by the EU, for the time being, both European and Chinese development aid remains largely fragmented. While the EU attaches great importance to multilateral frameworks and leaves the door open to cooperating with emergent donors, China seems less than enthusiastic with such an approach. In this context, the EU proposed a trilateral dialogue and cooperation, to which the chapter now turns.

THE EU, CHINA AND AFRICA: TOWARDS TRILATERAL DIALOGUE AND COOPERATION

In response to the rise of China as a key development actor in Africa, the Commission, in 2008, published *The EU, China and Africa: Towards Trilateral Dialogue and Cooperation* (European Commission, 2008). The Commission firstly articulated the changing landscape of EU–China–Africa trilateral geopolitics with reference to key events such as: the birth of the African Union (AU); the formulation of New Partnership for African Development (NEPAD); the EU–Africa Summit in Lisbon and the Joint Africa–EU Strategy; the evolution of the FOCAC; and the publication of *China's African Policy*. The Commission then stressed the need for trilateral dialogue and cooperation to complement bilateral partnerships (European Commission, 2008: para. 1). The Commission thus calls for gradual but progressive EU–China–Africa trilateral cooperation. The Commission then points to three guiding principles for this trilateral dialogue and cooperation and proposes four specific sectors. The three guiding principles are: a pragmatic and progressive approach; a shared approach; and effective aid. Four sectors are then pinpointed: peace and security in Africa; support for African infrastructure; sustainable management of environmental and natural resources; and agriculture and food security (European Commission, 2008: para. 2.2). In order to achieve these objectives, development policy dialogue and partnership are to be encouraged at the continental, regional and national levels. It is also suggested that African policy is to be regularly placed on the agenda of the EU–China Summit. The Commission concludes that this trilateral dialogue and cooperation could address global development challenges in an effective multilateral way and contribute to sharing the responsibility for global governance and development (European

Commission, 2008: para. 3). In the end, the Commission invites EU member states, African and Chinese partners to consider, *inter alia*:

- organising an annual meeting of senior officials (EU–AU–China) to coordinate dialogue and cooperate strategically;
- inviting the AU troika to join the EU–China annual dialogue on Africa; and
- entering into specific agreements between agencies, institutions and associations to facilitate results-oriented joint initiatives.

(European Commission, 2008: para. 3)

In focusing on the EU–China Summit, one should note the inclusion of African development policy in the Summit since 2006. In the 2006 joint statement, the EU and China committed to working together on peace, stability and sustainable development in Africa, while differing as to the norms and values informing their development assistance. The EU attached great importance to the principles of good governance and human rights, whereas China upheld its 'Five Principles of Peaceful Coexistence', particularly the non-interference principle (EU–China Summit, 2006: para. 15). In order not to marginalise Africa, the EU and China also agreed to cooperate with Africa in a spirit of partnership with the support of, *inter alia*, the NEPAD, and with the aim of realising the Millennium Development Goals (MDGs) (EU–China Summit, 2006: para. 15).

In the *2007 EU–China Joint Statement*, the two sides stopped clinging to their ideological and values preferences. Instead, they concentrated on the importance of the MDGs and sustainable development. They praised the efforts and progress made in resolving the Darfur crisis and sought to explore effective ways and means of cooperation with each other and Africa. China was thus invited to participate in the EU–Africa Summit as an observer (EU–China Summit, 2007: paras 9–10). This trilateral approach seems to have garnered a somewhat positive response from China. In the 12th EU–China Summit held in Nanjing, China on 30 September 2009, the EU and China 'welcomed trilateral dialogue between the EU, China and Africa, and agreed to explore appropriate areas for cooperation' (EU–China Summit, 2009: para. 13). They further reaffirmed their commitment to the full and timely realisation of the MDGs and support for African sustainable development and early economic recovery (EU–China Summit, 2009: para. 13).

In pursuing trilateral dialogue and cooperation, the EU and China may avoid adopting more confrontational approaches. The EU may also present an alternative model for the 'China in Africa' debates: the integration of China into African development programmes and political processes. This alternative model necessitates a self-critical recognition of the weaknesses of EU development policies and prohibits the adoption of a lecturing tone on the assumption that the European values are representative of universal values (Asche and Schüller, 2008: 74). Such a trilateral approach should also help to exploit the synergies and complementarities of EU and Chinese policies for Africa, as Africa will suffer first and foremost from EU–China antagonism.

From a practical perspective, a trilateral approach might be seen as being motivated by the fact that the EU, China and Africa are interlinked by global trade and investment patterns. In order to ensure that benefits derived from trade and investment activities are shared equally, and that challenges are effectively addressed, a trilateral approach wherein the EU, China and Africa have their respective roles may contribute to a constructive dialogue and positive solutions (Davies, 2009: 6). However, it must be stressed that such trilateral dialogue should be based on genuine interest in learning from one another, with the objective of realising fair and sustainable development; moreover, the process should be steered by Africa. The dialogue should go beyond government bodies; all stakeholders such as parliaments, local authorities and civil society organisations should be included in order to ensure that each assumes a proper degree of ownership of the development policies (Davies, 2009: 7–8).

Despite these virtues, some key challenges persist in relation to this trilateral approach. Firstly, one has to be cautious in making assumptions regarding the extent to which the EU and China can cooperate in Africa as part of their strategic partnership, given their contradictory positions on development. Secondly, a key challenge lies in the capacity of Africa to deal with multiple partnerships in ways that will advance its agency in international relations and avoid casting it as merely an arena for great power games. The third challenge relates to how China, while maintaining its economic and trade interests in Africa, will meet the expectations of traditional donors and prevent conflict on critical issues with other actors (Davies, 2009: 7–8).

CONCLUSIONS

The high profile of China's development activities in Africa alarms most Western countries and stokes the 'China in Africa' debate. China's engagement with African countries poses challenges not only to the development policies of traditional actors, but also to the effectiveness of existent regulatory regimes. This chapter examines the major legal and policy instruments governing African development policy for both the EU and China and compares their approaches. It is argued that between the two extremes of European conditionality and Chinese non-interference, a middle way can be found. Not all European instruments are based upon strict political conditionality, and Chinese adherence to the principle of non-interference is not as firm as often portrayed. This chapter argues that trilateral dialogue and cooperation will help to reconcile the two extremes of values-based premises and lessen the EU–China antagonism which might result from their confrontation over development in Africa. This chapter further argues that such EU–China–Africa trilateral dialogue and cooperation would contribute to African development only when it is steered by Africa. The capacity of African countries remains the major obstacle.

NOTE

1 In addition, African countries also reiterate their adherence to the 'one China policy' and support the peaceful reunification of China.

REFERENCES

Asche, Helmut and Schüller, Margot (2008) *China's Engagement in Africa: Opportunities and Risks for Development*. Hamburg: Deutsche Gesellschaft für Technische Zusammenarbeit.

Babarinde, Olufemi (2005) 'The changing environment of ACP–EU relations', in Olufemi Babarinde and Gerrit Faber (eds), *European Union and the Developing Countries: The Cotonou Agreement*. Leiden, Netherlands and Boston, MA: Martinus Nijhoff.

Babarinde, Olufemi and Faber, Gerrit (2005) 'From Lomé to Cotonou: EU–ACP partnership in transition', in Olufemi Babarinde and Gerrit Faber (eds), *European Union and the Developing Countries: The Cotonou Agreement*. Leiden, Netherlands and Boston, MA: Martinus Nijhoff.

Bretherton, Charlotte and Vogler, John (2006) *The European Union as a Global Actor*. New York: Routledge.

China's Information Office of the State Council (2010) White Paper on China-Africa Economic and Trade Cooperation. Available at: http://english.gov.cn/official/2010-12/23/content_1771603.htm (accessed 20 January 2012).

China's Ministry of Foreign Affairs (2006) *China's African Policy*. Available at: http://www.fmprc.gov.cn/eng/zxxx/t230615.htm (accessed 21 March 2011).

Cotonou Agreement (2000) *Partnership Agreement between the Members of the African, Caribbean and Pacific Group of States of the one part, and the European Community and its Member States, of the other part*, signed in Cotonou on 23 June 2000, OJ L317/3, 15 December 2000, last revised on 23 June 2010, *OJ* L287/3, 4 November 2010.

Davies, Penny (2009) *Think Piece on Aid and Development Cooperation Post Accra and Beyond – Steps Towards a Development Dialogue in 21st Century: The Example of EU, China, Africa*, EURODAD Report. Available at: http://www.eurodad.org/whatsnew/reports.aspx (accessed 7 February 2011).

EU–China Summit (2006) *Joint Statement of 9th EU–China Summit*, Helsinki, 6 September.

EU–China Summit (2007) *Joint Statement of 10th EU–China Summit*, Beijing, 28 November.

EU–China Summit (2009) *Joint Statement of 12th EU–China Summit*, Nanjing, 30 September.

European Commission (2008) *Communication from the Commission to the European Parliament, the Council, and the European Economic and Social Committee and the Committee of Regions, the EU, China and Africa: Towards trilateral Dialogue and Cooperation*, COM (2008) 654 final, 17 October.

European Consensus on Development (2006) *Joint Statement by the Council and the Representatives of the Governments of the Member States Meeting Within the Council, the European Parliament and the Commission on European Union Development Policy: 'The European Consensus'*, *OJ* C 46/1, 24 February.

FOCAC (2000) *Beijing Declaration of the Forum on China–Africa Cooperation*, 10–12 October. Available at: http://www.focac.org/eng/ltda/dyjbzjhy/DOC12009/t606796.htm (accessed 8 November 2009).

FOCAC (2006) *Declaration of the Beijing Summit of the Forum on China–Africa Cooperation*', 5 November. Available at: http://www.focac.org/eng/ltda/dscbzjhy/DOC32009/t606841.htm (accessed 8 November 2009).

FOCAC (2009) *Forum on 'China–Africa' Cooperation Sharm el-Sheikh Action Plan (2010–2012)*. Available at: http://www.focac.org/eng/zxxx/t626387.htm (accessed 14 November 2009).

Hoelbink, Paul (2005) 'European development aid in transition', in Olufemi Babarinde and Gerrit Faber (eds), *European Union and the Developing Countries: The Cotonou Agreement*. Leiden, Netherlands and Boston, MA: Martinus Nijhoff.

Hu, Jintao (2006) Speech: 'Address by Hu Jintao, President of the People's Republic of China, at the opening ceremony of the Beijing Summit of the Forum on China–Africa Cooperation', 4 November. Available at: http://www.focac.org/eng/ltda/dscbzjhy/SP32009/t606840.htm (accessed 8 November 2009).

Joint Africa–EU Strategy (2007) *The Africa–EU Strategic Partnership: A Joint Africa–EU Strategy*, Lisbon, EU–Africa Summit.

Minson, Adam (2008) *China's Preferential Trade Policy for Africa*. Johannesburg: South African Institute of International Affairs. Available at: http://www.cebri.com.br/midia/documentos/313.pdf (accessed 8 November 2009).

OECD (2005) 'Paris Declaration on Aid Effectiveness'. Available at: http://www.oecd.org/dataoecd/15/3/46874580.pdf (accessed 20 January 2012).

PART 3

The world financial and monetary system

7. A monetary G3 with a multilateral perspective

Pierre Defraigne[1]

INTRODUCTION: TAMING GLOBAL FINANCE AND COPING WITH MONETARY POLYCENTRISM

The world economy is heading towards a new balance in which emerging economies are increasing their share of global GDP while Western countries' share, caught in the eddies of the 2008 financial crisis, is shrinking (48 per cent) and the least developed countries are lagging behind. The change is not just quantitative: the Organisation for Economic Cooperation and Development (OECD) countries share about the same institutions and values while the BRICS display with the Group of Seven (G7) countries and among themselves significant differences in their governance and development models. While real convergence between advanced and developing countries makes multilateral governance more inclusive and fairer, these differences also make it more difficult to organise.

The passing of the baton from the West to an emerging Asia is above all the result of the intrinsic dynamics of market capitalism in its quest for efficiency, lower labour costs and higher profits, combined with effective although diverse development strategies in Asia. It also reflects diverging demographic trends and the savings patterns attached to them, as well as the change in sources of global labour supply whose productivity has been raised by the diffusion of technology worldwide. But the shift from the West to the East has been accelerated by severe market and policy failures: emphasis put on debt-driven growth led to an underestimation of both the financial instability risks and the impact of aggravating inequalities on household indebtedness and purchasing power. The main responsibility of the financial crisis lies with the United States (US), but the European Union (EU) has imported it. It rests upon both an oversized financial industry caught in the dynamics of competition for the highest returns on investment and bonuses on the one hand, and on complacent or deficient monetary policymakers and financial supervision authorities on the other.

What the financial crisis has dramatically brought to light is the difficulty for today's democracies to keep the balance between market forces and politics when the latter is confronted with the growing complexity of advanced systems whose keys are in the hands of experts. This has proved particularly conspicuous in the case of finance where 'hyper-financialisation' has been outweighing political decision-making and bureaucratic management capacities, at both national and multilateral levels. This loss of control over finance has allowed it to generate instability and to aggravate social inequalities in both advanced and emerging economies. There is indeed a direct link between the deregulation of global finance and the deterioration of the social contract which in all countries should provide the key to domestic stability, market openness and peace.

Since finance and money are intertwined realities, they must be tackled together. The taming of global finance by national and EU authorities, and the setting up of a genuine multilateral monetary system in line with the world economy's new balance, should therefore be addressed through a twin-track approach. There is a difference though. On the one hand, while financial norms and rules should be discussed within the multilateral Basel framework, they actually remain within the remit of national or, in the case of Europe, EU authorities, because there are no alternative last-resort lenders in case of a liquidity crisis, nor any alternative rescue authority in case of a solvency crisis. On the other hand, although an effective international monetary system requires a global institution, there is no prospect of an international sovereign authority which would be entrusted with the responsibility of issuing international liquidity, which is also the condition of acting as a last resort lender. Intergovernmentalism will keep prevailing in the International Monetary Fund (IMF) and the Group of Twenty (G20). Therefore before a new credible international monetary system (IMS) is put into place, a muddling through phase is unavoidable focusing on an effective ad hoc cooperation on macroeconomic and financial policies among the three major economic blocs which dispose each of an international currency: the US, the EU and China. Only such a voluntary coordination among the 'Big Three' can give a direction to and secure the effectiveness of multilateral cooperation in monetary and financial matters.

CURRENCY AND IMS

While the criss-crossing of global firms' output chains across borders and the increase of intra-firm trade are driving markets towards more globalisation, trade multilateralism is levelling off, and competitive liberalisation brings back trade bilateralism, which undermines the World Trade Organization (WTO). The financial sphere of the economy is also characterised by a growing contrast between the global functioning of financial markets and the move from a dollar-based international monetary order towards a complex system combining 'monetary polycentrism' – as coined by Aglietta (Aglietta et al., 1990) – with a wide array of floating and pegged exchange rates, hooked either to the dollar or to dominant regional currencies such as the euro, the renminbi (RMB) or currency baskets.

Unless multilateralism is given a serious boost, creeping continentalism, resulting from increasing bilateralist and regionalist trends, might eventually prevail as the shaping force of the world economic system, raising the prospect of protectionism and conflicts. Let us see how the rise of finance has damaged the IMS with financial markets taking over from multilateral institutions and curbing more and more the autonomy of government policies.

A currency fulfils three functions over the territory of one single country: a unit of account, a means of payment and a store of value. But international trade and capital flows between countries raise the issue of convertibility among currencies and therefore of their exchange rates. The use of one or several dominant national currencies in international transactions reduces the need for currency conversion and eases trade, foreign direct investment (FDI) and portfolio investment.

The IMS provides precisely for a workable framework facilitating the interaction between national currency systems and international trade and financial transactions. The IMS rests upon three forces whose relative importance has varied over time: governments in charge of national monetary regimes and particularly of international currencies, global markets that determine the hierarchy among international currencies, and international institutions, i.e. the IMF with regard to monetary and financial stability and the Basel G20-led Financial Stability Board (FSB) with regard to the production of financial norms. These institutions formalise the operational cooperation among countries under the guidance of the G7 yesterday and the G20 today, but with an intellectual and political leadership exerted by Anglo-Saxon academics and US Treasury officials.

The IMS fulfils three major roles:

- the supply of international liquidity in the right proportion for financing world growth through enhancing international transactions, without fuelling either inflation or deflation;

- the smooth and fair adjustment of external imbalances so as to prevent structural exchange rate misalignments which act as an aggravating factor for such imbalances;
- the handling of financial crises including coping with the issue of an ultimate resort liquidity provider, either directly by governments or through the IMF's stewardship.

In that way, the IMS would prevent or limit:

- the volatility of exchange rates caused by destabilising capital flows;
- the accumulation of international reserves through undervalued currencies by emerging economies which they have used as an insurance policy against both trade protectionism (from the US Congress against Chinese exports) and conditionality attached to liquidity provided by the IMF in the Asian 1997–98 crisis.

Actual incarnations of the IMS have never fully achieved satisfactory results. The gold standard was too 'mechanical' and came to a brutal end in the wake of the First World War which it had eventually contributed to bringing about. Bretton Woods I (BWI) worked for the benefit of the few and was soon led astray by its guardian, the US. The floating exchange rates and the abolition of capital controls under Bretton Woods II (BWII) kept world growth going and supported real convergence, but through the severe dysfunctions of the system as witnessed by huge structural imbalances. Current monetary polycentrism is leading the world economy into uncharted waters. Let us go through a quick review of these historical episodes in the quest for an explanation of the dynamics at work: the red thread is to be found in unsolved social conflicts in which finance played a decisive role, and in the strategic rivalry for resources and markets between the established economic powers and the latecomers. The sharing of the seigniorage attached to an international currency status is also a stake in this competition.

THE GOLD STANDARD, MORE THAN MEETS THE EYE

Industrial and financial market capitalism, born in the late eighteenth century in England, has definitely increased the pace of productivity growth in Europe and thereby has established its domination over the rest of the world for two centuries through technological superiority and colonial rule. Yet no multilateral system presided over that dramatic evolution: trade liberalisation triggered by the unilateral repealing of the

Corn Laws by the United Kingdom in 1846 led gradually to generalised free trade through the conclusion of a web of bilateral treaties which included the decisive Most Favoured Nation clause. In parallel, the gold standard secured both an international payments system and an adjustment mechanism for correcting external imbalances. As John Williamson pointed it out, the gold standard was no hydraulic system[2] (Aglietta et al., 1990: 309) 'along the lines of Hume's price-specie-flow mechanism' (Williamson, in Kenen, 1993: 54): on the one hand, the pound – deemed 'as good as gold' – played a key role in payments while the world's long-term interest rate was determined by the Bank of England's discount rate policy; on the other hand, capital flow mobility was the rule and governments could rely on private international loans for funding temporary deficits or delaying adjustments. The path was far from smooth though: firstly, financial crises were not rare and on several occasions the Bank of England had to suspend the convertibility of the pound; secondly, protectionism was lurking in the background. Indeed, in the course of the nineteenth century, organised labour started to hinder the return to equilibrium. Growing resistance to brutal job and wage cuts running consecutive to a restrictive monetary policy entailed by an outflow of sterling or gold reserves gradually made automatic adjustment more difficult and this fed bouts of protectionism.

Last but not least, the competition for resources and markets among the established powers and the latecomers – Germany, Japan and Italy – turned into military rivalry, in particular between the British Royal Navy and the German Imperial fleet for the control of sea routes. The First World War broke out under these circumstances.

The interwar period saw neither the restoration of the previous order nor the birth of a new one. In fact it had no system at all. The desperate attempts by international bankers to restore the gold standard, anxious as they were to resume their pre-war international financial business, did not prevent the final collapse of the system in 1931.

In the absence of an institutionalised cooperation among major economies, the 1929 Wall Street crash triggered off a domino effect: the lack of an adequate reaction from the US Federal Reserve (Fed) and the prohibitive tariffs imposed by the Congress led to an extension of the crisis to the whole global economy which became pulled into a spiral of beggar-thy-neighbour policies. Output and employment fell across the world and policies proved helpless. Massive rearmament initiated by the Nazis, eventually followed by democracies, led to an arms race, which tragically proved the ultimate answer to growing and lasting unemployment.

It is the lack of a coordinated policy answer to the crisis of the 1930s which eventually resulted in an apocalyptic conflict, no longer just between countries, but between systems – between fascism, a form of authoritarian capitalism, communism, a form of state capitalism, and the New Deal model of market capitalism initiated by Roosevelt in the USA.

BRETTON WOODS I: A PROMISING ATTEMPT AT MULTILATERALISM

In the wake of the Second World War the Bretton Woods regime, inspired by the New Deal experience, was established under US leadership. Often referred to as the first attempt at multilateral governance for enhancing world growth through a more efficient division of labour and allocation of resources thanks to free trade and FDI, the BW system calls for two qualifications: on the one hand, it was a US-led system because the US was then the largest trading economy, the largest provider of aid[3] and, through trade, the largest supplier of international liquidity; on the other hand, it did not have a universal membership but was circumscribed to most like-minded market democracies, with about the same level of development, sharing the same opposition to communist expansion and adhering to the same belief in Keynesian economics as a way to reconcile capitalism and democracy. In fact most of them, except in Latin America, trusted Roosevelt's embedded liberalism.

BWI proved successful for the West because it combined the gradual return to free trade and the space for full employment domestic policies. Capital controls eased the capacity of monetary policies to pursue internal and external stability and to reconcile the convertibility of currencies with the stability of exchange rates. Growth, full employment and a reasonably fair income and wealth distribution prevailed for three decades among participants in the system, mainly advanced Western countries. These remarkable achievements rested on the benefits of the centennial colonial rent in terms of a monopoly of manufacturing jobs and low commodity and energy import prices.

The BW system therefore proved effective in guiding OECD countries through the 'golden sixties' in America and the 'glorious thirties' in Europe. But success varied from one branch of the BW system to another. Among the BWI's three pillars of multilateral governance, trade thrived best through the General Agreement on Tariffs and Trade's (GATT) successive rounds of liberalisation and shared rules and disciplines now embodied in the WTO Charter; the norms setting pillar extended progressively its scope from labour to health, food safety, the environment and other innumerable standards, but the monetary and financial pillar soon drifted towards a chaotic path paved with both real successes and severe failures.

BWI provided an ambivalent multilateral IMS since it put the new gold exchange standard and the twin BW international financial institutions (IFIs) under US monetary hegemony. The US currency became indeed a legal surrogate for gold and this made the US the ultimate international liquidity provider bestowed with the discretionary power to choose between domestic and international priorities within a wider margin secured by seigniorage.[4] The existence of an implicit but effective pact, between free world countries and Washington, linking the dollar and the security of the West, Japan and South East Asian countries, provided the rationale for the new 'multilateral' BW regime.

The dollar-anchored exchange gold standard secured on the one hand currency convertibility, key to the return to free trade, and financial stability through fixed but adjustable exchange rates. Internal stability between employment and inflation was achieved through Keynesian policies made compatible with external stability through capital controls.

BWI proved effective and resilient until the early 1970s when the original fault-lines of the system started to outweigh its benefits. These fault-lines resulted mainly from its asymmetrical character. As the last-resort international liquidity issuer, the US enjoyed an 'exorbitant privilege' from the start since the need from third countries for additional liquidity, entailed by growing trade and financial transactions, fuelled an almost inextinguishable demand for the dollar. High world growth depended on the right supply of international liquidity. Paradoxically, as the recovery took place in Europe and Japan, the richest and largest economy of the world had gradually to switch from creditor to debtor status for supplying the necessary international liquidity. Relying on gold would have amounted to placing the world economy at the mercy of the two main gold sources: communist Soviet Union and South Africa, then still marred with apartheid.

This pattern fitted in perfectly with Washington's own economic and strategic design. Besides being the largest and the most advanced economy of the world, the USA also indeed fulfilled the critical strategic role of containing communism both in Europe and Asia: the implicit deal struck with Western Europe and Japan as a counterpart for American protection was their acceptance to accommodate the constraints of a unilateral dollar policy.

Bretton Woods remains, in the collective memory of the West, a beacon on the hill because it was the first attempt ever to provide a strong institutional framework for reconciling free trade and full employment through multilateral governance. Understanding its failure is therefore critical.

The system eventually broke down because the US shifted gradually from a benevolent economic hegemon to an abusive one. They issued too much liquidity in the 1960s in order to meet their domestic (social programmes), international (American FDI towards a nascent EU) and strategic (the Vietnam War and the nuclear race with Russia) objectives, dodging the trade-off between 'guns and butter'. Excessive liquidity fed worldwide inflation which, as a response from OPEC to the devaluation of their financial and oil reserves, brought about two oil shocks which proved, along with wage indexation, the major source of stagflation in the 1970s as well as discrediting Keynesian policies for three decades.

Central to the evolution of BWI had been the growing gap between the volume of dollars in circulation and US gold reserves, which made the initial official price of gold in dollars ($35 per ounce) a virtual one as a double gold market set in. Triffin summed up the US predicament in the form of a dilemma: the choice for the US was between bringing down the dollar's volume in line with gold reserves, or adjusting the dollar to the real price of gold. For the world, the first option meant massive deflation and the second a financial crisis comparable to that witnessed in 1931. But the US dodged the dilemma[5] first by making the dollar non-convertible and imposing a temporary 15 per cent import tax on 15 August 1971, then by devaluing their currency in December that year and eventually by letting it float in 1973. This episode led both to the collapse of BWI and to a reversal of Keynesian policies to supply-side and monetarism.

AN INTERNATIONAL MONETARY NON-SYSTEM AGAIN:[6] TOWARDS FINANCE'S DOMINANCE IN THE ANCHOR COUNTRY

The breaking of the link between the dollar and gold in August 1971 marked the end of BWI and the transition to BWII through the decisive switch from the fixed to the floating exchange rate system.

The dynamics sparked off by this systemic change soon forced European and other OECD countries to liberalise their own capital accounts, paving the route for global finance to emerge as a shaping force of the world economy and as a substitute for the BW IFIs in providing finance for developing countries and emerging economies. Behind the radical change of tack from the anchorage country with the shift to floating rates and capital deregulation, several factors were at work: the fast increase of international trade flows,[7] technological innovation both as a tool and a market for innovative finance, and the growing demands of governments confronted with both development needs and new financial volatility constraints caused by liberalisation.

But the two main reasons for this silent revolution were eventually political. Firstly, the balance of bargaining power changed in the US between liberals, and especially 'embedded liberals', and conservatives to the advantage of the latter, with growing acrimonious criticisms addressed to the New Deal legacy especially from Wall Street bankers. Then, enthused by the tremendous breakthrough of the IT revolution with its huge economic, financial and strategic implications, the leading forces in the US, both within and outside the government, undertook drastic transformations in their domestic model and international strategy under the influence first of neo-liberal and later of neo-conservative thinking. Reagan in the US and Thatcher in the UK were the emblematic figures of the conservative turn. Market fundamentalism inspired by Hayek and Friedman put its faith into 'efficient markets'. It focused on growth through supply-side and neutral monetary policies, insisting on tax cuts, labour flexibility and keeping social welfare to a minimum, relying on the 'trickle down benefits of growth' for lifting the poor. The neo-cons undertook to turn the 'indispensable Nation' into a 'hyperpower', after the collapse of the USSR whose back, severely weakened by bureaucratic totalitarianism, had been broken by the threat of an elusive Strategic Defence Initiative (the 'Star Wars project') from the US.

In that context, finance was seen as a source of growth and an engine of change, and therefore was given a priority. But the deregulation of finance amounted soon to handing over the responsibility for the economy from institutions to markets, from monetary policy to global finance. It did not harm the US economy. On the contrary, it freed the US government from the constraints attached to its former role as the official anchor country of BWI. But in a political system with strong lobbying influence over the Congress and the President due to the extravagant costs of political campaigning,[8] financial deregulation brought Wall Street back at the heart of US economic and monetary power and the rest of the world had to cope with the domestic and international choices of Washington. The liberalisation of finance, both through quick deregulation at home and with an abrupt end of capital controls among advanced countries, took place at a much faster pace than trade liberalisation because, as pointed out by Eric Helleiner (1994: 196), 'unilateral liberalization and deregulation constituted what John Plender has called a state's "mercantilist" strategy to maximize its own benefits from the open system at other states' expense'.

Moreover, thanks to financial liberalisation and deregulation, the US retained their privilege of remaining the main international liquidity supplier and this allowed them at the same time to expand domestic consumption and to conduct an ambitious and expensive military build-up strategy. High interest rates in America in the late 1970s and early 1980s allowed the US to attract huge capital inflows from the oil exporting countries and from wealthy people in developing countries. This permitted them to start up a huge current account deficit and a massive external debt denominated in dollars. Later, the IT revolution boosted productivity and provided the fuel for stock-exchange booms fed by an accommodating monetary policy. In such a way and despite the piling up of either private or public debt, or of both at the same time as is the case today, the US remained through the 1990s until recently an attractive place for portfolio investment. Tax cuts and the highly safe investment environment acted in the early 2000s as a new incentive for capital inflows despite the modest interest rates practised by the Fed.

Easy money was allowed through two main factors: on the one hand, cheap manufactured goods imported from China contributed as a key factor to low inflation in the West for two decades while, on the other hand, massive purchases of US T-bonds by China contributed to maintaining low long-term interest rates on the public debt and on mortgage loans, a factor that would play a role in the real-estate bubble and in the sub-prime crisis. But the main factor behind the Fed's accommodating monetary policy was the complacency of US monetary authorities vis-à-vis the 'irrational exuberance' of the stock exchange, as put by the then Fed Chairman Alan Greenspan himself.[9]

The faith put in the wealth effect generated by stock markets and real estate to support growth, which was reinforced by tax cuts instead of relying on steady wage increases in line with productivity, has been a central creed of US economic policy since Reagan until eventually the financial crisis broke out. There was indeed an acceptance that the growing inequalities did not matter for achieving high growth: the stagnating real wages of blue-collar workers for three decades contrasted blatantly with the capture of growth by the upper percentile of the income pyramid, be they asset holders or high-flying executives and entrepreneurs. Easy money was targeted both to households in order to allow them to satisfy their consumerist instincts – 'keeping up with the Joneses' – despite their relatively low income, and to institutional institutions and enterprises which used leverage as a major tool for increasing their return on investment (ROI) and share in the value-added.

Wall Street and the Pentagon have been the two main drivers behind the US easy monetary policy for two decades: it was mainly about making the rich richer and using strategic hegemony to make way for Western democratic values to win over Islamic fundamentalism or rogue states.

The dynamics of 'hyper-financialisation' in the US stemmed from technical and institutional changes which brought about policy changes initiated by conservative governments. They were soon imitated by progressive ones, as Blair succeeded Thatcher in the UK, and Clinton succeeded Reagan in the US, as the 'Third Way' made its way through Europe, whose elites adopted the neo-liberal creed, most often unknowingly. The information and communications technology (ICT) breakthrough and the move from banking to direct finance, especially in America thanks particularly to the removal of the Glass-Steagall Act in 1999, proved the prime drivers of financial revolution, but deregulation, which was revealed to be so decisive in the rise of finance, was a deliberate policy option. From these conditions a process of financial over-sophistication developed. But it embodied three major perilous mechanisms: firstly, ingenious and apparently innocuous securitisation provided the way to turn individual risk attached to a loan into systemic risk; then wrong incentives such as stock options and bonuses pushed for 'short-termism' and 'hit and run gains' that made the system more opaque, more speculative and more unstable, in a stealthy manner which escaped the vigilance of supervisory authorities; eventually the quick rise of banks' balance sheets soon erected moral hazard as a feature of financial and monetary governance because of the 'too big to fail' option. But in parallel, the multiplication of the activities of offshore financial centres and tax havens over the last two decades contributed to an aggravation of both global financial under-regulation and under-taxation.

The nexus of the crisis which took root in the IMS anchor country was therefore made of three factors which followed a specific sequence: firstly, the rising inequalities under the growing pressure of finance against a backdrop of technological innovation and the globalisation of production; then the Fed's easy money policy; and last but not least the unbridling of finance. The sub-prime episode, a massive Ponzi scheme of mortgage deals for poor households, ran into a major solvency and then liquidity crisis which called for massive interference from the state in order to rescue the banking sector. As the crisis extended like wildfire across most OECD countries, the same scenario was reproduced in several countries, although not all of them. But the negative wealth effect and the need to reduce indebtedness forced states to intervene further in the management of their economies through low interest rates and money supplies, and through huge fiscal stimulus in the framework of a G20 joint effort in order to prevent recession from turning into deflation and world depression. The debt extended to the government sector. But the new US predicament does not stop here.

POLYCENTRISM AS A RESPONSE TO THE DYSFUNCTIONING OF THE DOLLAR-BASED IMS

The benefits brought by global finance in terms of growth were never impressive while the final bill in terms of instability and inequality proved devastating for Western market capitalism, which is likely to cope with the long-term consequences of the 2008 financial crisis for at least a 'lost decade'. Yet a financial crisis was nothing new since financial crises had proliferated in the 1980s, mainly in developing and transition economies, and were dealt with by the IMF with mixed success, without any systemic damage.[10] The first serious backlash came when they hit the Asian emerging economies in 1997–98 partly because of domestic policy failures and partly because of a default of surveillance from the BW IFIs, too imbued with a neo-liberal trust in the virtues of financial market auto-regulation. Asian countries responded to the crisis and to the IMF's harsh treatment by building up strategic forex reserves, partly thanks to an undervaluation of their currencies. They did so in order to shelter themselves in the future from IMF tutorship, considered too much under US Treasury influence for their liking. But in 2008, the crisis broke out in Wall Street at the core of the Western capitalist system and it was of its own making because of the de facto collusion between Wall Street and US policymakers, the Fed and Treasury united in their quest for growth at any cost. The anchorage country being hit at its heart by the crisis, the IMS equilibrium was modified.

Meanwhile two important developments, which resulted partly from the IMS' dysfunctions, had taken place: the rise of China as a leading economy and as the main international creditor, and the monetary unification of Europe.

Today the world is therefore turning multipolar, including with regard to the IMS which has been characterised by Michel Aglietta (Aglietta et al., 1990) as 'monetary polycentrism' (dollar, yen, euro and gradually the RMB). Agnes Benassy-Quéré and Jean Pisani-Ferry (2011: 18–19) insist that the dollar will retain its dominant position despite the decline of the relative economic and strategic superiority of the US, since it remains an innovative and resilient economy able to deal with shocks, is financially open, is endowed with the most liquid and deepest bonds market of the world and is so far providing the guarantee of a predictable anti-inflation policy. None among the contenders, despite the internationalisation of the euro and to a lesser extent of the RMB, can pretend to offer the same set of characteristics for replacing the dollar as a dominant international currency. Yet the growing US indebtedness makes the dollar a potential target for speculation and a brutal depreciation would put even its dominant status at risk in a context of monetary chaos. Therefore one has to consider the rise of alternatives – not substitutes – to the dollar as desirable so as to prevent this chaos from occurring. But both the euro and the RMB have to strengthen their status as reliable international liquidity and as anchorages for their neighbouring currencies. Yet multilateral governance remains essential for preventing a drift towards inward-looking continental blocs. Multilateralism must rest upon cooperation among the three major currency suppliers as the core of the G20, and upon a strengthened role for the G20-dominated IMF.

The USA: Towards a Soft Landing of the Dollar

The US is both the pivotal global player and in fact the weakest link of the three major economic players because of the relative size of its private and mainly public debts which have been translated into a dollar-denominated external debt (94.3 per cent of GDP). Correcting the external imbalance (the current account deficit is 3.1 per cent of GDP in 2011) will therefore call for a severe adjustment in both households and the state. The first adjustment has already started to increase their savings rates if only because of the threat to jobs and wages, which slow growth prospects bring about. The challenge is more serious with the state deficit (8.9 per cent of GDP compared to 6.2 per cent in the eurozone) and public debt (93.25 per cent and 85.3 per cent respectively). The problem stems from the low level of the US budget as a proportion of GDP compared to the EU. As a proportion of collected taxes, the debt level is 216 per cent in the US against 191 per cent in the eurozone.[11] The reduction of the debt/GDP ratio will therefore call for an increase in taxes, which goes against the very deep instincts of a majority of US voters.[12]

If the American Congress proves unable to strike a bipartisan deal on restoring the health of the public finances, the risk, already evoked by some rating agencies, of a degradation of American debt is becoming a possibility for the first time ever. This could trigger the acceleration, despite the capital losses this would entail, of a restructuring of foreign portfolios away from the dollar, including China, the main creditor, and eventually a run on the dollar. The damage caused to the world economy is difficult to assess.

In reality the US is confronted with a triple challenge: (1) restoring a balance between debt and growth, i.e. giving up the recourse to debt as a way to stimulate growth; (2) as a consequence, making tough fiscal choices which imply both higher taxes and a trade-off between domestic expenditures, e.g. health, and strategic ambitions; and, (3) changing the American lifestyle to adjust it to the constraints of climate change while recognising that the country has been built up on fossil energy-based mobility.

These three drastic changes would be eased by a sharing of efforts with the rest of the world. Only a multilateral governance system can help the US in discharging their monetary, strategic and climatic responsibilities.

The Eurozone: Towards a Reliable Alternative to the Dollar as a 'Polycentric Currency'

The EU, confronted with the volatility of the dollar in the late 1970s, decided under a Jenkins-Schmidt-Giscard d'Estaing initiative to set up a European Monetary System (EMS) flanked by an Exchange Rate Mechanism. The latter aimed at stabilising intra-EU exchange rate variations within a narrow margin, which amounted to the establishment of a fixed exchange rate among European currencies pegged to a currency basket. In fact, the system operated like a D-mark zone, with the Bundesbank dictating the interest rate policy to the other countries, with high rates in the post-reunification phase. After ten years of functioning, the EMS confirmed the validity of the Padoa-Schioppa theorem, the so-called 'triangle of incompatibility': the combination of the free movement of capital, fixed exchange rates and autonomous monetary policies does not work, something must give. Eventually in the case of the EMS, it was the national monetary policies that were replaced by a single monetary policy. The switch from a multiple-currency system to a single one, the euro, took less than a decade between the collapse of the EMS in 1992 and the birth of the eurozone, regrouping first 11 EU countries in 1999 against 17 today.

The project, eased by German reunification and whose political motivation was the correlative need to anchor a larger Germany more firmly into Europe, was conceived first as a currency area, not as policy space. The main economic rationale of the eurozone was to tear down the last barriers to the four liberties of circulation (people, goods, services and capital) within the Single Market, i.e. the monetary transactions costs. The idea of sheltering the new bloc from external shocks was there too, but without specific additional tools. In fact the eurozone was a bold but hazardous project at the start: it was a currency without a government. Only an independent European Central Bank (ECB) was created as an institutional actor for the Economic and Monetary Union: moreover it was assigned the single and narrow objective of controlling the money supply and the short-term interest rates so as to keep core inflation at a low level (below 2 per cent). The hope of the 'euro fathers' – Delors, Kohl and Mitterrand – was that the dynamics of integration would gradually bring in the euro toolkit, i.e. the economic governance policy instruments and institutions needed for ensuring cohesion and growth. The bet was huge and risky since the eurozone, being rather a heterogeneous patch of countries, was not meeting the Mundell criteria for an optimum currency area: it was exposed to asymmetrical shocks, there was no mobility of labour across countries and nominal wages were rigid. The loss of the nominal exchange rate as an adjustment tool was therefore likely to prove expensive unless a federal budget would have acted as a redistribution mechanism between countries as they were confronted with different phases of the economic cycle, and as an instrument of real convergence acting upon the structure. But the EU budget remained stuck to a 1 per cent of GDP ceiling. In such conditions, it was obvious from the start that any serious difficulty in the world economy would put the eurozone in jeopardy. Its vulnerability was further aggravated by diverging competitiveness and fiscal performances between peripheral and core countries, under the umbrella of common low interest rates and strong exchange rates which eventually proved detrimental, respectively, for catch-up countries such as Spain and Ireland and non-competitive economies such as Portugal and Greece.

The current crisis brought about by financial markets' concerns for the sovereign debt sustainability of some peripheral countries is today forcing the EU to remedy the main fault-lines of the eurozone against a background of recurrent tensions on the financial markets. So far the EU leadership has been able to secure the necessary institutional changes on time, so as to resist attempts by market forces either to make a country default or to get it out of the eurozone, which could trigger off the unravelling of the eurozone and threaten the very unity of the EU. Since the launching of the euro, a huge enlargement of the EU has taken place (2004), bringing on board 12 more countries, most of them ex-communist countries from Central and Eastern Europe. The integration of these countries is taking time and for the time being, the EU–27's unity remains a challenge: the new member states are still in the process of absorbing the heavy pack of EU legislation and modes of operation, and they are not ready for the new quantum leap that progression to further integration would make necessary. Moreover, even within the historical hard core of founding countries, the mood is not presently in favour of new EU progress. Nevertheless, progress is made step by step under the leadership of the European Council. Yet the future remains fraught with dangers.

The EU-27 indeed carries the burden of an excessive public debt which is, in some countries, the legacy of an ill-functioning of democracy which has allowed structural deficits to build up, and in others the consequence of the 2009–10 anti-cyclical fiscal stimulus or, in some cases, the cost of rescuing the private banking sector. The ECB has been pursuing an accommodatory policy through low interest rates and refinancing the peripheral countries' debt, going up to the limit of its mandate. But growth prospects will remain low in the EU for the upcoming decade. Several factors are at work here, all of them exerting a deflationary pressure on global demand: the need to restore the health of public finances, the rising trends of commodities, food and energy prices, and the vulnerability of the banking system. The growing threat to jobs might also encourage precautionary savings. Moreover, the EU's growth performance will be handicapped by the combination of ageing and innovation deficits. But the main challenge for the EU will be to maintain its unity which is also the key to the openness of the EU market.

The EU is presently undertaking two main important legislative works both aimed at stabilisation: regulation and supervision of financial markets, and eurozone economic governance:

- The first is about stabilising finance through an EU-wide system of regulation and supervision in line with the Financial Stability Board's recommendations. The purpose of the legislation is key but limited: stability and more responsibility for the banks with the view of limiting moral hazard through a strengthening of their capital ratios and limitations on derivatives.
- The second is about strengthening the integrity and the viability of the eurozone: the efforts here are all geared towards greater fiscal discipline and labour flexibility, with a financial stability mechanism aimed at preventing sovereign defaults through joint EU/IMF interventions, a rather odd tandem.

Whether this will suffice to provide the basis for a stable and strong euro remains to be seen, or is the euro deemed to be strong only because the dollar is weak? On top of slow growth, a euro out of line with the competitiveness needs of the eurozone might eventually result in a protectionist backlash in the EU.

The Rise of China and the Emergence of an Additional International Currency

China's economic miracle, following the path of the flying geese pattern initiated by Japan in the 1960s, has been the real driver of global change, steering the BRICS in their emergence process. What makes the Chinese route to rapid and massive development so conspicuous is that China opted, in a very experimental and gradual fashion, for a heterodox development strategy by combining the strengths of global market capitalism and state capitalism. On the one hand, China would provide the necessary infrastructures in time and quality, and an educated and highly motivated labour force would be subject to the authoritarian rule of the CCP. On the other hand, foreign companies would act as vehicles for access to badly needed technology and as gates of entry into large foreign markets. The funding of massive investments in export industries has been ensured by the high savings of Chinese households through the state-controlled banking system. China's fast-rising trade surpluses stem mainly from its huge competitiveness differential, achieved until recently in the low segments of the global value chain which implies huge imports of components from neighbouring countries. But China is on the way to climbing up the technology ladder.

China has opted for a partial convertibility of the RMB, i.e. not extended to the capital account. It partly retains therefore the possibility of controlling its exchange rate through pegging the RMB to the dollar in varied guises.

Key to the pegging is the sterilisation of capital flows generated by China's current account surplus. Sterilisation was for a long time achieved though massive purchases of US T-bonds leading to the building up of huge foreign exchange reserves. This was a way for China to exploit the addiction of profligate American households to cheap manufactured exports from China while diminishing the risk of trade protectionism from the US Congress. The entry of China into the WTO in 2001 limited that risk. But the Asian crisis of 1997–98 and its handling by the IMF under US influence had been somewhat reminiscent of the vilified concessions episode in the recent history of China. During the crisis, China kept its currency at a steady level, not accompanying the depreciation of East Asian currencies and thereby relieving these economies of an additional concern. At the opposite end China promoted currency swap mechanisms among Asian countries in the framework of the Chang Mai Agreement (1998). This paved the way for further regional monetary cooperation in Asia with the view of sheltering their economies from US-led IMF intrusive tutorship in the future. Meanwhile several emerging economies opted for an under-appreciation of their own currencies in line with the depreciation of the dollar. Although the initial driver behind the huge structural current imbalances between America and China is the excessive US propensity to consume, leading to an excess of investment over savings, there is also some truth in the argument that the under-appreciation of the RMB, whose magnitude is highly controversial among specialists, did not ease America's efforts at adjustment, leaving imbalances at a dangerous level for the stability of the world economy.

Today China's growth performance remains both high and fragile. Despite very clever macroeconomic management by the Chinese authorities, as well as the long-term vision and planning of the CCP, China is confronted with huge short-term and structural challenges which might hamper its development potential in the future: among the first are domestic inflation, the slowdown in Western export markets and the potential volatility of the dollar; among the second are the shortage of arable land, the exposure to natural disasters, the large social and regional income gaps, and the severe degradation of the environment linked to both quick industrialisation and massive urbanisation.

China might also suffer from severe fault-lines in the financial sector which haven't surfaced yet, but which can be deduced from overcapacity in some sectors, including first and foremost real estate, and from the risk of a stock exchange bubble. China's central command of finance has proved a powerful tool of industrial policy, but it has certainly been diverted, through corruption or for political reasons, from a rational use of finance. This poses a twin problem: the real productivity of investment is sometimes questionable while the remuneration of households' savings is not high enough. The fragility of the financial sector which has been luckily sheltered from the Western financial crisis by capital controls, might appear to be the Achilles heel of China as it gradually opens up its capital markets and relaxes its controls in the decade ahead. China has indeed at least three reasons to envisage the gradual opening up of its capital account: (1) the strengthening of the RMB would help fight inflation; (2) the better functioning of the financial markets would ease the emergence of a more innovation-driven economy and relax the need to accumulate household savings; and (3) a stronger RMB and a better remuneration of savings would facilitate the move from an export-driven to a domestic-demand growth model. The first attempts made by China to test in Hong Kong and Singapore the international use of the RMB, suggest that the monetary authorities are envisaging this evolution in the near future. In fact, it has started in an experimental mode at a significant scale. China will then be confronted with the need to keep control over finance so as not to fall into the trap which the US and Europe have fallen. Strong ethics is indispensable for keeping the genie of finance in the bottle. This would be the reality check of the imprint of communism on market capitalism in China.

CONCLUSIONS

The abundance of liquidity left over from the bailing out of Western banks following Lehman Brothers' bankruptcy, and from post-crash stimulus measures such as quantitative easing both in America for rekindling growth and, to a lesser extent in Europe, for preventing a sovereign default within the eurozone, has left the world economy awash with cash with the inherent risks of new bubbles and increased speculation, particularly on commodity prices. Therefore market and policy failures in the monetary and financial sphere remain a serious risk for the world economy at large for the decade ahead. A strong and genuine IMS would certainly help to cope with this difficulty.

But the very idea of a centrally unified monetary system looks today more remote than ever despite the IMF's recent strengthening in terms of resources and rebalancing in terms of voting rights and presence on the Board. The IMF will matter more in the future as it regains its legitimacy, not only through this strengthening and rebalancing, but also by departing from the 'Washington Consensus'. But its role will be effective if the close macroeconomic cooperation of the three largest economies clears up the main difficulties that lie ahead.

The world economy must indeed first and foremost get rid gradually of the large structural current account imbalances on which real convergence has built up, in particular between China and the US, and gradually bring down the excess of liquidity. The world financial and monetary system will have therefore to go through a transition where cooperation among major currencies will have to pave the way for the emergence of a Bretton Woods III as a truly multilateral and universal SDR-based system.

Such trilateral coordination should aim at improving the world's stable growth prospects through policy adjustment in the three major economies. Firstly, there is a need to raise long-term savings rates and stabilise public finances in the US, since the 'exorbitant privilege' of the dollar seigniorage will be in the future severely restricted, even if the dollar remains an important international currency. Secondly, China will have to reshuffle its financial system so as to increase its effectiveness and resilience in order to move gradually towards the full convertibility of the RMB, whose appreciation would defuse the commodity-driven inflation and stimulate domestic demand, turning China from a surplus into a trade deficit country attracting foreign savings from the advanced countries. Thirdly, the EU must first and foremost turn the monetary union into a political union with the full attributes of a real power. This means encompassing both currency and defence, since the two are closely linked in the relationship of a country or a confederation of countries with the rest of the world. Growth in Europe must rest upon a robust and sustainable social model because cohesion in Europe is a condition of stability and openness. But this implies that Europe must circumscribe the oversized finance sector.

Hyper-financialisation, as it has developed over three decades, is incompatible with any social model since the sharing of the value added is too biased in favour of the global shareholder and of the global financial industry. So the genie of deregulated finance should be put back in the bottle, a very challenging task indeed. Ideally financial regulation standards and supervisory institutions should be agreed upon within the G20, through the normative work of the FSB in Basel. Nevertheless, regulatory convergence could prove unattainable because competition among established and rising global financial centres would fuel a regulatory race where the collective preferences with regard to financial risk aversion make a difference and the weight of the banking lobbies another. In such an occurrence, each global player should opt for the type of financial regulation and supervision that prevents destabilisation, tax evasion and criminal activities even if it implies strict surveillance of capital flows. The free movement of capital should indeed not be treated as an absolute must, but as a global public good once capital is neither under-regulated nor under-taxed. This condition implies that financial offshore centres opt for multilateral rules and norms in terms of financial regulation and cease to act as tax havens.

World peace and prosperity rests on strong multilateral governance for delivering key global public goods: free trade, fair use of natural resources, the climate, and an effective international monetary system encompassing finance. The deregulation of finance was a major mistake by the West. Without a disciplined and reasonable financial sector, no monetary system can work effectively.

NOTES

1. The paper stems from the final report of the Joint European and Chinese Study on Multilateralism under the activity entitled 'Global Governance: China–EU Cooperation in Multilateral Organisations' supported by the EU–China Policy Dialogue Support Facility project with the financial assistance of the European Union. The author wishes to convey special thanks to Professor Zhou Hong from the Chinese Academy of Social Sciences for her good cooperation and insightful comments, in particular the introduction.
2. 'Les auteurs n'ont pas constaté cette hydraulique des flux d'or avec ses mouvement symétriques entre pays excédentaires et pays déficitaires.'
3. The Marshall Plan for Western Europe was preceded by a massive support to Great Britain and the countries freed from Nazi invasion.
4. Privilege figured by the differential between interest paid and interest perceived today. See Eichengreen (2011: 4) and Stiglitz et al. (2010: 163).
5. Fred Bergsten challenged the relevance of focusing the intellectual debate in the 1960s around the question of the shortage versus excess of liquidity. He writes: 'I have great respect for Triffin but I think he derailed the world for a decade' (in Kenen, 1993: 44). The main issue for the US authorities was indeed the exchange rate flexibility of their currency

in order to recoup competitiveness and rekindle real growth.
6. Williamson, in Kenen (1993).
7. As Barry Eichengreen puts it: 'control on capital movements [...] provided the breathing space needed to organize orderly realignments [...]; they were also seen as necessary for the reconstruction of international trade [...] but the conjunction of free trade and fettered finance was not dynamically stable' (Eichengreen, 1996: 194).
8. Today market capitalism, under the irresistible pressure of global finance, has more influence than ever on the conduct of policies. Recent studies have highlighted the phenomenon in the US where lobbies call the tune on the Hill because of their huge outlays spent on influencing tax, trade, competition and/or foreign policies. International economic elites who meet in different circles (the Trilateral Commission, Bilderberg, Davos and Jackson Hole) exert an intellectual leadership over world governance. Until Wall Street's financial crisis broke out, thinking in the West had been dominated by the neo-liberal creed which exalts the superiority of the market over collective action, in particular because of its so-called self-regulating capacity. Nowhere more than in the financial sector has this laissez-faire vision been actually translated into liberalisation of capital flows, privatisation and deregulation with more radical determination. The link between the emergence of global finance and the degradation of the IMS is central to the analysis for triggering off new thinking about multilateral governance. On the role of lobbies in Washington and on the pervasive presence of neo-liberalism among leading international circles, see Reich (2008) and Rothkopf (2008).
9. 'We need a better cushion against risk' (Greenspan, 2009).
10. The scissor effect resulting from the combination of high rates imposed by the Fed's then Chairman Paul Volcker in order to eradicate inflation in the US in the early 1980s and the falling commodities prices crisis sparked off a major financial crisis among commodity exporting countries, mainly in Latin America and Africa, heavily indebted as a result of the massive recycling of petrodollars from OPEC countries towards developing economies a few years before. The IMF played a key role in providing a lever over these highly indebted countries to their public (Paris Club) and private (London Club) creditors to prevent defaulting on their debt but accepting a rescheduling.
11. Source: OECD Statistics online (2010).
12. Note the rather high level of non-voters among US citizens, mainly from the lower income range.

REFERENCES

Aglietta, M., Brender, A. and Coudert, V. (1990) *Globalisation financière: l'aventure obligée*. Centre d'Etudes Prospectives et d'Informations International (CEPII), ed. Economica.

Bénassy-Quéré, A. and Pisani-Ferry, J. P. (2011) *What International Monetary System for a Fast-changing World Economy?*, Working Paper 2011/6. Brussels: Bruegel.

Eichengreen, B. (1996) *Globalizing Capital: A History of the International Monetary System*. Princeton, NJ: Princeton University Press.

Eichengreen, B. (2011) *The Exorbitant Privilege: The Rise and Fall of the Dollar and the Future of the International Monetary System*. Oxford: Oxford University Press.

Greenspan, A. (2009) We need a better cushion against risk. *Financial Times*, 26 March.

Helleiner, E. (1994) *States and the Re-emergence of Global Finance*. Ithaca, NY and London: Cornell University Press.

Kenen, P. B. (ed.) (1993) *The International Monetary System: Highlights from Fifty*

Years of Princeton's Essays in International Finance. Boulder, CO: Westview Press.

Reich, R. (2008) *Supercapitalism: The Transformation of Business, Democracy, and Everyday Life*. New York: Vintage Books.

Rothkopf, D. (2008) *Superclass: The Global Power Elite and the World They Are Making*. New York: Farrar, Straus & Giroux.

Stiglitz, J. and the Members of a UN Commission of Financial Experts (2010) *The Stiglitz Report*. New York: New Press.

Williamson, J. cited in Kenen, P. B. (ed.) (1993) *The International Monetary System: Highlights from Fifty Years of Princeton's Essays in International Finance*. Boulder, CO: Westview Press.

8. Prospects for the international monetary system: key questions

Michel Aglietta

OVERALL ASSESSMENT: THE NATURE OF THE IMS

Let us consider the international monetary system (IMS) as a public good that should deliver two complementary outcomes: an adjustment mechanism to correct imbalances in the balance of payments between countries linked through international exchange on the one hand, and the provision of international liquidity that facilitates international payments on the other hand. They are complementary in the sense that the malfunctioning of one requirement hampers the effectiveness of the other. More specifically in a key currency system, the Achilles heel resides in the relationship between the issuer of the key currency and the demand for international liquidity by non-resident users. If the latter have no access to an alternative international currency which is able to fulfil the full range of monetary functions required by the international financial system, the former has no incentive to make allowances for the interest of economic agents in the rest of the world. There can be a mismatch resulting in either too much or too little international currency in relation to the demand of the rest of the world. Such an argument has been expressed in the Triffin (1960) dilemma whose relevance has been going on for the last 50 years.

Domestic preferences in the US (the issuer of the key currency) have tilted more often towards an excess supply of dollars than to the other side. This disequilibrium has destroyed the Bretton Woods system by forcing the accumulation of excess liquidity on Germany between 1968 and 1971, disturbing its anti-inflationary stance. The disequilibria arose in the capital accounts through a flow of hot money from the US despite capital controls that were multiplied in the Eurodollar banking system. It is interesting to notice that current accounts were lightly affected, at least compared with what has happened in the last decade! However, the exchange rate system blew out in 1971. The lesson is the following: *In a key currency system disturbances are more likely to propagate from the centre to the periphery than the other way round.* The US authorities have always confirmed this diagnosis by bluntly denying any responsibility: 'The dollar is our currency and your problem.'

It might be why an influential opinion at the beginning of this century has labelled the piling up of international imbalances 'Bretton Woods II'. This characterisation is true in the main lesson stated above: the disturbances the world has been suffering stem from the disruption in world liquidity and US authorities continued denial of any responsibility. But it is wrong in two respects: first the system is partly a flexible exchange rate system; second the US has had very large current account imbalances, whereas their current account had never been in deficit before the demise of Bretton Woods.

It ensues that it is justified to define the present IMS as a *semi-dollar standard:*

- A small number of currencies, but of countries that together make more than 50 per cent of world GDP, have moved to open capital markets and flexible exchange rates.
- A majority of currencies have opted for managed exchange rates and some degree of capital controls.

The result is the worst of both worlds:

- highly volatile exchange rates with persistent misalignments between convertible currencies; and
- the accumulation of balance of payment disequilibria transferred to the foreign exchange build-up that are fostered by mutually inconsistent economic policies.

This inconsistency was spelled out by Alan Greenspan in his most famous conundrum. From May 2004 to July 2007 the US Federal Reserve (Fed) raised its fed funds rate from 1 per cent to 5.25 per cent, but the long-term interest rates hardly bulged. The stickiness of US bond rates at very low levels for a very long period of time, while credit exploded much faster than GDP, was the main pillar of the leveraged real-estate price bubble that crashed in a full-fledged financial crisis.

This chapter will point out how far the design of the IMS was from delivering exchange rate stability and a proper supply of international liquidity.

OVERALL ASSESSMENT: EXCHANGE RATES AND WORLD LIQUIDITY

Exchange Rates

From the outset of the floating exchange rate period to the present, the three main currencies of the world (Deutschmark (DM) before the advent of the euro) have not displayed obvious trends in real, effective terms but instead have exhibited huge fluctuations (see Figure 8.1). There has not only been market volatility, but multi-year cycles that have fostered protracted misalignments. One should acknowledge that between mid-2002 and mid-2008 the dollar has depreciated 25 per cent in real, effective terms, while the current account deficit widened to 6 per cent of GDP in 2006 and diminished to 5 per cent in 2008 only due to the recession. It means that exchange rates are powerless when facing a reckless policy which encourages a runaway, credit-financed, consumption spree.

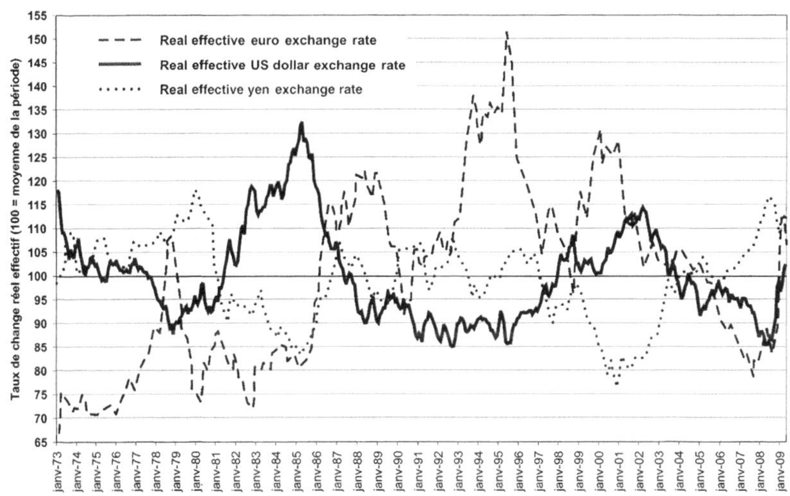

Source: Aglietta and Trainar (2009:11).

Figure 8.1 Real effective exchange rates of dollar, euro, yen in the long run

Focusing on China as an explanation for this imbalanced growth pattern in the key currency country is controversial, especially because one can see that China has sustained a robust, real, effective exchange rate appreciation since early 2005 (see Figure 8.2).

In the period where the real, effective exchange rate was flat, the trade surplus was about 3 per cent on average. It swelled to 10 per cent in 2008

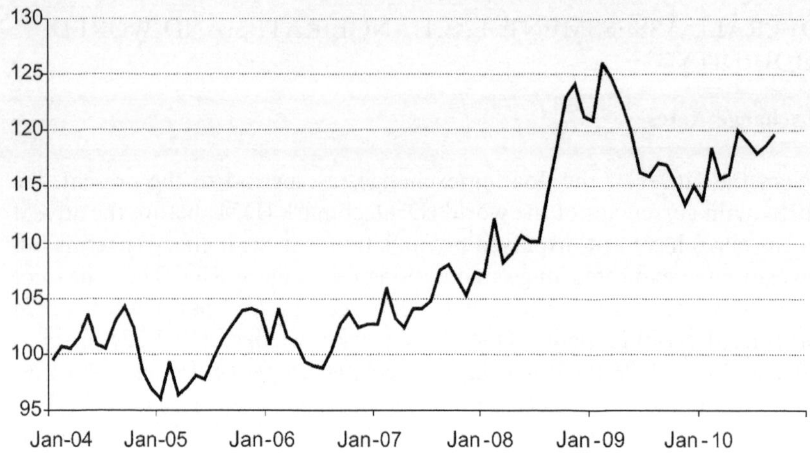

Source: CEIC, author's calculations.

Figure 8.2 Real effective exchange rate appreciation of the Yuan

while the RMB real, effective exchange rate appreciated 20 per cent. It then retreated to the range 4.5 per cent to 5 per cent in 2010 with a further appreciation. The reason why it swelled was the levelling off of imports, while Chinese firms had recovered their domestic market thanks to production capacities and enhanced productivity due to high rates of capital accumulation.

Therefore the conclusion is inescapable. *Imbalances had become unsustainable because economic policies had been unusually incompatible. No exchange rate adjustment whatsoever will ever be capable of providing smooth adjustment to such distortions.*

International Liquidity and World Money

Triffin's dilemma has reached a magnitude never before seen. In the latest decade the world monetary base has increased much faster than world GDP on a sustained basis (see Figure 8.3).

Until the crisis the growth of the world monetary base was highly correlated with the increase in world foreign exchange reserves that measures the rise in world liquidity. With the crisis foreign exchange reserves slumped with the heavy use of reserves by emerging markets' central banks which were trying to mitigate the freefall of their currencies. However, the increase in the balance sheet of Western central banks, fed by lender-of-last-resort operations followed by quantitative easing, was so large that it more than offset the plummeting official reserves.

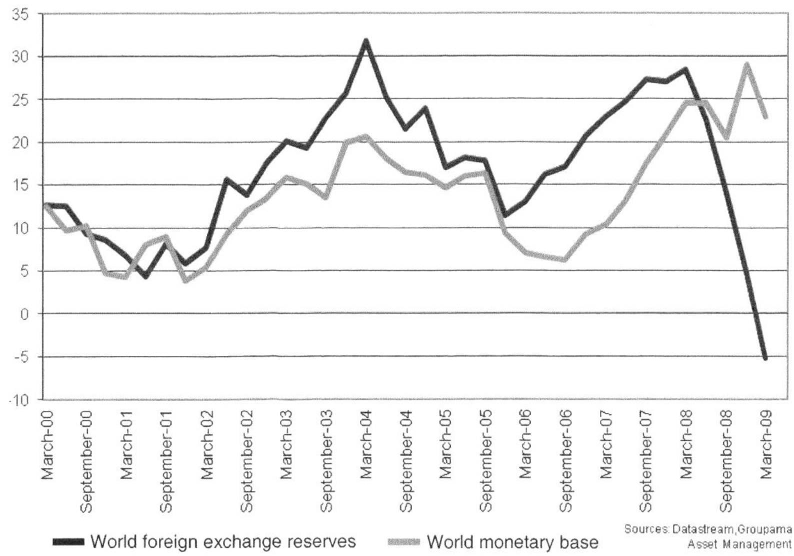

Source: Aglietta et al. (2010: 24).

Figure 8.3 World monetary base and foreign exchange reseve (y-o-y%)

The reason why foreign exchange (FX) reserves rose so fast is partly by design and partly due to constraints. First, after the string of crises at the turn of the century (Asian, Russian, Argentine), many emerging markets were determined to get out of the grip of the IMF and recover their autonomy in economic policy. They turned to export-led growth and accumulated enough reserves to stem a large external shock. This behaviour was validated by the spillover of the financial crisis in late 2008. Second, persistent current account surpluses need not automatically convert into FX reserves. There is the depth of capital account items in between. In principle financial investors might invest abroad foreign currency receipts that accrue in the domestic financial system when foreigners buy domestic bonds and equities in order to diversify their portfolios. Banks might indulge in dollar borrowing to hedge dollars deposited with them by economic agents that have gained dollar receipts in foreign trade. If, however, domestic financial systems are not well-developed, asset price changes within the system cannot smoothly adjust the inward and outward flows of foreign money. Capital controls are the only way to protect the domestic financial system from destructive asset price surges and slumps. Therefore financial institutions receiving dollar deposits have no way to hedge their holdings other than by selling them to the central bank. Capital restraints and FX reserve accumulation are the logical outcomes of uncompetitive domestic capital markets. Countries that open their capital accounts prematurely are vulnerable to speculative bubbles and capital flow reversals.

The conclusion is compelling. *The huge build up of FX reserves is the mirror of the unsettled regime of liquidity supply in the key currency issuing country, coupled with undeveloped financial systems in emerging market countries.*

The Problems Raised by US Quantitative Monetary Policy

The US and Europe are in the grip of a long-lasting balance sheet adjustment in the private sector. There is no way to avoid suboptimal economic growth for years to come. Therefore the objective of the Fed policy which makes it the dominant buyer of government securities cannot be to recover full employment. Rather, the objective is threefold: first lowering long-term interest rates on government bonds to keep the interest cost of government debt at a minimum; second ensuring a weaker dollar to alleviate the negative contribution of external trade to US growth; and third taking insurance against the risk of deflation and indirectly triggering higher medium-term inflation expectations.

One can argue that the last objective might have been better served by a shift to a price level target that would have impinged directly on inflation expectations. The most dangerous is the second objective which might heighten financial tensions with emerging market countries at the worst possible time to launch a reform process of the IMS.

If the Fed succeeds in lowering US government bond rates, which is not warranted considering the already unusually low level, it hopes to trigger a portfolio adjustment among financial investors towards corporate bonds and equities and eventually to real estate, so that a boost in asset prices fosters a wealth effect on domestic demand. The magnitude of this unusual approach is highly uncertain. It is more likely that the portfolio effect, if any, will spill over to commodity markets and emerging asset markets where yields are much higher than in the US. Not only might US financial investors increase the foreign share of their portfolios, but a much more worrisome move may occur. Hedge funds backed by their prime brokers could maximise their use of the dollar carry trade, borrowing dollars heavily since nothing has been done in financial regulation to prevent it, and selling the proceeds to buy any asset they see fit in emerging market countries and speculating in commodity futures markets.

Political bickering is inevitably heating up after the unilateral Fed decision. It will feed unilateral counter-decisions by governments wanting to protect their financial systems through capital controls. This ongoing episode once again shows that the difficulty of regulating world liquidity is paramount. Capital flows have become much more important than trade flows. Preserving competitiveness is surely in the minds of political leaders in emerging markets. But the principal goal is preserving their financial systems from another devastating bout of speculation triggered by US attempts to get rid of its liquidity trap.

WHAT IS REQUIRED AND WHAT IS POSSIBLE WHEN REFORMING THE IMS

The heaviest handicap to reforming the IMS stems from the radical divergence in diagnosis: the clash between the US and China stems from this divergence. If there are completely opposing views about what is the cause of the systemic problem, grounds cannot be found for a minimal common understanding about the improvements which are needed. More specifically, the US sticks to its view that the way international liquidity is supplied via the key currency system has nothing to do with global imbalances. Instead they see the distortions that plague the world economy as being due to the managed exchange rate policy of the Chinese government. For their part, the Chinese leadership bluntly rejects the US interpretation. They point out the disastrous hands-off financial policy that led to the explosion of credit worldwide as the main driver of global imbalance. They also blame unrelenting expansion of liquidity as the reason for renewed volatility in exchange rates.

With such an unfavourable point of departure, one should not hope for substantive reform straightaway. Bretton Woods was prepared for by three years of intensive work and bilateral negotiation between the only two countries in the world that had financial and monetary weight at the time and that shared the objective of supporting free trade. Many more powers are involved now, but they are all positively concerned with maintaining free trade. Moreover the International Monetary Fund (IMF) does not have to be created: it just has to adapt its mission and its statutes. Furthermore, the world is in the process of structural change which is modifying growth patterns. One must understand such organic endogenous forces and conceive the institutional reform that supports them.

Previously, one is used to analysing the structure of the IMS as a key currency system and to interpreting big changes as periods of competition between the established key currency and potential candidates, eventually leading to the restoration of the key currency or its replacement by another. One might be prepared to assume that the twenty-first century world will have a polycentric system without a key currency, where a key currency is a single national currency that fulfils all the functions of money in the international arena. These functions are summarised in Table 8.1.

Table 8.1 Functions of international money

Currency functions	Public actors	Private actors
Reserve of value	International reserves	Asset portfolios (currency substitution)
Means of payment	Vehicle currency for foreign exchange interventions	Currency of settlement in commercial and financial transactions
Unit of account	Anchor currency for exchange rate pegging	Numeraire in organised markets

Currency areas, for example regional monetary arrangements that do not necessarily have to reach the ultimate of monetary union with a single currency, will develop to support the means of payment function spurred on by private actor initiatives when trade flows shift. They can be boosted by clearing and settlement by governments issuing the currencies that fit the needs of these parts of international trade that decouple from the key currency. Such settlement mechanisms and platforms can either be located onshore or offshore depending on the will of sovereign states to loosen or maintain capital controls.

The means of payment function is the core function generating private international flows in a particular currency. The non-resident users will have cash balances in a currency they did not use beforehand. They need convenient yieldable assets to manage their cash accounts. A reserve of value function develops when deposits are accepted offshore by banks (like Eurodollar deposits in the 1960s) and bonds are issued by non-resident corporate entities, underwritten by investment banks and bought by qualified investors (like the Eurodollar bonds issued in London in the 1960s). The currency acquires the status of an international asset in non-resident private portfolios interested in diversification and in official reserve assets of central banks whose countries trade with the incipient new international currency.

DEVELOPMENT OF A REGIONAL ZONE IN ASIA, YUAN CONVERTIBILITY FOR NON-RESIDENTS AND A DUAL FOREIGN EXCHANGE MARKET

The impact of the crisis is an opportunity for the international monetary system to evolve. With the protracted weakening of growth in developed countries, the catching up by emerging markets will broaden (more countries involved) and be more based on endogenous forces within these markets and less on the pulling effect of export-led growth to the main OECD countries. The consequences for trade are already visible: increase in the share of inter-emerging market trade in world trade and faster economic integration in East Asia. China is the leading partner in both trends. It follows that economic agents involved in two-way trade flows with China (Brazilian exporters to China and importers of Chinese goods, Brazilian beneficiaries of Chinese FDIs for instance) have incentives to use the yuan as their means of payment, provided that facilities are established to manage yuan liquidities.

To accommodate these needs the CNH market is being organised in Hong Kong (HK). The CNH market is the yuan offshore market for non-residents in HK. It will develop yuan convertibility for non-residents compatible with capital controls for residents. The inescapable consequence will be a dual FX market for the yuan. Hong Kong will become the financial centre for the xeno-yuan as much as London was the financial centre for the Eurodollar.

The CNH market is mustering the following characteristics:

- a clearing and settlement system in yuan for offshore transactions, which will provide the base of liquidity;
- an agreement between the People's Bank of China (PBoC) and the Hong Kong Monetary Authority (HKMA) to allow non-bank non-resident agents without any direct trade links with China to open accounts in yuan with qualified banks incorporated in HK;
- access to the mainland monetary market restricted to banks participating in the settlement of offshore transactions;
- a *Dim Sun Bond market* issuing yuan offshore bonds has opened in HK to supply attractive assets to non resident investors; and
- as a consequence a dual foreign exchange market will develop in HK with a USD/CNY exchange rate for commercial transactions quoted with reference to the onshore market on one side and a USD/CNH exchange rate for non-commercial transactions that will be quoted endogenously according to the supply and demand of yuan liquidity.

Those structural developments foster a gradual process for an exit from the semi-dollar standard and a contribution to a polycentric system based upon an Asian-wide monetary area centred on yuan convertibility together with dollar and euro areas. The advantage of regional monetary zones is that they can take care of financial disturbances within the region and prevent them from spilling over to the wider IMS. An implicit subsidiary principle would apply.

The development of a monetary area in eastern Asia does not have to be as demanding and as formal as the one that created the European Monetary System (EMS) and subsequently the euro. Several processes are possible. One might build on the Chiang Mai Initiative and create an Asian Currency Unit (akin to the ECU for Europe in the 1980s). It would serve to denominate bonds appealing to institutional investors and financing infrastructure investments of central and local governments in the whole region. A monetary agreement might also be struck whereby all central banks agree to manage their exchange rates according to the ACU taken as their common benchmark in order to ensure consistency in their cross-exchange rates.

However, a recent Bank for International Settlements (BIS) paper shows that it is not even necessary to agree on the use of a common basket. Because the structure of foreign trade of the countries in the Asian region is similar enough, the only step needed is for each central bank to manage its currency according to its effective exchange rate. That would be enough to ensure consistency in cross-exchange rates. Because China has abandoned the dollar peg, the path is open to decouple smoothly from the dollar and separately adopt the guideline of the effective exchange rate.

MULTILATERAL SURVEILLANCE AND EXCHANGE RATES

The IMF is the institution dedicated to monitoring the monetary system's ability to deliver the dual services of a proper supply of international liquidity and smooth adjustment of balance of payments disequilibria. The objective is to achieve sustainable world growth and a fair sharing of the costs of achieving this global public good among countries. At best it can be said that the system has utterly failed to achieve the dual objective. Meanwhile the IMF has undergone changes to its mission via amendments to its statutes. In the Bretton Woods era, exchange rate policy was the linchpin of its activities because members had agreed to an exchange rate grid defined by dollar parities. The IMF was the referee which decided if a country was suffering from a fundamental deficit in its balance of payments when it asked for devaluation of its currency. The US was excluded from the procedure since the dollar was *de jure* the centre of the exchange rate system. Furthermore, because Keynes's proposals had been rebutted by the Americans, no rule was set to manage international liquidity. The devil was let loose in the system.

After the demise of Bretton Woods and the failure of the Committee of 20 in designing a new rule-based IMS, there was a complete renouncement of the political leadership. The exchange rates were entirely left to national sovereignty without any agreed-upon guidelines under the Jamaica amendments of 1976. That is why the accusation that China is today violating the rules is far-fetched; the rules do not exist. The IMF was given the mission of bilateral surveillance under Article 4. But the whole system was overhauled due to financial globalisation. The era of indebtedness and financial crises began. The IMF became, de facto, the mentor of indebted developing countries. Surveillance transformed into management of insolvency under concessionary loans. Meanwhile surveillance lost all bearing and significance for developed countries that had no need to borrow from the IMF.

The Asian and Russian crises were quite another matter. They were so-called third-generation crises, which called for multilateral action because they involved systemic risk. The tools were not at hand to deal with multiple insolvencies and minds were not prepared to handle the spillover of financial stress from one country to another. The aftermath left a lot of anger in public opinion in the many countries that had suffered the shocks. The governments of such countries changed policies drastically to eschew a renewed ordeal once and for all. Correlated with this, the massive outflow of capital from these emerging markets poured into developed countries' financial systems. It was the fuel that permitted Wall Street investment banks to design the deadly credit machine that extracted an extravagant amount of rent from the real economy and fed the global financial crisis. In the meantime an attempt at reform of the IMS was launched by the G7 in 1998 and failed lamentably in 2000 in both its objectives of setting up an international court of justice to resolve sovereign insolvency and embedding an international lender-of-last-resort responsibility in the IMF.

This concise historical recap is intended to highlight the pitfalls that await anyone who apprehends the formidable task of reforming the IMS in the present environment where there is a shaky financial system, weak growth and high unemployment in developed countries, coupled with bitter political disagreements. The only strategy that can succeed is the one that advances the underlying trend towards regional arrangements towards a polycentric system.

The G20 has agreed in principle to give the IMF the mission of multilateral surveillance under the Mutual Assessment Process. Assuming that the IMF has the political backing of its most influential members, it should provide substance to periodic multilateral debates on macroeconomic policy. The content of such analysis designed to feed multilateral political dialogue pertains to inconsistencies in macro policies which give rise to balance of payments distortions on the one hand, and to elaborating indicators of systemic risk on the other.

On the topic of macro policies, it is relevant to bring developments in real, effective exchange rates into the picture, while being aware of the uncertainty encompassing the measure of fundamental exchange rates. First, one must acknowledge that Purchasing Power Parity (PPP) is not a benchmark at all when assessing real exchange rates. Countries that are catching up with growth driven by productivity in manufacturing must have undervalued exchange rates against PPP. The real, effective exchange rate is a positive function of the ratio of real GDP per capita of the country to the leading country GDP per capita. The position of a particular country relative to this rule of thumb gives a clue to the eventual undervaluation or overvaluation of a particular currency. Second, in the process of catching up there is both a growth differential with the leading country and real appreciation of the currency in the country which is catching up. However, real wage increases and domestic price rises are much better ways to appreciate the real, effective exchange rate than nominal exchange rate variations. For instance, in the 1960s the yen appreciated continuously in real, effective terms at a fixed nominal exchange rate and pervasive competitiveness in the manufacturing sector thanks to a permanent rise in the relative price of non-traded to traded goods.

Besides, the present world is beset with disorderly capital flows. *It is crucial that countries keep their entire sovereignty in managing their nominal exchange rate and capital controls to mitigate fluctuations in asset prices. In emerging markets the exchange rate is a necessary pillar of macro prudential policy. It is linked to systemic risk prevention.*

Concerning alert indicators, the IMF must collaborate with the BIS which has the upper hand in gathering data on systemic financial entities and a better understanding of the spillover effects of financial fragilities such as counterparty risks and distress sales in the search for liquidity. The FSB (Financial Stability Board) is housed in the BIS and provides a forum for central gatherings on financial stability matters. Because central banks will improve their understanding of systemic risk formation in their macro prudential policy, an institutional mechanism must be found to link the knowledge that will be acquired by central banks with the knowledge and expertise of the IMF in international macro linkages.

However, the effectiveness of systemic risk prevention in multilateral surveillance will depend crucially on the strengthening of financial regulation in every financial centre of the world. One cannot but be pessimistic. After two years of work and recent enactments of legislation, financial regulation remains too far from being comprehensive and effective to be called a global process.

MANAGING INTERNATIONAL LIQUIDITY

It has been shown earlier that liquidity cannot be managed in the interest of the global community with a key currency system. The development of a polycentric currency world is the process that will move the world away from that system. Remember that key currency is not the same as dominant currency. A key currency system is a system where international liquidity is the liability of the issuer of the key currency. The Gold Standard was a dominant currency system because sterling was overwhelmingly the currency vehicle for settling international trade and the currency reserve of banks all over the world. However, it was not the ultimate means of settlement. The latter was monetised gold whose supply was not the debt of any country. It ensued that the issuer of sterling, namely the Bank of England, was subject to the constraint of convertibility. In a period of economic expansion, credit and bank deposits increased faster than the supply of gold in the banking system. The liability of the Bank of England swelled with the demand of the public for banknotes and with the reserves of the commercial banks deposited with the central bank. When the ratio of the gold stock to the amount of bank liability fell towards the legal minimum, the Bank of England raised the bank rate. It was immediately transmitted to the whole international banking system, firstly via British discount banks and secondly via their correspondents abroad. Therefore the supply of international liquidity responded to aggregate world credit in the international business cycle. There were successions of booms and recessions, but the business cycle was highly synchronised worldwide. Consequently there were little imbalances in the balances of payments and little gold was needed to settle imbalances between countries, unless the business cycle led to a banking crisis.

This little piece of international monetary theory means that the gold standard provided a mechanism to regulate world liquidity. When Keynes thought of the problem the world would have to face after the war, he understood very well that gold could not be the answer. Already the attempt of the UK government to re-establish the pre-1913 gold standard in 1926 was a disaster. Trying to re-establish gold after the Second World War would have triggered an abominable deflation. In this sense gold was a 'barbarous relic'. However, he thought of a mechanism that could tame the beast of liquidity in a world where all types of money were going to be man-made.

In his General Theory, Keynes had shown why and how liquidity preference was the most dangerous economic woe. Market liquidity is just a common belief. It is the belief of each market participant that it can sell to another market participant any asset held for cash without capital loss. Therefore liquidity does not have a social quality. Absolute liquidity preference is just a perversion of the market economy since the market collapses if everyone tries to sell simultaneously. It is why a sovereign entity must act as a lender of last resort. Who can do the job at the international level? A supranational central bank?

Keynes thought to suppress the problem in designing a settlement mechanism linked to rules that eschew the pathological demand for liquidity. He called it the International Clearing Union. The net multilateral balance of all transactions between countries (the variation of the net monetary position) is the balance of multilateral clearing registered by the clearing union as a surplus or a deficit of the country expressed in an international unit of account Keynes called the 'bancor'. The net balances are settled in units of credit allocated by the Clearing Union. As a result of any daily settlement the accounts of surplus countries are credited and the accounts of the deficit countries are drawn down. To avoid the accumulation of liquid balances over a maximum amount, surplus countries are required to spend more, while symmetrically, deficit countries whose balances decline under a minimum are required to save more. The constraints would be escalated on a graduated scale depending on the extent of violation of the balances. The total amount of international reserve assets would be the counterpart of the total amount of credit granted by the Credit Union. International liquidity and balance of payments adjustments are functionally linked to one another. The system provides collective insurance for participating countries, which is much cheaper than self-insurance and it limits the reserve hoarding race altogether. In a polycentric system with currency zones one might conceive of an application of the clearing union principle at regional level for intra-zone transactions and at international level when clearing and settling inter-regional transactions.

Of course the obstacles to such a system are formidable, but the principles are clear and they should inspire the lines of reform. They provide insight into US Secretary of the Treasury Geithner's proposal to set limits on current account balances. *It is the idea that deficit and surplus countries should be dealt with symmetrically,* a much better idea than China bashing! However, current account imbalances are not, by far, those that feed distortions in net monetary positions. Capital accounts are much more destabilising. Therefore, in the present globalised world, much tighter financial regulation that limits the leverage of financial institutions and the retention of capital controls are necessary tools to make the system work.

Another tool that Keynes had already pointed out is the regulation of the commodity market. With the huge amount of reserves already accumulated it is possible to make an international stabilising fund to intervene in crucial commodity futures markets in order to mitigate the wild volatility due to reckless speculation.

Akin to symmetric adjustments of deficit and surplus countries, a polycentric system would benefit from the creation of an international reserve asset that is not the debt of any country. The Special Drawing Rights (SDR) is precisely such an entity.

One must remember that SDR allocation is not money creation in the sense of issuing a debt on a financial institution. *SDRs are not liabilities but purely fiat assets.* They are potential claims on the freely usable currencies of IMF members. The sale of SDRs by one member to acquire reserve currencies creates an SDR claim to the counterparty in the transaction. The latter is offset by a mirror liability to the SDR Department of the IMF. As a result of their transactions, members have net claims and liabilities on the SDR Department, e.g. holdings above or below their allocations. Those net claims or liabilities carry market yields.

There are three reasons to enhance the role of the SDR. The first is to alleviate the shortcomings of the semi-dollar standard by reducing the incentive of central banks to acquire dollars. The second is to allocate enough reserves according to a rule-based issuance to avoid the precautionary pile-up of dollar reserves by countries whose currencies are weakly convertible. It will make the IMF an embryonic international lender of last resort. The third is the establishment of a Substitution Account in the IMF to enable countries loaded with an excessive amount of dollar reserves to diversify their foreign exchange off-market and therefore to preclude the disruption of exchange rates.

The first and the second objectives might be reached in developing the role of the SDR through contingent credit lines, which the IMF is already proposing (flexible credit line and precautionary credit line) without any *ex post* conditionality, augmented by an international lender of last resort facility. The third objective could be implemented by reviving the idea of the Substitution Account in the IMF.

To increase the attractiveness of the SDR, the People's Bank of China has suggested that future SDR allocations take the form of SDR bond issues by the IMF, instead of bilateral loans from countries contributing to the IMF. Those bonds would pay an interest rate based on the weighted rates of bonds of the SDR-constituent currencies. An SDR bond would be the first step in creating a market in invest-worthy assets, making it a true reserve currency. SDR-denominated bonds might be the counterpart of dollar reserves sold to a renewed Substitution Account. It would fulfil its role of facilitating the off-market diversification of reserve holdings.

As for the exchange risk borne by the Substitution Account, the best way to eliminate it might be for the administrators of the Account to diversify its dollar assets and to match currency compositions through off-market trades with central banks whose currencies are components of the SDR. Furthermore, a market hedge is possible if it is done dynamically. It should be recalled that the dollar does not fall continuously; instead it shows a cyclical pattern as highlighted above. Suppose, for instance, that the Account was created in 1980 just before the dollar began its five-year rise. The Account would have got fat profits from a 28 per cent appreciation of its dollar-denominated assets over its SDR-denominated liabilities. The Account administration could have invested the profits in a large array of financial assets to make a reserve that would have covered the exchange risk for a long period ahead. Finally the Fund can sell its remaining gold stock and invest the proceeds in an array of diversified financial assets matching the composition of the SDR to immunise its liabilities.

THE GOVERNANCE OF THE IMF

If the IMF is to get the mission of preventing global macroeconomic imbalances and overseeing common factors of financial instability, it had better strengthen its political weight. This will involve changes in the Fund's governance to enhance the weight of emerging markets and to improve the backing of the Executive Director.

An increase in the voting rights of some emerging markets is already under way but bolder steps are needed. The formula which defines quotas according to the political bargaining strengths of countries and alliances circa 1944 must be discarded for an objective formula entirely based on economic and financial indicators.

IMF governance reform will be half-baked, however, as long as the eurozone has no political representation for its currency. Currently, an array of governments, who no longer have a currency to speak for, sit in a monetary institution with voting rights dating from 1944, while the second most important currency in the world has no one to speak for it. Therefore the euro does not have the full attributes of an international currency. No substantial reform of international monetary governance can occur as long as this anomaly persists.

Other changes to the management of the IMF are also needed for a comprehensive reform. The capacity of a single country to veto the votes of a qualified majority should be repealed by lowering the required majority to pass new initiatives. The Executive Committee should be upgraded to a political council, a gathering of higher level officials mandated by their respective governments. It should meet monthly and be able to back up quickly the initiatives of the Executive Director. The designation of the latter should be open and the current exclusivity of European and, for that matter, Western candidates (it is coupled with the American exclusivity of heading up the World Bank) repealed.

REFERENCES

Aglietta, M. (2009) 'Evolution du système monétaire international: persistances historiques et enjeux à venir', *Géopolitique*, July.

Aglietta, M. and Trainar, P. (eds) (2009) 'Dollar: fin de règne?', *Revue d'Economie Financière*, no. 94, June, Introduction, p. 11.

Aglietta, M., Cohen, A.and Berrebi, L. (2010) *Banques Centrales et Globalisation*, Expertise No. 7, Groupama-am, p. 24.

Brender, A. and Pisani, F. (2007) *Les déséquilibres financiers internationaux*. Paris: La Découverte.

Eichengreen, B. (2011) *Exorbitant Privilege*. Oxford: Oxford University Press.

Hongyi, Chen, Peng, Wensheng and Shu, Chang (2009) *Renminbi as an International Currency: Potential and Policy Considerations*, HKIMR Working Paper No. 18.

MacKinnon, R. (2005) *The World Dollar Standard and Globalization. New Rules for the Game?* Stanford, CA: Stanford University.

Triffin, R. (1960) *Gold and the Dollar Crisis: The Future of Convertibility*. New Haven, CT: Yale University Press.

Truman, E. (2009) 'The G20 and international financial institution reform: unfinished IMF reform', *VOX Europe*, 28 January.

9. Is the renminbi undervalued?

Sylvain Plasschaert

INTRODUCTION

Whether or not the Chinese national currency, the renminbi (RMB), is undervalued remains a real bone of contention. Loud voices are raised not only in the American Congress but also by opinion-makers and even in some academic circles; they advocate for protectionist measures to be taken against the onslaught of imports from China, which, buttressed by low wages and an intentionally weak local currency, is indicted with causing the loss of numerous jobs in the US. The increasingly politicised dispute has inflamed the official circles in both countries.

The Chinese leadership maintains that China's surplus is not primarily shaped by the exchange rate, and that, unless the RMB was appreciating intolerably, the US deficit vis-à-vis China would not be cured in essence.

In the same context, it is noteworthy that, whereas official IMF statements express the view that the RMB is somewhat undervalued, the IMF Executive Board, in its conclusions on the 2010 Article IV Consultation, frankly confessed to dissension among its members.

Admittedly, the facts to which the critics of China refer cannot be denied. Indeed, the deficit of the bilateral trade accounts between the USA and China (and to a smaller extent the external current accounts) has grown ominously in recent years.

As can be inferred from Table 9.1, in the 2007–10 period, annual US exports to China amounted to less than a quarter of imports. In 2009, trade was still affected by the international recession and Chinese exports to the USA declined by 12 per cent; the resulting deficit was still 3.2 times larger than US exports to China.

Over the same period, as shown in Table 9.2, the EU-27 also ran a substantial external deficit in its bilateral relationship with China – barely lower than that of the USA. For EU-27 exports, China holds fourth place, behind the USA, Russia and Switzerland. When imports are aggregated China is now the largest supplier country for the EU-27.

Another strand in the debate relates to the rapid build-up of official foreign exchange ('forex') reserves by the Central Bank of China, which

Table 9.1 Bilateral trade between the People's Republic of China and the USA (billions of US dollars)

Year	Export from China to the USA	Export into China from the USA	Balance
2007	322	63	+259
2008	338	70	+268
2009	296	69	+227
2010*	229	56	+178

*First eight months of 2010

Source: US International Trade Commission.

Table 9.2 Bilateral trade between the People's Republic of China and the EU (billions of US dollars)

Year	Export from China to the EU	Import into China from the EU	Balance
2007	233	72	+161
2008	248	79	+170
2009	215	82	+133
2010*	125	53	+72

*First half of 2010

Source: Eurostat.

are projected by the World Bank Quarterly Update of November 2010 to be at more than US$2.8 trillion by the end of the same year.

An appreciation of the Chinese currency vis-à-vis the US dollar would end the RMB's pegging with the US dollar. This tie was abandoned in July 2005 but renewed in September 2008 at the outbreak of the international financial crisis; during that period, the RMB appreciated by 21 per cent against the US dollar but depreciated against the euro. In July 2010, it was announced that the RMB would again be allowed to fluctuate slightly against a basket of currencies and no longer be strictly tied to the dollar. From 5 September to early November 2010 the RMB gained almost 2 per cent to the dollar.

The controversy surrounding the appropriate forex rate for the RMB readily derails into boundless and emotional argumentation. Hence, the first section of this chapter will briefly comment upon commonly overlooked but relevant features which seriously qualify China's impressive export trade. It may already be noticed that most of the topics covered in this first section do not require lengthy development as they are amply substantiated in theory and supported by empirical evidence. Subsequently, this chapter documents that the massive foreign exchange reserves of the Chinese Central Bank are not fundamentally derived from the country's trade surplus. And, finally, this chapter submits some critical comments about the macro saving and consumption positions in the USA and China (obviously from opposite perspectives) which will feed discussion around the current account imbalance of both countries.

In this present analysis, the focus is on the relationship between China and the United States. As a matter of fact it is this bilateral relationship which appears to be the most strained and most unbalanced. But the analysis attempted here is also largely applicable, *mutatis mutandis*, to the EU–Chinese trade relationship.

A CLOSER LOOK AT CHINA'S EXPORT STATISTICS

The Exceptional Growth of China's Economy

Since 1980, the Chinese economy has experienced exceptional growth of around 10 per cent per year, in real terms. One should remember that this double-digit benchmark is an average, covering the whole time span since 1980 for a territory of continental dimensions! Per capita income is now close to US$3,000, which already puts China in the World Bank's rank of lower-middle-income countries.

Yet, although several industrial sectors in China have reached a high degree of sophistication, China still has many features of an (albeit rapidly) 'developing' country. The huge rural interior sector, where agriculture still performs a pivotal role, has a much lower income level than that of the urban centres and more particularly than that of the coastal areas, although one should remember that the de facto privatisation of the cultivation of the agricultural sector – and not of the ownership pattern – in the early 1980s has provided the initial and major push along China's growth path (see, for example, Naughton, 2007).

The Record Growth of Chinese Exports

Another principal engine of growth relates to the spectacular rise of China's export trade, starting in the early 1980s, but exploding after China joined the WTO in 2002. In 1980, China's exports totalled just US$20 billion. At that time, as was typical for Soviet-type economies, interaction with the outside world was minimised. By 2005, the value of exports had reached US$762 billion (according to China's Customs Statistics).

In 2008, China's aggregate exports rose to US$1,429 billion but then dived to US$1,202 in 2009, a fall of 16 per cent, on account of the worldwide financial crisis. The ensuing global recession took a heavy toll on Chinese exports, especially those to the USA and the EU. The trade surplus (exports minus imports) of China vis-à-vis the USA declined in 2009 from US$268 billion to US$227 billion. As from the latter part of 2009, China's overall export trade has recovered strongly.

The Close Link with Inward Foreign Direct Investment and the Issue of 'Relocation'

The, at first glance, overwhelming performance of China's exports must nonetheless be considerably qualified by several highly relevant features of China's international trade.

A major part, around 60 per cent, of Chinese exports, are operated by 'foreign invested enterprises' (FIEs). This concept comprises both joint ventures between Chinese and foreign companies and fully-owned affiliates of foreign enterprises. In other words, the label 'made *in* China' is not synonymous with 'made *by* Chinese firms proper'. One must thereby recall that firms in Hong Kong and Macao are also recorded as FIEs (see section below on 'The significant role of Hong Kong and "overseas Chinese"').

The uninformed 'man in the street' may view the production facilities which FIEs establish in foreign 'host countries' as substitutes or alternatives to the products that would otherwise originate in the home country. This view often prompts the complaint that such outward foreign direct investment (FDI) entails the relocation of production capacity from the home to the host country. The host country is then mistakenly indicted with destroying a considerable number of jobs at home, say in the USA.[1] Therefore a digression on the relocation of productive capacities abroad appears appropriate.

Genuine relocation occurs when a firm stops producing at home and starts the same production abroad. The assertion that firms in China are 'stealing' production and jobs in the United States may then be valid. The trade balance of the home country would be even more impaired whenever the FDI is availed of to produce goods that are re-exported to the home country.

Counterfactual analysis – 'what would have happened to the firm, in the absence of such relocation?' – is obviously fraught with doses of guesswork. Yet quite a number of firms contend that they would not have survived in an intensely competitive international environment if they had not moved their manufacturing to low-wage cost countries (such as China) or subcontracted production to unaffiliated, so-called 'contract manufacturers' (under Chinese or non-Chinese ownership).

When, however, the output of foreign multinationals in China is destined to serve the Chinese internal market, the claim of harmful relocation is not warranted. Indeed, any firm with an appealing product naturally strives to expand its sales into foreign markets. But often this cannot be achieved from an export platform in the home country, and a production facility in the host country may prove itself as the most efficient alternative. The motivations thereto are diverse, among them: prohibitive transport costs or import duties; the prior move by a major customer firm; and the urge to expand the scale of production, which can then be located more appropriately to the market.

The accusation of unfair relocation is particularly unfounded when the manufacturing of the goods in question has already essentially been terminated in the home country, as is the case for footwear in the USA. Relocation, in the above strict sense, occurs especially as regards labour-intensive end or intermediate products, such as the production of apparel, shoes and toys, in which China played a prominent role in the early years of its 'opening to the outside world'.

However, against the direct loss of jobs in the home country, one must consider that: (1) when the lower wages and other production costs in China result in lower sales prices (at a given quality) in the home country, they enhance the real incomes of consumers (for final goods) or of further processors (as regards intermediates); (2) home-country economies benefit from downward pressure on the overall price level and contain inflationary tendencies, with resulting positive effects on investments and growth; and (3) the cost advantage reaped in low-wage jurisdictions refers essentially to the manufacturing stage which typically only represents a low proportion of the value added in the total production chain. This sequence extends to the servicing of the final customer at the retail stage, and also involves pre-manufacturing activities such as design.[2]

Yet, already in the early days of China's opening-up gambit, inward FDI was, in the majority, aimed at nascent market outlets in China itself instead of being involved in the cheaper production of export-bound goods. Today, the rapid extension and enormous potentialities of the Chinese market mean that this is even more the case.

The Significant Role of Hong Kong and 'Overseas Chinese'

It was already mentioned that, with respect to trade, Hong Kong (and in a much more modest role) Macao are viewed as foreign territories by China. Both 'special administrative zones' run their own customs and currencies, but there are dense and deepening links between them and China proper. Thus Hong Kong is a major (immediate) destination for Chinese exports, amounting to 14 per cent of total export value in 2009, although much of this export flow only transits through the former British colony on its way to other destinations.[3] Besides, Hong Kong represents by far the largest geographical source of inward FDI in China.[4]

It follows that much of the outward trade of China is carried out by entrepreneurs and traders who belong to the large 'overseas Chinese' community in East Asia. Thus, since the early 1990s, the manufacturing of toys has predominantly been relocated from Hong Kong to Shenzhen or other 'special economic zones' which featured lower wages and welcomed FDI with favourable incentive schemes.

More recently, and for essentially the same motive of a cheaper labour supply, the manufacturing of electrical appliances and electronic goods, particularly in their final stages of production, has largely been relocated from Taiwan to sites in mainland China. This happened even prior to the recent political thaw in the relationship between the two regimes on either side of the Taiwan Strait.

From the above it follows that if East Asia were considered a single area, Chinese export levels would seem less impressive as part of it results from manufacturing production that has been relocated to mainland China.

The Upgrading of Technological Quality

Another noteworthy development is the continuous upgrading of the product quality and of the degree of sophistication of China's export assortment. In the initial years of its 'opening to the outside world', China, thanks to its abundant supply of unskilled labour drawn from the tens of millions of otherwise under-employed people in the rural interior, has fast become a major manufacturer of simple, labour-intensive goods. Over the years, firms in China, confronted with fierce competition and often benefiting from the inflow of FDI, enhanced their productivity and have been able to muster the production of higher-value goods.

This rapid climb along the technological ladder has been documented in several studies. Recently, Ma and Van Assche (2010), adopting the four-level OECD classification of technological prominence, found that the share of low technology (with textiles, apparel and leather as the main subsets) in total exports fell from 53 per cent in 1992 to 27 per cent in 2007, whereas the high technology segment (with radio, TV and communications, and office and computing machinery) jumped from 10 per cent to 31 per cent.

However, we must immediately stress that international trade statistics assign the geographical origin and the total value of the final product to the country where the last substantial processing is performed. This is often the case with firms in China (whether in domestic Chinese or in foreign ownership), to which the assembly of the various parts and components is typically entrusted. This remark is closely linked to the subsequent one about the widespread geographical fragmentation in today's production sequence.

The Substantial Role of 'Processing Trade'

The customs statistics of China distinguish between 'processing trade' and 'ordinary or general trade'. In processing trade, components and other intermediates are imported from abroad, prior to their further elaboration and finishing. Processing trade accounts for more than half of China's overall exports, although its relative importance now appears to be shrinking somewhat.

The fragmented manufacturing sequence has expanded rapidly in recent years, as can be inferred from successive annual UNCTAD Investment Reports. This is especially discernible in the East Asian region, where intra-regional trade acts as a major stimulus to economic integration, even prior to the Free Trade Agreement between ASEAN countries and China which became effective as of January 2010 and has thus created an immense free internal trade bloc.

Processing trade partakes in the phenomenon of internationally fragmented production, whereby firms from different countries are involved in the manufacture of the end product, which is then exported, say, from China – not including the activities involved in the further commercialisation of such final goods on their way to the final customer. The incorporation of intermediate inputs, sourced from foreign countries, into the final product significantly increases the import content of the exported products.[5] An iconic, and perhaps extreme example, is that of Apple's video iPod. Researchers at Berkeley University have figured out that out of the iPod, sold at US$299 in the American market, US$ 163 are captured by American companies, US$132 by part makers in other Asian countries and only US$4 by Chinese workers who are employed at the final assembly stage.[6]

Complaints from the Chinese side are frequently voiced that such fragmentation results in a very modest value-added in the Chinese stages of the manufacturing process. Firms in China quite often intervene in the finishing stage, especially when manual labour can still be usefully applied. The complaints relate mainly to 'contract manufacturing' (which involves only the manufacture, in line with specifications ordered by their principal, of labour-intensive goods or components). These sectors have attracted numerous entrepreneurs from China and elsewhere; they face fierce competition and low profit margins. In recent years, such profits have been further eroded by the appreciation of the RMB in the 2005–8 period, and by an upward push in wages now in progress. The recent international financial tsunami, and the related interruption of large orders from American or European firms and supermarkets, has resulted in the loss of 20 million jobs in the coastal areas.

An interesting finding of Ma and Van Assche (2010: 14) is that 'while China's export growth has been concentrated in the higher technology sectors, these are precisely the sectors in which China's domestic content is small'. The authors link this phenomenon to two properties of information technology processes, namely their modularity and 'separability'. Multiple but standardised and loosely coupled components are thereby involved (Ma and Van Assche, 2010: 14 note 2).

They also notice that the limited local content in China with respect to its high-technology exports implies that, generally speaking, China has not yet reached the pinnacle of technological mastery, which the crude export data tend to suggest.

There can be no doubt, nonetheless, that China is making great strides in assimilating technological knowledge and steadfastly entertains high ambitions thereto. Clearly, as firms in China increasingly source components and parts from within China thereby substituting for imports, the local content of production in China is also bound to be enhanced.

China's Import Trade

Another important aspect of the debate also tends to be overlooked, namely that the exports out of China are largely offset by its imports. Since it embarked on its successful opening-up strategy, China's imports have in most years been somewhat, but not substantially, lower than the value of its exports. As will be recalled below, it follows that the phenomenal ballooning of China's official reserves has not been fed primarily by highly positive trade balances.

Moreover, as is the case in most countries, the composition of China's imports differs greatly from that of its exports. Raw materials and equipment stand out in the import trade statistics whereas, as mentioned earlier, the processing trade results in entries on both sides of the trade balance, especially as regards textiles and electronics.

Chinese Multinationals on the March

A brand-new phenomenon is unfolding, namely the outward thrust by a growing number of Chinese enterprises, mostly still under government control. A few years ago, the Chinese authorities started loosening some restrictions on capital outflows.

Thus Chinese firms are investing in African and Latin American raw materials sectors. In the manufacturing sector, Geely, although small even by Chinese standards, recently took over the Volvo business from Ford. A few years ago, Lenovo acquired the PC section of IBM. Other firms such as Haier, Huawei and BYD are on their way to building household names in the international marketplace; in this regard they have established commercial and even production affiliates abroad.

The outward thrust of Chinese firms is likely to gather more momentum. The entry of Chinese firms abroad is explicitly encouraged by the Chinese government. Moreover, Chinese firms are eager to gain access to top-notch technology by way of the purchase of patents or the takeover of foreign firms. The abundant forex reserves (partly set aside in 'sovereign funds') provide a potent instrument to finance China's outward FDIs.

This rapidly growing outward FDI flow is bound to counteract somewhat the presently unbalanced bilateral trade and financial accounts between China and the USA (and the EU).

Bilateral Trade Balances are Misleading

The last, but not least criticism of the prevailing American stance regarding the RMB is an obvious one, namely that it makes no sense to myopically focus on bilateral trade figures. Admittedly, the US trade balance with China is highly negative, as is that of the EU-27, but only the overall trade balance vis-à-vis all other countries matters when looking at the positioning of a country's currency in the forex markets or when assessing the competitiveness of its businesses in the international marketplace. China's overall stance is much more balanced. Its surplus vis-à-vis the developed economies, more particularly the USA and the EU, is largely offset by a deficit against other countries, especially those from which it imports crude oil and other raw materials, or from East Asian countries which supply it with parts and components.

Summarising the Erroneous Obsession with Gross Exports

The main conclusion from our first section is that the almost exclusive concern which in most countries political leaders and public opinion attach to the maximisation of export earnings – thus imprinting a mercantilist bent to trade policies – is much overdone, as it is at odds with the present-day workings of the international business world.

Without doubt, a country would reap maximum economic benefit, if it – or more precisely if its enterprises – succeeded in conquering markets abroad for goods composed wholly of domestic parts and components. The value added during the production process would then accrue fully to the home country and this would be particularly welcome in terms of jobs created.

As amply analysed here, however, this myopic and almost obsessional view of gross export values is mistaken. Today, even large countries cannot be fully self-sufficient, as some natural resources must be sourced from abroad. Besides, domestic firms are often unable to serve foreign markets by way of exports from their home base, but are led to install a 'foreign direct investment' base in the host, or destination, country. As an illustration, the Bureau of Economic Analysis has figured out that, in 2007, the sales of foreign affiliates of American firms tripled that of exports from the USA. The frequent fragmentation of the manufacturing sequence across a number of countries adds another break to the traditional analysis which tends to view trade as consisting of the exchange of goods whose full value-added is created in a single country.

THE GIGANTIC FOREIGN EXCHANGE RESERVES OF THE CHINESE CENTRAL BANK

The Relevance of Trade Balances?

The forex reserves[7] of the Bank of China are presently about US$3 trillion. China recently dethroned Japan from the top rank in the league of foreign reserves. This outstanding position is often invoked as an argument for a significant appreciation of the RMB. It is held that such an event would, in turn, narrow the imbalance in trade and current balances, between the USA and China.

This argument is weak, because it basically attributes the explosive growth of the forex reserves to the rapid expansion of the export earnings of China over the payments for its imports – or in other words to China's net trade balance.

Even a quick look at the trade balance of China shows that, while vis-à-vis the USA annual export proceeds have generally exceeded China's import values, the net positive values over the last years cannot possibly explain the rapid build-up of the forex stance of China vis-à-vis the USA. The trade surpluses over the 2000–9 period results in an aggregate surplus of around US$1 billion, or not even 40 per cent of the actual total amount of the official reserves at present. Hence other relevant factors ought to be taken into account.

The Role of Net FDI Inflows

At present, China has become the principal destination of inward FDI, which mainly materialises in 'greenfield' projects and, to a smaller extent, acquisitions of firms in China. The flow of such financial resources has become larger in the wake of China's accession to the World Trade Organization (in 2002), and has only shrunk during the short-lived impact of the international financial tsunami in 2008–9. Prospective inflows of FDI look equally favourable for China.

Yet an opposite flow of outward FDI is also gathering momentum. In 2009, substantial outward FDI by Chinese firms counteracted the still huge inward flows and the net FDI inflow declined to US$37 billion. Significantly, the IMF 2010 article IV Consultation Staff Report (IMF, 2010a) projects that for 2011 FDI flowing out of China, at US$62 billion, will slightly exceed the inward flow.

Such inflows of FDI from abroad (again counting Hong Kong and Macao as foreign trade partners) are recorded in the country's financial or capital account. China's initial intention, expressed around 1997, to introduce convertibility for capital transactions by the turn of the century has been sidelined due to the damage inflicted by the East Asian financial crisis on neighbouring countries that had heavily relied on borrowing from abroad. Since then, China's financial account has remained under rather strict government control.

Hot Money Inflows

Another conduit whereby funds, denominated in US dollars (or other convertible currencies), get converted through the banking system into RMB and added to the forex reserves is most often referred to as 'hot money flows'. These movements are not easily traceable.

Although China's capital account remains supervised by the 'State

Administration of Foreign Exchange', such funds can sneak into the Chinese financial system by various channels, even if they do not transgress the applicable regulations. The anticipated appreciation of the RMB – a safe one-way bet in the case of China in recent years and for the immediate future – induces circumvention of the restrictions on capital movements proper. Thus the acceleration ('leading') of payments connected with exports to China, or conversely, the postponement of payments ('lagging') for imports into China, may aim to achieve more favourable conversion rates into RMB. Also the timing, or the amounts, of dividends remitted and of interest payments can be modulated so as to enlarge the funds available in RMB. In passing, and without further expanding on a related item, recently some controls on capital outflows have been softened and the RMB is even, to some extent, performing a role in international trade deals, especially with Hong Kong or East Asian countries (as explained in an IMF paper of October 2010: IMF, 2010b).

THE CURRENT ACCOUNT CONUNDRUM

Much of the debate about the 'correct' level of the RMB against major currencies concerns the current account positions of China and other countries, particularly the USA.

China's and America's Imbalances

Current account data measure the net international flows of goods and services that are composed of two subcategories whereby 'trade in goods and services' exceeds by far the other rubric of 'net current factor payments' such as dividends and remittances. As, in the Chinese case, those factor payments and receipts are so far much lower than the trade flows, and moreover were recently almost in balance, the preceding analysis of China's trade flows and of the resulting balance is relevant to a discussion in terms of current accounts.

However, there is another reason why current accounts are looked upon with keen interest by many analysts. Indeed, the current accounts provide a lens for assessing the appropriateness of forex rates between countries. Moreover, in terms of traditional macroeconomic identities, an imbalance in a country's net current account position also signals a divergence between its macroeconomic domestic gross savings vis-à-vis its gross domestic investments. Thus a country with a savings surplus normally builds up claims on the rest of the world when it makes its surplus savings available to parties in other countries. The reverse holds for a country with a deficit on its current account that is financed by funds procured from abroad. It also follows that the current account balance of a country in a given year equals a change in its net foreign assets.

The debate about the appropriate forex rate of the RMB was exacerbated in 2008 when the USA had the highest current account deficit, in absolute terms, estimated at US$673 billion, whereas China topped the league of the surplus countries with an estimated US$426 billion surplus (Monga, 2009). In terms of their respective GDPs, the deficit and the surplus stood respectively at −4.7 per cent and +9.8 per cent (ECB, 2010). The imbalance has since narrowed between the two countries, thanks to the financial crisis and the serious downfall in international trade, but further developments may show that this outcome is cyclical and reversible.

China's Record Savings Ratio

China's gross macro savings ratio to GDP reached a record rate of 59 per cent in 2008, which still outstripped the macro gross investment ratio of 49 per cent (Bank for International Settlements, 2009). It should be stressed, however, that, until the recent financial crisis, savings in China were not only generated by the household sector (in which they stood at a comparatively high level of around 20 per cent of GDP) but were amassed even more by the business sector, all subcategories included (for more details, see Ma and Yi, 2010). Thus state enterprises which survived the drastic reform and thinning of their numbers in the first years of the new century are enjoying high profit margins in an often oligopolistic market constellation. Besides, they pay almost no dividends to the state-shareholder and are often groomed by the state as national champions, called upon to flourish in international markets.

The motivations for the high savings in households are linked to the absence, so far, of a functioning social security system, particularly in the rural areas, and to the wish to provide a fruitful education to their (often sole) offspring. There are also indications that a high propensity to save is inherent in East Asian cultures. Until the recent financial tsunami, the government sector was able to generate a surplus, i.e. to finance a portion of public investments out of current public revenues. The mammoth stimulus programme to revive the economy has brought the government sector into deficit, but it is a position which has remained modest and sustainable, at −2.8 per cent of GDP in 2009 and −1.8 per cent in 2010 (World Bank's Quarterly Update, November 2010).

Conversely, the overall savings ratio in the USA stood at 12 per cent in 2008 as against 16 per cent in 2001. The huge deficits both in the current external accounts and in the public finances are covered by foreign savings, largely provided by the placement of China's forex reserves in American treasury bonds.

Paradoxically, the respective positions of China and the USA contradict the tenets of economic theory, namely that a capital-rich country should invest its current account surplus in a capital-poor country. But China is awash with capital which it is now even capable of exporting in large amounts.

Conceptual Weaknesses of the Current Account Yardsticks

The framework surrounding the dispute about the valuation of the RMB is open to some serious conceptual frailties. For one, the traditional dividing line between savings and non-savings, or consumption, is largely predicated on conventions. Savings are defined, and measured, as the subtraction of consumption outlays from income. Thus consumer durables, such as a refrigerator or car, are treated as a consumption outlay, whereas the purchase of a home is recorded as a constituent of savings, even though the motivation to acquire such goods and to set aside a portion of one's income is similar in both cases.

Besides, one can at length discuss which level of imbalance is optimal or acceptable. If all countries were achieving a zero outcome in their current account, there would be no room for the international transfer of surplus savings to countries that wish to complement their domestic savings by foreign ones. Hence, zero balances are not ideal in an open economy. Another consideration is that 'specific trade-related factors cannot by themselves explain large and sustained current account balances, which are in fact determined by many other variables, including foreign and domestic incomes, asset prices, interest rates, exchange rates' (Monga, 2009: 12). In a global financial arena, in which market participants gauge risk-adjusted returns across borders, 'global imbalances (may) become a balanced outcome of differences in potential growth rates and asset supplies' instead of being anomalous (Xafa, 2007: 17).

Finally, the impact of current account developments on the economies concerned depends essentially on the destination of the surplus or of the funds borrowed to cover the deficit. If foreign savings are availed of to strengthen the recipient country's infrastructure, even a substantial current account is much more acceptable than if the borrowing from abroad has been solicited to boost consumption – as was the case in the USA. Whereas the surplus countries such as China and the oil exporters face the question whether there are rational alternatives to the amassing of large reserves and their redeployment by way of financing deficits abroad, there may indeed be few alternatives. Finally, developing countries may rightly deem that they cannot yet allow capital account convertibility as their financial systems are still weak.

The Up-valuation of the RMB as a Cure for Imbalances?

Yet one must admit that persistent large imbalances between the USA and the EU, on the one hand, and China, on the other, tend to destabilise the world economy. This would certainly be the case, with disastrous results, if the creditors, namely China and Japan not forgetting the oil-producing countries, were no longer willing to finance the deficits of the main debtor country and no longer had confidence in the US dollar.

A crash of the American dollar would also spell disaster for China, which not only carries a huge stock of dollar assets, but also has a vested interest in the US market as an outlet for its exports. The two countries, their disagreements notwithstanding, appear condemned to coexist and seek cooperative schemes.

Obviously, one highly relevant peculiarity is that the United States enjoys the privilege of seigniorage: it can pay its debts in its own currency which, to an extent, it can create itself, whereas creditor countries, such as China, are, in the words of McKinnon (McKinnon and Schnabl, 2009) 'immature creditor countries' that cannot lend their surpluses in their own currency.

For many years to come, the US dollar, notwithstanding the terrible crisis in its financial system and the weak performance of its economy, will remain the predominant international currency in its multiple roles of invoicing currency, exchange market medium and reserve currency (Forbes, 2009).

Analysts of the present systemic balances in the world rightly recommend that each major participant should shoulder its part of the rebalancing task. This is no doubt advisable and was underwritten at the G20 Pittsburgh Summit in September 2009, and recently again at the Seoul Summit in November 2010.[8]

Whether the revaluation of the RMB would make a major contribution to a collective rebalancing exercise is nonetheless doubtful, in light of the preceding analysis. To achieve an effective impact on trade flows the up-valuation would have to be sizeable, which the Chinese leadership, engaged in a growth marathon, would not accept. Besides, facing more expensive 'made in China' goods, importers in the USA could easily switch to other suppliers, for example Vietnam. Anyhow, the widespread 'processing trade' would partially blunt the resulting price increase of China's exports when expressed in dollars, as the burden of adjustment on

Chinese exporters would largely be shifted to suppliers in adjacent countries (Ma and Van Assche, 2010). Finally, as already noticed, the Chinese export basket contains many items that no longer face competition from producers in the USA.

Another consideration is that the absence of clear indications about the equilibrium level for the forex rate in current exchange markets renders it difficult to derive a reliable yardstick. As a matter of fact, exporters from China and investors into China must deposit their forex assets in an account with a bank in China, which in turn must transform them into RMB. As one of the transacting parties thereby acts as a monopolist and, in fact, imposes the 'price' of the transaction, no genuine forex market exists in China. Moreover, in the present global financial arena, even functioning forex markets are no longer reliable gauges for forex rates that would bow to the market forces involved in international trade. Short-term non-trade transactions by powerful financial groups nowadays overwhelm the forex markets.

Hence a significant reduction in the US macro consumption ratio, accompanied by a resumption of positive savings on the one hand, and a relative inflexion of the high savings ratio in China and a move towards more consumption on the other, are advisable, although the effects of such policies will take time to materialise. In fact, these rebalancing sequences appear to be taking hold already, even without any conceivable commitments thereto at the G20 level. The deep recession in the USA, epitomised by an unprecedented unemployment rate and the steep declines in property values, render households much more prudent in their consumption behaviour, thereby dampening the recovery of the American economy. On the other hand, in China, the shift in the overall strategy decided some years ago, which aims to benefit the vast rural areas is bound to stimulate basic consumption and hence to downgrade the relative role of exports as a primary engine of growth.

In the author's view (Plasschaert, 2007), such reorientation of the Chinese development strategy away from an export-led growth path is not only economically meaningful, as it can galvanise much potential in the rural areas, but it is also socially, and hence politically, of crucial importance. As a matter of fact, the wide gap vis-à-vis the East and the urban population is deeply resented by the rural population, not primarily on account of their lower per capita income, but perhaps even more so because of their inadequate access to public health and educational facilities.

However, contrary to what Western commentators tend to project and hope for, the new strategy may not be highly instrumental in abating the very high investment ratio in Chinese rural areas. As a matter of fact, there are still large unmet investment needs, both public and private, in China's hinterland. Besides, it is too frequently overlooked that investment expenditures are equally a vector of immediate 'effective demand' with favourable capacity-enlarging effects on the economy, which consumption outlays cannot possibly claim.

Yet, a gradual revaluation of the RMB appears plausible, less because of insistence from abroad, but in the light of some solid arguments and likely developments. The renewed rapid growth carries the threat of some degree of price inflation and a higher value for the RMB would cheapen China's imports somewhat. Breaking the link with the dollar would also render monetary policy in China less dependent on US monetary parameters. Finally, in the longer run, and with the gradualism that has been a hallmark of China's remarkable growth journey, greater freedom for Chinese citizens and firms, as regards international capital transactions, is in the offing.

As argued earlier, the remodelling of the development pattern to the benefit of the rural sector can be expected to enhance consumption outlays thus reducing the sky-high savings ratio. Several influential Chinese economists are advocating for this change, to which they add worthwhile arguments. Thus, according to Justin Lin (Lin, 2009), now chief economist at the World Bank, the next steps in China's reform saga should aim to enhance the incomes of the wage-earners, who, today receive a smaller slice of GDP than some years ago. This upgrade in the relative position of labour income is now acknowledged by the leadership and appears to be underway. Moreover, it is facilitated by the overall rapid enhancement of the productivity in the Chinese economy. Another economist, Yiping Huang (2009), pleads for the liberalisation of prices in factor markets such as oil, gas and electricity, which are rather cheap and which foster high profits and associated savings in the corresponding business sectors.

ADDITIONAL SIDELINE REMARKS

This chapter has dealt with a single question, namely whether the RMB, as officially quoted by the Chinese Central Bank, should be considered as being seriously undervalued as is contended by influential circles in the USA. It reaches the conclusion that indictments of intentional manipulation of that exchange rate are poorly founded and overlook a number of specific features of the Chinese economy and financial system.

This conclusion should not be construed as implying that complaints in the USA or the EU about some policies in China or postures by Chinese authorities are groundless. Thus counterfeiting and violations of industrial property rights are rife. Public procurement practices tend to discriminate against foreign firms. Protectionism against foreign firms occurs quite often, especially at local government levels. But such and other areas of friction between China and the USA (and the EU) fall outside the parameters of this chapter.

NOTES

1. Although outward FDI indirectly generates some exports of intermediate goods and services.
2. For a detailed analysis of the value chain as regards the manufacturing of shoes in China and its impact on the competitiveness of EU firms see Kommerskollegium (2007).
3. Thus Hong Kong statistics show that in 2009 only 13 per cent of exports from Hong Kong represented 'domestic exports', the latter have been dominated since the early 1980s by the re-exports of goods produced by Hong Kong-owned firms in China. On the import side, Hong Kong represents only 9 per cent of the overall value of imports by China. This statistic highlights the rapid expansion of the capacity of Chinese harbours along its east coast.
4. A non-negligible portion of such FDI must be attributed to firms headquartered in the People's Republic of China, which 'round-tripped' their own investments through Hong Kong subsidiaries in order to benefit from tax incentives granted to foreign-invested enterprises. But recently, the tax treatment in China of foreign and domestic firms has been harmonised.
5. The international fragmentation of the production sequence also results in an artificial inflation of the overall international trade statistics, as compared to the case in which the value added towards a final product would be built up in a single country.
6. This, and other examples, are cited in the EU Trade Policy Study Group paper (2010).
7. The broader concept of 'official international reserves' also encompasses gold, SDRs and the reserve position at the IMF.
8. However, Simmons (2006), who studied previous episodes of major imbalances in international finance, is sceptical about the chances of reaching a multilateral consensus.

REFERENCES

Bank for International Settlements (2009) *79th Annual Report 2008/2009*. Basle: BIS.

EU Trade Policy Study Group (January 2010) *A Modern Trade Policy for the European Union*. Online at: http://www.ecipe.org/tpsg/A%20Modern%20Trade %20Policy%20for%20The%20European%20Union.pdf (accessed 12 January 2011).

European Central Bank (ECB) (2010) *Prospects for Real and Financial Imbalances and a Global Rebalancing*, European Central Bank Monthly Bulletin, April, pp. 91–100.

Forbes, Kristin (2009) 'Financial network effects and deepening', in Jean Pisani-Ferry and Adam Posen (eds), *The Euro at Ten. The Next Global Currency?* Wahington, DC : Brussels: Peterson Institute for International Economics, pp. 41–52.

Goldberg, Linda and Dillon, Eleonor W. (2007) 'Why a dollar depreciation may not close the U.S. trade deficit', *Current Issues in Economics and Finance*, 13 (5): 1–7.

Huang, Yiping (2009) 'Fixing China's current account surplus', *East Asia Forum*. Online at: http://www.eastasiaforum.org/2009/12/13/fixing-chinas-current-account-surplus (accessed 12 January 2011).

International Monetary Fund (2010a) *People's Republic of China: Staff Report for the 2010 Article IV Consultation*, IMF Country Report No. 10/238, July. Washington, DC. Online at: http://www.imf.org/external/pubs/ft/scr/2010/cr10238.pdf (accessed 12 January 2011).

International Monetary Fund (2010b) *Review of the Method of Valuation of the SDR*, 26 October. Online at: http://www.imf.org/external/np/pp/eng/2010/102610.pdf (accessed 12 January 2011).

Kommerskollegium – National Board of Trade (2007), *Adding Value to the European Economy*. Online at: http://www.kommers.se/upload/Analysarkiv/Arbetsomr%C3%A5den/EUs%20yttre%20handelspolitik/Addingvaluetothe Europeaneconomy.pdf (accessed 12 January 2011).

Lin, Justin Y. (2009) *Economic Development and Transition*. Cambridge: Cambridge University Press.

Ma, A. and Van Assche, A. (2010) *China's Role in Global Production Networks*, mimeo. Montreal: HEC.

Ma, Guanan and Yi, Wang (2010) *China's High Saving Rate: Myth and Reality*, Bank for International Settlements Working Paper No. 312. Basle: BIS.

McKinnon, Ronald and Schnabl, Gunther (2009) *China's Financial Conundrum and Global Imbalances*, Bank for International Settlements Working Paper No. 277. Basle: BIS.

Monga, Celestin (2009) *Hegelian Macroeconomics. The Dialectics of Global Imbalances*, World Bank Working Paper Series No. 5175. World Bank.

Naughton, Barry (2007) *The Chinese Economy. Transitions and Growth*. Cambridge, MA: MIT Press.

Plasschaert, Sylvain (2007) *China: Inzicht in zijn Doorbraak*. Leuven: Davidsfonds.

Simmons, Beth A. (February 2006) *The Future of Central Bank Cooperation*, Bank for International Settlements Working Papers n. 200, February. Basle: BIS.

World Bank (2010) *China Quarterly Update, November 2010*. Online at: *web.worldbank.org/WBSITE/EXTERNAL/COUNTRIES/EASTASIAPACIFICEXT/CHINAEXTN/0,,contentMDK:22502137~pagePK:1497618~piPK:217854~theSitePK:318950,00.html* (accessed 12 January 2011).

Xafa, Miranda (2007) *Global Imbalances and Financial Stability*, International Monetary Fund Working Paper 07/111. Washington, DC: International Monetary Fund.

10. Dynamic engagement: China's participation in international monetary institutions

Qu Bo[1]

DANGEROUS DICHOTOMY

Against the backdrop of the 2008 financial crisis, the policy choices of the Chinese government concern many observers and policymakers in developed countries. They hotly debate whether China is a status quo state (to help the US maintain the existing system) or not and the appropriate policy responses to China's rise. This kind of division is dangerous and unhelpful. It assumes that China has opposing policy positions to developed countries and attributes this difference to the nature of power transition and the type of Chinese government. This judgement ignores the fact that China as a new emerging power has interests in reforming the international institutions as well as maintaining them. It is hard to explain why China's behaviour in international institutions varies by issue area and over time. In some fields, China makes strong policy assertions, such as against the Bilateral Surveillance 2007 of the International Monetary Fund (IMF). At the same time, in other areas, China seems indifferent to these institutions: for example, China is less enthusiastic about the IMF reform before 2008. This kind of dichotomy is likely to view the relationship between China and the Untied States as a double gamble (Lampton, 2008). America has bet that China will be a responsible stakeholder in the international system and accept rather than overturn the international principles and norms as it grows in power. And China has bet that Washington will not seek to systematically frustrate the development of China. 'These "bets" have been placed not only by the leadership of each country but by their middle classes and societal organizations as well, and the stakes are high' (Lampton, 2008: 274).

But the problem actually is not whether China would change the international institutions or whether the international institutions and their developed founding countries would 'tame' China. The problem is how to understand the formation of Chinese policy toward the international institutions. Has China attempted to or successfully altered, more or less, the international norms and rules? If so, on what terms and how has China responded to the international institutions? What factors affect China's preferences and policies toward the international institutions?

This chapter uses the example of China's participation in the international monetary institutions to illustrate the process and driving forces in China's policy formation. The paper argues that China's preferences toward the international monetary institutions are the function of its domestic reform process and rationale. In particular, the paper explores the conditions under which China would accept international norms and rules, as well as the conditions under which it would tend to propose its own agenda.

The chapter begins with the argument that the domestic reform process and rationality are key factors needed to understand Chinese reactions to the international monetary institutions. In the subsequent section, the analysis of three cases shows the conditions under which China accepts the international norms and rules and the factors that affect the terms of China's reform demands. The concluding section discusses the implication of understanding China's post-crisis behaviour towards international monetary cooperation.

DOMESTIC REFORM AND INTERNATIONAL PARTICIPATION

China's participation in the international economic institutions is a function of the process and dynamics of its domestic reform. The way in which China's reform has unfolded gives Chinese leaders lessons in how to integrate into international institutions. From China's own reform process and characteristics, it will be more helpful to explore the conditions under which China will accept international norms and to estimate the demands China will probably propose due to its economic growth. A small amount of existing research has already paid attention to the domestic political dimension. For example, Susan Shirk (1993, 1996) points out that the leadership competition within the Communist Party of China (CPC) is the source of policy innovation. The following section summarises the process, characteristics and dynamics of China's reform, and recognises those factors affecting China's behaviour in international economic institutions.

THE PROCESS AND CHARACTERISTICS OF CHINA'S REFORM

China's economic reform is seen differently from the big bang which took place in East European countries, and is a process of propagation in which regions and sectors reform one after another. In general, there are at least three characteristics of China's reform process (Wu, 2005; Naughton, 1995, 2007).

First, the reform began without a blueprint. There was no carefully plotted reform strategy. China's reform did not pursue an ideal or pre-designed framework or timetable. In the initial phase of reform, Chinese leaders just had some sort of general picture and simple objectives: to double the size of the national economy at the end of the twentieth century and to realise middle income levels by the middle of the twenty-first century. But there were no strategies designed to achieve these objectives. Deng Xiaoping describes the reform process as 'crossing the river by groping stones'. With no blueprint, the promotion of experimentation is the specific pattern of how China pushed its reform forward.

Second, the reform process is mainly driven by the specific problems during the transition. China has designed many interim institutional arrangements. The dual-track system is to ensure the survival and development of non-traditional sectors and actors in the command economy system. In a planned economy, almost all capital and materials are allocated by administrative order. But when non-state enterprises developed, central government needed to design special institutional arrangements to ensure that these economic actors were able to access resources and foreign currencies. Thereby, at the beginning of the reform, the dual-track price system and foreign exchange system appeared. The dual-track system played a positive role in the rapid development of non-state sectors and the smooth transformation from a centrally planned economy to a socialist market economy. The Chinese leaders adopted new institutional arrangements by practice and when facing specific problems in the reform process. The central government takes responsibility for identifying problems and making policy choices. For Chinese leaders, reform is a process of self-promotion and development during complex international and domestic challenges.

Third, China's reform is incremental. After the experiment with increased enterprise autonomy failed, China adopted some patch-up measures to keep the state sector running and switched its main efforts to non-state sectors for new growth. This strategy is called incremental reform (Wu, 2005: 57). Incremental reform means that the reform does not deal with the redistribution of asset stocks during the initial phase but focuses on using market mechanisms to allocate the incremental asset.

Moreover, the reform process was gradual. China's reform process took on expansive characteristics: from the agricultural sector to the industrial sector, from rural to urban areas, from special economic zones to coastal provinces and then to all regions, from non-state enterprises to state-owned enterprises, and from tax and fiscal to financial and trade liberalisation, etc.

China's behaviour in the international economic institutions is influenced by these reform characteristics. Firstly, China has no clear and definite picture for the reform and restructuring of international institutions as is the case for its domestic reform process. Secondly, China's demands to international institutions unfold on the basis of domestic reform. When domestic reform requires more participation in the international institutions, China's choices are aimed at helping achieve domestic reform objectives. Thirdly, Chinese leaders try to actively identify the challenges in the international arena, and then make decisions about whether to accept international norms and rules. Finally, China will insist on an incremental approach when proposing its requirements for reform to the international institutions.

THE DYNAMICS OF CHINESE REFORM

For those concerned by China's rise, there is uncertainty about the future Chinese reform. Will China continue its economic reform? Is it possible that China will reverse its reform process? Will China accept international principles, norms and rules, or overturn them? For the pessimistic observers, there is a high risk that China will face serious challenges in deepening its reform because of its domestic political conflicts and authoritarian regime type. But the optimistic observers believe that the reform process is hardly reversible. The internal logic of how reform has unfolded creates autonomous momentum for pushing reform forward. This dynamic is relevant to what China will become and what Chinese preferences toward the international institutions could be.

In the late 1980s, China experienced economic and political disturbances. Against this background, Harold Jacobson and Michel Oksenberg (1990: ix) predicted that the process of Chinese participation in international institutions would be 'more protracted, more difficult, and more internally divisive than in the early and mid-1980s', because its domestic political situation became more conservative. However, when Deng Xiaoping made his famous Southern journey speeches on reform and socialist market economics in early 1992, the reform and opening-up policy regained momentum. In 1992, the 14th National Congress of the

CPC set forth the reform target of establishing a socialist market economy. These speeches and decisions marked a new stage in China's reform.

Some economists argue that China's gradual reform is irreversible because of the internal logical sequence (Lin et al., 1994: 246–66). They emphasise the path-dependence effects. When China adopted initial reform steps, the macroeconomic planned system could not accommodate the new non-state sectors, market-oriented micro-management and a resources allocation system. As a consequence of these changes, decentralisation and part marketisation made the reform process irreversible. From a political economy perspective, Gabriella Montinola et al. (1995) argue that the special federalism provides political foundations for China's economic reform. This kind of market-preserving federalism has made the Chinese reform process hard, if not impossible, to reverse. They believe this institutional change will guarantee the reform moves forward. Li, Junru (2007: 29–30), an official Chinese theorist, holds similar arguments about the irreversible process of reform. He believes the logical sequence of reform will deepen and promote political development.

Here, the author of this chapter argues that China has made a series of political institutional adjustments and explains how these adjustments protect the whole reform and reduce opportunities to organise anti-reform coalitions. These institutional reforms are more important than the so-called Chinese-style federalism or merely economic logic. These adjustments have two aspects: the restructuring of the highest decision-making institutions and a series of 'administrative system reforms'. With these adjustments the pro-reform leaders and bureaucrats are empowered.

THE HYPOTHESES

To construct the argument that China's participation in international economic institutions is a function of the processes and dynamics of its domestic reform, the author draws on a number of hypotheses to explain how domestic reform affects China's international behaviour.

When domestic reform policy conforms with international principles and norms, China is likely to accept these principles and norms; when the rules and decision-making procedures of international institutions are restructured in a way which constrains the autonomy of ongoing domestic policies, China is likely to oppose these reforms. The Chinese government will adopt its reform policy based on the domestic and international situations and China is likely to insist on incremental and gradual reform of the international economic institutions.

In the following section three cases on China's participation in international monetary cooperation are selected to illustrate the process and rationale behind China's behaviour. The first case concerns China's convertibility of its current account in 1996, by which the logic of Chinese acceptance of international norms is shown clearly. The second case shows the conditions under which China will oppose efforts to reform the international economic institutions. The third case is about China's policy choices after the 2008 financial crisis so as to show the logic underlying these decisions. Through this case, the chapter attempts to provide some insight into the way in which China could influence the international monetary institutions.

THE REALISATION OF CURRENT ACCOUNT CONVERTIBILITY

The initial engagement between China and the IMF was seen as successful for both sides (Jacobson and Oksenberg, 1990: 57–9). Some researchers underscore the role the IMF played in China's reform process. For this perspective, the interaction between China and the Fund was much like a learning process for Chinese authorities, with the Fund exporting its expertise and providing technical assistance. But the reality seemed much more complicated. In 1980, China introduced an internal settlement rate on foreign exchange without notification of the IMF. Before 1994, China had adopted a dual-track system of foreign exchange. In 1996, China finally realised its current account convertibility. What were the real reasons which pushed China to conduct foreign exchange, banking and financial sector reform? Under what conditions did China accept the norm of current account convertibility?

China participated in the Fund and the World Bank in 1980 and notified the Fund it would realise current account convertibility, which means removing restrictions on current international payments and transfers. However, China took 16 years to fulfil its commitment to current account convertibility. During the period, China made various institutional adjustments in order to adapt to the consequences of domestic reform. The process of China's acceptance of Article VIII is a clear example which shows the conditions under which China would accept international norms and rules.

THE PROCESS OF INSTITUTIONAL ADJUSTMENT

When it adopted opening-up and reform policies after the Third Plenary Session of the 11th Central Committee of the Communist Party of China (CCCPC) in December 1978, China had to reform and restructure its government processes to respond to the pressures and challenges released by the reform. The administrative decentralisation in the initial reform phase led to increasing economic activities among new actors and in new sectors. And the Chinese authorities made a series of institutional adjustments, some of which were interim and others of which conformed to market principles. These reforms laid the foundation for the realisation of current account convertibility. There were two major reforms of banking and foreign exchange management institutions related to current account convertibility.

The banking and financial institutions of China's planned economy were not able to adapt to the administrative and economic decentralisation which occurred in the late 1970s. As long as the allocation of capital was determined by a central planner in the form of fiscal appropriations, state-owned enterprises were the sole form of production unit and the banks were the only form of financial intermediary the planned financial system could sustain. But when the right of collectives in rural areas to self-management was reaffirmed by the central government and agricultural procurement prices increased, the monetary activities around agriculture expanded; when non-state enterprises and commercial enterprises were allowed and encouraged, the financial demands of these sectors emerged and strengthened; and when the state-owned enterprises got more autonomous decision-making power, the People's Bank of China (PBC) had to streamline and design its loan policies. The banking sector's institutional adjustments were coincidently in accordance with the principles and norms of a market economy.

In the context of a planned economy, the PBC was the only bank in China.[2] With further reform, the PBC evolved to exclusively have the functions of a central bank. The first step was to separate commercial financial business from the PBC. In September 1983, the State Council decreed *The Decision Regarding the PBC Exclusively Playing the Role of the Central Bank*. According to this decision, the PBC as an administrative institution would exclusively handle the problems of financial regulation and enacting and implementing monetary policies. In 1995, *The People's Bank of China Law* was enacted and implemented, which formally and legally established the PBC as the central bank.

China's commercial banks emerged from the functional transformation of the PBC. Since 1979, the Agricultural Bank of China (ABC), Bank of China and the (People's) Construction Bank of China (CBC) have successively separated from the PBC to serve agricultural production, foreign exchange management and business investment financing, respectively. In 1983, the State Council decided to establish the Industrial and Commercial Bank of China with which to support industrial development. The establishment of commercial banks reflected general Chinese economic reform, from agriculture, foreign exchange and investment financing to industrial and commercial sectors. Since 1986, the Chinese authorities allowed the big four state-owned banks to cross their traditionally defined division of sectors when conducting their business. At the same time, the State Council approved the entrance of commercial banks and a number of joint-venture commercial banks were set up.[3]

The second major reform related to current account convertibility was that of foreign exchange management. Since 1949, China has successively chosen a self-seclusion development strategy (1949–71, including an interlude between 1950 and 1960 during which China built close economic relations with the USSR) and an import substitution strategy (1972–78). And China has suffered with a shortage of foreign exchange for a long time. Against this background, Chinese policy was strict control of foreign exchange. The Chinese authorities required that all foreign exchange earned from exports be surrendered at the official exchange rate and allocated the foreign exchange rates according to administrative order. Overvalued Chinese currency (renminbi or RMB) resulted in importers having an advantage over exporters. When China opened its doors, the foreign trade priority was to solve the shortage of foreign exchange. In 1979, the State Council passed *Some Rules Regarding Greatly Developed Foreign Trade and Increased Foreign Exchange*, by which a new internal settlement foreign exchange rate was created and would be implemented as of 1981. This decision actually devalued the renminbi.

At the same time, in order to encourage enterprises to export and build foreign exchange, the Chinese authorities introduced a foreign exchange retention arrangement, meaning that enterprises could keep a share of foreign earnings. The foreign exchange retention system could be used for enterprises' imports or sold on the swap market. With the growth of foreign trade and the increasing size of the swap market, the Chinese authorities gradually devalued the RMB and the gap between the official and swap market foreign exchange rate decreased. By 1993, 80 per cent of foreign trade was settled at the swap market price. In 1993, at the Third Plenary Session of the 14th CCCPC it was presented that the Chinese government would create the conditions to realise the convertibility of the renminbi. The results of previous policy choices and institutional adjustments made it possible and necessary to unify the official and swap market foreign exchange rate. From January 1994, China adopted a new foreign exchange rate management system introducing: a unified, managed floating foreign exchange rate regime; a system of exchange settlement and sale to replace foreign exchange retention; the establishment of a foreign exchange market mainly through banks; and the abolition of the command order for the allocation of foreign exchange (prior to 1994, all foreign exchange earnings were allocated by quotas). These developments laid the foundation for current account convertibility. Soon after, China notified the IMF that it would accept the IMF's Article VIII and realise current account convertibility as of 1 December 1996.

It is true that China's acceptance of the IMF's Article VIII (norms to realise current account convertibility) was the result of persuasion by the IMF and other organisations. Some scholars note that the IMF had played a critical role at certain junctures (Jacobson and Oksenberg, 1990). But the process of current account convertibility realisation shows a much more complicated policy landscape. Domestic economic decentralisation and corresponding institutional adjustments were the driving force for China's realisation of current account convertibility. The final commitment to Article VIII was the result of the prior institutional adjustments and reflected China's domestic reform's demands.

AGAINST THE 2007 DECISION ON BILATERAL SURVEILLANCE

Surveillance is one of the core functions of the IMF. There are two aspects to surveillance: bilateral surveillance, which evaluates the exchange rate policies of individual member countries; and multilateral surveillance, which monitors the world economy and financial stability. The task of bilateral surveillance is to evaluate whether the exchange policies of individual member states are consistent not only with its own interests but also with the interests of the international financial system. IMF surveillance is based in law on Article IV of the Fund's Articles of Agreement and the 1977 Decision on Surveillance over Exchange Rate Policies.

Article IV is naturally in favour of industrialised countries which have adopted a floating foreign exchange rate regime. It legalises the market-driven exchange rate fluctuations. Thus, it actually benefits those countries which have adopted a floating exchange rate regime as regards the obligations of Article IV, especially when the surveillance focuses on foreign exchange rates. On the contrary, countries which still maintain a fixed exchange rate regime are in a disadvantageous position in the Fund's surveillance framework, as the term external stability implies that the exchange rate and balance of payments flows are two sides of the same coin.

When Mr Rodrigo de Rato came into office as the new IMF Managing Director in 2005, he launched a strategic review to consider how to reform and restructure the Fund and make the Fund relevant to globalisation. After research and discussion, de Rato proposed a medium-term reform strategy. One of the core points was to strengthen the Fund's surveillance. Later, the IMF Executive Board approved a new Decision of Bilateral Surveillance in 2007.

The 2007 Surveillance Decision introduced the concept of external stability as the bilateral surveillance principle which is about the imbalance of current and capital accounts. Moreover, the decision clearly defines exchange rate manipulation. Under the 2007 Surveillance Decision, the foreign exchange rate becomes the core surveillance objective. Meanwhile, the 2007 Decision depreciates the position of members with fixed exchange rate polices. These countries shoulder the major burden of having to adjust their foreign exchange rate policies when confronting trade imbalance problems. On the contrary, the floating exchange rate countries have much more autonomy, for their exchange rates are determined by the market.

China has strongly opposed the 2007 Surveillance Decision. As Deputy Governor of the PBC Hu Xiaolian puts it, 'in strengthening surveillance, the Fund should be realistic and not overestimate the role of exchange rates. Biased advice would damage the Fund's role in safeguarding global economic and financial stability' (IMF, 2007: 104). Even after the 2007 Decision was passed, China continued its opposition. At the International Monetary and Financial Committee (IMFC) meeting in 2009, Deputy Governor of the PBC Yi Gang said 'the 2007 Decision distracted the attention of the Fund and the international community from the real systemic risks, and delayed policy responses . . . We call for a timely and thorough review of the 2007 Decision in order to avoid a recurrence of past mistakes' (Yi, 2009: 3). It is obvious that China is worried that the 2007 Decision could be used against it.

In essence, China supports the strengthening of IMF surveillance, especially after the Asian financial crisis in 1997, and it is willing to solve the global imbalance as well. So, why has China opposed the 2007 Bilateral Surveillance? What factors could help explain China's preference for stability of exchange rate policy? First, Chinese officials have a different explanation for the prerequisites of maintaining the stability of international monetary relations. They tend to separate the trade surplus from the exchange rate policies. Chinese officials argue currency appreciation may not rebalance international trade. The examples of Japan and Germany already demonstrate this point. China would like to solve trade imbalances by other measures rather than with a floating exchange rate or the appreciation of the RMB.

Moreover, China insists that the focus of surveillance should be the industrialised countries' macroeconomic policies and short-term capital flows. From China's perspective, these are the potential risks to the stability of the international monetary system. Thus, the main mandate of the Fund should be to maintain international financial stability and stable foreign exchange rates among industrialised countries. At almost every International Monetary and Financial Committee (IMFC), Chinese representatives have emphasised that the IMF should monitor capital flows and enhance surveillance over the major industrialised countries.

CHINA'S CHOICE AFTER THE FINANCIAL CRISIS

China's economic growth stands out in the context of the financial crisis. The industrialised countries have agreed to allocate more quotas of the IMF and the World Bank in order to better reflect the contemporary realities of economic power. China, with other new emerging powers such as Brazil, India and Russia, has played a great role in the recent global political efforts to regenerate economic momentum. These developments have intensified some observers' anxieties about China's threat or challenge to the international institutions. For China, on the one hand it gets more of a voice in the international economic institutions, but on the other it is also confronted with much stronger pressure to restructure and transform its policies and institutions. What are the implications of the financial crisis for China? Is it an opportunity for China to rise as a global power or not? What will China probably do to respond to the consequences of the financial crisis?

In retrospect, three important events have heavily influenced China's engagement in international monetary cooperation: the Asian financial crisis in 1997; China's entry to the World Trade Organization (WTO) in 2001; and the financial crisis of 2008. As discussed in the previous section, one of the main functions of the CPC is to identify the problems relevant to Chinese economic development and to figure out solutions to these problems. These three events made Chinese authorities redefine the problems and challenges of globalisation. The Asian financial crisis prevented China from realising capital account convertibility. The commitment to the WTO to open financial sectors led to reform of the banking and financial institutions. And the 2008 financial crisis will accelerate the speed of making the RMB convertible and of financial sector restructuring. The rationale and process of domestic reform will make China's transformation conform to international principles and norms.

The Asian financial crisis of 1997 impeded China from achieving capital account convertibility, but promoted financial sector reform. China has tried to realise capital account convertibility, but the 1997 Asian financial crisis altered China's policy preference. In their statement to an annual meeting of the IMF, Chinese representatives expressed that capital account convertibility should be carried out in an orderly and well sequenced manner. Furthermore, the financial crisis prompted the Chinese government to accelerate its financial reforms. In 1997, a National Financial Working Meeting was held for the first time.[4] The working meeting is a form of political mobilisation, by which the CPC coordinates and informs high-level leaders to ensure compliance with the Party's policy priorities. Thus the Chinese authorities adopted a series of reforms to invigorate the banks and financial institutions. First, measures had been taken to enhance the authority of the central bank. Second, the functions of financial supervision and insurance supervision were separated from the central bank and the Securities Regulatory Commission and the Insurance Regulatory Commission were created. Third, the Ministry of Finance issued bonds worth 270 billion RMB to increase capital for the commercial banks. In 1999, four financial asset management companies were set up in order to purchase and deal with bad loans from the big four state-owned banks. As a result of the reform, the main banks' capital adequacy ratio was over 8 per cent.

China's accession to the WTO in 2001 was another major driving force of financial sector reforms. Facing the pressure of gradually opening up the financial sector over five years, the Second National Financial Working Meeting was held in 2002. The threefold purpose of the meeting was to enhance the competitive capacities of the financial sector, to strengthen supervision capacity and to promote the financial market. To these ends, the Chinese government first adopted measures to transform the state-owned commercial banks into joint-stock banks and then listed them on the stock exchange. Second, the Bank Supervision Commission was established in 2003. Third, the authority and level of the central bank was promoted further. The Third National Financial Working Meeting of 2007 focused on the exchange rate and foreign reserves. China's reform is a continuous reformulation process adapting to changing international and domestic circumstances. The government goals for financial reform evolved continually as economic reform deepened. The accession to the

WTO was a strong driving force which led China to establish its market-oriented preference for financial system reform.

China has responded to prior shocks along similar lines. The 2008 financial crisis made the Chinese government consider conducting further and deeper domestic reform as well. This is the Chinese style when confronting new challenges. While China complains about the weakness of the existing international monetary arrangements, it will adapt instinctively to weakness with domestic reforms.

The ongoing financial crisis has tended to increase China's voice in the international economic institutions. At the same time, it also poses great challenges, including appreciation of the RMB, trade protectionism and threats to China's financial security. In this controversial context, China resumed discussion about the direction of international monetary arrangements and the reform strategy China should undertake. Chinese authorities will adapt to the changing international and domestic environment when designing its agenda for further reform and formulating its preferences for international monetary cooperation.

INTERNATIONALISATION OF THE RMB OR THE ASIAN MONETARY COOPERATION MECHANISM

The financial crisis exposed the weakness of the existing international monetary arrangements. The non-reserve currency countries are disadvantaged in the international monetary system. Such countries have to accumulate reserve currencies and the value of the reserve is influenced by the reserve currency country's monetary policy. Chinese scholars and policymakers are discussing two policy options to respond to the problem. Some scholars argue that China should learn from the European monetary cooperation experience to establish an Asian monetary cooperation mechanism. They note that Asian monetary cooperation already has a good basis which has developed since the Asian financial crisis in 1997. Others emphasise the importance of diversification of international currencies and argue that China should accelerate its speed to internationalise the RMB. The final objective of China's financial reform is to transform the RMB into one of the key international currencies. No matter which approach prevails, China is likely to promote its financial reforms and gradually achieve a modern, flexible and competitive financial system in the next ten years. Specifically, there is a great possibility China will realise capital account convertibility, achieve RMB convertibility, adopt a more flexible foreign exchange rate and build up Shanghai as an Asian, or even international, financial centre.

China acknowledges the importance of reforming the international monetary system, but feels that the existing reform efforts overlook systematic vulnerability. For China, it would be better to strengthen its own capacity through further domestic reform than to depend on protracted and controversial reforms to the existing international monetary system.

CONCLUDING REMARKS

The rationale and process of Chinese domestic reform affect its participation in the international economic institutions. It is true that China is learning how to cope with the international institutions by practice. Only when the institutions' recommendations are compatible with its internal reform direction will China be easily able to accept these norms and rules. The domestic reform rationale and process can better explain why China participated in the international institutions in the first place and how its participation will unfold in the future.

Moreover, China sees itself as a transition economy. The reform is a process of self-development and self-promotion. This identity is helpful for China to accept the international norms and rules. Finally, though China has had no Western-style democratisation until now, the market-oriented reform is likely to proceed. Throughout its reform process, China has adopted a series of institutional adjustments which provide the basis for further pro-market reform. Such domestic explanations complement a structural analysis of China's strategies.

NOTES

1. I am grateful to Robert Keohane and Ngaire Woods. Thanks also to Helen Milner and Rosemary Foot for their helpful and constructive comments.
2. By name, there were also the People's Construction Bank of China, the Agricultural Bank of China and Bank of China, but these were actually directly or indirectly affiliated to the PBC. During 1969–78, the PBC was integrated into the Department of Finance.
3. Besides these banks, there are medium-sized and many local banks in China, such as rural credit cooperatives, rural commercial banks, urban credit cooperatives, postal savings banks, etc. At the same time, a few foreign-funded financial institutions operated in China.
4. The national working meeting or the central working meeting focusing on a specific issue area is the highest-level meeting in certain issue areas. In general, it consists of members of the Central Committee of the CPC, including the Politburo members, ministers of the state council, secretaries of provincial committees of the CPC and governors of provinces. The Central Economic Working Meeting and Agriculture Working Meeting convene every year. The working meetings on other issue areas will convene according to the decision of the central committee or the Politburo.

REFERENCES

Dai, Xianglong (2009) 'Retrospect review of several critical financial decision-makings' ('Ruogan zhongda jinrong juce de huigu'), *China's Finance*, 19: 24–6.

Frieden, Jeffry (1991) 'Invested interest: the politics of nation economic policies in a world of global finance', *International Organization*, 45 (1): 425–51.

Goldstein, Morris and Lardy, Nicholas (eds) (2008) *Debating China's Exchange Rate Policy*. Washington, DC: Peterson Institute for International Economics.

Goldstein, Morris and Lardy, Nicholas (2009) *The Future of China's Exchange Rate Policy*. Washington, DC: Peterson Institute for International Economics.

IMF (2007) *IMF Survey*. Washington, DC: IMF.

Jacobson, Harold and Oksenberg, Michel (1990) *China's Participation in the IMF, the World Bank, and GATT*. Ann Arbor, MI: University of Michigan Press.

Johnston, Alastair Iain (1998) *Cultural Realism: Strategic Culture and Grand Strategy in Chinese History*. Princeton, NJ: Princeton University Press.

Johnston, Alastair Iain (2003), 'Is China a status quo power?', *International Security*, 27 (4): 5–56.

Johnston, Alastair Iain (2007) *Social States: China in International Institutions, 1980–2000*. Princeton: Princeton University Press.

Keohane, Robert (1984) *After Hegemony: Cooperation and Discord in the World Political Economy*. Princeton, NJ: Princeton University Press.

Kim, Samuel (ed.) (1998) *China and the World: Chinese Foreign Policy Faces the New Millennium*. Boulder, CO: Westview Press.

Kugler, Jacek (2006) 'The Asian accent: opportunity for peace or precondition for war?', *International Studies Perspectives*, 17 (1): 36–42.

Laffont, Jean-Jacques and Qian, Yingyi (1999) 'The dynamics of reform and development in China: a political economy perspective', *European Economic Review*, 43 (4–6): 1085–94.

Lampton, David (2008) *The Three Faces of Chinese Power: Might, Money, and Minds*. Berkley, CA: University of California Press.

Lardy, Nicholas (1994) *China in the World Economy*. Washington, DC: Institute for International Economics.

Li, Junru (2007) *Contemporary China's Political Trend* (*Dangdai Zhongguo Zhengzhi Zouxiang*). Fuzhou: Fujian Renmin Press.

Lin, Yifu, Cai, Fang and Li, Zhou (1994) *China's Miracle: Development Strategy and Economic Growth* (*Zhongguo De Qiji*). Shanghai: Shanghai Sanlian Publishing House.

Montinola, G., Qian, Yingyi and Weingast, B. (1995) 'Federalism, Chinese style: the political basis for economic success in China', *World Politics*, 48 (1): 50–81.

Naughton, Barry (1995) *Growing Out of the Plan: Chinese Economic Reform, 1978–1993*. Cambridge: Cambridge University Press.

Naughton, Barry (2007) *The Chinese Economy: Transitions and Growth*. Cambridge, MA: MIT Press.

Rodrik, Dani (1996) 'Understanding economic policy reform', *Journal of Economic Literature*, 34 (1): 9–41.

Shirk, Susan (1993) *The Political Logic of Economic Reform in China*. Berkeley, CA: University of California Press.

Shirk, Susan (1996) 'Internationalization and China's economic reform', in Robert Keohane and Helen Milner (eds), *Internationalization and Domestic Politics*. Cambridge: Cambridge University Press, pp. 186–208.

Tsou, Tang (1994) *Twentieth Century Chinese Politics (Er'shi Shiji Zhongguo Zhengzhi)*. Hong Kong: Oxford University Press.

Weingast, Barry (1995) 'The economic role of political institutions: market-preserving federalism and economic growth', *Journal of Law, Economics and Organization*, 11 (1): 1–31.

Woods, Ngaire (2007) *The Globalizers: The IMF, the World Bank, and Their Borrowers*. Ithaca, NY: Cornell University Press.

Wu, Jinglian (2005) *Understanding and Interpreting Chinese Economic Reform*. Mason, OH: Thomson/South-Western.

Yi, Gang (2009) 'Statement at the Twentieth Meeting of the IMFC in Istanbul'. Online at: www.pbc.gov.cn/publish/english/956/2009/20091229123244738531637/20091229123244738531637_.html (accessed 14 January 2011).

PART 4

Climate change and energy

11. Global climate governance and the energy challenge: European and Chinese perspectives

David Belis and Simon Schunz

Faced with the rise of emerging economies such as Brazil, India and – particularly – China, the geopolitical and economic world order previously dominated by developed countries is being restructured. Two central, interrelated areas of global governance are especially influenced by this development: global climate change, widely recognised as one of the crucial challenges of our time, and the energy challenge, i.e. the task of transforming and finding sustainable pathways that will provide the energy needs for societies world-wide (Goldthau and Witte, 2010; Intergovernmental Panel on Climate Change, 2007; OECD, 2009).

This part of the book is dedicated to climate and energy governance in China and the European Union (EU), EU–China climate and energy relations and the evolving role of both actors in the global governance of climate change and energy issues. Different aspects are highlighted such as the various policy frameworks on climate change and energy in China and the EU and the specific role of the Clean Development Mechanism in EU–China relations, and there is a reflection on future energy security for China, Europe and the world at large.

The present, introductory chapter aims to identify some of the major challenges and recent developments in the field of global climate and energy governance, with a particular focus on the role of China and the EU. Emphasis will first be placed on the material realities in terms of energy needs and climate change in both China and the EU as well as on a discussion of their domestic policy responses. Subsequently, the global, multi-level and bilateral-level policymaking on climate change and energy will briefly be discussed and linked to the different contributions in this part of the book.

MATERIAL REALITIES AND POLICY RESPONSES IN CHINA AND EUROPE

The European Union and China face a twin crisis which they partly – albeit to varying degrees – contributed to and they will both bear the consequences. This crisis consists of (1) potentially devastating, human-induced climate change and (2) the energy challenge: an escalating dependence on and need to secure the provision of imported and finite energy sources.

Climate change, caused by current and historical emissions of greenhouse gases (GHG), has not been halted by the emergence of a United Nations (UN) climate regime in recent decades. As a result, trends such as the rise of the global mean temperature by around 0.75°C between 1906 and 2005 are bound to continue (Intergovernmental Panel on Climate Change, 2007: 2–4). The effects of these trends can already be felt across the planet in the form of changed weather patterns, which are impacting on human living conditions in various ways and sparking concerns about the possibly 'abrupt or irreversible' consequences of climate change (Intergovernmental Panel on Climate Change, 2007: 7–13).

Climate change is inextricably linked to the energy challenge: the combustion of fossil fuels is one of its major causes and needs to be seriously curtailed to attenuate future devastating climate impacts. Simultaneously, societies worldwide seem to be in dire need of ever-increasing amounts of energy to sustain their economies. For emerging economies and developing countries, it is especially the current shortage of energy supply that constitutes a major challenge, while for developed countries the dependence on external sources turns out to be most problematic. Urgent action is thus needed to set the world on a socio-economic development path that takes the limits of its current system of (energy) consumption and production into account (International Energy Agency, 2010; Meadows et al., 1972).

From a historical perspective, developed or OECD (Organisation for Economic Cooperation and Development) member countries, including the United States, Japan and various EU member states, are the world's major energy consumers and greenhouse gas emitters.

Table 11.1 shows that the US and the EU alone have contributed more than half (50.27 per cent) of total cumulative GHG emissions since 1950.[1] More importantly, per capita emissions in the industrialised world are also much higher than in developing and emerging countries. Even though China has overtaken the US as the most important GHG emitter in recent years, its per capita emissions are currently only half of those of the EU and a quarter of those of the US. The share of Chinese emissions

Table 11.1 Current and historical GHG emissions

	Share of global emissions (2005, CO_2eq)	Per capita emissions (2005, tCO_2eq)	Cumulative share of global emissions (1950–2005, CO_2eq)
EU	13.86%	10.1	23.8%
China	19.13%	5.5	10.90%
India	4.92%	1.7	2.64%
US	18.29%	23.4	26.47%

Source: World Resources Institute (2011).

continues, however, to rise at a breathtaking speed. Induced by China's fixed investment and export-driven economic boom in recent years, and especially since the latest round of economic reforms in the late 1990s (Akyuz, 2010; Zhu, 2011), emissions have increased heavily. In 2009, China emitted close to 8 billion tonnes of CO_2, up from 3 billion tonnes a decade earlier (see Figure 11.1).

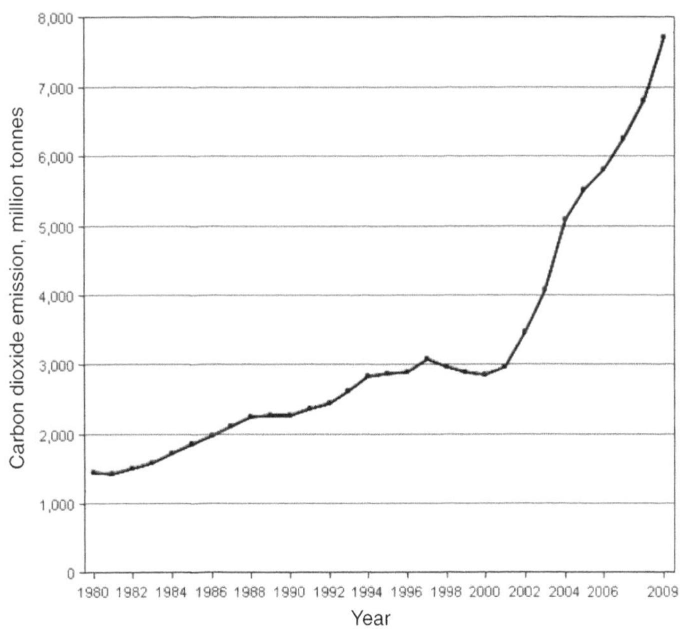

Source: Adapted from Energy Information Administration (2010).

Figure 11.1 Carbon dioxide emissions in China (1980–2009)

The rise of emissions in China is directly related to its booming energy demand. The International Energy Agency (IEA) calculated that China overtook the United States as the world's largest energy consumer in 2009. Total primary energy demand in China that year rose to more than 2.2 billion tonnes of oil equivalent (toe) versus 2.1 billion tonnes in the US. China's energy demand doubled in just ten years: total energy demand in 2000 stood at just over 1 billion toe (International Energy Agency, 2010). What is even more problematic, from a climate change perspective, is that between 60 and 70 per cent of Chinese energy generation relies on coal. It

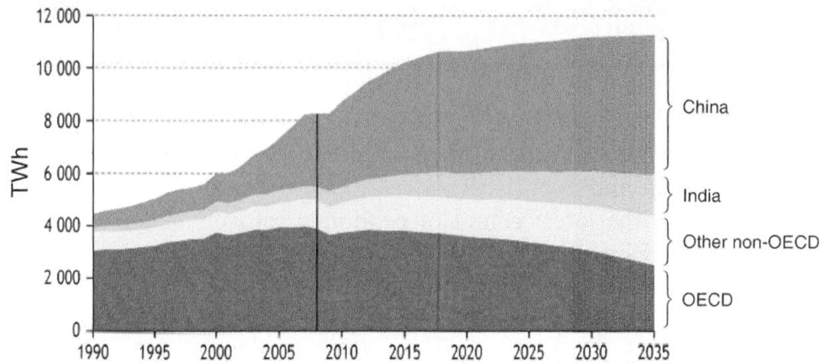

Source: International Energy Agency (2010).

Figure 11.2 Coal-fired electricity production by region

is precisely China's exploding coal use and coal-fired electricity production that adds to its rising contribution to climate change (see Figures 11.1 and 11.2; Yang, 2009).

The major increase in China's coal-fired electricity production offsets the projected drop in this area in OECD countries, as calculated by the IEA (Figure 11.2). Without measures to tackle unsustainable energy production both in the developed world and in emerging economies such as China and India, there is therefore little chance to achieve the targets set in the Copenhagen and Cancun climate deals of staying below a rise of 2°C (or even 1.5°C) compared to pre-industrial temperature levels (United Nations Environment Programme, 2010; International Energy Agency, 2010).

During the 2009 Copenhagen and 2010 Cancun climate summits, China promised to voluntarily reduce the amount of carbon emitted per unit of GDP by 40 to 45 per cent in 2020 based on 2005 levels – a step in the right direction, from a climate mitigation perspective, but far from sufficient in view of its rising CO_2 emissions. The target is, moreover, not as ambitious as it seems: it will most likely be reached by extending the previously existing energy efficiency targets. It is also a *relative* target, meaning that under the assumption of continued economic growth, absolute emissions would continue to rise.

The European Union is in a similar situation. Although member states had by 2009 already reduced domestic emissions by 17.3 per cent below 1990 levels, a reduction of 25–40 per cent in developed country emissions by 2020 and of 80–95 per cent by 2050 is required to remain below the 2°C warming limit (Intergovernmental Panel on Climate Change, 2007). The EU's current 20 per cent by 2020 target is thus well within reach. Heated debates are currently being held about whether it should be upgraded, however, to meet at least the minimum scientific requirements (European Commission, 2011; Climate Action Network Europe, 2010). A recent study on the carbon footprint of European countries, moreover, shows that the EU has actually exported a major part of its emissions reduction to emerging and developing countries, including China, by moving energy-intensive manufacturing abroad and importing the final products. The study estimates that the EU-15 had actually *increased* its carbon footprint by 47 per cent between 1990 and 2006, when taking consumption into account (Brinkley and Less, 2010). Interestingly, the study concludes that '[i]n 1990, net carbon flows embedded in trade were an insignificant proportion of global carbon emissions, *but have grown substantially since, and particularly sharply since around 2002*' (Brinkley and Less, 2010: 15, emphasis added). Viewed from the perspective of overall carbon impact, Europe's responsibility is thus much larger than commonly acknowledged. At the same time, however, there exists a complicated entanglement between Europe's emissions and global economic growth, and Chinese economic growth in particular.

The interplay between over-consumption in the West and export and investment-oriented economic growth in emerging economies is a problem that has been largely neglected in the climate debate thus far. Without denying the potentially major contribution to reducing emissions which can be made by increased energy efficiency, emissions trading and various measures in the transport, agriculture and construction sectors, the role of consumer behaviour remains highly underemphasised (Bruyninckx, 2010; German Federal Environment Agency, 2009). Despite valuable and widely acclaimed studies aimed at raising consumer awareness and transforming societal consumption patterns (Jackson, 2009; McKibben, 2010), no serious policy efforts have been undertaken in this area so far.

In addition to tackling over-consumption habits, one of the other central areas of climate-related action with much potential for emissions reduction in Europe is the limiting of energy consumption and transforming of the energy production sector. In contrast with consumption-related emissions, policy efforts to tackle the energy issue are under serious consideration (European Commission, 2011). Two major driving forces in this respect, apart from climate change, are energy security and economic competitiveness. With regard to energy security, European dependence on energy imports from the Middle East and Russia, in addition to the heavy reliance of some member states (notably France and Belgium) on nuclear energy, has caused serious concern due to the prolonged conflicts in the Middle East, recurrent gas- and oil-related disputes with Russia and the 2011 nuclear disaster in Japan. Most member states depend on external sources for more than 50 per cent of their energy, while some smaller members like Ireland, Cyprus and Malta even import up to 100 per cent of their energy needs (Eurostat, 2009). In the long-term, European energy independence would, moreover, guarantee a relatively cheap, green and safe basis for economic stability. Another driving force for renewable energy development is a growing concern about European competitiveness in the sector. Major competitors such as the United States and China are investing heavily in R&D, exploitation of rare-earth resources used in the production of wind turbines and solar panels, and domestic production development. China aims, for example, to increase the share of renewable energy in its total energy mix to 11.4 per cent by 2015 (as adopted in the 12th Five Year Plan) and 15 per cent by 2020, and has recently become the largest producer of solar cells worldwide (Central Committee of the Communist Party of China, 2010; China Renewable Energy Development Project, 2008).

In contrast to the EU's broader motivations, the main driving force behind China's renewable energy targets – in addition to competitiveness and climate change concerns – is to fuel domestic economic growth. China has abundant sources of coal, numerous oil fields and currently yields over 90 per cent of economically feasible rare-earth exploitation in the world (US Department of Energy, 2010). Energy dependence is thus less of a driver for China. It is energy security, on the contrary, that leads to the current build-up of wind and solar power technology and generation capacity. A large part of the renewable power equipment produced, however, remains destined for the American and especially the European market (China Renewable Energy Development Project, 2008). A second problem is that although the relative share of renewables in China is expected to rise significantly, so is its absolute demand for fossil fuels and especially coal, depending on the rate of economic growth (International Energy Agency, 2010).

Where China creates solutions while continuing to contribute to the problem of climate change, the composition of European gross energy consumption equally underlines that massive investment and effort are needed to move away from an unreliable and untenable energy system based on fossil fuels and nuclear power towards a fully renewable and clean energy system, including smart grid technologies, local and offshore

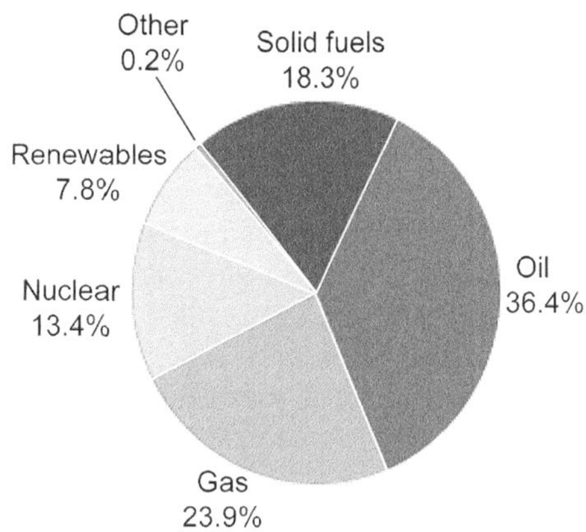

Source: European Commission (2010).

Figure 11.3 Gross energy consumption, EU-27 (2007)

wind parks and solar photovoltaic power. In 2007, fossil fuels including oil, natural gas, solid fuels (e.g. coal) and nuclear energy constituted 92 per cent of gross energy consumption in the EU, while renewables accounted for merely 7.8 per cent (see Figure 11.3).

The EU's current climate and energy policies put forward the objective of a 20 per cent share of renewables in the overall energy mix by 2020, a target that is part of the 2008 Climate and Energy Package. The package introduced the 20-20-20 by 2020 targets, i.e. 20 per cent reduction in emissions, 20 per cent increase in energy efficiency and a 20 per cent share of renewables in 2020 (European Parliament/Council of the European Union, 2009a, 2009b, 2009c). Like the emissions reduction target, and as in China, the Union's renewable energy objective seems to be well within reach and not even close to what science and experts in academia, civil society and even some business associations propose as the best way forward for both Europe and China – and for solving both the climate and the energy crisis: a gradual but urgent transition towards a sustainable energy system as a vital component of a future low-carbon society (European Commission, 2011; German Federal Environment Agency,

2009; International Energy Agency, 2010; World Wide Fund for Nature, Ecofys and Office for Metropolitan Architecture, 2011).

THE EVOLVING GLOBAL GOVERNANCE OF CLIMATE CHANGE AND ENERGY

To respond to the outlined climate and energy challenges, domestic action in China and the EU is vital and indispensable. As a global common goods problem, however, climate change also requires the collective action of all emitters and (major) energy consumers. In that regard, both China and the EU are crucial players in contemporary global climate and energy governance. Not the least as a result of China's rise as an energy-hungry economic and geopolitical power, these governance arenas are, however, currently undergoing significant and open-ended transformation processes (Schreurs, 2010; Zhang, 2010). These processes, their effects, dynamics and policy outcomes constitute the central themes of this part of the book.

For climate change, despite the emergence of fora such as the G-8 + 5, G-20 and the Major Economies Forum (MEF) of the world's 17 major emitters, the UN regime developed around the Framework Convention and its Kyoto Protocol currently remains the key arena for global climate governance. It is on two parallel tracks – the Ad Hoc Working Group on Long-term Cooperative Action (AWG-LCA) and the Ad Hoc Working Group on the Future of the Kyoto Protocol (AWG-KP) – that parties try to find consensus solutions, essentially on the form, magnitude and modalities of emissions reduction by different groups of parties. Yet, this over-complication of global climate policymaking – fuelled by and coinciding with geopolitical shifts related to the rise of the emerging economies – means that global climate governance is currently very much in a state of flux.

The shape global governance will ultimately take is bound to depend on the interplay of the three arguably most important players: China, the US and (still) the EU. Currently, there seems to be a trend toward a G-2 (China–US) type of arrangement that increasingly keeps the EU on the sidelines (Schunz, 2012). This constellation favours the emergence of an action-based multilateralism embodied in the 'pledge and review approach' of the Copenhagen Accord. This type of approach, which focuses on concrete policy actions rather than on binding targets, is advocated and elaborated upon by Richard Cooper in this part of the book. Should China, India and the other BASIC countries (Brazil and South Africa) decide, however, to join forces with the EU, a reinvigorated, treaty-based global multilateralism could become possible, in which continued US inactivity would not pay off. In both scenarios, cooperation and competition in the renewable energy and low-carbon technology sector is set to play a key role, as shown by the Cancun negotiations in December 2010 (Schunz and Belis, 2011).

Whether China will side with the EU or remain caught up in a G-2 relationship with the US is currently an open question. For a long time, the country has considered global climate negotiations primarily as a site for defending its status as a developing country and fending off emissions reduction obligations (Heggelund and Backer, 2007). This strategy was very effectively pursued in and since Copenhagen, through apt use of the G-77/China coalition of developing countries and by co-initiating the BASIC group of emerging countries as an interest-based phalanx against the demands of developed countries. For the time being, China considers its proposed actions, embodied in the above mentioned 40–45 per cent target, as voluntary, and does not want to submit them to stringent international verification. Furthermore, China remains vividly opposed to an internationally legally binding framework for global climate policies (Purvis and Stevenson, 2010). This approach gained the country very negative publicity during and after the 2009 summit in Copenhagen, when it was blamed for much of the failure of the talks by both European leaders and the media. In the year thereafter, a remarkable PR strategy sought to turn this situation around, with partial success. Although China's position has not really changed substantially, it has signalled openness toward a more inclusive and cooperative approach – as Jingquan Chen explains in detail in this part of the book. By organising the October 2010 preparatory meeting for COP 16 in Tianjin, China practically underscored this willingness.

In contrast to China and its opposition to a legally binding climate regime embodying solid emission reduction targets for all major emitters, the EU has long been among the key promoters of precisely such a regime (Schunz, 2012). Its position and attitude were recently expressed in its unilateral 20 per cent emissions reduction proposal (with a 30 per cent proposal hinging on similar actions by other industrialised countries) and its very proactive engagement in the regime discussions in line with its domestic policies, especially the market-based approach embodied in its Emissions Trading System (EU ETS). Although this approach meant, in the past, that the EU was arguably instrumental in assuring the continuity of the multilateral climate regime (Oberthür and Roche-Kelly, 2008), the Union has not had much leverage over the regime negotiations in recent times. At the Copenhagen Summit, it was sidelined notably by the Chinese, other BASIC countries and the United States. Since then, it has been much less vocal internationally, arguably also as a result of internal institutional conflicts over the implementation of the Lisbon Treaty, and more pragmatic in its outreach. As an expression of this pragmatism, the European Commission's draft 'Roadmap for Moving to a Competitive Low Carbon Economy in 2050', presented in March 2011, contains very few ideas on the future shape of the international negotiations besides 'the swift implementation of the pledges made since Copenhagen' (European Commission, 2011:13). An interesting issue in this context, linking the EU notably to China, is the future of the Clean Development Mechanism (CDM). While the CDM has had a certain effect on the promotion of renewable energy development in China – as outlined by Pei-fei Chang, David Belis and Hans Bruyninckx in this part of the book – an EU policy shift has taken place in recent years regarding the use of this mechanism. Within the European Commission and the Parliament, the CDM is currently seen as having too many environmental integrity and transparency problems, and as a direct subsidy to a main competitor in areas such as renewables and low-carbon technologies (European Commission, 2011; Delbeke, 2011). It remains to be seen what this potentially means for the EU's leverage in global climate negotiations, as the EU ETS was the main source of demand for – primarily Chinese – CDM reduction certificates Certified Emission Reductions (CERs).

While the further evolution of the climate regime still hangs very much in the balance prior to the 2011 summit in Durban and the 2012 Rio + 20 summit, the obvious divergences between China and the EU about all major issues under negotiation (form of the outcome, magnitude and modalities of targets) tends to mask the areas of convergence. The one area where both players recently seem to have converged concerns the necessity to start – and, to some extent, the modalities of – building a low-carbon society. The latest efforts in both China and the EU (China's 12th Five Year Plan and the EU Roadmap 2050) show that both powers are exploring pathways to a society sustained by low-carbon technologies. Internationally, however, it remains to be seen whether and how these efforts can be included in the United Nations Framework Convention on Climate Change (UNFCCC) negotiations in a serious manner. In some ways, however, China and the EU appear closer in their approach than the US and China or the EU and the US, which might open up perspectives for collaboration transcending purely technology-based exchange in the global governance of climate change.

For global efforts to deal with the energy challenge beyond climate governance fora, the picture is much less clear-cut: 'Energy is governed piecemeal, mostly in ad-hoc responses involving specific countries or groups of countries' (Florini and Sovacool, 2009: 5239). Energy governance fora at the global level typically include institutions as varied as the International Energy Agency, the G8 and development banks (Lesage et al., 2010, chapter 4). While China and the EU have been, to varying degrees, involved in these bodies, the difficulty in distilling a distinct system of global energy governance makes it almost impossible to determine the two parties' positions vis-à-vis this 'highly disjointed' form of global energy policymaking (Florini and Sovacool, 2009: 5247). What seems rather obvious is that both are in the first place strategically trying to assure their security of energy supply through bilateral and regional arrangements, often also in a piecemeal manner, rather than focusing on concerted global efforts to promote, for example, the development and dissemination of clean energy technologies. Bernard Snoy's contribution as well as the chapter by Bram Buijs and Lucia van Geuns elaborate specifically on these issues, scrutinising EU–China bilateral competition, but also instances of cooperation in the field of renewable energy, and set this into the broader context of the emergence of European and Chinese energy policies.

China's external energy policy, sometimes referred to as its 'global energy hunt', involves tapping into resource-rich states in all continents, with the country 'courting the governments of these states aggressively, building goodwill by strengthening bilateral trade relations, awarding aid, forgiving national debt, and helping build roads, bridges, stadiums, and harbours' (Zweig and Jianhai, 2005: 26). The EU, by contrast, has, first and foremost, looked to its neighbourhood to assure security of supply, often in return for preferential treatment (Youngs, 2009). Neither the depth nor the scope of the geopolitical approach taken by China has been matched by an EU that is still often struggling to define coherent positions in its internal and external energy policies. Regarding (existing and prospective) competition for resources, little common ground for the promotion of coherent and sustainable energy governance exists, regardless of the urgent need to tackle the twin challenges posed by climate change and energy security (Goldthau and Witte, 2010; International Energy Agency, 2010).

In synthesis, this chapter and this part of the book testify to the fact that China and the EU are not only key players in the contemporary economic and political world order, they are also key in terms of the environment. At the very least, both players are now starting to effectively recognise the importance of a profound transformation of global (energy) consumption habits and of the need to revolutionise the world's energy system. It is at all levels of governance that further action is required to tackle the complex challenges of climate change and energy, and both China and the European Union have the capacity to strongly contribute to the solution.

NOTE

1. The Kyoto Protocol to the United Nations Framework Convention on Climate Change (UNFCCC) covers six major greenhouse gases: carbon dioxide (CO_2), methane (CH_4), nitrous oxide (N_2O), hydrofluorocarbons (HFCs), perfluorocarbons (PFCs) and sulphur hexafluoride (SF_6), often jointly referred to as carbon dioxide equivalent or CO_2eq (United Nations, 1997).

REFERENCES

Akyuz, Yilmaz (2010) *Export Dependence and Sustainability of Growth in China and the East Asian Production Network*, Research Paper 27, April. Geneva: South Centre.

Brinkley, Andrew and Less, Simon (2010) *Carbon Omissions: Consumption-based Accounting for International Carbon Emissions*, Research Note, October. London: Policy Exchange.

Bruyninckx, Hans (2010) *Living in a Low-Carbon Society: A Sociological Perspective*. Presentation, High-level Workshop on Living in a Low-Carbon Society, 18–19 November, Brussels.

Central Committee of the Communist Party of China (2010) *Zhonggong zhongyang guanyu zhiding guomin jingji he shehui fazhan di shi'er ge wunian guihua de jianyi* [*Opinion of the Central Committee of the Communist Party of China on Establishing the 12th Five Year Plan*], 18 October. Available at: http://www.ndrc.gov.cn (last accessed 28 February 2011).

China Renewable Energy Development Project (2008) *Report on the Development of the PV Industry in China (2006–2007)*. China Renewable Energy Development Project.

Climate Action Network Europe (2010) *Why Europe Should Strengthen Its 2020 Climate Action*. Brussels: Climate Action Network Europe Report.

Delbeke, Jos (2011) Untitled. Intervention at the Stakeholder Conference on the Roadmap for Moving to a Low Carbon Economy in 2050. Brussels, 17 March.

Energy Information Administration (2010) *Carbon Dioxide Emissions in China (1980–2009)*. Available at: http://www.eia.gov (last accessed 28 February 2011).

European Commission (2010) *EU Energy in Figures 2010*. Directorate-General for Transport and Energy, European Commission.

European Commission (2011) *A Roadmap for Moving to a Competitive Low Carbon Economy in 2050*, COM (2011) 112/4. Brussels.

European Parliament/Council of the European Union (2009a) *Directive of 23 April 2009 amending Directive 2003/87/EC so as to Improve and Extend the Greenhouse Gas Emission Allowance Trading Scheme of the Community*, 2009/29/EC.

European Parliament/Council of the European Union (2009b) *Directive of 23 April 2009 on the Promotion of the Use of Energy from Renewable Sources and Amending and Subsequently Repealing Directives 2001/77/EC and 2003/30/EC*, 2009/28/EC.

European Parliament/Council of the European Union (2009c) *Decision on the Effort of Member States to Reduce their Greenhouse Gas Emissions to Meet the Community's Greenhouse Gas Emission Reduction Commitments up to 2020*,

406/2009/EC.

Eurostat (2009) *Panorama of Energy: Energy Statistics to Support EU Policies and Solutions*. Luxembourg: Eurostat Statistical Books.

Florini, Ann and Sovacool, Benjamin (2009) 'Who governs energy? The challenges facing global energy governance', *Energy Policy*, 37 (12): 5239–48.

German Federal Environment Agency (2009) *Role and Potential of Renewable Energy and Energy Efficiency for Global Energy Supply*, Report No. (UBA-FB) 001323/E. Berlin: German Federal Environment Agency.

Goldthau, Andreas and Witte, Jan Martin (eds) (2010) *Global Energy Governance: The New Rules of the Game*. Washington, DC: Brookings Institution Press.

Heggelund, Gørild and Backer, Ellen Bruzelius (2007) 'China and UN environmental policy: institutional growth, learning and implementation', *International Environmental Agreements*, 7 (4): 415–38.

Intergovernmental Panel on Climate Change (2007) *Climate Change 2007 Synthesis Report: Summary for Policymakers*. Cambridge: Cambridge University Press.

International Energy Agency (2010) *World Energy Outlook 2010*. Paris: International Energy Authority.

Jackson, Tim (2009) *Prosperity Without Growth: Economics for a Finite Planet*. London: Earthscan.

Lesage, Dries, Van de Graaf, Thijs and Westphal, Kirste (2010) *Global Energy Governance in a Multipolar World*. London: Ashgate.

McKibben, Bill (2010) *Earth: Making a Life on a Tough New Planet*. New York: Times Books.

Meadows, Donella H., Randers, Jorgen, Meadows, Dennis L. and Behrens, William W. (1972) *The Limits to Growth: A Report for the Club of Rome's Project on the Predicament of Mankind*. New York: Universe Books.

Oberthür, Sebastian and Roche-Kelly, Claire (2008) 'EU leadership in international climate policy: achievements and challenges', *International Spectator*, 43 (3): 35–50.

Organisation for Economic Cooperation and Development (2009) *The Economics of Climate Change Mitigation: Policies and Options for Global Action beyond 2012*. Paris: OECD.

Purvis, Nigel and Stevenson, Andrew (2010) *Rethinking Climate Diplomacy. New Ideas for Transatlantic Cooperation Post-Copenhagen*. Washington, DC: German Marshall Fund of the United States.

Schreurs, Miranda (2010) 'Multi-level governance and global climate change in East Asia', *Asian Economic Policy Review*, 5: 88–105.

Schunz, Simon (2012) 'The European Union in the United Nations climate change regime', in Jan Wouters, Hans Bruyninckx, Sue Basu and Simon Schunz (eds), *The European Union and Multilateral Governance: Assessing EU Participation in United Nations Human Rights and Environmental Fora*. Basingstoke: Palgrave.

Schunz, Simon and Belis, David (2012) *China, India and Global Environmental Governance: The Case of Climate Change*, Policy Brief. Leuven: Leuven Centre for Global Governance Studies.

United Nations (1997) *Kyoto Protocol to the United Nations Framework Convention on Climate Change*. New York: United Nations.

United Nations Environment Programme (2010) *Emissions Gap Report: Are the Copenhagen Accord Pledges Sufficient to Limit Global Warming to 2°C or 1.5°C? A Preliminary Assessment*. Nairobi: United Nations Environment Programme Report.

US Department of Energy (2010) *Critical Materials Strategy*. Washington, DC: US Department of Energy.

World Resources Institute (2011) *Climate Analysis Indicator Tools*. Available online at: http://cait.wri.org (last accessed 28 February 2011).

World Wide Fund for Nature, Ecofys and Office for Metropolitan Architecture (2011) *The Energy Report: 100% Renewable Energy by 2050*, International Report. Gland: World Wide Fund for Nature.

Yang, Ming (2009) 'Climate change and energy policies, coal and coalmine methane in China', *Energy Policy*, 37 (8): 2858–69.

Youngs, Richard (2009) *Energy Security: Europe's New Foreign Policy Challenge*. Abingdon: Routledge.

Zhang, Zhongxiang (2010) *Copenhagen and Beyond: Reflections on China's Stance and Responses*, Working Papers, Economic Series 111, June. Honolulu, HI: East-West Center.

Zhu, Andong and Kotz, David M. (2011) 'The dependence of China's economic growth on exports and investment', *Review of Radical Political Economics*, 43 (1): 9–32.

Zweig, David and Jianhai, Bi (2005) 'China's global hunt for energy', *Foreign Affairs*, 84 (5): 25–38.

12. China–EU and the challenge of global climate change and energy

Richard N. Cooper

We still live in a world in which national states are the key decision-makers on domestic and international issues. This is likely to remain the case for at least the next twenty years. Even though Europe's experiments in genuinely supranational decision-making, albeit through a painfully slow process, have resulted in notable successes, there is little reason why decision-making should be raised to higher governmental levels without a compelling reason to do so. Following the principle of subsidiarity, there is little reason for international governance unless a strong affirmative case can be made on the basis of greater effectiveness, cost efficiency and/or removing harmful deadlocks at national level. Where such a case can be made, then, each problem should be addressed on its merits, which typically will involve far fewer countries than the entire international community of over 200 states. And the appropriate grouping of relevant states will undoubtedly vary from issue to issue.

Given that each state has a single vote and most resolutions of the UN General Assembly and its various subsidiaries are passed by a simple majority, the formal UN system is 'democratic' at the state level in all issues except security. But with the arguable exception of the Law of the Sea treaty, this system has ensured deadlock on most issues of practical importance. Calls for greater 'democratisation' of the international system should therefore be better defined and clarified from a practical perspective. At the global level we should be driven to find practical solutions to practical problems, not engage in conceptual or abstract discussions of the definition of 'governance'.

Where energy is concerned there are currently two problems that require global solutions, or at least widespread international cooperation.

The first concerns *energy security*: oil and, for Europe and in future for China, natural gas. Projections up to 2030 by the US Energy Information Administration which assume a benign world and continued economic growth (EIA, 2009), show world dependence on oil from the Persian Gulf region – which contains most of the world's known oil reserves – continues to rise, the extent of the rise of course depending on the oil prices assumed to prevail over the next 20 years. Higher prices, for example, would result in a decrease in dependence due to the fact that less oil would be consumed while more oil would be produced in other regions.

This projection raises two questions. Firstly, will countries bordering the Gulf make the required investments in additional oil production to satisfy higher world demand, beyond the 2 million barrels a day increase in output which Saudi Arabia now plans? Secondly, would the world be comfortable with growing dependence on that region? The answer to the second question both in Washington and Beijing is no. Therefore what are the plans in case of a negative answer to both questions?

The problem is that incremental oil from the Gulf countries is far cheaper than oil from elsewhere, so Gulf countries could undercut prices required for profitability, as Saudi Arabia did in 1985 and again in 1998, thus discouraging investment in alternatives including non-oil alternatives. One idea to overcome this problem would be to put in place an international agreement on a *floor* price for oil. That *floor* price would not have to take the form of a global agreement, but it does need to cover all the major exporters of energy-intensive manufactured goods, including the European Union, China, the USA, Japan, Korea, etc. If the world price of oil drops below the agreed threshold, these countries would impose a tax on all users of oil. It would not be easy to agree on the threshold price, but this does not mean it should not be tried.

At a minimum, there is a need to set up a forum to discuss these issues, and it would be problematic to include major exporters of oil in that forum. The G20 includes Saudi Arabia, Russia, Indonesia (which will not be a major exporter for long), and Brazil (which may soon become a major one) and these countries should certainly not have veto power over an agreement to assure oil security.

The second issue is climate change, for which use of coal is central. Here, a simple syllogism may help: one cannot seriously mitigate climate change without help from all the rapidly growing developing countries, China being quantitatively the most relevant (plus of course the United States); however, these countries cannot accept a meaningful quantitative ceiling on their respective levels of greenhouse gas emissions which they fear would threaten their economic growth. What is needed therefore is to change the conceptual framework from an international agreement based on quantitative targets to an international agreement based on meaningful actions.

One concrete, action-based, proposal which should be considered seriously is for a harmonised charge on greenhouse gas (GHG) emissions imposed by every country, or at least by all the countries that either now or in the coming years will make a quantitatively important contribution to GHG emissions, with each country keeping the revenue it collects. This should appeal to finance ministers everywhere, who would welcome a new, internationally sanctioned, trade-neutral source of revenue. The key issue, however, is to shift the negotiating framework from targets to actions, not this particular action.

When a delegation of senior officials from the European Commission visited Harvard in fall 2008 to outline the EU approach to the upcoming Copenhagen negotiations, I had argued that the EU approach would fail not on procedural but on substantive grounds. But when asked if there was a Plan B, officials replied firmly that there was no Plan B. This is an example of the fact that the EU is so involved in its internal decision-making that it is not paying attention to the priorities, constraints and limitations of the rest of the world, whose cooperation is nonetheless necessary to attain the desired objective, that is to reduce GHG emissions.

Where can the world negotiate an agreement on climate change? The UNFCCC Conference of the Parties demonstrated at Copenhagen its incapability of reaching an agreement on this important topic. Developing countries are stuck in the mindset that only developed countries should take on commitments to reduce emissions and they should be free to pursue their own objectives unconstrained by a climate agreement. But this position is not tenable if mitigation of climate change is to be taken seriously. Today's developed countries could reduce their CO_2 emissions to zero by 2020 – something that is surely not going to occur – and on plausible projections world CO_2 emissions from developing countries alone would be above the worldwide level of 1990, the base year for the Kyoto Protocol, and on a steeper trajectory (EIA, 2009). The unpleasant reality is that without active participation by key developing countries soon, climate change will not be seriously abated.

China and the United States – the two largest GHG emitters, whose participation is essential to any workable agreement – need to agree on the boundaries of an agreement that is acceptable to both of them. This is not to suggest a generalised G2, which should be opposed as both unworkable and undesirable, but on this particular issue bilateral discussions would be internationally helpful – indeed, may be necessary. After the United States and China agree on the acceptable boundaries, negotiations could take place in a larger group, such as the G20, although European representation there needs to be drastically reduced, at least for this issue. After the negotiation has been completed, it can be presented to the UN Conference of Parties for their endorsement or at least acquiescence.

The international trading system is seriously at risk if countries take a piecemeal, uncoordinated approach to mitigation of climate change. It is unclear at this time what the United States will do, but it can be forecast that if it does something alone it will include trade restraints against countries that have not taken 'comparable measures', and the EU will follow soon thereafter. This will provide a field day for protectionists on both sides of the Atlantic which will not be in the interests of China or other emerging markets.

To conclude, even with vigorous measures to develop hydro-, wind-, nuclear-, and solar-power, China's demand for coal to generate electricity will continue to rise, implying under one projection that by 2030 China will account for over half of the world's coal consumption (EIA, 2009). The world's dependence on coal will continue for at least another two decades, perhaps longer. If the world wants to seriously mitigate climate change, mastering carbon capture and storage will be essential. Europe has carbon capture technology; China continues to build coal-fired power plants at a rapid pace. Carbon capture has not been proven yet on a commercial scale; we do not know which is the most workable, and least costly, of several possible approaches. As one possible practical suggestion for EU–China cooperation, the EU should offer to provide the technology for carbon capture and to pay the incremental costs in some of China's new coal-fired plants, as a large-scale experiment to find out how best to do it on a commercial scale. With little time to waste, this project should start as soon as possible.

REFERENCE

Energy Information Administration (EIA) (2009) *International Energy Outlook*, May.

13. Climate change, technology transfer and low-carbon economy development in China

Jingquan Chen

THE DILEMMA OVER CARBON EMISSION REDUCTION IN CHINA

I would like to begin this part with the following piece of news from China: the local government of Anping County in Hebei Province planned to implement a county-wide power-cut starting from September 2010 in order to meet its emission reduction requirements. Not only were businesses involved in this plan, but ordinary people were also to face 22-hour blackouts every three days in their homes. Even hospitals and traffic lights were included in the power-cut plan. Fortunately, this plan was criticised first by the media then by the central and provincial government, and it was subsequently amended by the local government. Only then were hospitals, people and traffic lights spared from the plan.

This case reflects the dilemma of the Chinese government over carbon emission reduction. Evidently, the Chinese government is very serious in its commitment to the emission reduction goal. China pledged to cut energy consumption per unit of GDP (energy intensity) by 20 per cent from 2006 to 2010 (equivalent to a 23 per cent carbon intensity target). In recent years, the Chinese government has been exhausting all means to meet this goal. For example, China has stepped up efforts to eliminate outdated production capacity since 2007, and has phased out small coal-fired power plants with 70 MKW generating capacity by July 2010. And premier Wen Jiabao has said: 'We are willing to slow down the GDP growth rate to meet the target if it is necessary' (Xinhua News Agency, 14 September 2010). Despite all of this, it seems very difficult to reach the target. Actually, the energy consumption per unit of GDP has even increased slightly in the first half of 2010, due to the economic stimulus plan. Facing the pressing task of emission reduction, the central government ordered more than 2,000 companies with low production capacities to close by the end of September. This has encountered the resistance of some local governments, who are willing to sacrifice citizen power supply to maintain employment and GDP growth as their prime priorities.

As the 20 per cent energy intensity target by 2010 seems to be an arduous task for China, we could imagine how formidable it would be to meet the 2020 emissions intensity target of 40–45 per cent reduction compared with 2005. Meeting this target will require an additional 22–29 per cent reduction compared with 2010 (Jimin, 2010). Actually, many officials and companies in China said that they have already done all they can to meet the 2010 target and there is not much space left for further reductions by 2015 because all the low-hanging fruit has already been picked (Jimin, 2010). Anyway, it will not be sustainable to reduce carbon emission by power-cuts. A long-term and systematic approach is necessary. The key to energy conservation and emission reduction should be the transformation of the development paradigm and increasing production efficiency. But this is a long process, and if the cost is too high, the process will be unsustainable in undeveloped regions.

China's dilemma is common for undeveloped countries which face a gap between the requirement to cut emissions and their technology capacity as well as financial support. Without the support of new technology and aid from outside, the undeveloped regions have no other choice than to cut power or close the small plants with low production efficiency, even when that means the unemployment of hundreds of thousands of people. In this context, any extra emission-cutting requirement seems to become a sort of constraint on development, even a constraint on survival. That's why the technology transfer mechanism is so important in the global effort to tackle climate change, and why most parties in the international negotiations have great expectations of making a breakthrough in technology transfer issues in the coming Cancun conference.

EMISSION REDUCTION AND TECHNOLOGY TRANSFER

According to International Energy Agency statistics, China has become the biggest CO_2 emitter, surpassing the US for the first time in 2007 (IEA, 2009). China and the US are respectively responsible for about a fifth of global annual emissions of the most important greenhouse gas. But if the historical accumulations of CO_2 emissions over the past century are taken into account, China's contribution to global CO_2 emissions sinks to around 10 per cent. On the other hand, the contribution of industrialised countries, with long-accumulated emissions of CO_2, increases significantly. For example, the US's contribution to global warming approaches 30 per cent (Höhne et al., 2010: 19).

If the whole history of CO_2 emission since the Industrial Revolution began is taken into account, the scenario differs more and China's contribution descends to 7 per cent.

As the developed countries have already finished the process of industrialisation and play a leading role in low-carbon technology development, they are also anticipated to play a leading role in addressing climate change. That's the basic principle of nations' 'common but differentiated responsibilities', which was first formulated in the context of the 1992 Rio Earth Summit and endorsed by the United Nations Framework Convention on Climate Change (UNFCCC) and the Kyoto Protocol. According to this principle, the developed countries have a duty to cut emissions first and to provide the funds and technology for developing nations' emission cuts.

Surely China and other developing countries cannot avoid their responsibility to reduce emission. But measures based on their own capacities are far from that which is demanded in addressing global climate change. The challenge of climate change is so urgent that we have no more time to wait. We need actions on a global scale to address climate change. Low-carbon technology needs to be transferred and deployed as widely as possible and as quickly as possible. Article 4.5 of the UNFCCC states that developed country parties should take 'all practicable steps to promote, facilitate and finance, as appropriate, the transfer of, or access to, environmentally sound technologies and know-how to other Parties, particularly developing country Parties' and that they should 'support the development and enhancement of endogenous capacities and technologies of developing country Parties', and calls on other parties and organisations to assist in facilitating the transfer of such technologies.

However, cases of successful technology transfer under the UNFCCC are rare up to now. That's because there is a paradox in practice. The governments of developed countries say that they intend to promote technology transfer but have no technology in hand as the technology is owned by the private sector. And private sector companies say that they would like to spread their technology, but that without a profits innovation will be unsustainable. It seems that they are both right. That's why there is little progress for technology transfer under the UNFCCC. So what's the way out?

One of the solutions is that governments of developed countries set up a co-fund to support undeveloped countries looking to buy and deploy low-carbon technologies. The Copenhagen Accord made progress in this regard, by emphasising, 'the collective commitment by developed countries to provide new and additional resources of 30 billion dollars for the period 2010–2012 and mobilizing jointly 100 billion dollars a year by 2020 to address the needs of developing countries and to establish the Copenhagen Green Climate Fund.' It is expected that a significant portion of such funding could be used for technology transfer. In this way, the deployment of low-carbon technology could be sped up with the intellectual property rights (IPR) of the private sector protected well.

Another solution involves reframing the politics and policy of IPR in climate change areas. The action of addressing climate change is to protect the atmosphere – a global public good – and it is important to ensure that there is a correct balance between protecting IPR and ensuring rapid diffusion of new technology to mitigate and adapt to climate change (Tomlinson et al., 2008: 83)

Maybe the compulsory licence mechanism for exploitation of the AIDS medicine patent could be a reference. Given the global public good nature of low-carbon innovation, action is required at the multilateral level to build on national policies and correct market failures. In this aspect, an international 'Protect & Share' IPR and Licensing Framework Agreement would be helpful. But it's a pity that negotiation in this area has made little progress.

As far as China is concerned, it seems that China has become strong enough in low-carbon technology innovation. For example, China led the world in 2009 in terms of installed hydropower capacity, nuclear power capacity under construction, the coverage of solar water heating panels and cumulative solar photovoltaic power capacity. Yes, the data are correct. But sometimes data can be misleading. For instance, China has also led the world in terms of high-tech production exports since 2006. However, looking into the data one finds that about 68 per cent of high-tech export in China was created by wholly foreign-owned enterprises, and another 16 per cent was created by sino-foreign joint venture enterprises (Figure 13.1). In another words, almost 84 per cent of core patents for Chinese high-tech products belong to foreign companies.

So we can see that China's development is largely credited to foreign partners. But on the other hand, the concentration of innovation capacity in developed countries does not match the global need for diverse mitigation and adaptation technology. Up to now, the transfer of low-carbon technology still follows the traditional trade approaches (i.e. international commodity trade, international technology trade and foreign direct investment), and this will limit its spread because the undeveloped regions can't afford it. In an area where the market might fail, governments can't fail to do something. All governments should play

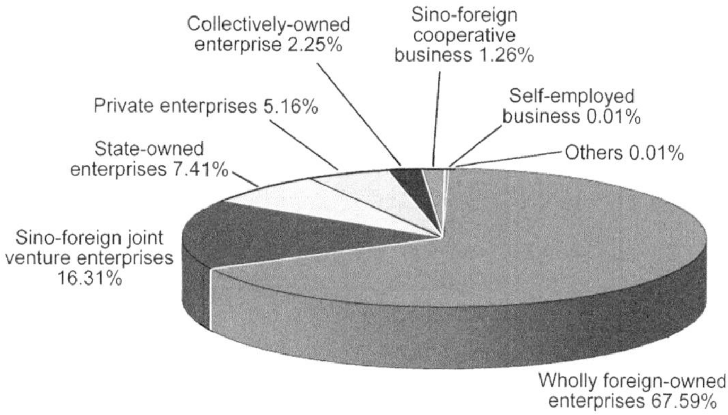

Source: National Bureau of Statistics of China and Ministry of Science and Technology (2009).

Figure 13.1 The ratio of contribution of different types of companies to China's high tech production export (2008)

a more ambitious and effective role in advancing technology transfer that addresses climate change.

LOW-CARBON ECONOMY DEVELOPMENT IN CHINA

China faces a huge challenge to transform its economic development onto a low-carbon track. China is still in the process of industrialisation and urbanisation and ranks behind 100 countries in terms of per capita GDP. Judging by the UN standard, 150 million Chinese people are still living in poverty. In terms of resource consumption, coal accounts for 70 per cent of China's energy mix and is responsible for 80 per cent of greenhouse gas emissions (Figure 13.2). In this context, there will still be quite some time for China to fundamentally break away from coal-produced energy. Despite this, China has made rapid progress in shifting to a low-carbon economy.

First, China has set binding targets for carbon intensity and taken credible steps to achieve that goal. In outlining the 11th Five Year Plan for national economic and social development back in 2006, China set a target of decreasing energy intensity by 20 per cent and basically reversing the trend of further deterioration of the environment by 2010. For the first four years of the 11th Five Year Plan up to the end of 2009, energy consumption per unit of GDP dropped by 14.38 per cent cumulatively, and chemical oxygen demand (COD) and SO_2 emissions were down by 9.66 per cent and 13.14 per cent respectively. That's equivalent to reduced

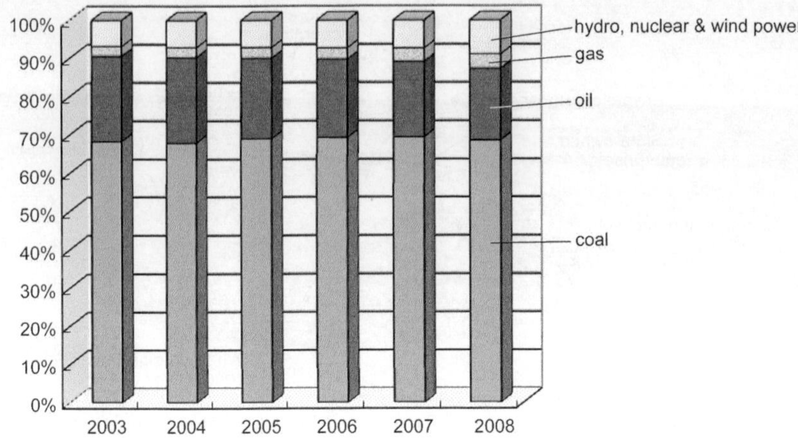

Source: National Bureau of Statistics of China (2009).

Figure 13.2 Energy consumption structure in China (2003–8)

emissions of nearly 900 million tons of CO_2 in comparison with the business as usual scenario. Furthermore, the targets released by China in 2009 require that by 2020, CO_2 emissions per unit of GDP should go down by 40–45 per cent from the 2005 level, non-fossil energy should make up about 15 per cent of primary energy consumption, and forest coverage should increase by 40 million hectares and forest stock volume by 1.3 billion cubic metres, both from 2005 levels. All the targets will be written in China's 12th Five Year Plan as a binding requirement. The measure to lower energy consumption alone will help save 620 million tons of standard coal in energy consumption over the next five years, which will be equivalent to the reduction of 1.5 billion tons of CO_2 emissions in comparison with the business-as-usual scenario.

Second, China has made great efforts to speed up the structural adjustment of its industry in shaping an energy- and resource-efficient and environment-friendly economy. China has stepped up efforts to eliminate outdated capacity since 2007, and closed a large number of heavily polluting, small, coal-fired power plants, small coal mines and enterprises in the steel, cement, paper-making, chemical and printing and dyeing sectors. In September 2010, China enacted a regulation to require compulsory energy-saving assessments for new fixed asset investments; all new investments must undergo independent assessment and government review of whether they are energy-saving or not before being approved by the government. As an important low-emission industry, high-speed rail is booming in China. In recently years, China has built the world's longest high-speed rail network with about 7,400 km of routes in service as of September 2010. China will spend 800 billion RMB (US$120 billion) as part of an ambitious plan to double the size of its high-speed rail network by 2012 (Xin, 2010). Moreover, according to the new five-year plan proposal, China will make progressive efforts to boost energy efficiency, promote low-carbon technology and establish carbon trade markets.

Third, China is striving to develop new energies and renewable energies. China plans to increase the share of new energies in its primary energy mix to 10 per cent in 2010 and to around 15 per cent by 2020. Actually, China is on safe ground to achieve the 10 per cent goal this year (2010), because in 2008 the figure had already hit 9 per cent, equivalent to 250 million tons of standard coal. Of this 9 per cent share, hydropower installed capacity contributed 172,000 megawatts and wind power 121,700 megawatts, ranking China, respectively, first and fourth in the world in terms of power produced by these means. China's collective solar water heater panels totalled 130 million square metres and in cumulative terms, PV power generation has produced 150 megawatts of electricity, both measures being the highest among all countries globally. At this point, China is formulating a Development Plan to Revitalize New Energy Industries. The purpose of this plan is to give stronger support to the development of wind, solar and biomass power, smart grids and new fuel materials for automobiles. According to the final draft of this plan, hydropower installed capacity will reach 380 GW by 2020, wind power 150 GW, nuclear power 80 GW, biomass power 0.3 GW and solar power 0.2 GW.

China is the beneficiary of globalisation, and will undertake its responsibility to contribute to the global efforts to address climate change. China was the first developing country to endorse Agenda 21 and to elaborate a Comprehensive Work Plan for Energy Conservation and Emissions Reduction and a National Climate Change Programme. China attaches great importance to developing practical cooperation with Europe on environment protection and energy and climate change issues and China always supports efforts to jointly cope with the challenges of climate change through solid and effective international cooperation.

REFERENCES

Höhne, Niklas., Blum, Helcio., Fuglestvedt, Jan., Bieltvedt Skeie, Ragnhild., Kurosawa, Atsushi., Hu, Guoquan., Lowe, Jason., Gohar, Laila., Matthews, Ben., Nioac de Salles, Ana Claudia., Ellerman, Christian. (2010) *Contributions of Individual Countries' Emissions to Climate Change and Their Uncertainty*, Climatic Change Online First^{TM}, 24 September.

International Energy Agency (2009) 'CO_2 emissions from fuel combustion', in IEA,

Highlights 2009. Paris: IEA.

Jimin, Zhao (2010) *Climate Change, Energy, and Low-Carbon Economy in China*. Presentation at the 'Dialogue with China on Harmonious Society: Governance, Participation and Social Cohesion', Wiston House (UK), organised by Wiston Park, 4–7 November.

National Bureau of Statistics of China (2009) *China Statistical Yearbook 2009*. Beijing: China Statistics Press.

National Bureau of Statistics of China and Ministry of Science and Technology (2009) *China Statistical Yearbook on Science and Technology: 2009*. Beijing: China Statistics Press.

Tomlinson, S., Zorlu, P. and Langley, C. (2008) *Innovation and Technology Transfer: Framework for a Global Climate Deal*. E3G and Chatham House, November.

Xin, Dingding (2010) 'China's high-speed rail links to be doubled by 2012', *China Daily*, 29 July.

Xinhua News Agency (2010) 'Wen Jiabao's answers to the questions on the Opening Ceremony of Summer Davos and Entrepreneur Forum', 14 September. On-line at: http://www.gov.cn/ldhd/2010-09/14/content_1701849.htm (accessed 13 January 2011).

14. EU–China climate relations: the Clean Development Mechanism and renewable energy in China

Pei-fei Chang, David Belis and Hans Bruyninckx

INTRODUCTION

This chapter studies the use, role and validity of the Clean Development Mechanism (CDM) in European Union relations with China on climate change, with a particular focus on the renewable energy (RE) sector. The relationship between the EU and China on climate mitigation is a significant one, since both are key players in global climate governance. The European Union is by far the largest economic bloc engaged in the Kyoto Protocol in the developed world (Jordan et al., 2010) and it is responsible for one of the largest shares of historical emissions worldwide, while China is the largest political and economic power among developing countries and the largest source of greenhouse gas emissions at present and for the foreseeable future (Netherlands Environmental Assessment Agency, 2007). The CDM plays a controversial role in this relationship, providing finance for renewable energy technology development in China on the one hand (EU–China CDM Facilitation Project, 2009), while posing various problems linked to environmental integrity, transparency and EU–China competition in the RE sector on the other (Delbeke, 2011; Wuppertal Institute for Climate, Environment and Energy, 2011; interviews, Beijing).

This chapter aims to uncover a number of basic insights into the rather technical and at times opaque nature of the CDM as part of EU–China climate relations. A comprehensive account of the problems related to EU–China CDM cooperation, however, falls beyond the chapter's scope. The focus is narrowed to the following three issues: (1) the regulatory frameworks for EU–China CDM cooperation; (2) the role of finance in CDM project development compared to other determinants; and (3) concrete linkages between the CDM and the energy policy aspirations of China and the EU. For the latter two, China's wind power sector is selected as a case study in view of its relative importance compared to other Chinese renewable energy CDM projects (e.g. solar or biomass).

The first section presents the relevant regulatory frameworks governing EU–China CDM cooperation and provides a rationale for looking at the CDM in the context of renewable energy development in China. There are two major frameworks involved: the international regulatory framework for the CDM, and the rules and regulations governing the CDM in China which are framed in its domestic climate and renewable energy policies. Internationally, the CDM constitutes a significant element of the UN framework to combat climate change, allowing Annex I Parties (developed countries) and non-Annex I Parties (developing countries), as defined by the United Nations Framework Convention on Climate Change (UNFCCC) and its Kyoto Protocol, to undertake activities that reduce emissions in non-Annex I Parties and contribute to sustainable development (United Nations, 1992, 1997). Annex I Parties use Certified Emission Reductions (CERs) resulting from CDM projects to meet their reduction targets. CERs are bought and sold on the global carbon market, based on the procedures of the Kyoto Protocol's International Emissions Trading Mechanism (Yamin, 2005). An important reason for looking at the market for emission reduction certificates lies in the fact that the EU and China host, respectively, the largest sources of demand and supply for CERs. The European Union's Emission Trading System (EU ETS) is the single largest source of demand for CERs resulting from CDM projects, while Chinese projects currently supply the biggest amount of CERs worldwide (UNFCCC, 2011; Point Carbon, 2010). The second set of regulations pertains to the regulatory framework for the CDM in China and its role in Chinese renewable energy policy. The key document here is the 2005 Measures for the Operation and Management of Clean Development Mechanism Projects, establishing national CDM management institutions and setting standards for CDM project approval.

In the second section, this chapter looks at the wind power sector to examine the importance of finance as a driver for CDM project development compared to other possible incentives and determinants and to delineate concrete linkages between the CDM and Chinese and European RE development. Wind power projects and the wind power sector are selected because of the impressive growth rates in the sector in recent years, the large amount of wind projects in China's CDM portfolio, the substantial involvement of European wind companies in the sector and the amount of CERs originating from Chinese wind projects that are traded in the EU ETS (Lewis, 2010; Li, 2010).

THE REGULATORY FRAMEWORKS FOR EU–CHINA CDM COOPERATION

The following subsections introduce the two main regulatory frameworks that define EU–China CDM cooperation. The first section presents the relevant institutions, procedures and regulations that govern the CDM internationally. The second section introduces the Chinese domestic regulatory framework covering the CDM in relation to its renewable energy policies. A comprehensive bilateral EU–China CDM framework does not exist.

The Clean Development Mechanism

With 2,950 registered projects (as of April 2011), 581 million issued CERs (theoretically equivalent to 581 million tonnes of CO_2), and more than 2.7 billion CERs expected from registered projects by the end of 2012, the CDM is exceeding initial expectations as regards both the amount of projects and the certificates issued (UNFCCC, 2011).

The Kyoto Protocol (1997) defines the CDM in a rather flexible way. Article 12.2 and Article 12.3 of the Protocol allow for both unilateral, bilateral as well as multilateral (or portfolio) approaches to CDM projects. The bilateral approach involves Annex I and non-Annex I Parties cooperating in partnership, the unilateral approach consists of entities from non-Annex I Parties that undertake CDM activities without foreign partners, and the multilateral/portfolio approach refers to the case where an intermediary constructs a range of complementary CDM activities on behalf of others (Yamin, 2005: 30). Strictly speaking, technology transfer can only take place in bilateral and multilateral projects, although the development of specific technologies can be stimulated in unilateral projects through cash flows from (future) CER revenues. The establishment of CER sales agreements during the design of a project can, to a certain extent, ensure this cash flow prior to the actual issuance of CERs.

The most important actors, terms and processes involved in the mechanism can be concisely summarised by explaining the CDM project cycle (see Figure 14.1). The latter can be divided into five steps: (1) project design; (2) validation and registration; (3) monitoring; (4) verification and certification; and (5) CER issuance.

The Project Design Document is the key document involved in the first two steps of the project cycle. It is written by the Project Participants (PPs) and describes all the relevant details of the project, including the baseline (or 'business-as-usual scenario') against which the 'additionality' of the

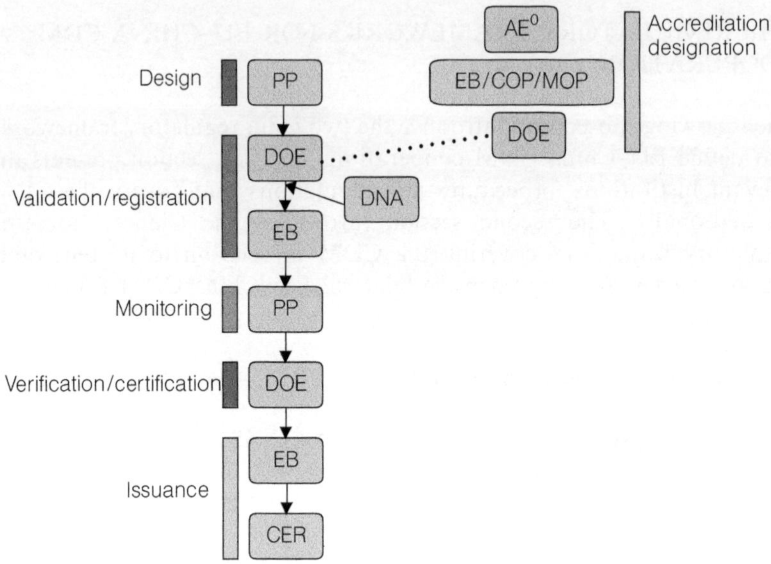

Figure 14.1 The CDM project cycle

targeted emission reductions is established. An independent third party (known as a Designated Operational Entity (DOE)) validates the project after the Project Design Document has been approved by the Designated National Authority of the host country (e.g. China). The CDM Executive Board (EB), the international body that supervises the CDM, officially registers the project when validation is completed. Monitoring of emission reductions is performed by the PPs themselves, according to the procedures mentioned in the Project Design Document. A second Designated Operational Entity performs verification and certification of the monitoring results, leading to the issuance of CERs by the Executive Board. Issued CERs are forwarded to the accounts of the relevant entities in the CDM registry, held by the UNFCCC Secretariat, from which a link is established to the International Emissions Trading Mechanism, commonly referred to as the 'global carbon market' (CDM Rulebook, 2010).

The EU Emissions Trading System (EU ETS), a European company-level system linked to the international trading mechanism since 2008, provides the single largest share of demand for CERs in the global carbon market (Point Carbon, 2010). A maximum of 1.4 billion CERs are expected to enter the EU ETS during the first commitment period (2008–12), while the UNFCCC expects the issuance of 2.7 billion CERs by 2012 from projects registered by April 2011 (Chevallier, 2010; UNFCCC, 2011).

Total CER demand from the EU is, moreover, driven by both EU ETS and non-EU ETS sources. The latter refers mainly to individual EU member states that need reduction certificates to comply with their Kyoto targets. An additional 0.7 to 1 billion CERs could potentially enter the European carbon market in this way (Chevallier, 2010).

Table 14.1 Host country ranking (April 2011)

Host country	Issued CERs	Registered projects	Global share of issued CERs
China	48,167,650	1299	55.25%
India	93,303,692	636	16.06%
Republic of Korea	66,955,940	53	11.52%
Brazil	51,612,683	188	8.88%
Others	8,244,877	774	8.29%

Source: Adapted from: UNFCC (2011).

China, on the other hand, provides the single largest share of CER supply worldwide. It hosts 1,299 registered CDM projects as of April 2011, with another 1,188 projects at the validation phase (UNFCCC, 2011; UNEP Risoe Centre, 2011). Table 14.1 shows that China is currently the most important host country in the world, both in terms of CERs issued and registered projects. The CDM registry has issued 581 million CERs so far, of which China has produced 320 million or 55.25 per cent. India, the second largest country in the CDM, hosts only 636 projects, about half China's amount. More significantly, India only produces 93 million CERs, or 16 per cent, of the global market.

It is clear that at least regarding the first commitment period of the Kyoto Protocol (2008–12), the European Union and China are by far the most important blocs involved in CER trading, the former on the demand-side and the latter on the supply-side of the global CDM market. It is mostly the EU's company-level trading system, the EU ETS, that drives global CER demand.

CDM Rules and Regulations in China

This section explains the regulatory framework for the CDM in China and its role in Chinese renewable energy policy. On 12 October 2005, the Chinese government issued the Measures for the Operation and Management of Clean Development Mechanism Projects (the 'CDM Rules'). The latter is the only legal document on the CDM in China and it is mainly concerned with the management institutions and domestic approval procedures for CDM projects (NDRC & WB, 2009: 27).

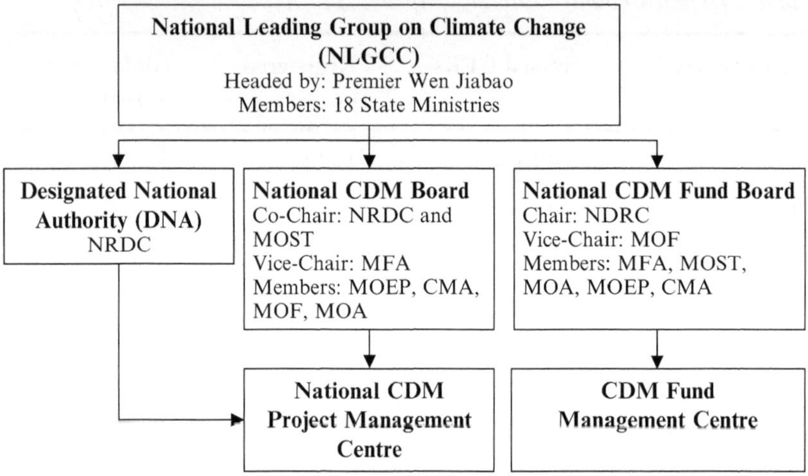

Source: EU–China CDM Facilitation Project (2009: 21).

Figure 14.2 CDM management institutions in China

The major institutional actors of CDM management in China are the National Leading Group on Climate Change (NLGCC), the Designated National Authority (DNA), the National CDM Board and the National CDM Fund Board (see Figure 14.2). The NLGCC holds the ultimate authority over the CDM in China, coordinating important CDM policies and approving members of the National CDM Board. The group was established in 2007 and consists of the Chinese Premier and members of 18 state ministries. The National CDM Board functions as an advisory body for the NLGCC and is involved in CDM approval procedures. The National Development and Reform Commission (NDRC), one of China's most influential and powerful ministries, acts as China's DNA. It is in charge of the acceptance of applications and the issuance of letters of approval, the basic requirement to enter step 2 (validation) of the CDM Project Cycle. The National CDM Fund Board governs the CDM Fund, set up to promote sustainable development, climate adaptation and mitigation in China. The CDM Project Management Centre and the

CDM Fund Management Centre provide operational and administrative assistance to the DNA, the NLGCC, the National CDM Board and the National CDM Fund Board.

The CDM Rules favour projects that promote 'energy efficiency, renewable energy development and methane recovery and utilization through transferring environmentally sound technology' (CDM Rules, Art. 4). CDM projects in these three priority areas are encouraged by the government and pass approval procedures more easily. Other major elements of China's generally very efficient CDM Rules include:

- *Eligibility requirements.* Only Chinese companies or Chinese holding companies are eligible for CDM projects (CDM Rules, Art. 24). A Chinese holding company refers to a joint venture where the Chinese entity controls a minimum of 51 per cent of the shares. This rule limits the access of foreign companies to CDM development in China and is thus an important element in the discussion on technology transfer.
- *CER price guidance.* The DNA performs a price review before issuing the letter of approval, de facto establishing a CER price floor.
- *Tax levies.* The Chinese government levies a tax of 2 per cent of the CER transfer price on priority area projects, 30 per cent on N_2O projects and 65 per cent on HFC and PFC projects. Tax revenues are collected in the CDM Fund, governed by the National CDM Fund Board.

These rules, particularly the tax levies based on the three priority areas, indicate the Chinese government's urge to promote technology transfer and to develop renewable energy technology in China through the CDM.

The overall regulatory framework of RE development is governed by the 2005 Renewable Energy Law and a number of targets issued in various policy documents in the following years. These include primarily the following: a 10 per cent share of renewable energy in primary energy consumption by 2010, an 11.4 per cent share of non-fossil fuels in primary energy consumption by 2015 and a 15 per cent share of non-fossil fuels by 2020. Note the difference in language – probably referring to the use of nuclear energy and large-scale hydropower energy – in the first compared to the latter two targets. The 10 per cent by 2010 target was first issued in the 2007 National Climate Change Program (CNCCP) and reiterated in the 2007 Mid- and Long-Term Renewable Energy Development Plan and the 11th Five Year Plan (2006–10) for Renewable Energy Development. The 15 per cent target was first adopted in the 2007 Mid- and Long-Term Renewable Energy Development Plan and later on formed one of China's voluntary international pledges in Copenhagen and Cancun. The 11.4 per cent by 2015 target was included in China's 2011–15 12th Five Year Plan, adopted in March 2011. Table 14.2 summarises China's renewable energy and non-fossil fuels targets.

Table 14.2 China's renewable energy and climate mitigation targets

Policy document	Year	Target
China's National Climate Change Programme (CNCPP)	2007	10% RE by 2010
The Mid- and Long-Term Renewable Energy Development Plan	2007	10% RE by 2010 and 15% non-fossil fuels by 2020
The 11th Five-Year Plan (2006–10) for Renewable Energy Development	2008	10% RE by 2010
Copenhagen Accord, Appendix II; Cancun Agreements, Decision 1/CP.16	2009/ 2010	15% non-fossil fuels by 2020
The 12th Five-year Plan (2011–15)	2011	11.4% non-fossil fuels by 2015

Compiled by the authors.

The general picture that emerges from China's recent policy initiatives shows a modest aspiration to change current energy production and consumption patterns and move away from over-reliance on fossil fuels towards a moderate increase in the use of non-fossil fuel energy. The CDM is mainly perceived as a complementary vehicle to enhance technology transfer and facilitate financial flows and is only sporadically referred to in policy documents. As both finance and technology are key issues in the development of the renewable energy sector in China, however, the CDM potentially touches upon aspects of each of the above mentioned renewable energy policy frameworks.

EU–CHINA CDM COOPERATION: THE CASE OF WIND ENERGY

From a developing country's perspective, the CDM offers two major resources: finance and technology. It is widely perceived that of these two, only financial resources flow to the developing world as foreseen.[1] As a matter of fact, studies on technology transfer show that CER revenue is actually one of the main reasons why technology is transferred at all, as it financially enables investment in equipment and know-how (Lewis, 2010; Wang B, 2010; Schroeder, 2009). The following subsections look at the wind power sector in terms of the weight of finance as a driver of CDM project development compared to other determinants and reveals concrete linkages between the CDM and the energy policy aspirations of China and the EU.

Wind Energy in China

The Renewable Energy Law is an important driving force of China's wind market expansion. Since 2005, when the law introduced various targets and (market) mechanisms, the growth of wind installation capacity in China is evident compared to earlier periods. After it took effect in January 2006, 1,337 megawatts (MW) were added in one year and the accumulated installed capacity reached 2.6 gigawatts (GW). The following years witnessed an equally impressive growth rate, leading to an installed capacity of 12.8 GW in 2008 and nearly 25 GW by the end of 2009 (see Figure 14.3). Initial figures for 2010 point to another massive year-on-year increase, reaching over 41 GW of installed wind power capacity (Xinhua, 2011).

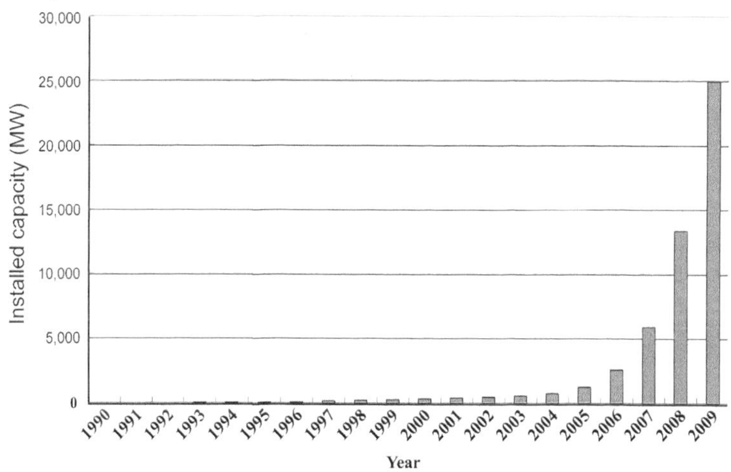

Adapted from NREL (2004); Lema and Kristian (2007); Zeppezauer and Carnabuci (2009).

Figure 14.3 Wind installation capacity in China 1990–2009

With regard to the CDM, the share of wind projects in China has been relatively large, with 366 out of 1,299, or about 30 per cent, of China's registered CDM projects belonging to this type as of April 2011

(UNFCCC, 2011). Interviews with the central government, industry and academics show that without the CDM, the wind power sector would probably not have developed as quickly as it did up until today. To a certain degree, it facilitated the rapid development of China's wind-power sector and enhanced wind power technology transfer – particularly in a quantitative sense.

Finance as the Key Determinant

CDM funding is a key element in making several hundreds of Chinese wind projects profitable – at least if the financial additionality claims in the Project Design Documents correspond with reality. Interviews show that the 366 CDM wind-power projects would not be economically competitive and would have an internal rate of return that is lower than the benchmark price (meaning the lowest acceptable price set by the NDRC) without CER revenues. Projects that have registered under the CDM reach a greater internal return rate than the benchmark by relying on the revenue transferred from the expected CO_2 emission reductions (compared to business-as-usual).

The problem of proving financial additionality is best illustrated by a dispute between the Chinese government and the CDM Executive Board in 2009. In June that year, the Chinese government carried out a major wind electricity price reform by introducing fixed feed-in-tariff prices in regions with rich wind capacity. The purpose of introducing fixed prices by region was to ensure profit, but how they are effectively being operated is unclear. At the end of the year, the Executive Board rejected 50 Chinese wind projects based on concerns about financial additionality because wind-generated electricity prices appeared to be much lower than those previously approved. The Board suspected that the Chinese government intentionally fixed a very low price, so that CDM project developers could falsely claim financial additionality, i.e. that they need the additional revenue from CER sales for the project to be financially feasible (Shanghai Financial News, 2009; Xinhua, 2009). As a matter of fact, a study by Michael Wara and David Victor demonstrates that between one- and two-thirds of the entire CDM market is in fact non-additional, meaning that these projects would have taken place anyway. The environmental integrity of the CDM is therefore highly questionable (Wara and Victor, 2008).

The fact remains, however, that the CDM leads to a significant financial flow towards China's domestic wind-power sector. This finance stems from CER sales mainly destined for the European market (Delbeke, 2011; Point Carbon, 2010). Of the two main 'engines' of the CDM (finance and technology), it is the financial flow resulting from the sale of CERs that essentially drives the Chinese CDM wind-power market (interviews, Beijing).

Insights from the level of the renewable energy sector in general support this finding. Most importantly, interviews with European experts have brought to light that Europe and European companies have decided to become involved in the domestic renewable energy market in China regardless of expected breaches in the intellectual property rights (IPR) of imported technology – as opposed to choices made by US government and industry (interviews, Beijing). The main rationale for European companies to do so is access to the Chinese market. Technology development or transfer (of important technologies) that takes place through CDM projects must mainly be seen in this light – and is certainly not a driver of CDM project development.

Other insights from the general state of affairs of China's wind-power development sustain the view that finance is the primary driver of the CDM. There are two such insights that deserve some closer attention: (1) different views on technology transfer; and (2) the Chinese concession system for wind power.

A central point of disagreement is the definition of technology transfer – a point that is of general importance in the climate debate and connected to the problematic issue of IPR as mentioned above. China's central government supports the view that key technological know-how should be transferred to developing countries to support mitigation activities. With regard to the wind-power sector, these technologies are still mainly controlled by European companies based in Denmark, Germany, the Netherlands and Spain, in addition to a number of US companies. European industry, on the other hand, emphasises the need for a balance between technology transfer and competition. If the Chinese government were to ask foreign investors to reveal their central control systems or core technology, the latter would quickly be out of business.

The issue was further complicated by the '70 per cent local content rule', established in 2005 but cancelled in 2009. The rule was intended to stimulate technology transfer to local wind turbine manufacturers and to reduce production costs (Pan and Zhu, 2006). Before 2005, the major challenge for wind-power development was that most wind turbines and generators relied heavily on foreign imports, which were expensive and made investment costs high. To reduce the burden on investors, the Chinese government decided that 70 per cent of wind turbine components should be produced locally. The rule did not mean that turbines had to be produced by Chinese companies, but it obliged products to be made locally, either by domestic or foreign industries. This rule enabled Chinese industry to learn from European and other foreign investors about how to produce turbines and other wind technology, and it was actually one of the main drivers of the sector's development boom over the past five years. The major disadvantage of the local content rule, however, was that companies used cheap materials to drive down costs, which, combined with a lack of government funding on R&D, caused severe wind turbine quality problems. Poor quality led to production losses and increased repair costs, which in turn led to investment losses (Nao, 2006). As a result, the central government decided to abandon the rule in 2009. That decision was beneficial to EU businesses, which can now compete in the market with quality turbines and it has also opened up more possibilities for various kinds of joint ventures with domestic partners.

The wind concession system, initiated by the central government in 2003, is another important issue for European and other foreign investors in China's wind-power sector (Schroeder, 2009; Wang, Q., 2010). The concession system consists of two different bidding rounds for wind power development projects, *national* and *local* bidding rounds. Both bidding rounds are open to foreign investors and Chinese companies. Problems arise mainly in the national bidding rounds, which are very rarely won by European players. National biddings are based on the price per kWh and do not take into account quality factors such as turbine longevity, know-how related to optimal windmill placement and so forth. The European technology giants, champions in high-quality turbines, simply cannot compete with the cheap but relatively low-quality Chinese turbines and are cut off from participation in major domestic projects as a result.

The observations from the sector-level contacts between European and Chinese wind developers show that both sides attach a lot of importance to core technology. European industry clearly has the technological expertise and capacity to build high-quality wind turbines, and is eager to hold on to its key assets while China attempts to build up technology both qualitatively and, more succesfully, quantitatively. Simultaneously, the EU expects future revenues for its companies from access to the Chinese wind-power market and is therefore willing to risk losing part of the IPR on (lower value) technologies. Technology development/transfer through the CDM is likewise a by-product of the financial flow generated through CER sales.

One of the key consequences of this finding is that a very peculiar situation has arisen in recent years with regard to the CDM in EU–China RE relations. The billions of euros that flow through the mechanism actually contradict Europe's overall economic and climate strategy: money – from European taxpayers and industry – is flowing directly to Chinese competitors without added-value in terms of technology. For individual companies it might be rational to invest in CDM projects and profit from the sale of CERs to the European market, but it is a waste of resources for the European wind industry and the European Union at large. Especially in view of long-term climate action in the EU – envisaged in the proposed Roadmap for a low-carbon society in 2011 – it becomes meaningless to subsidise a competing sector in China while finance is highly needed for domestic wind-power and low-carbon technology development (Delbeke, 2011; European Commission, 2011).

Waste of financial resources becomes a misdemeanor against the global environment if one takes into account the environmental integrity concerns related to, among other reasons, weak additionality claims (Delbeke, 2011; Ruthner et al. 2011; Wara and Victor, 2008). This is a direct consequence of the fact that the CDM's relative emission reductions are calculated against an imaginary, hypothetical projection or baseline, as opposed to absolute emission reductions, as in the EU ETS, where they are calculated vis-à-vis an actual historical amount (see above).

The final argument against the validity of the CDM is the following: the CDM allows Europe, historically greatly responsible for climate change, to partly continue to pollute instead of taking more drastic and urgent action domestically. Reflecting this truism, Connie Hedegaard, European Commissioner for Climate Action, stressed the importance of domestic action to reach Europe's climate goals during her 2011 presentation of the *Roadmap for Moving to a Competitive Low Carbon Economy in 2050* (Hedegaard, 2011; European Commission, 2011). European mitigation postponement behaviour increases the long-term economic, societal and ecological costs of building a European low-carbon society – exactly the opposite of an argument that is often raised in favour of the CDM: that it would supposedly be a cost-effective solution to tackle climate change.

CONCLUSIONS AND FUTURE OUTLOOK

This chapter has studied the role, use and validity of the CDM by looking at EU involvement in Chinese CDM projects in wind power. The first section introduced the two main regulatory frameworks that govern EU–China CDM relations, i.e. the international CDM rules and China's domestic CDM measures and related renewable energy policies. These frameworks establish the legal boundaries within which Chinese and European businesses engage in joint or unilateral CDM projects, buy and sell CERs, and transfer advanced technology and/or know-how. The section section empirically investigated the wind-power sector in China. In addition to the evolution and size of the sector and CDM projects implemented, the chapter has looked at the role of finance and technology in the CDM. The most straightforward conclusion is that the attraction/

absence of financial flows is the single most decisive factor for CDM development in the wind-power sector. The sale of CERs into the European Emissions Trading System stimulates China's wind-power expansion and facilitates technology development (or transfer, depending on how 'transfer' is defined) as a by-product.

Insights from the general situation of the renewable energy sector in China underscore that finance is the driver while technology is in the back seat, and reveal a number of significant linkages with Chinese and European renewable energy policy and company/industry behaviour. European companies aim to gain access to the Chinese wind-power market and are willing to cope with potential breaches of IPR on (lower value) technologies. Access is limited by the Chinese government, however, by the former 70 per cent local content rule and the wind concession system, installed to protect its own industry. The difference of understanding with regard to what 'technology transfer' actually means adds to the mix of divergent interests and actors at work.

In combination with both inherent and particular flaws of the CDM – mainly environmental integrity concerns related to (financial) additionality, ethics and long-term economic costs – it is concluded that the CDM does not work in favour of European industry, the European taxpayers nor the EU at large, except for those companies that benefit directly and in the short term from CER revenue. Since the CDM contributes to mitigation postponement behaviour within the EU, and taking into account the flaws of the mechanism, the CDM might be a harmful instrument for China in the long-term as well. If climate change is not seriously abated, China is projected to suffer from severe climate impacts such as extreme weather events, droughts, floods, imperiled food and water supply, the spread of vector-borne diseases and biodiversity losses (IPCC, 2007).

In a first attempt to tackle the issue, the EU issued more stringent regulations for Phase III (2013–20) of its emissions trading system in 2009. Current EU ETS legislation for that period only allows post-2013 CERs from projects in Least Developed Countries or from third countries that establish a bilateral agreement with the EU (European Parliament/Council of the European Union, 2009). A large amount of CERs from China, however, produced by already registered projects before the end of 2012 will still be allowed to flow into the EU in both Phase II and Phase III under current regulations. The key message is that domestic efforts to tackle climate change are the best way forward in the construction of a European and a Chinese low-carbon society, not only for taxpayers and the general public, but also for the credibility of governments and the economic future of both China and the EU.

INTERVIEWS

Beijing, May 2009–February 2011:

- Business representatives: 17
- Academics: 10
- Officials: 10
- Members of international organisations: 2
- Total: 39

Note: Strict anonymity rules are applied to all interviewees due to the sensitive economic and political context of the research topic. In total, 39 interviews were held during three research visits in Beijing (China) in May 2009, June 2010 and February 2011.

NOTE

1. Information in the following sections is based on interviews with Chinese and European business representatives, officials, academics, and members of international organisations. See list of interviews, Beijing, May 2009 – February 2011, at the end of the chapter.

REFERENCES

'CDM Rulebook' (2010). Online at: http://cdmrulebook.org (accessed 16 November 2010).

Chevallier, Julien (2010) 'Price relationships in the ED emissions trading system', *Centre pour la Communication Scientifique Directs*. Online at: http://halshs.archives-ouvertes.fr/docs/00/45/87/28/PDF/Chevallier170210.pdf (accessed 16 November 2010).

Delbeke, Jos (2011) Intervention at the Stakeholder Conference on the Roadmap for Moving to a Low Carbon Economy in 2050, Brussels, 17 March.

EU–China CDM Facilitation Project (2009) 'Technology Transfer in CDM Projects in China'. Online at: http://www.euchin-cdm.org (accessed 16 November 2010).

European Commission (2011) *A Roadmap for Moving to a Competitive Low Carbon Economy in 2050* (COM (2011) 112/4). Brussels.

European Parliament/Council of the European Union (2009) *Directive of 23 April 2009 amending Directive 2003/87/EC so as to Improve and Extend the Greenhouse Gas Emission Allowance Trading Scheme of the Community* (2009/29/EC).

Han, Jingyi (2009) *Renewable Energy Development in China: Policies, Practices and Performance*. PhD dissertation, Netherlands Research School for the Socio-Economic and Natural Sciences of the Environment, Wageningen University, Netherlands.

Hedegaard, Connie (2011) *Keynote Speech*. Stakeholder Conference on the Roadmap for Moving to a Low Carbon Economy in 2050, Brussels, 17 March.

IPCC (2007) 'Summary for policymakers', in M. L. Parry, O. F. Canziani, J. P.

Palutikof, P. J. van der Linden and C. E. Hanson (eds), *Climate Change 2007: Impacts, Adaptation and Vulnerability. Contribution of Working Group II to the Fourth Assessment Report of the Intergovernmental Panel on Climate Change.* Cambridge: Cambridge University Press, pp. 7–22.

Jordan, A., Huitema, D., van Asselt, H., Rayner, T. and Berkhout, F. (2010) *Climate Change Policy in the European Union: Confronting the Dilemmas of Mitigation and Adaptation?* Cambridge: Cambridge University Press.

Lema, Adrian and Kristian, R. (2007) 'Between fragmented authoritarianism and policy coordination: creating a Chinese market for wind energy', *Energy Policy*, 35 (7): 3879–90.

Lewis, Joanna (2010) 'The evolving role of carbon finance in promoting renewable energy development in China', *Energy Policy*, 38 (6): 2875–86.

Li, Jun (2010) 'Decarbonising power generation in China: is the answer blowing in the wind?', *Renewable and Sustainable Energy Reviews*, 14: 1154–71.

Li, Jungfeng and Wang, Z. (2007) *China Renewable Energy Industry Development Report*. Beijing: National Development and Reform Commission.

Nao, Nakanishi (2006) 'China Wind Power Boom May Bust Without Policy Change'. Online at: http://www.planetark.com/dailynewsstory.cfm/newsid/37362/story.htm (accessed 1 September 2010).

National Development and Reform Commission (2005) *Measures for Operation and Management of Clean Development Mechanism Projects in China*. Beijing: National Development and Reform Commission.

National Development and Reform Commission (2006) *China's Eleventh Five-Year Social and Economic Development Plan*. Beijing: National Development and Reform Commission.

National Development and Reform Commission (2007a) *Introduction to the Eleventh Five- Year Plan on Energy Development*. Beijing: National Development and Reform Commission.

National Development and Reform Commission (2007b) *National Evaluation Report of Climate Change*. Beijing: National Development and Reform Commission.

National Development and Reform Commission (2007c) *Medium and Long-Term Development Plan for Renewable Energy in China*. Beijing: National Development and Reform Commission.

National Development and Reform Commission and World Bank (2009) *CDM in China: Five Years of Experience (2004–2009)*. Beijing: National Development and Reform Commission.

National People's Congress (2005) *The Renewable Energy Law of the People's Republic of China*. Beijing: National People's Congress.

National People's Congress (2009) *Renewable Energy Law of the People's Republic of China (Revised)*. Beijing: National People's Congress.

National Renewable Energy Laboratory (NREL) (2004) 'Grid Connected Wind Power in China'. Online at: http://www.nrel.gov/docs/fy04osti/35789.pdf (accessed 22 June 2010).

Netherlands Environmental Assessment Agency (2007) 'China Now No.1 in CO_2 Emissions, USA in Second Position'. Online at: http://www.pbl.nl/en/news/pressreleases/2007/20070619Chinanowno1inCO2emissionsUSAinsecondposition.html (accessed 2 January 2009).

Pan, Jiahua and Zhu, X. (2006) *Energy and Sustainable Development in China: Sustainable Energy Watch 2005–06*. Beijing: Helio International.

Point Carbon (2010) 'Carbon 2010: The Return of the Sovereign'. Online at: http://www.pointcarbon.com/polopoly_fs/1.1420234!Carbon%202010.pdf (accessed 15 October 2010).

Ruthner, L., Johnson, M., Chatterjee, B., Lazarus, M., Fujiwara, N., Egenhofer, C., Monceau, T. du and Brohe, A. (2011) *Study on the Integrity of the Clean Development Mechanism (CDM)*, Final Report to the European Commission, Directorate-General Climate Action, December, Ref.: CLIMA.B.3/ETU/2010/0020r. London: AEA.

Schroeder, Miriam (2009) 'Utilizing the Clean Development Mechanism for the deployment of renewable energies in China', *Applied Energy*, 86: 237–42.

Shanghai Financial News (2009) 'NDRC: Price Setting is Irrelevant to CDM'. Online at: http://www.gerun369.com/news/mast/200911272148.htm (accessed 20 June 2010).

UNEP Risoe Centre (2011) 'UNEP Risoe CDM/JI Pipeline'. Online at: http://cdmpipeline.org (accessed 6 April 2011).

UNFCCC (2008) 'Analysis of Technology Transfer in CDM Projects'. Online at: http://cdm.unfccc.int/Reference/Reports/TTreport/index.html (accessed 16 November 2010).

UNFCCC (2011) 'CDM Project Search'. Online at: http://cdm.unfccc.int/index.html (accessed 6 April 2011).

United Nations (1992) *United Nations Framework Convention on Climate Change*. New York: United Nations.

United Nations (1997) *Kyoto Protocol to the United Nations Framework Convention on Climate Change*. New York: United Nations.

United Nations (2009) *Copenhagen Accord, Appendix II: Nationally Appropriate Mitigation Actions of Developing Country Parties*. United Nations.

United Nations (2010) *The Cancun Agreements: Outcome of the Work of the Ad Hoc Working Group on Long-term Cooperative Action under the Convention*, Decision 1/CP.16. New York: United Nations.

Wang, Bo (2010) 'Can CDM Bring technology transfer to China? An empirical study of technology transfer in China's CDM projects', *Energy Policy*, 38: 2572–85.

Wang, Qiang (2010) 'Effective policies for renewable energy: the example of China's wind power – lessons for China's photovoltaic power', *Renewable and Sustainable Energy Reviews*, 14: 702–12.

Wara, Michael and Victor, D. (2008) *A Realistic Policy on International Carbon Offsets*, PESO Working Paper 74. Stanford, CA: Stanford University.

Wuppertal Institute for Climate, Environment and Energy (2011) 'Using the CDM beyond 2012', *Mo Info*, 1 (11): 1, 5–7.

Xinhua (2009) 'UN Suspended 50 CDM Wind Power Projects'. Online at: http://www.caijing.com.cn/2009-12-03/110327621.html (accessed 20 June 2010) (in Chinese).

Xinhua (2011) 'China Has World's Most Installed Wind-Power Capacity'. Online at: http://www.china.org.cn/business/2011-01/13/content_21733120.htm (accessed 7 April 2011).

Yamin, Farhana (ed.) (2005) *Climate Change and Carbon Markets: A Handbook of Emissions Reduction Mechanisms*. London: Earthscan.

Zeppezauer, Christian and Carnabuci, C. (2009), 'A New Revolution: China Hikes Wind and Solar Power Targets'. Online at: http://www.renewableenergyworld.com/rea/news/ article/2009/10/a-new-revolution-china-hikes-wind-and-

solar-power-targets (accessed 21 April 2010).
Zhang, Zeming, Wang, Q., Xing, Z., Hamrin, J. and Baruch, S. (2009) 'Renewable Energy Development in China: The Potential and the Challenges'. Online at: http://www.frankhaugwitz.info/doks/general/2001_China_RE_Situation_Report_full_EF.pdf. (accessed 14 November 2010).
Zhang, Zhongxiang (2010) *Copenhagen and Beyond: Reflections on China's Stance and Responses*, Working Papers, Economics Series 111. Honolulu, HI: East-West Centre. Online at: http://www.eastwestcenter.org/fileadmin/stored/pdfs//econwp111.pdf (accessed 18 November 2010).

15. The energy challenge: China, the EU and the restructuring of global governance

Bernard Snoy

THE NATURE OF THE CHALLENGE

One of the most significant facts of today's global economy is the emergence of China, together with India, as the new giants of the world economy and the international energy markets. However, we are only becoming aware of the alarming consequences for China, for the other emerging countries and for the USA, the European Union (EU) and the rest of the world that unfettered growth in global energy demand – a growth that is expected to exceed 50 per cent between 2005 and 2030 – could have in terms of both energy security and environmental sustainability. In terms of energy security, the key issues are depletion of non-renewable resources and increased dependence on Middle Eastern and Russian fossil-fuel sources. As concerns environmental security, the main issue is climate change provoked by CO_2 and other greenhouse gas (GHG) emissions. The key challenge therefore for all countries, including the EU member states and China, is to put in motion a transition to a more secure, lower-carbon energy system, without undermining economic and social development.

CHINA'S PRIMARY ENERGY DEMAND AND RESOURCES

According to the International Energy Agency (IEA, 2007: 262):

> [. . .] in less than a generation, China has moved from being a minor and largely self-sufficient energy consumer to become the world's fastest growing energy consumer and major player on the global energy market. Soaring energy use is both a driver and a consequence of the remarkable growth in the country's economy – especially in heavy industry. For many years, China was able to meet its rapidly growing energy needs entirely from domestic resources, so its impact on global markets was minimal. That has changed dramatically in the last decade and national concerns about supply security have grown in parallel.

Rising fossil-fuel use has worsened already acute local pollution and driven up greenhouse-gas emissions, casting doubts on the sustainability of China's pattern of development.

The breakdown of total primary energy demand in China by energy source is illustrated in Figure 15.1, provided by the IEA.

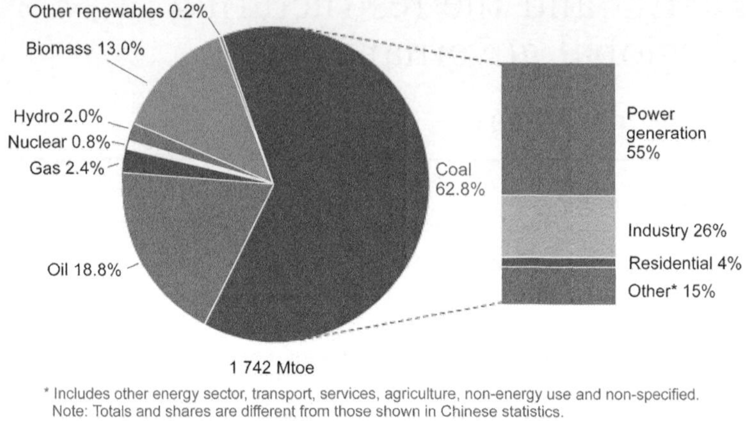

Source: World Energy Outlook 2007 © *'China and India Insights'*, OECD/International Energy Agency (2007: 262, Figure 8.1).

Figure 15.1 Total primary energy demand in China (2005)

As can be seen, coal is the backbone of China's energy system, meeting just over 60 per cent of the country's primary energy demand, providing most of the fuel used by power stations and much of the final energy used by industry, commercial businesses and households. According to the IEA, coal's importance in the overall fuel mix has in fact been growing in recent years, due to booming demand for electricity, which until recently was 80 per cent coal-based. Oil demand is also growing quickly, with a share in primary demand reaching 19 per cent in 2005. Because of the continued use by so many rural households of wood fuel and crop wastes for cooking and heating, biomass remains an important source of energy. In 2005, natural gas, nuclear power, hydropower and renewable sources including wind and solar power constituted only very small proportions of total primary energy demand but, of course, this is bound to change in the future.

China's per capita energy use remains less than 30 per cent of the OECD members' average; it is modest particularly in comparison with per capita energy use in the USA (see Figure 15.2) but it is higher than in most other developing regions because of the importance of heavy industry.

China is generously endowed with energy resources, particularly coal

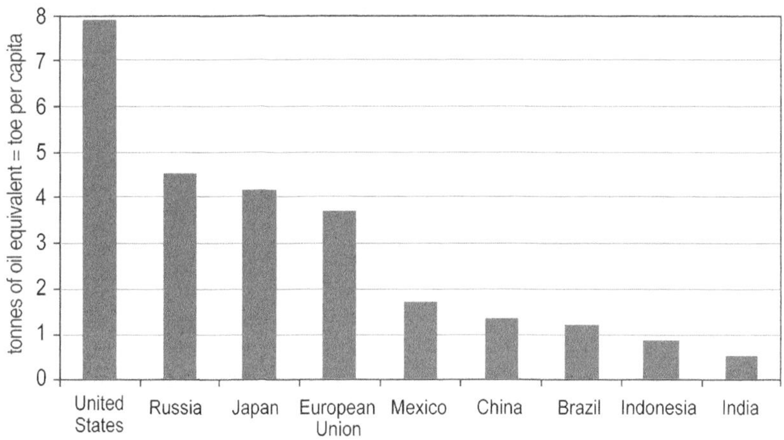

Source: World Energy Outlook 2007 © *'China and India Insights'*, OECD/International Energy Agency (2007: 266, Figure 8.2).

Figure 15.2 Per capita primary energy demand in China, India and other selected countries (2005)

and renewables, such as hydropower, wind, biomass and solar. However, while China possesses significant oil and gas resources and continues to enjoy some success in exploration within its territory, according to the IEA, its resources are insufficient to match the projected demand through to 2030. The government is encouraging its national oil companies to invest in developing oil resources abroad (for example in countries such as Kazakhstan, Nigeria, Sudan and Angola) – a policy referred to as 'going out' (IEA, 2007: 272).

OUTLOOK FOR ENERGY DEMAND AND SUPPLY IN CHINA

According to the IEA, China's primary energy needs will, under a reference scenario which predicts the outcome were there to be no change to current government policy, expand from 1,742 million tonnes of oil equivalent (Mtoe) in 2005 to 3,819 Mtoe in 2030, an average annual rate of increase of 3.2 per cent. In recent years, China has already overtaken the US to become the world's largest energy consumer.[1] Consequently, the reference scenario finds that the combined projected share of China and India in the increase in world primary energy demand over the 2005–30 period will be 45 per cent for all sources of energy and 82 per cent for coal only (see Figure 15.3). Oil demand for transport in China, spurred by rapidly expanding passenger and

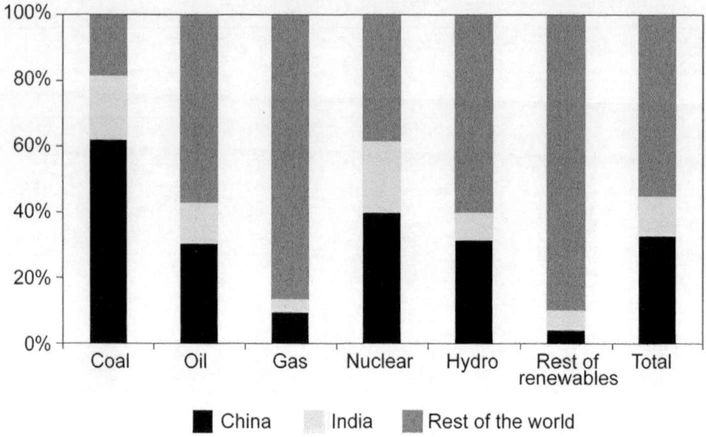

Source: World Energy Outlook 2007 © *'China and India Insights',* OECD/International Energy Agency (2007: 118, Figure 2.1).

Figure 15.3 Shares of China and India in the increase in world primary energy demand by fuel in the reference scenario (2005–30)

freight vehicle fleets, could almost quadruple between 2005 and 2030, contributing to more than two-thirds of the overall increase in Chinese oil demand. This is based on the assumption, among others, that new car sales would increase from 4.4 million in 2006 to about 18 million in 2030, with the vehicle stock increasing from 37 million in 2006 to about 270 million in 2030, by which time the ownership level – at 260 vehicles per 1,000 people – would be close to that of South Korea. Rising incomes would also underpin strong growth in housing, the use of electric appliances and heating and cooling requirements.

Faced with this booming energy demand, China's own energy resources will not be sufficient. Chinese resources – especially coal – are extensive but will not be sufficient to meet the growth in China's energy needs. Oil imports could jump from 3.5 mb/d (millions of barrels per day) in 2006 to 13.1 mb/d in 2030, while the share of imports in demand could rise from 50 to 80 per cent. Natural gas imports will also increase quickly, with the share of imports in demand also exceeding 50 per cent. China will need to add more than 1,300 GW to its electricity-generating capacity, which is more than the total current installed capacity in the US. Coal will remain the dominant fuel in power generation. The IEA reference scenario also calls for cumulative investment by China in energy-supply infrastructure of around 3,740 billion dollars (in year-2006 dollars) for the period 2006–30, out of a world total of around 22 trillion dollars (see Figure 15.4).

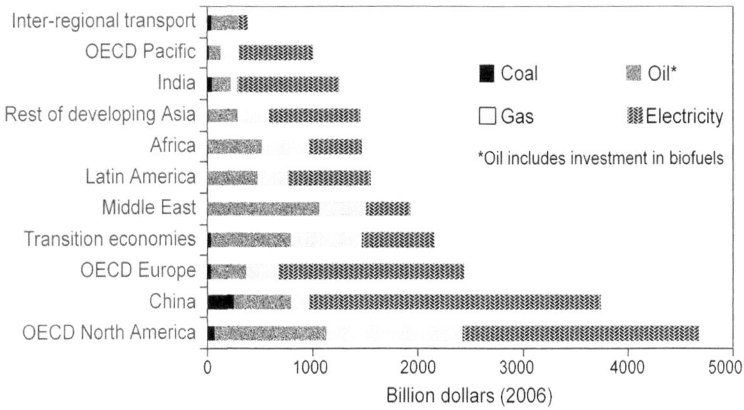

Source: World Energy Outlook 2007 © *'China and India Insights'*, OECD/International Energy Agency (2007: 96, Figure 1.13).

Figure 15.4 Cumulative investment in energy infrastructure in the reference scenario by fuel and region (2006–30)

More than two-thirds of these investments in China would need to take place in the power sector. The consequences of the IEA's reference scenario for CO_2 emissions are shown below (see Figure 15.5). With 11.4 gigatonnes (billion tonnes) China will become in 2030, by far, the biggest emitter of energy-related CO_2 emissions, although on a per capita basis its emissions, at 7.9 tonnes, will be very close to the EU level and would still be less than half of those of the USA.

These overwhelming projections make clear that stronger action is needed. In fact, China is already making efforts to address the causes and consequences of burgeoning energy use, particularly in the area of energy efficiency, but even stronger measures will be required. Government action must focus on curbing the rapid growth in CO_2 emissions from coal-fired power stations, the primary cause of the surge in global emissions in the last few years. It is encouraging to note that many of the policies available to alleviate energy insecurity can also help mitigate local pollution and climate change, and vice versa. There are large potential gains for OECD countries, including the EU, on the one hand, and China and other emerging countries, on the other hand, from enhanced policy cooperation.

The Emerging EU Energy Policy

The formulation of a common EU policy has been a long and arduous process due to the fact that, except for the provisions of the European Coal

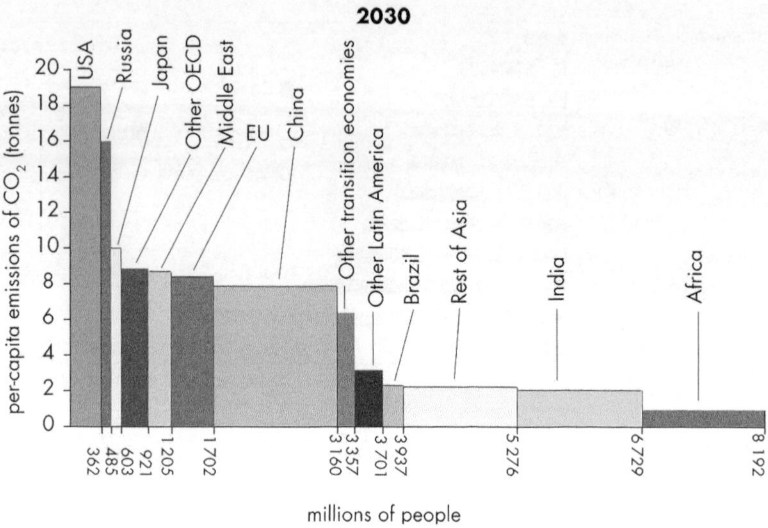

Source: World Energy Outlook 2007 © *'China and India Insights'*, OECD/International Energy Agency (2007: 203, Figure 5.10).

Figure 15.5 Per capita energy-related CO_2 emissions and population by region in the reference scenario

and Steel Treaty and those of the Euratom Treaty, energy policy has remained for a long time an area in which member states have been eager to maintain their national, sovereign prerogatives. It is only recently, due to the new Article 194 of the Lisbon Treaty (Treaty on the Functioning of the European Union (TFEU)), that majority decision-making can occur when it is deemed necessary to reach EU objectives in areas such as the functioning of the energy market, security of energy supply, energy efficiency, new and renewable energy development and network interconnections. National sovereignty is, however, maintained as far as the choice of the national policy mix and the exploitation of national energy resources are concerned. Furthermore, the framework under which EU energy policy has been formulated in recent years (see, for instance, the 2007 Energy Green Paper) brings together the three dimensions of energy security, overall competitiveness and environmental sustainability.

On 10 November 2010, the European Commission issued a new Communication to the European Parliament, the Council, the European Economic and Social Committee and the Committee of the Regions, on *Energy 2020: A Strategy for Competitive, Sustainable and Secure Energy* (SEC(2010)1346). There is also a related Communication, dated 17 November 2010, on *Priorities for 2020 and Beyond – A Blueprint for an*

Integrated European Energy Network (SEC(2010) 1395). These documents constitute important steps in the formulation of a common EU energy policy.

The creation of a common EU external energy policy has been equally arduous and agreement so far is primarily on rather broad principles. These principles were articulated for the first time in a paper *An External Policy to Serve Europe's Energy Interests*, issued jointly by the European Commission and the High Representative/Secretary General of the Council in 2006. These principles are as follows:

1. Promoting transparency and improved governance in the energy sector through energy partnerships with third countries, the objective being to create mutually beneficial, open, transparent, non-discriminatory and stable conditions for energy investment and trade;
2. Improving production and export capacities in producer countries and developing and upgrading energy transportation infrastructure in producer and transit countries;
3. Improving the climate for European companies' investments in third countries and opening up the production and export of energy resources to EU industry;
4. Improving conditions for trade in energy through non-discriminatory transit and third-country access to export pipeline infrastructure;
5. Enhancing physical and environmental security as well as the energy infrastructure safety;
6. Encouraging energy efficiency, use of renewable energies including bio-fuels, low emission technology and rational use of energy worldwide;
7. Implementing the relevant Kyoto Protocol mechanisms;
8. Diversifying energy imports by product and country;
9. Creating an international regime for the supply of enriched uranium to countries that have chosen the nuclear option, in line with non-proliferation commitments and taking into account the Euratom Treaty provisions; and
10. Promoting strategic reserve stocks and encouraging joint stock holding with partner countries.

To deal with the energy dimension of its relationship with China, the EU has set up the EU–China Energy Conference, which gathers together high-level European and Chinese representatives from industry and the public sector every two years, alternating between China and Brussels. It is co-organised by the Chinese Ministry of Sciences and Technology and the European Commission's Directorate General Energy.

At the EU–China Energy Working Group meeting in March 2005, two new initiatives were agreed.[2]

1. *Action Plan on Clean Coal.* The objective is to provide a sound set of information to decision-makers at political/ministerial/corporate level about how to develop policies and implement Clean Coal Technologies in China that are available or are currently being developed in Europe.
2. *Action Plan on Industrial Cooperation Energy Efficiency and Renewable Energies.* The objective is to establish closer contacts and to support the efforts in China to promote industrial cooperation in order to increase the use of energy efficiency and the use of renewable energies in China.

A Memorandum of Understanding establishing an 'EU–China Dialogue on Energy and Transport Strategies' between the European Commission and the National Development and Reform Commission (NDRC) was signed on the occasion of the EU–China Summit on 5 September 2005 in Beijing. The first meeting took place in Brussels on 21 March 2006, with energy discussions focusing on: (1) energy policies; (2) energy efficiency, energy savings and the environmental impact of energy; and (3) technology co-operation and renewables.

A Joint Declaration on Climate Change between China and the EU was issued on the occasion of the same summit, setting a cooperation goal for 2020 of developing and demonstrating in China and the EU advanced near-zero emissions coal technology through carbon capture and storage.

The sixth EU–China Energy Conference, which took place in Shanghai on 20 and 21 February 2006, saw presentations and discussions focus on five main themes:

- reinforcing the security of energy supply;
- promoting renewable energy;
- increasing energy efficiency;
- strengthening nuclear safety and security; and
- interactions between energy policy and research and environmental policies (EEP).

The seventh EU–China Energy Conference took place in Brussels on 6 and 7 November 2008 and had the following themes:

- renewable energy for power generation (solar and wind);
- the increasing role of bio-fuels;

- promoting hydrogen energy and fuel cells;
- coal and gas hydrates;
- carbon capture and storage; and
- nuclear energy.

When on 30 November 2009, the 12th EU–China summit was held in Nanjing, the respective leaders' common statement welcomed

> The recent deepening of their Energy Dialogue, with a view to enhancing the use of clean and sustainable energy as well as global energy security. They also welcomed concrete co-operation in the fields of renewable energy, clean coal, bio-fuel and energy efficiency. They thus called for further deepening of co-operation in the energy field. (Council of the European Union, 2009: point 10)

A concrete outcome of the summit was the signing of a Memorandum of Understanding (MoU) on Energy Performance and Quality in the Construction Sector. This initiative will create a platform for bilateral cooperation and involve joint projects in the building sector with a view to enhancing energy efficiency in China. China's current 40 billion m^2 of building stock has low energy-efficiency records and requires urgent action. China's construction market is booming: by 2020, 30 billion m^2 of building stock will be constructed and 13 billion m^2 of the old stock will be improved.

With successive conferences, with the adoption of the Action Plans on Clean Coal and on Industrial Cooperation, and with the signing of MoUs related to the transportation and construction sectors, the EU has managed to set up concrete co-operation programmes for the highest energy-consuming sectors in China.

Of course the task is huge. The challenges are daunting. But at least a framework exists in which the most important issues of the EU–China relationship can be discussed, leading to mutually advantageous cooperation projects and addressing the key objectives spelled out in the EU Energy 2020 strategy.

NOTES

1. International Energy Agency (2010); World Energy Outlook (2010); see also online at: http://www.iea.org/index_info.asp?id=1479.
2. For more details see online at: http://ec.europa.eu/energy/international/bilateral_cooperation/china.

REFERENCES

Council of the European Union (2009) Joint Statement of the 12th EU–China Summit (Nanjing, China), 30 November, available online at: http://www.consilium.europa.eu/uedocs/cms_Data/docs/pressdata/en/er/111567.pdf

European Commission (2010) Communication to the European Parliament, the Council, the European Economic and Social Committee and the Committee of the Regions on *Energy 2020: A Strategy for Competitive, Sustainable and Secure Energy* (SEC(2010) 1346), 10 November.

European Commission (2010) *Priorities for 2020 and Beyond – A Blueprint for an Integrated European Energy Network* (SEC(2010) 1395), 17 November.

European Commission and High Representative/ Secretary General of the Council (2006) *An External Policy to Serve Europe's energy interests.* Brussels.

International Energy Agency (2007) *World Energy Outlook 2007. China and India Insights*. OECD/IEA.

International Energy Agency (2010) *World Energy Outlook 2010*. OECD/IEA.

16. China, the EU and sustainable energy: cooperation, competition or conflict?

Bram Buijs and Lucia van Geuns

INTRODUCTION

Climate change and energy security are global concerns, as problems in the climate system and energy markets touch every country around the world. In theory, these shared concerns could bring the European Union (EU) and China together as they face similar challenges in achieving a sustainable and secure energy system. Energy, and especially sustainable energy, might serve as an excellent field for cooperation and both parties could potentially benefit a lot, possibly complementing each other in some aspects. However, despite some government initiatives towards closer cooperation in the energy field, this chapter will argue that in reality EU–China relations concerning sustainable energy development are quite complicated. Although interaction in the private sector has been rapidly growing, the results of official collaborative projects have been rather limited when compared to the scale of the challenges ahead. Furthermore, friction seems to be emerging due to concerns over competitiveness in the field of low-carbon energy technologies. How such trends will develop in future, and whether the emphasis will remain on cooperation rather than conflict, will be vital for both markets as they address such global challenges as climate change and energy security.

This chapter starts with an introduction to Chinese energy policy and developments within its energy sector. EU–Chinese interaction in the energy field is subsequently evaluated, firstly from a policy and governmental perspective and then by a discussion on the economic opportunities offered by China's developing energy market. Finally, the causes of emerging friction are analysed.

CHINESE ENERGY POLICY: PROGRESSIVE AND PRAGMATIC

China's energy system is still dominated by coal, which accounts for 70 per cent of the primary energy consumption and circa 80 per cent of generated electricity. However, in recent years, China has gained quite broad acclaim for its progressive energy policy that emphasises energy efficiency and the development of low-carbon energy sources.

Energy policy in China is driven by three main factors. The first is energy security, from both an internal and external perspective. On the one hand, being able to secure a sufficient supply of energy domestically is already a major challenge given the extremely rapid growth of China's economy and its skyrocketing demand for energy. This holds especially for the domestic supply of coal, given infrastructural bottlenecks, and for the necessary expansion of China's power sector in order to keep up with demand. On the other hand, its rapidly growing energy demand is also making it more dependent upon foreign, imported energy sources, a matter of increasing concern to the Chinese government: for crude oil, import dependency stood at 56 per cent for 2009 and is expected to surpass 75 per cent within the next two decades; for natural gas, it stood at 10 per cent and might reach 30 per cent by 2015 according to some observers.[1]

Second, environmental concerns are playing an increasingly important role. The Chinese media and public have become more vocal about environmental problems, putting the government under pressure to address these issues. One of the main concerns is the pollution associated with the enormous use of coal in China's economy, causing problems such as air pollution, acid rain and severe public health problems.

The third motivation for China to push forward with a progressive energy policy is the economic opportunity which it sees in developing low-carbon energy technologies. In recent years, China has been striving to develop indigenous manufacturing and R&D capabilities in industry sectors ranging from wind turbines to solar panels to electric cars to advanced nuclear reactor technology (Buijs, 2009).

These combined reasons have resulted in quite progressive energy policy being put forward in China. The recent 11th Five-Year Plan for the period 2006–10 included several ambitious targets on renewable energy and energy efficiency. One key goal has been to reduce overall energy intensity, i.e. the amount of energy used to produce one unit of GDP, by 20 per cent by 2010 compared to the 2005 level, which is estimated will save 1.5 billion tons of CO_2 emissions. China's industrial sector, which originally deployed rather outdated technologies, still has major potential for improved energy efficiency: overall, the energy intensity of China's economy is still estimated to be about four times as high as for its Western counterparts.[2] Implementation measures taken in order to meet the intensity target include energy conservation programmes such as the 'Top-1000 Enterprises Programme' that aims to save energy in China's one thousand largest industrial energy users and shut down old and inefficient small-scale industrial users and power plants.

Concerning China's power supply, the main renewable energy contribution comes from hydropower, which accounted for 15 per cent of electricity generated in 2007. Nuclear power stood at 2 per cent and non-hydro renewable energy sources, such as wind and solar, contributed less than 1 per cent. However, the latter shares are set to increase as China has embarked upon a rapid development of renewable energy sources and nuclear power. The Chinese government has set official targets to raise the share of non-fossil energy sources in its primary energy consumption to 15 per cent by 2020 and to decrease greenhouse gas emissions relative to its GDP (i.e. the carbon intensity of its economy) by 40–45 per cent by 2020 compared to the 2005 level.

SIMILAR CHALLENGES: A GOOD FOUNDATION FOR COOPERATION?

Although their domestic circumstances are obviously very different, China and the European Union face quite similar challenges in transforming their fossil fuel-based energy system into a more sustainable system based on low-carbon energy sources.

A technical example is the need to improve the electricity grid and construct more interconnection capacity. Similar to Europe, China is starting to experience difficulties in accommodating the intermittency associated with wind energy. It is estimated that one-third of all Chinese wind farms are not connected to the grid and there is a need for more interconnected networks since areas that are advantageous for wind energy, such as Inner Mongolia, are far removed from demand centres in the coastal regions. Similar to Europe, flexible 'back-up' generating capacity and advanced 'smart grid' systems will be required to achieve the successful integration of large amounts of intermittent renewable energy in China.

The field of policymaking is another example. In many cases, the cost barriers for renewable energy deployment in China are even more prohibitive than in European countries. Hence there is a need to design supportive policies and learn from best practices, in which Europe has broad experience. In fact, Europe has clearly served as a model for China in policymaking and many examples can testify to this. First, feed-in tariffs have been established in China for wind power, following the very successful promotion of renewable energy sources through such policies in Germany and other EU member states. For solar energy such feed-in tariffs are under consideration. Another policy measure introduced in China is the renewable portfolio standard (RPS) that requires power and grid companies to purchase a certain percentage of renewable energy. Third, China has set strict fuel efficiency standards for cars following European legislation and these standards are already stricter than those in the US.

Apart from this dialogue on best practices in policymaking, however, a survey of the energy field shows that EU–China cooperation has had only limited impact up to now. European policy documents indicate that one of the main focus areas is cooperation in the field of carbon capture and storage (CCS), both on legal matters and technology transfer. One example has been the $STRACO_2$ project: Support to Regulatory Activities for Carbon Capture and Storage. Its aim was to support the development of a regulatory framework for CCS in the European Union and to investigate the possibilities of applying EU and international regulation to the development of CCS regulation in China.[3] Second, there is the current Near Zero Emissions Coal (NZEC) initiative, a shared UK–China and EU–China project which aims to build a CCS-equipped coal-fired demonstration power plant.[4] It runs alongside the COACH project, which aims to establish broad cooperation between China and the EU in the field of CCS. The declared goal of COACH is to prepare the ground for implementation in China of large-scale polygeneration energy facilities with options for coal-based electric power generation as well as the production of hydrogen and synthetic fuels.[5]

The above-mentioned initiatives on CCS followed from the EU–China Summit of September 2005, in which a partnership on energy and climate change was announced. The initial joint declaration was followed by a Memorandum of Understanding during an EU–China Energy Conference, in February 2006, and the final report of the $STRACO_2$ project was published in July 2009. However, progress in terms of making China's energy sector development more sustainable, appears to have been very slow.[6] On the Near Zero Emissions Coal demonstration plant, the preliminary phase has been finished, with research results having been presented in October 2009, including research on the geological storage capacity in China. The intention is now to prepare groundwork for the construction of the demonstration plant, which should be ready by 2015.

However, taking into account the enormous speed with which China's energy sector is developing, it becomes apparent that there is a massive gap between what the aims of EU–Chinese cooperation are on energy and what is happening on the ground. In the period 2005–10, China added more than 300 GW of fossil-fired capacity to the grid, almost completely dominated by coal: total conventional thermal power-generating capacity was expected to reach 700 GW by the end of 2010 (Xinhua News Agency, 2010; Energy Information Administration of US Department of Energy, 2010). A comparison of EU–China projects with China's own initiatives in the field of CCS shows that they already run the risk of being surpassed by developments within China's own coal R&D sector (Morse et al., 2009: 7–8). For instance, China was building a 250 MW coal-fired integrated gasification combined cycle (IGCC) demonstration power plant near Tianjin, GreenGen, which was expected to attain first-phase operation in 2011 and should include CCS in a later stage. Moreover, a CCS project was being pursued at a Shenhua coal-to-liquid plant in Inner Mongolia, which should capture 100,000 tons of CO_2 per year initially, was slated to come online in 2010.[7] Moreover, in other sectors, especially such as renewable energy, China was surging ahead at a pace and scale which leaves the EU–China cooperative projects in the shade: for instance, over the period 2005–9 installed wind power capacity has doubled each year, increasing from 1.3 GW in 2005 to 25.8 GW in 2009.[8] Also, in other fields, China was pushing for sustainable energy policies, such as promoting 'new energy vehicles' such as hybrid and electric cars, establishing high-speed rail links between major cities and constructing extensive metro-line systems to improve public transport.

THE IMPORTANCE OF CHINA AS A SALES MARKET FOR EUROPEAN AND OTHER INTERNATIONAL ENERGY COMPANIES

In contrast with the limited scope of government-level official cooperation, business contacts in the private sector have rapidly developed. Given the tremendous growth of China's power sector and China's interest in advanced technologies, business opportunities have emerged for European companies both in the field of conventional (fossil) energy and renewable energy. Companies such as Shell and Siemens have traditionally had a large presence in China and they are, for instance, working on advanced coal technologies together with Chinese partners. Framatome, a French nuclear firm that later became part of Areva, has played a key role in the initial development of nuclear power in China, supplying most of the key technologies for the first few nuclear reactors that came online in China in the mid-1990s.

For renewable energy in particular, China has emerged as one of the biggest growth markets. According to a report by UNEP, China gained the top spot globally for overall sustainable energy investment in 2009. Out of $119 billion invested worldwide by the financial sector in clean energy companies and utility-scale projects, $33.7 billion took place in China, an increase of 53 per cent compared to 2008 (New Energy Finance and UNEP, 2010: 5–10). It illustrates that while European and American markets suffered from the impact of the recession, investment remained strong in China.

Many companies in the renewable energy sector have set up manufacturing operations in China which has become a major sales market for many of them. The wind sector in China can serve as an example. Due to strong government support, China's wind sector has grown exponentially for the past couple of years and foreign companies have been very much involved in developing this market. Vestas, the world's leading wind turbine manufacturer from Denmark, had already established five factory complexes in China by 2009, including their largest integrated manufacturing complex globally. Total investment reached 3 billion yuan and their workforce in China exceeds 3,000 workers. For some of the turbines manufactured in China, the localised content has surpassed 90 per cent. Vestas's Annual Report for 2009 showed that the Asia-Pacific region accounted for 14.3 per cent of exported capacity, generating 11 per cent of the total revenue. However, the contribution of the region is expected to rise to 20 per cent by 2010 in terms of received orders (Vestas, 2010: 23, 27, 28). For Gamesa, the Spanish wind turbine manufacturer, Asia has already become its top market. International sales accounted for 89 per cent of sales in the first half of 2010, of which Asia accounted for 34 per cent (China 25 per cent and India 9 per cent), up from 13 per cent in the first half of 2009 (Pardo, 2010; Harvey, 2010).

Another example is the renewable energy firm Enfinity. The Belgian company won a prestigious tender to develop China's first large-scale solar energy project in the desert town of Dunhuang in the western Gansu Province. The first phase consists of 10 MW, but total capacity should later increase incrementally to 100 MW, making it one of the largest solar energy projects worldwide. Enfinity clearly sees Asia as one of their biggest growth markets, considering the amount of additional electricity generating capacity that still needs to be installed. In 2009, the regional distribution of revenue was still focused on Europe, which accounted for 90 per cent of the total, versus 10 per cent for Asia and the US combined. However, this balance is expected to shift rapidly. Already by 2011, their revenue distribution is estimated to be Europe 60 per cent, US 20 per cent, and Asia 20 per cent.[9]

FRICTION AND INCREASING COMPETITION

From a global climate perspective, Chinese involvement in low-carbon energy sectors and their rapid growth is very positive news. However, this development is causing increasing political friction due to the economic interests involved. Most certainly the growth of China's power sector and its renewable energy market has offered new market opportunities for foreign companies. However, complaints have also sprung up about restricted market access, forced technology transfer, lack of transparency and unfair competition vis-à-vis Chinese domestic competitors.

The wind energy sector provides a key example of how the Chinese government has implemented rather strategic policy measures to facilitate the build-up of its domestic industry. In the first phase, China's wind energy market was completely dominated by international companies and the first few Chinese domestic firms teamed up mostly with European companies through partnerships or technology licensing when starting manufacturing operations. However, in just a few years the dominant market share held by international wind turbine companies in China dropped very quickly, falling from 75 per cent in 2004 to less than 20 per cent in 2009 as they yielded to domestic competitors (Li and Gao, 2007; CREIA, 2010: 5). Some factors played a role in this. First of all, the Chinese government issued a localisation requirement for the wind energy sector. It stipulated that for all turbines being built, at least 70 per cent of the components (measured by value) should be locally manufactured. The implication of this policy was that international firms had to set up factories and manufacturing operations in China to meet this requirement, which indirectly increased technology transfer and capacity building. Second, the tendering process which has been used to select companies to develop wind farms has focused mostly on price and less on quality, performance and service aspects. In effect this has favoured Chinese companies which might not yet be equal to their international counterparts from a quality or technology perspective, but which can produce cheaply and thus underbid international manufacturers. As a consequence, international wind turbine firms, while in some cases still being able to increase their sales in absolute terms, have lost market share rapidly. The largest Chinese manufacturers have now started to look abroad for export opportunities: having acquired certain technologies through mergers and acquisitions they are well-positioned to extend competition to the global market.

These aspects of Chinese wind sector development are not isolated, as China's similarly keen interest in achieving technology transfer has been driving cooperative deals in nuclear power, solar energy, high-speed railways and many other sectors. Technology transfer requirements have often been an essential part of the contracts signed with foreign partners. Gradually, the increasing competition of Chinese companies is leading to more friction and it is eroding the willingness of industrialised countries to give financial support to the development of renewable energy in China. One example has been that in the run-up to the Copenhagen COP-15 summit of the UNFCCC, the UNFCCC Executive Board for Clean Development Mechanism (CDM) projects announced that they were reconsidering the application of Chinese wind farms for CDM emission reductions credits. While the CDM flexible mechanism has been installed to allow developed countries to invest their money in more cost-effective emission reduction activities in developing countries, the Executive Board deemed it necessary to re-evaluate whether China should be eligible for such support, given that their wind energy sector is growing so quickly and no additional funding seems to be needed (He and Morse, 2010). The negotiations in Copenhagen and other UNFCCC summits also showed that the willingness of developed countries to somehow support China with building its renewable energy sector, either by financial support or technology transfer, has greatly decreased even though it is recognised that accelerating a low-carbon transition in China will be crucial to achieving global climate change objectives and that this transition is not even close to moving fast enough by itself.

More recently, the issue of competitiveness versus Chinese support for its renewable energy sector has resurfaced in the WTO probe launched by the US Trade Representative, upon a complaint filed by the US Steelworkers Union (*New York Times*, 2010). According to the petition, China's support schemes for its renewable energy sector are giving its low-carbon products an unfair advantage in the global market, leading to financial losses and unemployment in the US renewable energy sector. With many countries still suffering from the economic crisis and seeking to frame investments in renewable energy as policies to secure 'green jobs' for their own workforce, importing low-carbon technology products from China is becoming more and more sensitive politically. An interesting case in point has been the green energy policy launched by the Ontario provincial government in Canada, which also included a 60 per cent local content requirement for renewable energy projects, which has run into WTO complaints from Japan, the US and the European Union (Reuters, 2010). If a global trend towards 'green protectionism' further materialises causing trade barriers between countries to rise, it might offset the benefits of increasing economies of scale and the downward pressure on prices induced by global competition, benefits that are so much needed in order to make sustainable low-carbon energy more competitive. In the end, it will be critical for the European Union to find an approach towards China which can balance these interests and incorporate all considerations at the global, member state and company level, in order to ensure that the emerging competition for green energy provides incentives for innovation and progress rather than a protectionist response.

NOTES

1. Data for 2009 based on *BP Statistical Review of World Energy June 2010*. Projections for oil taken from International Energy Agency, *World Energy Outlook 2010* (2010b: 135), and for gas: *Financial Times*, 'Gas: home supplies to cut imports', 12 September 2010. Available at: http://www.ft.com/cms/s/0/aa3b6988-bc71-11df-a42b-00144feab49a,dwp_uuid=8992c4a2-bc70-11df-a42b-00144feab49a.html.
2. According to the *Key World Energy Statistics 2010* from the International Energy Agency (IEA, 2010a), total primary energy supply divided by nominal GDP stood at 0.75 tonnes of oil equivalent per thousand US$2,000 for China, compared to 0.17 toe/000 US$2,000 for the OECD average.
3. The Synthesis and Final Reports of the STRACO_2 project (published July 2009) can be downloaded from the website: http://www.euchina-ccs.org/ (accessed 24 December 2010).
4. More information available at: http://www.nzec.info (accessed 24 December 2010).
5. COACH stands for 'Cooperation Action within CCS China–EU'. Official website available at: http://www.co2-coach.com (accessed 20 October 2010). COACH is partially funded by the EU under the 6th Framework Programme. According to the website the COACH project addresses three issues: coal gasification for appropriate polygeneration schemes with CO_2 capture and storage; identification of reliable geological storage capabilities of CO_2 in China, and societal anchorage including legal regulatory and public issues.
6. If the activity on the COACH website is any measure to go by, it does not bode well: only two publications have been put online since its inception (one from June 2007 and one from February 2009), and only two news items (dated June 2008 and February 2009).
7. MIT CCS project database (last update July 15, 2010), available at: http://sequestration.mit.edu/tools/projects/ordos.html (accessed 25 October 2010).
8. Global Wind Energy Council (GWEC, 2010), available at: http://www.gwec.net/index.php?id=125 (accessed 25 October 2010).
9. Personal communication with Gino van Neer, CEO Enfinity Group Asia.

REFERENCES

BP Statistical Review of World Energy (June 2010).

Buijs, Bram (2009) *China, Copenhagen and Beyond*, Clingendael International Energy Programme, September 2009.

Buijs, Bram (2012) *China and the Future of New Energy Technologies*. Clingendael International Energy Programme, March 2012 see http://www.clingendael.nl/ciep/publications/?id=8850&&type=summary

China Renewable Energy Industries Association (CREIA) (2010) *China Wind Power Outlook 2010*. Beijing: CREIA.

Energy Information Administration of US Department of Energy (2010) *International Energy Statistics*. Available at: http://www.eia.doe.gov/cfapps/ipdbproject/iedindex3.cfm?tid=2&pid=28&aid=7&cid=&syid=1980&eyid=2007&unit=MK (accessed at 20 October 2010).

Financial Times (2010) 'Gas: home supplies to cut imports', 12 September. Available at: http://www.ft.com/cms/s/0/aa3b6988-bc71-11df-a42b-00144feab49a,dwp_uuid=8992c4a2-bc70-11df-a42b-00144feab49a.html (accessed 24 December 2010).

Harvey, Fiona (2010) 'Unexpected lull after decade of following wind', *Financial Times*, 13 September.

He, Gang and Morse, Richard (2010) *Making Carbon Offsets Work in the Developing World: Lessons from the Chinese Wind Controversy*, Stanford Program on Energy and Sustainable Development (PESD), Working Paper No. 90, March.

International Energy Agency (IEA) (2010a) *Key World Energy Statistics 2010*. Paris: IEA/OECD.

International Energy Agency (IEA) (2010b) *World Energy Outlook 2010*. Paris: IEA/OECD.

Li, Junfeng and Gao, Hu (2007) *PR China Wind Power Report*, China Renewable Energy Industries Association (CREIA). Beijing: China Environmental Science Press.

Morse, Richard K., Rai, Varun and He, Gang (2009) *The Real Drivers of Carbon Capture and Storage in China and Implications for Climate Policy*, Stanford Program on Energy and Sustainable Development (PESD), Working Paper No. 88, August. Available at: http://iis-db.stanford.edu/pubs/22621/WP_88_Morse_He_Rai_CCS_in_China.pdf (accessed 25 October 2010).

New Energy Finance and UNEP (2010) *Global Trends in Sustainable Energy Investment 2010*. Available at: http://bnef.com/Download/UserFiles_File_WhitePapers/sefi_unep_global_trends_2010.pdf (accessed 24 December 2010).

New York Times (2010) 'U.S. to investigate China's clean energy aid', 15 October.

Pardo, Francesca (2010) 'Turbines: Gamesa has big ideas', *Financial Times*, 13 September.

Reuters (2010) 'Ontario's green energy push draws fire from Japan, U.S. and E.U.', 12 October.

STRACO$_2$ Project (July 2009) Synthesis and Final Reports. Available at: http://www.euchina-ccs.org/ (accessed 24 December 2010).

Vestas (2010) *Annual Report 2009*. Available at: http://www.vestas.com/Admin/Public/DWSDownload.aspx?File=%2fFiles%2fFiler%2fEN%2fInvestor%2fCompany_announcements%2f2010%2f100210-CA_UK_AR.pdf; http://www.vestas.com/en/investor/financial-reports/financial-reports-2009.aspx (accessed 25 October 2010).

Xinhua News Agency (2010) 'Update: China's power installed capacity to hit 950 mln kW in 2010', 8 April 2010. Available at: http://www.istockanalyst.com/article/viewiStockNews/articleid/4012420 (accessed 20 October 2010).

Websites

Cooperation Action within CCS China–EU (COACH): http://www.co2-coach.com (accessed 20 October 2010).

Global Wind Energy Council (GWEC) (2010): http://www.gwec.net/index.php?id=125 (accessed 25 October 2010).

MIT CCS project database (last update 15 July 2010): http://sequestration.mit.edu/tools/projects/ordos.html (accessed 25 October 2010).

NZEC: http://www.nzec.info (accessed 24 December 2010).

PART 5

Security and politics

17. The US–Japan alliance and the rise of China: implications for the East Asian security order and the EU's regional role

Elena Atanassova-Cornelis

INTRODUCTION

This chapter takes a closer look at the geo-strategic environment and evolving regional order in East Asia with the aim of contributing to a better understanding of the current restructuring in the global governance system, especially in the area of security. Indeed, as China rises and consolidates its status as a major power in Asia, it challenges the US hegemonic position in the region. This, in turn, has implications for America's global primacy, the international strategic order and the role of the European Union (EU) in global governance.

The US regional dominance in East Asia rests on the so-called 'hub and spoke' security system, which comprises a set of post-war bilateral military alliances between Washington and regional states, notably including Japan. The US–Japan alliance has been a major pillar of the American-led order, checking the rising power of the People's Republic of China (PRC) and deterring conflicts in the Taiwan Strait and the Korean Peninsula. Regional uncertainties concerning China's strategic intentions have led to a strengthening of US–Japan security ties in the 2000s, which Beijing has interpreted as being directed at China and as a tool of Washington's strategy of maintaining its primacy in East Asia. While the resulting security dilemmas and mutual hedging strategies have come to define the regional order, the increasing focus in East Asia on multilateral cooperation and non-traditional security has tempered the potential for instability.

Against this background, the purpose of this chapter is to examine how the dynamics between the US–Japan alliance and China are shaping the evolving security order in East Asia, as well as to explore the opportunities for strengthened European multilateral engagement in the region in light of the changing geo-strategic environment.

The chapter first analyses the manifestation of strategic mistrust and the security dilemmas between Tokyo and Washington, and Beijing, and then moves on to explore recent trends of engagement and cooperation between the three powers. Subsequently, the discussion examines the primary components of the evolving regional security order and looks at the EU's policy towards East Asia. The chapter concludes by arguing that while the US-led security system continues to be a main provider of East Asian stability and hence ensures America its regional primacy, it is increasingly complemented by regional multilateralism in non-traditional security areas. In turn, this opens up the way for Europe's strengthened engagement with the region, including with China, and hence for the EU's implementation of a more multilateral approach to global governance.

SECURITY DILEMMA DYNAMICS IN EAST ASIA

Changes in the US–Japan Alliance and Distrust of China

The strengthening of the US–Japan alliance since the late 1990s and Chinese responses to it have been at the centre of the current security dynamics in East Asia. The strategic convergence of Tokyo and Washington on traditional security issues was accentuated, especially in the wake of 9/11, while Japan under Prime Minister Koizumi Junichiro (2001–6) unquestionably emerged as a reliable ally of America. A strong advocate of Tokyo's more robust foreign policy, Koizumi dispatched Japanese Self-Defence Forces (SDF) on non-combat missions to the Indian Ocean and Iraq, revised the country's national security doctrine to introduce a new global role for Japan, and accelerated the deployment of a Ballistic Missile Defence (BMD) system in Japan. The US focus under Bush on enhanced military partnership with Tokyo and its open support for Japan's more assertive security role reflected the strategic convergence of the two allies. This was also seen in their shared threat perceptions, especially concerning the Democratic People's Republic of Korea (DPRK or North Korea) and China, as well as in the US–Japanese consensus on the (military) means to tackle security challenges (Bisley, 2008). Indeed, a main incentive in upgrading the alliance, including the ongoing joint research on BMD, has been the DPRK's provocative behaviour since the 1990s. In this context, both Washington and Tokyo have repeatedly emphasised the threat North Korea's missile and nuclear programmes pose to stability in East Asia, as well as to the entire international community.

Shared concerns about the rise of Chinese military power have acted as an additional stimulus for Japan and the US to deepen their military cooperation. Tokyo has questioned if the objective of Beijing's military modernisation is the mere resolution of the Taiwan issue, for China's accelerated missile deployment has not only increased its ability to strike Taiwan, but also Japan and some of the main US military bases in East Asia. Additionally, a perceived lack of transparency into the PRC's (People's Republic of China) national defence, as well as the double-digit growth of its defence spending from the late 1990s on, has influenced the emergence of a perceived 'Chinese threat' in Japan. For example, the 2009 Japanese White Paper on Defence underlined that 'China has not yet achieved the levels of transparency expected of a major regional power' (Ministry of Defence, Japan, 2009: 49–50).

Similarly in the US, the perception of a 'Chinese threat' has gradually gained ground over the last decade. Uncertainties concerning Beijing's both short-term and long-term goals have led to worries in Washington that China, as it becomes stronger, might seek to alter the structure of the regional order, and hence challenge the US leadership position and interests in East Asia (Medeiros, 2005). Indeed, America has sided with Japan by expressing concerns that China's military modernisation has implications going beyond the PRC's 'immediate territorial interests' (i.e. the Taiwan issue) and has repeatedly pointed out the limited transparency in Beijing's defence policy.[1]

China's successful anti-satellite weapon test in 2007 intensified the debate among US analysts concerning Chinese 'anti-access strategies' designed to deter the US from intervening in a Taiwan crisis, strategies seen by some observers as an indicator of a shift in the military balance of power in East Asia (Saunders, 2008).

America's security strategy in East Asia, seen in the reinforcement in the 2000s of the hub and spoke system in general and the alliance with Japan in particular, clearly shows that Washington has remained committed to sustaining its military primacy. To be sure, the US has increasingly come to recognise China's growing regional influence and the need for Beijing's cooperation in tackling regional challenges (e.g. North Korea's nuclear ambitions). Nevertheless, America has not shown willingness to share its leadership in East Asia with China, i.e. to establish a kind of condominium of power, but has rather expected Beijing to be 'fully cognizant' (Pei, 2007: 104) of US intention to preserve its regional primacy and hence a Pax Americana.

Chinese Worries about and Responses to US–Japan Alliance Strengthening

From a Chinese perspective, the strengthening of the US–Japan alliance has been largely directed at the PRC and seeking to constrain its rising power. In this context, China's view of Japan's changing security posture has mirrored Tokyo's mistrust of Beijing. Chinese analysts have repeatedly expressed concerns regarding Japan's alleged re-emergence as a major military power by emphasising Tokyo's drive to acquire new military capabilities such as BMD systems. Especially under Koizumi, Japan was seen as 'fabricating' threats coming from the PRC's military build-up and abandoning 'its post-war path of peaceful development to pursue political and military power' (Xinhua, 2005). Additionally, Sino-Japanese relations in the politico-military area deteriorated to unprecedented levels during Koizumi's term in office due to bilateral disputes over history and small islands in the East China Sea. Negative popular perceptions in Japan and China as well as mutual animosity only served to exacerbate the security dilemma in the region.

Strategic mistrust also underpins China's relations with the US, with Beijing wary of America's strategic intentions in East Asia. As discussed elsewhere in this volume, China has been a strong supporter of multipolarity, both at the regional and global levels. The PRC's official documents underscore the destabilising impact of 'hegemonism and unilateralism' (clearly with reference to US policy under Bush) on international security, and point to the eventual 'world multipolarisation' in global politics (Chinese Government's Official Web Portal, 2004, 2006, 2008). Despite its rhetoric about multipolarity, Beijing has largely accepted the inevitability of continued US dominance (Foot, 2006) and a Pax Americana in East Asia, at least for now. At the same time, while the PRC has sought to accommodate US hegemony, it has also hedged against a possible negative impact of America's regional dominance on Chinese interests (Foot, 2006). Two important components of this hedging strategy have been Beijing's more active regional diplomacy and its military modernisation programme. In this way, China has sought to reduce the risk of containment by the US and its East Asian allies, most notably Japan, as well as raise the costs of involvement by Washington (and Tokyo) in a potential conflict over Taiwan.

There is no doubt that the Taiwan issue has remained a major factor that could destabilise relations between the US and Japan, and China. The PRC has repeatedly criticised the bilateral military cooperation between Washington and Taipei, and strongly protested against US arms sales to Taiwan, seeing them as interference in China's internal affairs. However, as was reaffirmed by the Obama administration on the occasion of its January 2010 arms sales package to Taiwan, the US has argued that the provision of arms seeks to preserve the military balance in the Strait. For Washington, this is consistent with its long-standing policy of recognising only Beijing, but providing Taipei with defensive weapons.[2] US policy on Taiwan is largely perceived in China as the basis of America's alleged containment of the PRC, with the strengthening of the US–Japan alliance seen as one of the major aspects in Washington's efforts in this regard (Medeiros, 2005).

Against this background, Beijing has come to interpret the expansion of the security cooperation between Tokyo and Washington as joint interference in Chinese domestic matters. The PRC has worried that US–Japanese development and deployment of a BMD system in East Asia, especially a mobile and sea-based one, could be extended for the defence of Taiwan and hence prevent reunification with the mainland. In this sense, by reinforcing the alliance in order to tackle the threat from the DRPK, Tokyo and Washington have faced a security dilemma with Beijing with regard to the Taiwan issue (Atanassova-Cornelis and Mendes, 2010). While pursuing economic interdependence with the island, Beijing has sought a more coercive approach to the reunification issue by means of reinforcing Chinese military capabilities and becoming more serious about the use of force. In this context, the PRC's modernisation of its nuclear and missile arsenal has been particularly important, while the enactment of the Anti-Secession Law in 2005 underscored the PRC's intention to employ 'non-peaceful means' in order to 'protect China's sovereignty and territorial integrity' (National People's Congress, 2005).

The security dilemma dynamics between the US–Japan alliance and the PRC defines the mutual hedging between these powers. Washington, while emphasising common interests and bilateral cooperation with Beijing, has reinforced its security alliances and partnerships in Asia, with its alliance with Japan playing a central role in this hedging strategy (Medeiros, 2005). For Tokyo, its close security relationship with America has been a major component of its own external balancing behaviour vis-à-vis Beijing.[3] Finally, China's 'hedged acquiescence' towards the US has been motivated in part by the unprecedented expansion of US–Japan security ties under the Koizumi–Bush partnership, as well as by its recognition of the strategic advantage enjoyed by the US as a balancer (notably with Japan) in Asia's geopolitics (Pei, 2007). In addition to its military modernisation efforts and active regional diplomacy, Chinese hedging has included the development of new strategic partnerships beyond East Asia, including with the EU.

ENGAGEMENT AND COOPERATION BETWEEN THE US, CHINA AND JAPAN

The diplomatic priorities of the Obama administration in East Asia and the generally stable US–China relations since the Bush era suggest a positive trend for regional stability. America under Obama is seen to have increased its focus on non-traditional security issues, including poverty, development and climate change. Furthermore, a major departure from Bush's policies, notably his 'go it alone' approach, is Obama's call for multilateral solutions to global problems and, specifically, his focus on engaging East Asia multilaterally. More specifically, the US has strengthened its relations with ASEAN by holding in 2009 its first ever summit with the organisation and by signing ASEAN's Treaty of Amity and Cooperation the same year. America has also officially joined the East Asia Summit in 2011. Not only has Washington been determined to pursue multilateral diplomacy in Asia based on dialogue and cooperation, it has also stressed its expectation to be a fully-fledged participant in various regional institutions.

Obama's focus on multilateral cooperation for tackling new threats and protecting the 'global commons', as defined in the 2010 Quadrennial Defence Review (United States Department of Defense, 2010), is positive for the relations between Tokyo and Washington, and Beijing. As the US–Japan alliance is redefined to cope with new security challenges, including natural disasters and maritime piracy, its cooperation with other major powers, especially China, will be increasingly important. The fact that the three countries have already agreed to conduct a trilateral policy dialogue to discuss various issues of common concern is also a positive sign of trust-building efforts in the region.

Obama's approach towards China reflects US emphasis on cooperation and engagement in its East Asia strategy. The US president has reassured Beijing that America is not seeking to contain the PRC and stressed, instead, that the cultivation of 'spheres of cooperation – not competing spheres of influence' would lead to progress in the region (Murayama, 2009). This has been welcomed by Chinese leaders who, themselves, view the bilateral relations as contributing to regional and global stability and emphasise the need to develop them from a strategic and long-term perspective. In this regard, the 2009 US-initiated, high-level US–China Strategic and Economic Dialogue is a clear expression of Obama's determination to elevate the bilateral partnership to one addressing a variety of global issues (Cossa, 2010a). In East Asia, China's role as a key player in the six-party talks (SPT) seeking North Korea's denuclearisation will continue to be crucial for American interests. For the PRC, on the other hand, US non-support of unilateral Taiwanese change of the status quo in the Strait and Washington's willingness to treat China as a partner rather than rival will further allay Chinese fears about perceived US–Japanese containment. This is not to say that tensions between the US and China may not arise. Indeed, the bilateral row over the Obama administration's arms sales package to Taiwan was a case in point.[4] However, the row did not signify a major change in relations, but showed a familiar dynamic at work. While the US demonstrated its commitment to regional stability and its determination, as stressed by President Obama, 'to be an Asia-Pacific power' (Cossa, 2010b), China, by suspending bilateral military exchanges, defended what it regarded as its core national interest of sovereignty and territorial integrity. The resumption in October 2010 of US–China military dialogue is a confirmation of both side's willingness to maintain a stable and cooperative relationship.

The rather positive Sino–Japanese relations in the post-Koizumi era also give grounds for optimism for a stable regional order in East Asia. While historical and territorial disputes between the two neighbours have not been resolved, both Tokyo and Beijing have tended to emphasise mutual engagement and cooperation in their relations. In the security area, for example, Japan and China have undertaken a number of steps towards enhancing military transparency and confidence building, such as regular high-level defence meetings and mutual visits by naval ships. The Chinese Communist Party (CCP) government has focused on promoting a positive image of Japan, while generally controlling the anti-Japanese sentiments within Chinese society. On the Japanese side, the Democratic Party of Japan (DPJ), under the administration of former Prime Minister Hatoyama Yukio (2009–10) underscored a proactive diplomacy towards East Asia, especially China. This was in stark contrast with the traditional US-centric foreign policy of the successive Liberal Democratic Party (LDP)-led governments. Indeed, Hatoyama advocated the formation of an 'East Asian community' and invited Beijing, in particular, to cooperate with Tokyo in the realisation of this initiative. Japan's proposal drew upon the European experience whereby the existing cooperation among Asian countries in areas such as climate, natural disasters and maritime security would lead to a multilayered network for a functional community, with political cooperation seen as a long-term objective. At the same time, Hatoyama's focus on China, as well as the tensions between Japan and the US over his decision to review a bilateral agreement (signed by Bush and Koizumi in 2006) on the realignment of US military forces in Japan, seemed to suggest a weakening of the alliance and, by extension, of the American-led regional order.

The foreign policy of the current democratic administration in Tokyo of Kan Naoto (May 2010–present), while still too early to evaluate, has arguably dissipated the above perceptions. At the moment, Kan seems focused on repairing Tokyo's damaged ties with Washington rather than following through on Hatoyama's East Asian community initiative. For their part, the Sino–Japanese tensions over the September 2010 collision in the East China Sea exposed once again the fragility of their bilateral relations. Finally, the recent US–Japanese agreement to strengthen bilateral strategic consultations concerning China's military build-up and its increasing maritime presence in the East and South China Seas suggests that hedging will remain an important component of regional order in East Asia in the years to come.

EVOLVING EAST ASIAN SECURITY ORDER

As this chapter demonstrates, the US hub and spoke system in East Asia centred on the US–Japan alliance remains a main component of the regional security order and hence ensures America its primacy. As long as Tokyo considers its bilateral arrangements with Washington as the cornerstone of Japanese and regional security, the US-led system will surely have a stable pillar to stand on.

Looked at from another perspective, the alliance has put a cap on Japan's potential rearmament (feared by Beijing) and has made American power 'more predictable', thereby reducing (Chinese/regional) uncertainties as to how it may be exercised (Ikenberry, 2004). Even though the alliance enhancement under the Bush–Koizumi partnership came to be regarded by Beijing as a threat to its interests, the PRC has recognised the overall benefits of the US-led security system. Indeed, the stability in East Asia based on that system has created an environment in which China has been able to focus on its primary goal of economic development (Shambaugh, 2006). Beijing is also seen to be using the hub and spoke arrangements to its own advantage by seeking to establish 'an informal Chinese spoke' in the system, i.e. a 'special bilateral relationship' with Washington, and thereby maximise its diplomatic manoeuvrability (Ikenberry, 2004). This suggests that, while the PRC will continue to hedge against a possible downturn in its relations with the US (and Japan), it will not seek, at least in the foreseeable future, to overthrow the existing order altogether.

For East Asian states, as they remain wary of China's long-term strategic goals in the region, the hub and spoke system and the US forward military presence continue to be seen as major guarantors of their security needs. To be sure, most Asian countries (and Japan no longer seems to be an exception) recognise the growing influence of the PRC, which is now a major driving force of the region's economic development, and seek cooperative relations with Beijing. Although the improvement, since the late 1990s, in regional perceptions of China, especially in South East Asia but not in Japan, has been a significant change, some ASEAN states encourage Washington and Tokyo to assume a larger regional role in order to balance Beijing (Saunders, 2008). Finally, territorial and sovereignty disputes, the rise of nationalistic sentiments and mutual distrust between countries in East Asia (notably Japan and China) underpin the view in the region that the US military presence and America's role as a 'stabiliser' are indispensable to East Asian security (Sutter, 2008). Indeed, no other major power, neither Japan nor China, is trusted by Asian states to assume such a role, and the US remains for now the only power both able and willing to provide the public good from which all in the region benefit (Sutter, 2008).

Since the mid-1990s, however, a new trend has emerged in the evolving regional order in East Asia, which in many ways has complemented America's role rather than represented a direct alternative to the US-led system. The region has seen a mushrooming of multilateral fora and dialogues which have helped build mutual trust and confidence. Their main characteristic is a focus on economic and non-traditional security areas of cooperation. To be sure, in North East Asia, 'hard security' concerns about North Korea's nuclear programmes have drawn Asian countries closer to one another, as seen in the US–Japan–ROK (Republic of Korea) security consultations (known as the Trilateral Coordination and Oversight Group) and the (currently stalled) SPT. The future possibility that another multilateral security framework in North East Asia could emerge from the SPT should not be ruled out, and it may offer opportunities to strengthen cooperation, especially between Japan and China, on less sensitive, non-traditional security issues (Atanassova-Cornelis and Mendes, 2010). The three-way talks among Tokyo, Beijing and Seoul, which were established in 2008, are already an indicator that such concerns as natural disasters and infectious diseases are leading to greater intra-regional collaboration.

In the wider East Asian region, it is ASEAN that has been the driver of institution building. The ASEAN Regional Forum (ARF), the only region-wide security dialogue, has focused on developing security cooperation and confidence-building, as well as provided the EU with an opportunity to strengthen its involvement in Asia. The ASEAN + 3 (APT) process, for its part, has contributed to deepening regional ties, primarily in the economic, monetary and financial fields, with its major achievement being the 2000 Chiang Mai Initiative for currency swaps. The APT is significant in that it has brought together only states from North East and South East Asia, thereby playing an important role in building intra-regional relations. Regional calls for the creation of an East Asian community also suggest a more clear trend towards 'Asian only' multilateralism (i.e. without the US), although Japan's support for an expanded East Asia Summit and a more inclusive membership in the envisaged community indicate that balancing Chinese influence remains important for Tokyo. Indeed, Beijing's active involvement in and promotion of various regional multilateral fora has placed it at the centre of East Asian regionalism. The PRC's regional diplomacy of engagement has aimed to reduce the perceived 'Chinese threat' in Asia and to reassure China's neighbours, and, as mentioned earlier, has been part of its hedging strategy towards the US.

The growth of regional multilateral fora and dialogues does not necessarily suggest that East Asia is likely to establish, in the foreseeable future, a security community which would replace the current American-led system with a multilateral security order centred on a political community. Indeed, the diversity of political systems, centrality of the nation-state and presence of competitive identities and parochial nationalism are major barriers to the formation of a political community and hence a 'Europeanisation' of East Asia (Ikenberry, 2004). Regional security organisations, namely the ARF, have so far failed to institutionalise the process that would lead to an effective resolution of conflicts, and thus they remain limited in their ability to tackle serious security issues, especially in North East Asia. Finally, the lack of strategic trust and mutual suspicion between the two major powers, i.e. Japan and China, result in their rivalry for influence and make joint leadership in furthering regional institution-building a difficult task.[5] All of which leads to the observation that an alternative to the US-led order has not materialised yet.

THE EU'S REGIONAL STRATEGY IN EAST ASIA

Europe has a strong interest in promoting regional cooperation in East Asia as this reflects the EU's multilateral approach to global governance. Furthermore, the support for region-building activities in other parts of the world has been an important policy objective for Brussels, as this is regarded as a means to enhance peace and stability both regionally (e.g. in Asia) and globally. The EU's policy towards Asia, as outlined in the Commission's Asia Strategy papers of 1994 and 2001, emphasises the need for Europe's strengthened engagement in the region's political and security dimensions (European Commission, 1994, 2001). While not completely excluding hard security issues, as reflected in the EU's concerns regarding the DPRK's nuclear programmes, the documents prioritise a number of non-traditional security areas of cooperation, including promotion of development, reduction of poverty, protection of human rights and tackling environmental problems.

The Commission's latest Asia paper indicates support for regional integration as one of the EU's strategic priorities for cooperation in the region (European Commission, 2007). With regard to East Asia, that support envisages enhanced dialogue in the framework of the Asia–Europe Meeting and the ARF, as well as with ASEAN. Finally, the 2003 European Security Strategy (ESS), which proposed that the EU develop strategic partnerships with Japan and China (among others), is yet another signal that Europe is seeking to deepen its involvement in Asia's political and security issues (European Council, 2003, 2008). While the nature of that involvement is yet to be further clarified, a major indicator of the EU's future role in East Asia is Europe's multidimensional approach to security stressed in the ESS, i.e. one that emphasises non-traditional security threats along with traditional ones.

It should be emphasised that the EU's respective security relations with East Asia's two major powers, i.e. Japan and China, have developed largely outside of the framework of hard security issues, while not excluding them altogether.

The most institutionalised bilateral link in Europe's relations with East Asia is the one with Japan, which reflects the shared democratic values between the two actors. Euro-Japanese cooperation since the 1991 Hague Declaration has primarily evolved as a partnership in the area of 'soft security', focusing, for example, on climate change, foreign aid and economic development. To be sure, Tokyo and Brussels have also tackled hard security issues through joint initiatives on nuclear non-proliferation and disarmament. Japan and the EU have further cooperated in non-military crisis management and post-conflict reconstruction, which have been identified in the 2001 Japan–EU Action Plan (along with the above-mentioned issues) as some of the major areas for deeper cooperation in the twenty-first century.[6]

The EU's relationship with China is still not as mature as the one with Japan and contains some important areas of divergence, especially with regard to views on democracy and human rights. As discussed elsewhere in this volume, the political dialogue between Brussels and Beijing has undergone significant evolution from the end of the 1990s on, which has increasingly reflected a number of common interests shared by the two partners. The EU has supported China's transition towards a more open society and has sought its full integration into the international community. This has been welcomed by Beijing as it hedges against US regional dominance in East Asia and looks for recognition as a responsible great power. A basis already exists for expanding EU–China cooperation in non-traditional areas, such as environmental protection and climate change. Brussels and Beijing have also shown a willingness to deepen their consultations with regard to hard security issues, including nuclear non-proliferation.

In contrast to the relations between the US–Japan alliance and China, Europe's respective interactions with Japan and the PRC are not party to the geopolitical rivalries in East Asia, nor do they exacerbate regional security dilemmas. In fact, Brussels has been conspicuously absent from the region in strategic terms, something the EU has arguably been seeking to change. Europe's soft power and comprehensive approach to security, including its civilian-centred approach to peacekeeping and experience in anti-terrorism, is welcomed in East Asia (Von Hoffman, 2007). By contrast, the US–Japan alliance (or America's other 'spokes' for that matter) with its focus on the military dimension of security seems not so well suited to addressing the growing number of non-traditional challenges faced by states in the region, notably in South East Asia (Bisley, 2008). Obama's East Asia policy suggests that Washington has recognised the shortcomings of its approach to regional commitments, as well as become more attentive to Asian multilateralism. The US may now be developing what has been described as the 'missing element' in its relations with China, i.e. a parallel multilateral engagement with East Asia (Bersick, 2006). As Beijing plays a central role in Asian institution-building processes, America may learn from the EU's approach of opting for soft power and promoting regional cooperation when interacting with China and the region (Bersick, 2006). Finally, in East Asia, the growth in recent years of multilateral groupings and dialogues reflects the understanding by regional states that closer collaboration is the best way to tackle transnational threats. This only strengthens the argument that Europe's greatest potential for expanding its security engagement with East Asia and furthering regional cooperation is in the area of non-traditional security.

CONCLUSION

In the twenty-first century the regional security order in East Asia continues to be largely underpinned by bilateralism rather than multilateralism and guided more by the logic of power-balancing than regional integration. Indeed, nearly sixty years after the signing of the original US–Japan Security Treaty, the bilateral alliance between Tokyo and Washington remains a major provider of stability in East Asia, as well as a main pillar of the American-led security system in the region. Japan's willingness to enhance its regional role has strengthened the deterrent effect of the US forward deployment in East Asia, thereby ensuring Washington its regional primacy. As Asian states remain wary of China's long-term strategic goals, they continue to see the hub and spoke system as indispensable to their security needs. Finally, America's role as a stabiliser of major power relations, notably those between Tokyo and Beijing, remains important as well.

The post-Cold War dynamics between the US–Japan alliance and China indicates that strategic mistrust and security dilemmas are defining features of the evolving order in East Asia. The potential remains for instability in the relations between Tokyo and Washington, and Beijing, and a shift towards major-power rivalry would definitely have serious regional repercussions. On the other hand, Obama's focus on greater US engagement in regional multilateralism and the relatively stable US–China and Japan–China relations indicate a positive trend towards cooperation and alleviation of the security dilemma. Indeed, while mutual hedging continues to define the interactions between the US and Japan, and China, the emphasis at the moment in all three capitals seems to be placed on the cooperative dimension of this hedging strategy. Economic interdependence and the need for collaboration with regard to a number of common global challenges are important factors underpinning this.

Developing outside of the traditional and more sensitive area of hard security, there is a new trend in the evolving East Asian order, i.e. a growing focus on institution-building. This trend reflects the priority that Asian states place on economic development and their increased concern about non-traditional security challenges. Given that an EU-style regional order for East Asia is unlikely to emerge in the coming decades, regional multilateralism in many ways complements the US-led system rather than presents an alternative to it, by addressing those concerns that are perceived not to be sufficiently dealt with by America.

It is in this context that the EU, with its experience of multilateralism and reliance on soft power in foreign policy, has strong potential to boost East Asian regional cooperation efforts in non-traditional security areas. Indeed, Europe's strengthened involvement with Asian states will further exemplify the benefits of a coordinated approach to tackling issues of common concern. The EU's multidimensional conceptualisation of security and the increasing importance placed on transnational challenges in East Asia are areas of convergence. Furthermore, it is on non-traditional issues that Europe may arguably work with both Japan and China, and thereby help them build mutual trust and enhance cooperation. Finally, the current positive trends in the relations between Tokyo and Washington, and Beijing, present perhaps a unique opportunity for the EU to strengthen its role in that part of the world and thereby promote its multilateral approach to global governance. While the American-led regional order is set to continue, Europe has much to offer for maintaining stability in East Asia.

NOTES

1. See United States Department of Defense (2006: 29); see also *Annual Report to Congress: Military Power of the People's Republic of China*, various years.
2. This policy is based on the Taiwan Relations Act passed by Congress in 1979 and the simultaneous recognition by Washington of the government in Beijing as the only legitimate government of China. The Act does not officially commit the US to intervene militarily on Taiwan's behalf in case of an attack by the mainland.
3. For an argument concerning the shift of Japanese policy towards China from accommodation during the Cold War to a mixed strategy of engagement and balancing under Koizumi, see Mochizuki (2007).
4. Obama's arms package did not include submarines and advanced fighter aircraft, the F-16 C/D, regarded by Taiwan as a high priority for its defence. China objects to the fighters, in particular, as it does not consider them to be defensive weapons.
5. On Japanese and Chinese approaches to multilateralism in East Asia and Sino–Japanese rivalry, see Atanassova-Cornelis and Mendes (2010).
6. Japan and the EU are currently negotiating a new Joint Action Plan, as the present one expired at the end of 2010. For the original text, see: http://www.mofa.go.jp/region/europe/eu/summit/action0112.html (accessed 21 November 2010).

REFERENCES

Atanassova-Cornelis, E. (2010) 'Foreign policy instruments and factors for policy change: Japan's security "normalisation" reconsidered', *Asian Journal of Social Science*, 38 (2): 279–306.

Atanassova-Cornelis, E. and Mendes, C. A. (2010) 'Dynamics of Japanese and Chinese security policies in East Asia, and implications for regional stability', *Asian Politics and Policy*, 2 (3): 395–414.

Bersick, S. (2006) 'Strategic considerations in the US–China relationship and the role of European soft power', *Asia-Europe Journal*, 4: 251–64.

Bisley, N. (2008) 'Securing the "anchor of regional stability"? The transformation of the US–Japan alliance and East Asian security', *Contemporary Southeast Asia*, 30 (1): 73–98.

Chinese Government's Official Web Portal (2004, 2006, 2008) 'White Paper on National Defence'. Online at: http://english.gov.cn/official/2005-08/17/content_24165.htm (accessed 27 November 2010).

Cossa, R. A. (2010a) 'Obama's East Asia policy: so far, so good', *Pac Net*, 5. Pacific

Forum CSIS. Online at: http://csis.org/publication/pacnet-5-obamas-east-asia-policy-so-far-so-good (accessed 17 November 2010).

Cossa, R. A. (2010b) 'US–China relations on a downward slide', *Pac Net*, 4A. Pacific Forum CSIS. Online at: http://csis.org/publication/pacnet-4a-us-china-relations-downward-slide (accessed 19 November 2010).

European Commission (1994) *Towards a New Asia Strategy*, COM (94) 314 final, 13 July, Brussels.

European Commission (2001) *Europe and Asia: A Strategic Framework for Enhanced Partnerships*, COM (2001) 469 final, 4 September, Brussels.

European Commission (2007) *Regional Programming for Asia: Strategy Document 2007–2013*, 31 May, Brussels. Online at: http://ec.europa.eu/external_relations/asia/rsp/07_13_en.pdf (accessed 21 November 2010).

European Council (2003) *A Secure Europe in a Better World – The European Security Strategy*, 12 December, Brussels. Online at: http://www.consilium.europa.eu/uedocs/cmsUpload/78367.pdf (accessed 21 November 2010).

European Council (2008) *Report on the Implementation of the European Security Strategy – Providing Security in a Changing World*, 11 December, Brussels. Online at: http://www.consilium.europa.eu/ueDocs/cms_Data/docs/pressdata/EN/reports/104630.pdf (accessed 21 November 2010).

Foot, R. (2006) 'Chinese strategies in a US-hegemonic global order: accommodating and hedging', *International Affairs*, 82 (1): 77–94.

Ikenberry, J. G. (2004) 'American hegemony and East Asian order', *Australian Journal of International Affairs*, 58 (3): 353–67.

Medeiros, E. S. (2005) 'Strategic hedging and the future of Asia-Pacific stability', *Washington Quarterly*, 29 (1): 145–67.

Ministry of Defence, Japan (2009) *Defence of Japan* (Annual White Paper). Online at: http://www.mod.go.jp/e/publ/w_paper/2009.html (accessed 25 November 2010).

Mochizuki, Mike M. (2007) 'Dealing with a rising China', in T. U. Berger, M. M. Mochizuki and Jitsuo Tsuchiyama (eds), *Japan in International Politics: The Foreign Policies of an Adaptive State*. Boulder, CO and London: Lynne Rienner, pp. 229–55.

Murayama, Y. (2009) 'U.S. engagement in Asia relies on Japan as partner', *Asahi Shimbun*, 16 November. Online at: http://www.asahi.com/english/Herald-asahi/TKY200911160077.html (accessed 7 April 2010).

National People's Congress, People's Republic of China (2005) *Anti-Secession Law*, 14 March. Online at: http://www.china.org.cn/english/2005lh/122724.htm (accessed 22 November 2010).

Pei, Minxin (2007) 'China's hedged acquiescence: coping with US hegemony', in Byung-Kook Kim and A. Jones (eds), *Power and Security in Northeast Asia: Shifting Strategies*. Boulder, CO and London: Lynne Rienner, pp. 99–125.

Saunders, Paul C. (2008) 'China's role in Asia', in D. Shambaugh and M. Yahuda (eds), *International Relations of Asia*. Lanham, MD: Rowman & Littlefield, pp. 127–49.

Shambaugh, D. (2006) 'Asia in transition: the evolving regional order', *Current History: A Journal of Contemporary World Affairs*, 105 (690): 153–9.

Sutter, Robert (2008) 'The United States in Asia', in D. Shambaugh and M.Yahuda (eds), *International Relations of Asia*. Lanham, MD: Rowman & Littlefield, pp. 85–103.

United States Department of Defense (2006, 2010) *Quadrennial Defense Review*.

Online at: http://www.defense.gov/qdr/ (accessed 17 November 2010).
United States Department of Defense (various years) *Annual Report to Congress: Military Power of the People's Republic of China*. Online at: http://www.defense.gov/pubs/china.html (accessed 12 November 2010).
Von Hoffman, N. (2007) 'How do Asians evaluate Europe's strategic involvement in East Asia?', *Asia-Europe Journal*, 5: 187–92.
Xinhua (2005) 'Japan's "sense of crisis" pure imagination', 4 November. Online at: http://news.xinhuanet.com/english/2005-11/04/content_3729035.htm (accessed 15 November 2010).

18. The EU vis-à-vis China: a question of power and coercion?

Tanguy de Wilde d'Estmael[1]

INTRODUCTION

The European Union (EU) and China share at least two common points in international relations: in the latter part of the twentieth century, they embodied, each in their own very different way, a kind of third way in the then bipolar world; and in the twentieth-first century, they leave some doubt about the kind of power they are developing. It is this unique facet of these two atypical powers that this paper intends to clarify before moving on to a more controversial aspect of their relationship: coercion by the EU through the continuing 1989 arms embargo against Beijing. This latter situation is quite paradoxical: this use of coercion remains a stain on the otherwise carefully woven fabric of multifaceted cooperation.

THE EUROPEAN UNION – A 'MODEL' WORLD POWER?

The relationship of the European Union to the rest of the world opens a debate about its identity and the 'clout' it exerts on the international stage. This is not new. As soon as the presence of the European Communities was clear in the global arena, questions were raised. In the twentieth century, throughout the 1970s and 1980s the question was to find either a third way or at least 'another way' that would provide some direction for European integration in a bipolar world. For the last two decades, the relevance of the EU's role in a globalised but insecure world has inspired this thinking. What remains of all the excitement of when the Treaty of Lisbon came into force, a treaty which, to some extent, reinforces the politico-strategic dimension of the EU?

Institutional reform, painstakingly undertaken since 2002, removes any doubt about the need to consider the EU as an effective actor on the international stage. But that doesn't mean it can be approached like any other actor, and especially not as any other state. The unusual and atypical nature of the EU prevents any comparison or inclusion in what is habitually called statehood.[2] Ipso facto, it is almost impossible to elucidate the type of 'power' that will arise. It may seem incongruous to call the external dimension of the EU 'power', given the historical pride on which it was built in order to overcome the 'power politics' (*Machtpolitik*) known only too well after two bloody continent-wide wars. Certainly, the EU presents itself as, by its very nature, a paragon of a 'postmodern' system in which relations among member states are not based on force or power, but have reached a turning point because of freely agreed common values (Cooper, 2003). But, in the outside world, the EU must deal with 'modern' world powers who view state sovereignty, cooperation based on consensus and balance of power as being very important. Whether the EU likes it or not, it is part of a 'power politics' world, even if it has an opportunity to advance a different conception of power.[3] In this sense, European 'power' is less frightening than in yesteryear; the EU wants to reassure the world around it through the use of its abilities in the service of certain values, while taking into account its own interests.

How then, to qualify this power? It is important to distinguish the elements of analysis which are often muddled up and have led to confusion. Here three levels of reflection – the means, method and context for the deployment of power – must first be separated to be properly understood and recombined thereafter.

At first glance, in its early days, the EU, which was limited to the Communities, acquired a de facto status as a market force through the extent of its economic and financial means. The commercial importance and the network of relationships from which it grew reinforced an international presence initially characterised by the absence of any serious military capacity. Hence, the concept emerged of the EU as a civilian power. If the limited means the developing EU had at its disposal perfectly justified the civilian character of its role, this approach did not provide insight into what kind of power it should be: merely attractive 'soft' or coercive through economic pressure and therefore 'hard' (Burckhardt, 2004)? A lack of military means, contrary to popular belief, does not imply soft power which is only capable of attracting cooperation. Sanctions and economic incentives, conditional aid and bi/multilateral agreements,[4] for example, are vectors of coercion and for the imposition of certain norms. In this sense, if the EU was initially only a civilian power, it was so through a combination of methods (soft, hard, normative) in a context that lent itself to the expression of this particular approach. And if it was a civilian power with means at its disposal, it aimed to 'civilise' or tame international relations through the dissemination of values and principles.

Have the end of the East–West confrontation and the acquisition of its own military capabilities for crisis management changed things? Only in part. The EU remains a civilian power, which is more credible since it has acquired other ways and means to intervene in world affairs, and more attractive in its immediate environment. But it must be understood that it is in a less comfortable position now than during the Cold War, when its status as a purely civilian power was an original and defining characteristic. The tragedy of the Balkans in the early 1990s, demonstrated forcefully the inadequacy of purely civil crisis management. However, the Union ceased to be considered as a purely civilian power by those with such a restrictive definition (of power) that it barely applied to the EU, namely a power that was neither military nor coercive, only attractive (Smith, 2000, 2005).

The gradual development of the ESDP (European Security and Defence Policy/1999–2009) has produced the CSDP (Common Security and Defence Policy) in the Treaty of Lisbon. However, it should not lead to any illusions as to the emergence of a military power. The resources available limit its possibility of using force; the Union is not as such a military alliance and ultimately offers no guarantee of territorial integrity to member states. This is a distinguishing feature of the EU in relation to other centres of power in the world. To suggest that the EU could become a military power is a too literal reading of the ESDP-CSDP, which postulates that the means it adopts would eventually bring a certain military might.[5] This clearly does not match the current situation. If the EU is no longer a civilian power and is less than a military power, what is it?

The notion of normative power is fashionable (Manners, 2002; Laidi, 2008) and, while not without certain internal contradictions, can combine the methods of soft and hard power. As the EU attracts, it can impose its standards in various ways. The EU expansion amply demonstrates this desire through the strengthened Copenhagen criteria, and also to a lesser extent the European Neighbourhood Policy (ENP). Furthermore, the EU tries to promote its standards where it can (from principles of democracy to environmental standards) with a mixture of attraction, pressure and their own presence. This combination echoes the concept of smart power, power targeted by design and intelligent through the multitude of its methods, both soft and hard. The export of its norms is not without neo-imperialist hints in the eyes of certain states feeling the impact of the importance of EU trade coupled with policy injunctions. But democratic 'messianism', dear to the European Union, is faltering at the start of the twenty-first century. The Iraqi example has shown that this is a kind of conceit: establishing a democracy in a sociocultural soil that is not ready. West Germany and Japan after 1945 were only possible because of the magnitude of the disaster and of the abominations committed by the defeated regimes. And in more general terms, the appeal of the democratic model needs to be rebuilt. The image conveyed in the media and on the web is often that of a hedonist West, caught up in the pursuit of pleasure and ease where individualism vies with consumerism. This perception, which could certainly be more nuanced, is not likely to instil a sense of human rights and human dignity. The West also appears inconsistent with its purported principles when 'realpolitik' prevails, such as when the red carpet was rolled out for the fickle Colonel Gaddafi, as the Libyan leader had distanced himself from terrorist movements and halted his nuclear weapons programme, but all the while continued to persecute Bulgarian nurses and Swiss businessmen.

The European Union follows the contours of the present order in international politics in permanent tension between cooperation and conflict, fed by various realities, interests, ideas and values. In this context, it attempts a synthesis between Marshall and Metternich – one might argue these historical references are applicable to the present reality. The EU is the largest global provider of development aid, hence the comparison with the Marshall Plan, which rebuilt by promoting cooperation among the recipients of American largesse and stabilising democracies. The EU promotes effective multilateralism internationally,[6] thus the evocation of Metternich and the Concert of Europe, whose updated principles the EU would like to transpose to the world community.

Ultimately, the EU seeks to be an 'exemplary' power in three different senses. Firstly, the Union itself provides an example: it is a successful model of democratic post-conflict integration transposable *mutatis mutandis* to other regions. Secondly, by its actions or foreign policy options, the EU leads by example, showing the way: it expects to attract and rally others to its policies. Thirdly, when faced with harsh realities which are impermeable to persuasion, the EU needs, from time to time, to 'make an example of', by imposing strict conditions or penalising through diplomatic and economic sanctions, or intervene to manage a crisis, preferably in concert with the UN, but without ever succumbing to motivations other than benevolence inspired by a desire for peace and democracy. In this context, the challenge for the EU is both the mobilisation of all appropriate means at its disposal and the consistency of its overall international effort to underline its greater effectiveness compared to the typical foreign policy of most states. The tension is palpable, however, when the Union's interests push it in directions inconsistent with its values, or when the promoted values incline it to neutrality or withdrawal within an existing relationship. It is difficult to be exemplary in a world that is not. But international affairs have long faced this difficulty. Sometimes there is no other way than 'to put into these diplomatic conversations the same ardour that others reserve for the field of battle' and to believe that, as in the time of the Pax Romana, 'each hour of calm' is 'a victory gained, though precarious like all victories; each dispute arbitrated [serves] as precedent and pledge for the future', and that 'good like bad becomes a routine, that the temporary tends to endure, that what is external permeates to the inside, and that the mask, given time, comes to be the face itself' (Yourcenar, 1982: 359–60).

CHINA, PEACEFUL RISING POWER?

China for its part is also a land of paradoxes. An economic power through impressive external trade, it remains nevertheless a developing country. Domestic demand is not (yet) at the height of the potential economic output: for the moment more than half of China's wealth comes from exports. Anxious to establish itself as an attracting 'soft' power, China nevertheless turns away from any global leadership role, preferring to introduce itself and its concerns into the processes of global governance. Ipso facto, China does not want a messianic role while remaining attached to the sacrosanct state sovereignty. This particular choice of not presenting itself as a 'normative' power is a source of success in any state wary of political and economic conditionality. At times we might even ask if China is not the distant heir of the principles espoused by George Washington in his famous farewell address, when he advocated an increase in economic relations, but a form of political isolationism for the US, then a future world power.[7] Comparison can, however, be misleading, and conduct toward the outside world has a particular Chinese characteristic contained in another famous line from Deng Xiaoping, shortly after his return to power and the launch of major reforms: 'Keep a cool head and maintain a low profile. Never take the lead – but aim to do something big.'

Since then, China can no longer hide or adopt a low profile. It simply insists on the peaceful nature of its rise to power, only showing its teeth on the Taiwan issue. Beijing clearly announces, right up the highest levels, the policy it will follow to improve its appeal internationally (Wang, 2008: 258).[8] In addition, China has rethought the well-known principles of peaceful coexistence, and conceptualised the idea of 'peaceful development'.[9] The latter, according to one Chinese scholar (Wu, 2008: 15), implies three types of renunciation: (1) the renunciation of expansion, thus removing the possibility of Chinese colonisation; (2)the renunciation of hegemony, stating what is widely understood, namely that the Chinese lay no claim to leadership or domination outside their borders; and (3) the renunciation of any alliances to prevent the formation of blocs, a grim memory from the Cold War. The political leaders in China regularly reaffirm this option of peaceful development. Based on the position of the President, Vice-Minister of Foreign Affairs Du Qiwen stated in particular that, 'China will never seek hegemony or engage in expansion.' And continued: 'China [. . .] will never seek benefits for itself at the expense of others or shift its troubles onto other countries.'[10]

In fact, China rejects any movement towards uni-polarity or 'uni-multipolarity' (Huntington, 1999: 35–49) to advocate a truly multipolar world. The line is fairly consistent with the Chinese denunciation of hegemony and its reluctance to assume leadership. In this context, effective multilateralism, for China, does not really resemble that which is promoted by the EU. This latter sees it as a teleological mechanism, serving some kind of global governance. Realism is certainly a feature in Beijing's vision of international relations, where power is shared among states finding a new equilibrium in the system that is, de facto, not (yet) multipolar. China is emerging in the trend observed by one author that 'international regulation has become the functional equivalent of the fervent tradition that balance is established through treaties and arms' (Joffe, 2006: 70). Here multilateralism is somewhat manipulated to reduce the place of other powers, with little regard for the socio-political objectives of international organisations or for collective security (Struye de Swielande, 2009: 10). In this sense, multilateralism is effective in Chinese eyes if it leads to multipolarity. Beijing approaches multilateral exercises with its eyes wide open and with its interests and those of its main partners clearly in mind. This *modus operandi* reaches its limits in Beijing; not yet an actor on the world stage, it is unable to make or even influence substantially the rules of the game in the international arena.

MEANING OF COERCION IN THE COOPERATION BETWEEN POWERS

China and the EU, two comparable powers but with sometimes divergent objectives, formed a strategic partnership in 2003. In the European Union jargon, this signals the prospect of a global partnership. Nevertheless, the arms embargo established in 1989 by the then EU-12 shortly after the events of 4 June was maintained. Over twenty years after the brutal crackdown on students, orchestrated by the Chinese authorities in Tiananmen Square, what is the meaning of this continued coercion – couldn't a doubt as to the EU's motivation be reasonably expected? For the European Union, the use of coercive diplomacy has become a common practice over time and refined through a variety of measures to target more and more clearly the policies of any state subject to its disapproval. The impact of this diplomacy is really felt when the Union's action is independent, that is when the CFSP initiates an action without any resolution from the UN, which is obviously the case when the EU admonishes a member of the Security Council such as China or Russia. The study of the origins of this policy of coercion and a thorough examination of its evolution (de Wilde d'Estmael, 1998, 2000a, 2000b) has helped develop analysis of the individual cases of autonomous EU sanctions. The proposed analysis schema sets out three types of objective (primary, secondary, tertiary) believed to induce three types of function or effects of the same sort (see Table 18.1).[11] The primary objective of the sanction directly affects the target: it is principally a measure to concretely condemn a particular action. But this punitive objective is coupled with the idea of transformation: change in the behaviour of the target through pressure. The secondary purpose of sanctions is in reference to what the sanctioning actors want to express about themselves, in this case, a demonstration for EU public opinion that the member states are ready, willing and able to act collectively. Finally, the tertiary objective pursued enlarges the field of action, not to the target or those sanctioning, but to the international system as a whole, a signal that coercive action is supposed to produce. This analysis schema provides an initial gauge of the political impact of the sanctions adopted in the short or long term, and may also elucidate why sanctions are not adopted in some circumstances where they could be envisaged.

Looking at the Chinese arms embargo, it is better to divide the analysis into the short and medium term, that is the immediate impact following June 1989 until about 2003, and afterwards, at which time the renewed vigour of the EU–Chinese partnership put in question the continuation of a perhaps obsolete embargo.

By adopting, among other measures,[12] an arms embargo against Beijing, the EC-12 agreed within the framework of European Political Cooperation (EPC) to exert pressure jointly and to take measures at the state level, since arms sales remain a national and not a Community matter. Achieving unanimity in this case was not a done deal; the United Kingdom in particular did not want to target China given the pending return of Hong Kong to Beijing's control scheduled for 1997. So, the EC-12 quickly agreed that London could pursue high-level contacts in this area, even though they were otherwise suspended (Baker, 2002).

In and of itself, the existence of this joint action was therefore a first success for EPC. It also showed that the EC-12 were not reluctant to confront any power that did not respect the principles that the European

Table 18.1 Incidents of independent EU sanctions: identfiying the objectives and effects of political coercion?

Primary objectives		**Secondary objectives**		**Tertiary objectives**	
(the target: states, autonomous areas, groups, individuals)		(vis-à-vis sanctioning party, in this case the EU itself, first through the European Political Cooperation (EPC) then the CFSP, the member states)		(vis-à-vis international partners, allies, third states, the UN and the international community)	
Punishment: Concrete measures which coincide with the condemnation of the behaviour	*Transformation*: Transform the political attitude and/or policy of the target	Demonstrate an ability to work together despite a lack of enthusiasm of member states Demonstrate innovation or creativity	'Do something' to appease public opinion or to respond to certain requests of the European Parliament	Remind the international community of the principles (*erga omnes*) defended by the EU through its approach to foreign affairs, its objectives and its coherence	Trigger actions by the UN
Primary effects		**Secondary effects**		**Tertiary effects**	
The result is always reached	The efficiency does not depend solely on the action of the EU	If sanctions are adopted, they in fact demonstrate the capability to work together	The result depends on the perception of the EU action	The function of sanctions as an example is always fulfilled	Solidarity is shown with third-party states or rallying them to the action proposed by the EU
Long-term effects on relations between the EU and the target		Long-term effects on the CFSP development of increasingly refined coercive practice		Effects in the short or medium term on the UN decisions or on foreign policy decisions taken by third-party states	

Community (EC) promoted in its external relations in general. In the following months, all the agreed economic restrictions were put in place, with the exception of those concerning arms. However, there was no discernable impact on Beijing's attitude towards its rebellious youth. The effect of the coercive measures was in fact non-existent, but in the years that followed some openings for dialogue on the issue of human rights in China appeared, which could be seen as a concession from Beijing in part due to European pressure. But it was also initially a signal for other EC/EU partners. It indicated that the USSR, then in the midst of turbulent changes, needed to continue with its reforms or risk seeing EC aid dry up. And above all, the EC-12 were aligned with Japan and the United States, all of whom were anxious to limit Chinese military capacities which could permit, for example, a military adventure against Taiwan. Over time, the events of Tiananmen Square disappeared as a motivator for the EU member states given the significant changes in the Chinese and international contexts. However, some points will renew the debate on whether or not to continue the embargo, for example Beijing's openness on the issue of human rights, its level of aggression towards Taiwan and the impact of the EU's Chinese policy on transatlantic relations. Table 18.2 below summarises the key elements.

In the medium-term, it is possible to consider the dialogue between the EU and China on human rights a result of the embargo, whose success remains otherwise limited. Non Governmental Organisations (NGOs) are very active in the field of human rights but do not yet participate in the dialogue and the EU has failed to convince Beijing to ratify the UN's International Covenant on Civil and Political Rights (ICCPR). As for the lifting of the embargo, since 2003, a series of arguments have been put forward, principally by France and Germany and at the highest levels by President Jacques Chirac and Chancellor Gerhard Schröder. It is true that a strategic partnership was established at that time by the EU and China, accompanied by military cooperation with some member states, particularly France and Germany. More generally, the spectacular increase in cooperation in a range of areas, which from 2008 have made China the largest importer of EU goods and its second largest trading partner,[13] raises questions as to the continuing coercion which is viewed unfavourably by Beijing. China considered that the EU was treating it like the pariah states of Burma, Sudan or Zimbabwe. But the Franco-German support to which some members of the Commission were sensitive did not have unanimous support among member states, some Nordic countries in particular continuing to oppose the lifting of the embargo.[14] They were not convinced by the bulwark that had been put forward: the arms sales code of conduct, in force since 1998 and subsequently strengthened. This

Table 18.2 Incidents of independent EU sanctions: application to China, post-Tiananmen Square 1989 (arms embargo)

Primary objectives		**Secondary objectives**		**Tertiary objectives**	
Punishment: Condemnation of the murderous repression of peaceful demonstrators	*Transformation*: 1. Peaceful solution and discussion with students 2. Attention to human rights in China	Common action despite British reservations	Maintain at least one enforcement measure	Reminder of the inseparable nature of human rights policy of the EU	A signal for the USSR Not frighten the United States or Japan Relationship to the Taiwan issue
Primary effects		**Secondary effects**		**Tertiary effects**	
The result is achieved in any case: punitive stigma	1. None 2. Privileged EU–China dialogue on human rights since 1995	OK for a while	Relatively little practical impact but great symbolic importance	OK	Tri-party debate EU–US–China
Limits on EU–China dialogue regarding human rights (no NGOs) No ratification of the UN ICCPR treaty		Code of Conduct for arms exports Franco-German and Commission discussions about lifting of the embargo – under debate		Ongoing discussions	

instrument, gradually integrated into the CFSP,[15] would suspend arms sales if the buyer was at war. This did not, however, reassure the concerned states which noted in 2005 a Chinese law legitimising the use of force by Beijing in the case of a declaration of independence by Taiwan.[16] The problem thus resurfaced and the clearly expressed reservations of the US assured the preservation of the status quo. Maintaining the embargo on arms clearly shows the different perspectives of international relations held by the two powers. For China, the 'peaceful development' of its power is a corollary to a world where the five principles of peaceful coexistence (Wen, 2004) permit cooperation between states with different political systems. In this context, the embargo does not respect the principle of mutual benefit, the reciprocal advantage for states of non-interference in one another's internal affairs. The EU, on the other hand, looks to use its economic and political weight to both 'enlighten' international relations and to pacify them, but in a more dynamic manner than the maintaining of the status quo as contained in the concept of peaceful coexistence. The EU is more in favour of 'peacemaking' coexistence. To this end, an embargo on military materiel is applied, even if for reasons appertaining uniquely to the internal situation of the country concerned.

CONCLUSIONS

In summary, the continuation of the EU embargo in 2011 is linked to considerations far removed from the events of Tiananmen Square in 1989. The lack of unanimity among member states, the importance of maintaining leverage even if it has little practical effect on a seemingly menacing China (i.e. questions around Taiwan, Tibet, the Uighur population) and the desire to soothe public opinion, the European Parliament or the United States are all factors that explain the ongoing presence of this coercive measure in an otherwise highly cultivated relationship. In the future, the EU may be able to demonstrate that the weak character of its embargo and a limited ability to ensure real control over arms sales (including the code of conduct) by other means are worth the constraint, which in the eyes of its target has a strategic importance less for its army than for its global image. The difficulty for the EU may be in depriving itself of a convenient instrument of power with which it can react both internally and externally. The embargo is indeed an easy weapon to brandish when the Union is pilloried because of the intensity of its relations with a regime that does not share European values.

NOTES

1. The author expresses his acknowledgements to his colleagues T. Struye (Louvain-la-neuve) and J. Burns (Namur) for their help and comments (both scientific and linguistic) in the writing of this paper.
2. The Common Foreign and Security Policy (CFSP) of the EU has not been set up to replace national foreign policies. Cf. the warning launched at the beginning of the process by Hill (1990: 54).
3. The EU has to tackle with the 'issue' of others' power. This is unavoidable. For an example of this kind of 'problem' concerning the US, see Andréani (2006).
4. See, for example, de Wilde d'Estmael (1998) and Portela (2010).
5. This is the opinion of certain American thinkers. Such thinking has been clearly criticised by Howorth and Menon (2009: 221–38).
6. From the adoption of the European security strategy by the European Council ('A secure Europe in a better world', 12 December 2003), effective multilateralism is celebrated as a means to challenge the new threats in the international arena.
7. George Washington pronounced the following assumptions on 19 September 1796: 'The

great rule of conduct for us in regard to foreign nations is, in extending our commercial relations, to have with them as little political connection as possible. So far as we have already formed engagements, let them be fulfilled with perfect good faith. [. . .] Europe has a set of primary interests, which to us have none or a very remote relation. Hence she must be engaged in frequent controversies, the causes of which are essentially foreign to our concerns. Hence therefore it must be unwise in us to implicate ourselves, by artificial ties, in the ordinary vicissitudes of her politics or the ordinary combinations and collisions of her friendships or enmities.'

8. Wang indicates that President Hu Jintao did not hesitate, during the 17th Congress of the Chinese Communist Party, to encourage his country 'to enhance culture as part of the soft power of our country to better guarantee the people's basic cultural rights and interests'.
9. Struye de Swielande mentions that during the winter 2003–4, the expression 'peaceful rising' appeared to be too aggressive and became 'peaceful development' (Struye de Swielande, 2009: 16).
10. Du Qiwen at the High-Level Seminar on Chinese Foreign Policy, February 2008, Brussels Institute of Contemporary China Studies.
11. The distinction first established by Barber (1970: 370) is here reshaped and implemented for the EU. For a broader analysis of economic sanctions in international relations, see de Wilde d'Estmael (2004: 373–97).
12. These other measures (restrictions in the military; cultural, scientific, technical cooperation; reductions of political contacts;. . .) have been progressively lifted since 1990.
13. According to the figures given by the DG Trade (European Commission) on its website, in 2008 China became the second trade partner of the EU (11.4 per cent of the trade exchange) behind the US (15.2 per cent) but ahead of Russia (9.7 per cent); China represents 16 per cent of imports into the EU, ahead of the US (12 per cent) and Russia (9.2 per cent). The US remains the top export partner of the EU (19.1 per cent), but China (6 per cent) is in fourth place, close to Russia (8 per cent) and Switzerland (7.5 per cent). The EU is the top trade partner of China (17 per cent of the trade exchange) ahead of the US (13.9 per cent) and Japan (10.6 per cent). In 2009, EU–China trade was still rising: China has become the third placed export partner (7.9 per cent) but remains the top import partner (17.8 per cent) and, in general, the second trade partner of the EU (12.9 per cent of the total exchange).
14. On these issues and for different approaches, see, for example, Casarini (2007), Remond (2008), Zhimin (2008) and two views from Taiwan by Tang Shao (2005) and Tai-Lin (2006–7).
15. Adopted on 8 June 1998, The code of conduct has been revised several times before its integration into a CFSP Common Position 2008/944/CFSP, 8 December 2008 *OJUE*, L 355/99, 13 December 2008.
16. On 14 March 2005, the Chinese National People's Congress adopted the Anti-Secession Law which recalls the legitimacy of a military intervention if Taiwan intends to declare independence.

REFERENCES

Andréani, Gilles (2006) 'L'Europe et le problème de la puissance américaine', in M. Zaborowski (ed.), *Friends Again ? EU–US Relations After the Crisis*. Paris: Institute for Security Studies, pp. 83–109.

Baker, Paul (2002) 'Human rights, Europe and the People's Republic of China', *China Quarterly*, 2: 45–63.

Barber, James (1979) 'Economic sanctions as a policy instrument', *International Affairs*, 55 (3): 367–84.

Burckhardt, Christian W. (2004) *Why Is There a Public Debate About the Idea of a*

'Civilian Power Europe'?, EI Working Paper, 2004-2. London: London School of Economics and Political Science, European Institute.
Casarini, Nicola (2007) 'The international politics of the Chinese arms embargo issue', *International Spectator*, 42 (3): 371–89.
CFSP Common Position 2008/944/CFSP, 8 December 2008 *OJUE*, L 355/99, 13 December 2008.
Cooper, Robert (2003) *The Breaking of Nations: Order and Chaos in the Twenty-First Century*. London: Atlantic Books.
de Wilde d'Estmael, Tanguy (1998) *La dimension politique des relations économiques extérieures de la Communauté européenne. Sanctions et incitants économiques comme moyens de politique étrangère*. Brussels: Bruylant.
de Wilde d'Estmael, Tanguy (2000a) 'L'efficacité politique de la coercition économique exercée par l'Union européenne dans les relations internationales', *Annuaire français de Relations internationales*, 1: 502–21.
de Wilde d'Estmael, Tanguy (2000b) 'Une continuité dans le changement: les mesures de coercition économiques de l'Union européenne à l'égard de l'URSS et de la Russie', in T. de Wilde and L. Spetschinsky (eds), *Les relations entre l'Union européenne et la fédération de Russie*. Louvain-la-Neuve: Institut d'études européennes, pp. 165–85.
de Wilde d'Estmael, Tanguy (2004) 'Les sanctions économiques comme moyens de politique étrangère', in C. Roosens, V. Rosoux and T. de Wilde d'Estmael (eds), *La politique étrangère. Le modèle classique à l'épreuve*. Brussels: P.I.E.-Peter Lang, pp. 373–97.
European Council (2003) *A Secure Europe in a Better World*, 12 December.
Hill, Christopher (1990) 'European foreign policy: power bloc, civilian model or flop?', in Reinhardt Rummel (ed.), *The Evolution of an International Actor: Western Europe's New Assertiveness*. Boulder, CO: Westview Press.
Howorth, J. and Menon, A. (2009) 'Sécurité européenne et relations transatlantiques: pourquoi l'Union européenne n'est pas en train d'équilibrer les Etats-Unis', in F. Mérand and R. Schwok (eds), *L'Union européenne et la sécurité internationale. Théories et Pratiques*. Genève/Louvain-la-Neuve: Académia-Bruylant, pp. 221–38.
Huntington, Samuel (1999) 'The lonely superpower', *Foreign Affairs*, 78 (2): 35–49.
Joffe, Josef (2006) *Hyperpuissance*. Paris: Odile Jacob.
Laidi, Zaki (2008) *La norme sans la force*, 2nd edn. Paris: Presses de Sciences Po.
Manners, Ian (2002) 'Normative power Europe – a contradiction in terms', *Journal of Common Market Studies*, 2: 235–58.
Portela, Clara (2010) *European Union Sanctions and Foreign Policy: When and Why Do They Work?* London: Routledge.
Remond, Mathieu (2008) 'Ventes d'armes à la Chine: la fin de l'embargo européen?', *Politique étrangère*, 2 : 307–18.
Smith, Karen (2000) 'The end of civilian power EU: a welcome demise or cause for concern?', *International Spectator*, 35 (2): 11–28.
Smith, Karen (2005) 'Beyond the civilian power EU debate', *Politique européenne*, 3 (17): 63–82.
Struye de Swielande, Tanguy (2009) 'La Chine et le 'soft power': une manière de défendre l'intérêt national de manière douce', *Notes d'analyse de la chaire InBev-Baillet Latour 'UE–Chine'*, No. 2. Louvain-la-Neuve: UCL.
Tai-Lin, Cheng (2006–7) 'L'embargo européen contre la Chine: le point de vue de Taïwan', *Monde Chinois*, 9 : 89–96.

Tang Shao, Cheng (2005) 'The EU's Policy towards China and the arms embargo', *Asia Europe Journal*, 3: 313–21.

Wang, Yiwei (2008) 'Public diplomacy and the rise of Chinese soft power', *Annals of the American Academy of Political and Social Science*, 616 (1): 257–73.

Wen Jiabao (2004) 'Carrying forward the Five Principles of Peaceful Coexistence in the promotion of peace and development', *Chinese Journal of International Law*, 3 (2): 363–8.

Wu, J. (2008) 'Past, present and future', *China Security*, 4 (3): 14–15.

Yourcenar, Marguerite (1982) *Mémoires d'Hadrien*, in *uvres romanesques* (first published 1951). Paris: Gallimard, Collection La Pléiade.

Yourcenar, Marguerite (1990) *Memoirs of Hadrian Followed by Reflections on the Composition of Memoirs of Hadrian*. New York: Noonday Press (first published 1963).

Zhimin, Cheng (2008) 'The limits of the EU as a strategic actor: the case of ending the EU's arms embargo on China' , in R. Seidelmann and A. Vasilache (eds), *European Union and Asia: A Dialogue on Regionalism and Interregional Cooperation*. Baden-Baden: Nomos, pp. 264 *et seq*.

19. The EU and China: emerging global powers capable of balancing US hegemony and shaping a new world order?

Hanne Cuyckens

INTRODUCTION

The world order that has emerged since the Cold War is characterised by US hegemony. Even though some authors believed that the distribution of powers among states and other international players following the end of the Cold War was going to lead to a more balanced world order, US hegemony had been showing no signs of decline. The financial crisis has strongly reminded us of the extent to which the post-Cold War world is increasingly interconnected and interdependent. An increasing number of issues can no longer be tackled by a single country alone. US dominance has been more and more put into question by an increasing number of emerging global powers, such as the EU and China. These two actors strongly believe that a more balanced multipolar system will provide for a more secure and stable world. More concretely, recent events, such as the global financial crisis and the negotiations at the Copenhagen climate change conference, have shown a possible geo-strategic shift in the world's balance of power.

In this chapter the question is raised as to whether the EU and China, who are both emerging global actors, are capable of balancing US hegemony and shaping a new world order. In order to do so, it is useful to first give a brief overview of the legal framework of EU–China relations. Then both actors' view of multipolarity and the relationship between the EU, the US and China will be analysed. Finally, it will be argued that, even though the US remains the most important global actor, the world order is evolving towards a more multipolar balance of powers and emerging actors such as the EU and China will definitely, even if it is yet unclear to what extent, have a role to play in the redefinition of this new world order.

A BRIEF OVERVIEW OF THE FRAMEWORK OF EU–CHINA RELATIONS

Formal relations between the EU and China were first established in 1975. The momentum for starting this relationship was there for both the EU as well as for China. In fact, China had just signed an anti-soviet partnership with the US and on the EU side the beginning of the European Political Cooperation (EPC) process, the predecessor of what was to become the Common Foreign and Security Policy (CFSP), was being witnessed (Casarini, 2009: 25). In 1985, the then European Economic Community (EEC) and China signed a Trade and Cooperation Agreement. This agreement was primarily adopted in the framework of the Common Commercial Policy. Even though the relationship has nowadays evolved to include issues other than the economic, the 1985 Trade and Cooperation Agreement still remains the main legal framework for the EU's relations with China. In order to adapt the legal framework to this new reality, the EU and China have, since 2007, started to negotiate a Partnership and Cooperation Agreement (PCA), which besides the traditional economic issues will also include political and security issues.

The long-term strategy of the EU vis-à-vis China has also been set out in a series of communications by the European Commission (EC). A thorough analysis of these communications falls outside the ambit of this chapter, but it is interesting to briefly look at their recurring themes, which are: to engage China further, both bilaterally and on the world stage; to support China's transition towards an open society based on the rule of law and respect for human rights; to encourage China's integration in the world economy; and to raise the profile of the EU in China (Griese, 2006: 548).

China has also adopted a policy paper on its relationship with the EU, entitled *China's EU Policy Paper*. Adopted in October 2003, it was the first, and still the only, policy paper adopted by China in the area of bilateral relations. This document is quite an interesting one. It starts by recognising the importance of the EU, both as an international actor and as a partner for China. Statements such as '[t]here is no fundamental conflict of interest between China and the EU [. . .]' (Ministry of Foreign Affairs of the People's Republic of China, 2003: 2) and '[t]he common ground between China and the EU far outweighs their disagreements' (Ministry of Foreign Affairs of the People's Republic of China, 2003: 2) are made at the beginning of the paper. This very positive picture is later contrasted by a certain number of demands that China makes of the EU. For example, '[t]he Chinese side requests the EU side not to have any contact with the Tibetan Government in exile' (Ministry of Foreign Affairs of the People's Republic of China, 2003: 4). China's policy paper on the EU is thus a quite paradoxical document, because as Cabestan rightly mentions, '[o]n the one hand, it glorifies the EU's power and influence in the world as if the EU were a real political and military pole, a prerequisite that is far from being met [. . .] [and] [o]n the other hand, this document lists a series of odd-looking demands on Taiwan, Tibet, human rights, and the lifting of the arms embargo' (Cabestan, 2006: 17).

THE EU, CHINA AND THEIR BELIEF IN A MULTIPOLAR WORLD

Over the last decades, the emergence of the EU as an external actor and the rise of the People's Republic of China have greatly influenced world politics. Due to their size, their economic weight and their strategic importance, these new global actors are most likely to, and in a sense already have, become important players on the international scene (Casarini, 2009: 1). As such they provide an important challenge to the international order centred on the US.

The relationship between the EU and China has evolved over time and while it was initially primarily based on trade, it has now evolved to include issues as diverse as climate change, migration and the fight against organised crime. This evolution has to be seen in the light of broader global evolutions. We live in a world that has become more and more interconnected and globalised. The number of global issues has grown and global problems require global solutions. Both parties recognise the need for global problems to be addressed by global actors. Since they are both striving to find their place in a US-led world their relationship will 'inevitably impinge on (and have implications for) the emerging global order as well as the strategic state sitting on top of the international system' (Casarini, 2009: 11).

One of the main priorities for the EU in its relationship with China is the promotion of China's integration into the international community. The EU does not merely want to involve China in international affairs, it wants China to become a *responsible* actor on the international scene: '[t]he EU is eager to see China sharing in the opportunities and responsibilities at the heart of the international community, as China opens to a freer flow of ideas and cooperation, both in the key Asian region and globally' (Commission of the European Communities, 1998: 3). In order for China to be able to fulfil this role, the EU believes it is important to fully support China's internal development process. This objective has to be linked to what has been declared in the European Security Strategy (ESS): '[t]he quality of international society depends on the quality of the governments that are its foundation. The best protection for our security is a world of well-governed democratic States' (Council of the European Union, 2003: 10). The EU thus wants to help China in its internal reform process in order to make sure that it becomes a 'well-governed democratic state' capable of playing a role in international society. Next to its support of internal reform, the EU also finds it important to integrate China into as many international institutions as possible (Shambaugh, 2005: 8). One of the latest examples is, of course, China's accession to the WTO. To summarise, as Odgaard and Biscop rightfully put it, the EU 'expects China, as an emerging global power, to shoulder global responsibilities and to contribute actively and constructively to effective multilateralism' (Odgaard and Biscop, 2007: 62).

When we analyse the different EC Communications and China's EU Policy Paper, it seems that the promotion of multilateralism is very important for both actors. The 2003 EC Communication mentions that the 'EU and China share views on the importance of multilateral systems and rules of global governance, which includes the further strengthening of the United Nations system, its role in regional and global conflict resolution and in the co-ordination of actions addressing global concerns [...]' (Commission of the European Communities, 2003: 3). China's Policy paper states that '[b]oth China and the EU stand for democracy in international relations and an enhanced role for the UN' (Ministry of Foreign Affairs of the People's Republic of China, 2003: 2) and that one of the objectives of its relationship with the EU is to '[s]trenghten China–EU cooperation at the UN and work together to uphold the UN's authority, promote its leading role in safeguarding world peace [...] and support UN's reform' (Ministry of Foreign Affairs of the People's Republic of China, 2003: 2).

Both the EU and China are supportive of a balanced international system with different poles of power. But they have a different idea on how to realise this new world order. The vision of the EU on 'effective multilateralism' has been outlined in the ESS: '[I]n a world of global threats, global markets and global media, our security and prosperity increasingly depend on an *effective multilateral system*. The development of a stronger international society, well functioning international institutions and a rule-based international order is our objective [emphasis added]' (Council of the European Union, 2003: 9). In order to realise this objective of effective multilateralism, the EU is 'committed to upholding and developing international law' (Council of the European Union, 2003: 9) and 'want[s] international organisations, regimes and treaties to be effective in confronting threats to international peace and security and must therefore be ready to act when their rules are broken' (Council of the European Union, 2003: 9). Multilateralism from the EU point of view can be summarised as the importance of effective international (and regional) organisations and the importance of international law. What China refers to can be better qualified as multipolarity rather than multilateralism. Multipolarity refers to 'the balanced distribution of the ability of individual powers to prevent unilateral options from prevailing' (De Vasconcelos, 2008: 24). It is not exactly the same as multilateralism. China's focus lies more on the number of poles capable of contributing to the balancing of power rather than on developing effective multilateral institutions. China sees itself as one of those poles and wants to play a role in containing the more powerful states while at the same time asserting its own sovereignty (De Vasconcelos, 2008: 27). This is quite a long way from the concept of multilateralism promoted by the EU, as outlined by then External Relations Commissioner Ferrero-Waldner: 'For the EU [. . .] it is not the number of poles which count, but rather the basis on which they operate. Our vision is a world governed by rules created and monitored by multilateral institutions' (Ferrero-Waldner, 2005). The EU's conception of multilateralism seems to be difficult to reconcile with the strong adherence of China to the concepts of sovereignty and non-interference in domestic affairs (Narramore, 2008: 97). It seems difficult (if not impossible) to picture China pooling sovereignty and having to obey to decisions taken by international (or regional) organisations. It can be said that for the bottom line, China and Europe want to achieve the same goal. They both want to effectively balance US hegemony and build a world order based on a better distribution of power, but the ways in which they want to realise this differ. For the EU, this new world order should be based on better international norms and more effective international (and regional) organisations, whereas 'China's view of multilateralism seems to err more towards its long-cherished fidelity to multipolarization [. . .], whereby multiple mechanisms counter a hegemonic global order' (Shambaugh et al., 2008: 313). International institutions can constitute one of these mechanisms, but rising global powers such as China itself, and for example India and Brazil, can also constitute such poles of power. The EU as an important global actor is also seen by China as such a pole. The importance for China thus lies in a great multiplicity of poles rather than in the value of international law and effective international institutions.

THE FAILURE OF THE EU TO ACT AS A COHERENT ACTOR IN EU–CHINA RELATIONS

The relationship between the EU and China has not only become more intensive and more extensive but it has also become more complex over the years. The 'honeymoon period'[1] seems to be over and the growing disagreements on matters such as, for example, human rights, the future role of China in Africa and the lifting of the arms embargo have created tensions between the two actors. A change in tone can be measured in the latest communication from the EC in which it is stated that '[t]he EU's fundamental approach to China must remain one of engagement and partnership. But with a closer strategic partnership, mutual responsibilities increase. The partnership should meet both sides' interest and the EU and China need to work together as they assume more active and responsible international roles, supporting and contributing to a strong and effective multilateral system' (Commission of the European Communities, 2006: 2).

A major element contributing to the tensions in the EU's relationship with China is the incapacity of the EU to act as a coherent actor and to define a common policy vis-à-vis China. The debate surrounding the possible lifting of the arms embargo is an important illustration of this incapacity. Indeed, disagreements on this issue could be found at different levels of the decision-making process: there were disagreements between (and even inside) the different institutions at EU level, between the different member states and even inside some of the member states.

The decision to impose an arms embargo on China was taken in 1989 right after the Tiananmen incident. With the intensification of the relationship, the pressure to lift the arms embargo became more and more important. On the Chinese side, it is argued that 'the EU cannot be serious about building a strategic partnership with China while leaving it in the same category as Africa's and Asia's worst-run countries' (Barysch, 2005: 60–1). The lifting of the arms embargo is thus fundamental to the building of mutual trust and the emergence of a strategic partnership with China. On the EU side, France and Germany made an official proposal to lift the arms embargo in December 2003. A consensus in favour of lifting the arms embargo was found quite rapidly but things got more complicated in the beginning of 2005 (Men, 2008: 14). The adoption by the Chinese of the anti-secession law in March 2005, growing US pressure not to lift the embargo and the modification of the German position after the election of Angela Merkel altered the interests at stake in the debate.

At the EU level, there were some divergences in the positions of the different institutions. The European Parliament, which has an advisory role in CFSP matters, was strongly against the lifting of the arms embargo. In a resolution on EU–China relations adopted in 2005, it 'strongly recommend[ed] – as endorsed by numerous of its resolutions – that the EU arms embargo against China remain intact until greater progress is made on human rights issues' (European Parliament, 2005). The High

Representative for CFSP, Javier Solana, was in favour of lifting the arms embargo (Kreutz, 2004: 51). It can easily be assumed that Solana supported it in order to favour the development of the strategic partnership put forward in the ESS. Finally, the position of the EC is quite interesting. In fact, there seems to have been a difference in position between the President of the Commission, Romano Prodi, who was in favour of the lifting, and the Commissioner for External Relations, Chris Patten, who was against (Kreutz, 2004: 50). Not only did the different European institutions adopt different positions but there were even different positions within the same institutions.

Concerning more specifically the positions of the different member states, France and Germany were the strongest advocators of the lifting of the embargo. They argued that 'the embargo ha[d] become an "anachronism" in the EU's rapidly evolving partnership with China' (Barysch, 2005: 61) and that, in any case, the arms embargo did not prevent member states from selling arms to China because in the absence of a common list of embargoed goods 'the embargo never became EU coherent in implementation and scope' (Kreutz, 2004: 47). Although this was the official argument used, it can of course be supposed that the main driver behind this position was of a commercial nature. While most of the member states adhered to this position, not all of them were in favour of lifting the arms embargo. The Netherlands and Denmark were particularly opposed to it. Their main argument was the question of whether human rights in China had improved sufficiently in order to justify the lifting of the embargo (Barysch, 2005: 61). This position is in line with the more general foreign policy interests of these countries which tend to emphasise human rights. These member states are also 'less likely to win large-scale contracts in China' (Barysch, 2005: 61), consequently the commercial incentive is not so important to them. The influence of the US is an important factor in the position of some member states, especially those, such as the UK or some of the newer member states, which are traditionally close to the US. As we will see later on in this chapter, the US was strongly opposed to the lifting of the embargo and this has certainly played a role in the position of some member states. The position of some member states also evolved over time. The most striking example is Germany, whose position shifted from being an initial advocate for the lifting of the arms embargo to being against it, especially for human rights reasons, once Angela Merkel had been elected (Men, 2008: 15).

The EU's difficulty in being a coherent actor, which was highlighted by the debate surrounding the embargo, is a more generalised problem in its relationship with China. As Fox and Godement rightfully put it, it seems that the 'European divisions reflect a lack of faith among Member States that the EU can act as an effective guarantor of their national interests' (Fox and Godement, 2009: 30). The main problem is that this undermines the credibility of the EU in the eyes of its Chinese interlocutors. China no longer, at least for now, perceives the EU as a serious political partner (Fox and Godement, 2009: 33). Consequently, China has revaluated its approach to the EU and has moved some of the focus from the European Commission back to some key member states (Narramore, 2008: 94). China has also learned how to play the internal divisions and to use them to its advantage. In this sense, China has not hesitated to punish those member states who were interfering with its internal affairs, as was the case vis-à-vis the Netherlands and Denmark when they supported an attempted resolution to condemn China at the 1996 Annual Geneva Conference on Human Rights, and to reward 'the good Member States', such as France, with lucrative commercial contracts (Narramore, 2008: 94).

THE RELATIONSHIP BETWEEN THE EU, THE US AND CHINA

Having seen that both the EU and China want to promote a multipolar world and consequently balance US hegemony, it is accordingly important to analyse the potential influence of the US on the EU–China relationship. In order to do so, this chapter must look once again at the debate surrounding the lifting of the arms embargo. In fact, this debate has not only highlighted internal discrepancies inside the EU but has also clearly demonstrated that the US still has a big influence on the EU.

In order to establish the weight of the US on the EU–China relationship, it is first of all important to determine the relationship between the EU and the US and the vision of both actors vis-à-vis China. The ESS mentions that 'one of the core elements of the international system are transatlantic relations' (Council of the European Union, 2003: 9). The US is thus an important partner for the EU. This does not mean that there have never been any tensions between the two actors. Recently the relationship has been under a lot of pressure, especially on questions such as the war in Iraq and the global war on terror. Concerning their vision on China, the two actors more or less agree on the principal terms. They both want to successfully integrate China into the international community and to help it become a 'responsible stakeholder' in international affairs (Cabestan, 2006: 36). While their goal is more or less the same, the differences are to be found in the way they believe this goal can be achieved. This of course has to be linked with the fact that the US is a hard power and the EU is a soft power. Both actors do not have the same means at their disposal. From a more geopolitical point of view, the main difference between both actors is the fact that, in contrast to the US, the EU has no real security and defence interests in the region. In fact, the only security threats that the EU sees emanating from China are issues of 'soft security' such as human rights, environmental issues, economic competition, illegal immigration, organised crime and drugs smuggling or 'hard security' issues such as proliferation of weapons of mass destruction, which only constitute an indirect security threat (Gill, 2008: 278). The US on the other hand has defence responsibilities vis-à-vis Taiwan. It thus has direct security and defence interests in the area. This important military and political commitment made by the US to Taiwan makes its relationship with China much more complicated than the relationship the EU has with China (Gill, 2008: 279).

The fact that the EU, in contrast to the US, has no defence responsibility in the region was one of the main reasons why the US was so strongly opposed to the lifting of the arms embargo. In fact, the US warned 'that the EU should not upset the balance of power in a region in which it has no defence responsibilities' (Watts and Watt, 2005). Indeed, in the eyes of the US, the lifting of the arms embargo would most probably affect the military balance in the Taiwan Strait in favour of China and this would affect the balance of power in the region (Narramore, 2008: 100). This argument became even stronger after the adoption of the Chinese anti-secession law in March 2005.

As Swanström rightfully puts it, the EU found itself in a difficult position 'since the lifting or keeping of the embargo would deliver a political message to both the US and China' (Swanström, 2008: 163). Both China and the US are the EU's most important trade partners and the way the EU was going to handle this difficult situation would in any case affect its trade and political relationship with either the US or China. In the end, the EU gave in to US pressure and decided not to lift the arms embargo. The EU did not want to put its relationship with the US at risk and it thus preferred 'disappointing' their Chinese interlocutors instead of risking harm to the transatlantic relationship. To go even further, it could be said that they preferred to undermine their capacity to act externally, especially in the eyes of China, over upsetting the US. Indeed, the final outcome of this diplomatic defeat is precisely the weakness of the EU to act as a coherent and fully independent international actor.

After the debate concerning the lifting of the arms embargo, the EU realised the importance of its relation with the US and has renewed contact with its transatlantic partner. An example of this can be found in the EU's recent guidelines on its foreign and security policy in East Asia, where it has stated that '[t]he US security commitments to Japan, the Republic of Korea and Taiwan and the associated presence of US forces in the region give the US a distinct perspective on the region's security challenges. It is important that the EU is sensitive to this. Given the great importance of transatlantic relations, the EU has a strong interest in partnership and cooperation with the US on the foreign and security policy challenges arising from East Asia' (Council of the European Union, press release 2010). The arms embargo issue 'has served as a wake-up call for both the EU and the United States' (Cabestan, 2006: 36). They have realised that it was important to communicate regarding their respective strategies vis-à-vis China.

The issue of the arms embargo has yet to be fully resolved. It continues to be important for China and will most certainly be raised again. And indeed this has recently been the case. At the beginning of 2010, Spain, which was holding the EU presidency for the first half of 2010, indicated that 'it is willing to reconsider the bloc's arms embargo with China' (Willis, 2010). In light of some recent events we can wonder whether the outcome of the debate would be the same if it were to be put on the agenda again now. In fact, China has lately grown considerably on the international scene and might perhaps nowadays have a greater influence on the EU and the US. Two issues can be advanced in order to support this view: the global economic crisis and the negotiations at the Copenhagen climate change conference. The aim of this chapter is not to analyse these issues in detail but rather to demonstrate how they might affect the relationship between China, the EU and the US.

The financial crisis broke out in September 2008 and resulted in 'the near-collapse of the established world economic order' (Fouquet, 2009: 10). The EU, China and the US, as well as many other important powers, were deeply affected by this crisis (Fouquet, 2009: 10). Huge efforts were undertaken by all major powers in order to restore their systems and maintain stability (Fouquet, 2009: 10). Apart from affecting the economic system, the financial crisis has also had an impact in the world order and more specifically on the distribution of power. In fact, even though all major powers were deeply affected by the economic crisis, some were worse off than others. Whereas the financial crisis has 'diminish[ed] the status of the United States as the world's only superpower' (Reynolds, 2008), China confirmed its status as a crucial economic partner. Indeed, as a holder of huge current account surpluses China was able to help the rest of the world cope with the financial crises by lending them money (*The Economist*, 2008). China lent a huge amount of money to the US and to the IMF in order to allow the fund to assist the numerous countries suffering from the economic crisis (Fouquet, 2009: 12). China not only played a fundamental role in the resolving of the crisis but the US still owes China an important amount of money. This has without any doubt affected the balance of power between both countries and has pushed China towards a greater role on the international scene. This has of course also affected the EU–China relationship. As Fouquet aptly puts it: '[t]he [. . .] global crisis has [. . .] called into question the previous models and power-centres of economic and political development in the West and raises the issue of what new order and relations will emerge between China and its Asian neighbours and with the US and Europe.'

After having successfully negotiated the financial crisis, China has become more assertive on the international scene (*The Economist*, 2010). This has been clearly demonstrated during the Copenhagen climate change conference, where 'China single-handedly ruined any positive outcome' (Wacker, 2010: 58). The way the Chinese delegation behaved during the conference strongly demonstrates the role China wants to play on the international scene. They no longer want to be 'thwarted' (*The Economist*, 2010). A journalist who was present in Copenhagen mentions that 'China wrecked the talks, intentionally humiliated Barack Obama, and insisted on an awful "deal" so western leaders would walk away carrying the blame' (Lynas, 2009). Copenhagen clearly demonstrated that China is aware of the fact that it is becoming an uncontested superpower and as such it demonstrated 'its newfound muscular confidence' (Lynas, 2009). The conference also highlighted another important element: the EU failed to play a role in the Copenhagen event. This is particularly surprising since international climate policy has been a field in which the EU traditionally plays an important role. More importantly, it is also a field of external relations where it has managed to develop a coherent and consistent position (Geden and Kremer, 2010: 31). This makes us wonder whether the development of a coherent external relations policy would be enough for the EU to play a major role in world politics. To conclude, not only was no real solution on how to deal with global warming found in Copenhagen, but the weight or absence of weight of certain actors in the debate might demonstrate a potential shift in the distribution of global power.

CONCLUSION

Even though the US remains the most important global power for now, there are clear signs that the world order is evolving. Emerging global actors such as the EU and China are playing a more and more important role in world politics. Lately, this has especially been the case for China, which has emerged out of the financial crisis more powerful than ever and has shown that it is well aware of the fact that it is becoming an uncontested international actor. The way China took the lead in Copenhagen should serve as a wake-up call for both the US and the EU. If the US is most likely to remain the most important global power, it will not remain so in the way it was during the period immediately after the Cold War (Dellios and Field, 2002: 96). 'Close and friendly relations with both the EU and China will be necessary for it to retain its status as the prime superpower' (Dellios and Field, 2002: 96). The EU, on the other hand, has to become a more coherent external actor if it wants to play a real role in world politics. It is the EU's ambition that its situation will improve with the entry into force of the Lisbon Treaty. However, Europe needs to be aware that a clearer external representation and a better decision-making procedure cannot resolve all problems. If some member states want to continue pursuing their own national interests on certain issues, they will not be prevented from doing so by these new rules. Rules can only do so much. What is really needed for things to change is the political will to make it happen.

The world order seems to be shifting towards more multipolarity, characterised by the existence of different poles of power. These poles nevertheless do not all have the same power. For now, the US remains the most important pole, but it is not clear whether this will remain the case. It is of course too soon to draw conclusions from the way China has been demonstrating its power lately, but these signs should not be ignored. Different potential future scenarios have been advanced. Some have suggested the emergence of a new type of bipolar world composed of two superpowers: the US and China, while others visualise a 'triumvirate' composed of the previous two actors and the EU, or others see a major role for China and the other BRIC Countries (Fouquet, 2009: 10). It is, of course, still unclear as to precisely which way the world order will evolve, but it surely is changing and the EU and China (even if to different extents) will definitely play a role in the redefinition of this world order.

NOTE

1. The term that was used by some authors to qualify the period of intensification of relations between the EU and China.

REFERENCES

'Agreement on Trade and Economic Cooperation between the European Economic Community and the People's Republic of China', *OJ* L 250, 19 July 1985.

Barysch, Katinka (2005) *Embracing the Dragon: The EU's Partnership with China*,

CER Policy Brief, May.

Cabestan, Jean Pierre (2006) 'European Union–China relations and the United States', *Asian Perspective*, 30 (4): 11–38.

Casarini, Nicola (2009) *Remaking Global Order. The Evolution of Europe–China Relations and Its Implications for East Asia and the United States*. Oxford: Oxford University Press.

Commission of the European Communities (1988) *A Long Term Policy for China–Europe Relations*, COM(1998) 181 final. Online at: http://www.eeas.europa.eu/china/docs/com95_279_en.pdf (accessed 7 May 2010).

Commission of the European Communities (2003) *A Maturing Partnership – Shared Interests and Challenges in EU–China Relations*, COM(2003) 533 final, Brussels, 10 September. Online at: http://eur-lex.europa.eu/LexUriServ/LexUriServ.do?uri=COM:2003:0533:FIN:EN:PDF (accessed 7 May 2010).

Commission of the European Communities (2006) *EU–China: Closer Partners, Growing Responsibilities*, COM(2006) 631 final, Brussels, 24 October. Online at: http://eur-lex.europa.eu/LexUriServ/LexUriServ.do?uri=COM:2006:0631:FI-N:EN:PDF (accessed 10 May 2010).

Council of the European Union (2003) *A Secure Europe in a Better World*, 12 December. Online at: http://www.consilium.europa.eu/uedocs/cmsUpload/78367.pdf (accessed 7 May 2010).

Council of the European Union (n.d.) *Guidelines on the EU's Foreign and Security Policy in East Asia*. Press release. Online at: http://www.consilium.europa.eu/ueDocs/cms_Data/docs/pressdata/en/misc/97842.pdf (accessed 31 January 2010).

De Vasconcelos, Alvaro (2008) '"Multilateralising" multipolarity', in G. Grevi and A. De Vasconcelos (eds), *Partnerships for Effective Multilateralism. EU Relations with Brazil, China, India and Russia*, Chaillot Paper No. 109. Paris: Institute for Security Studies, May.

Dellios, Rosita and Field, Heather (2002) 'China and the European Union: potential beneficiaries of Bush's global coalition', *Australian Journal of International Affairs*, (56) 1: 83–98.

European Parliament (2005) Resolution on EU–China Relations (2005/2161(INI)). Online at: http://www.europarl.europa.eu/sides/getDoc.do?pubRef=-//EP//NONSGML+TA+P6-TA-2006-0346+0+DOC+PDF+V0//EN (accessed 10 May 2010).

Ferrero-Waldner, Benita (2005) *The EU, China and the Quest for a Multilateral World*, 4 July 2005 (speech), http://www.europa-eu-un.org/articles/en/article_4854_en.htm (accessed 10 May 2010).

Fouquet, David (2009) 'The economic crisis and a new balance of power?', *EU–China Observer*, 2: 10–15.

Fox, James and Godement, François (2009) 'A power audit of EU–China relations', *European Council on Foreign Relations*, April. Online at: http://ecfr.3cdn.net/532cd91d0b5c9699ad_ozm6b9bz4.pdf (accessed 10 May 2010).

Geden, Oliver and Kremer, Martin (2010) 'The European Union: a challenged leader in ambitious international climate policy', in S. Drogue (ed.), *International Climate Policy. Priorities of Key Negotiating Parties*, SWP Research Paper, Berlin, March.

Gill, Bates (2008) 'The United States and the China–Europe relationship', in D. Shambaugh, E. Sandschneider and Z. Hong (2008) *China – Europe Relations: Perspectives, Policies and Prospects*. London: Routledge.

Griese, Olaf (2006) 'EU–China relations – an assessment by the Communications of the European Union', *Asia Europe Journal*, 4 (4): 545–53.

Kreutz, Joakim (2004) 'Reviewing the EU arms embargo on China: the clash between value and rationale in the European security strategy', *Perspectives: Central European Review of International Affairs*, 22: 43–58.

Lynas, Mark (2009) 'How do I know China wrecked the Copenhagen deal? I was in the room', *The Guardian*, 22 December. Online at: http://www.guardian.co.uk/environment/ 2009/dec/22/ copenhagen-climate-change-mark-lynas (accessed 14 April 2010).

Men, Jing (2008) *EU–China Relations: From Engagement to Marriage?*, EU Diplomacy Papers, 7/2008.

Ministry of Foreign Affairs of the People's Republic of China (2003) *China's EU Policy Paper*, 13 October. Online at: http://www.mfa.gov.cn/eng/topics/ceupp/t27708.htm (accessed 7 May 2010).

Narramore, Terry (2008) 'China and Europe: engagement, multipolarity and strategy', *Pacific Review*, 21 (1): 87–108.

Odgaard, Liselotte and Biscop, Sven (2007) 'The EU and China: partners in effective multilateralism?', in D. Kerr and L. Fei (eds), *The International Politics of EU–China Relations*. Oxford: Oxford University Press.

Reynolds, Paul (2008) 'US superpower status is shaken', *BBC News*, 1 October. Online at: http://news.bbc.co.uk/2/hi/business/7645743.stm (accessed 14 April 2010).

Shambaugh, David (2005) 'The new strategic triangle: US and European reactions to China's rise', *Washington Quarterly*, 28 (3): 7–25.

Shambaugh, David, Sandschneider, Eberhard and Zhou, Hong (2008) 'From honeymoon to marriage. Prospects for the China–Europe relationship', in D. Shambaugh, E. Sandschneider and Z. Hong (eds), *China–Europe Relations: Perspectives, Policies and Prospects*. London: Routledge.

Swanström, Niklas (2008) 'EU–China relations: troubled relations?', *Quarterly Journal of Defense Policy Studies*, 24 (1): 153–75.

The Economist (2008) 'The financial crisis: into the storm', Issue 950, 25 October.

The Economist (2010) 'Geopolitics: facing up to China', Issue 950, 6 February.

Wacker, Gudrun (2010) 'Caught in the middle: China's crucial but ambivalent role in the international climate negotiations', in S. Droge (ed.), *International Climate Policy. Priorities of Key Negotiating Parties*, SWP Research Paper, Berlin, March. Online at: http://www.swp-berlin.org/en /common/get_document.php?asset_id = 6914 (accessed 14 April 2010).

Watts, J. and Watt, N. (2005) 'Rice tells EU: don't lift China arms ban', *The Guardian*, 21 March. Online at: http://www.guardian.co.uk/world/2005/mar/21/china.usa (accessed 10 May 2010).

Willis, Andrew (2010) 'EU presidency reconsidering China arms embargo', *EU Observer*, 27 January. Online at: http://euobserver.com/13/29343 (accessed 14 April 2010).

20. BRICs, China and the emerging world order: is the PRC writing a new global script?

Jagannath P. Panda

THE PREMISE

The phenomenon of the emerging economies of Brazil–Russia–India–China (BRIC)[1] has driven the academic and policy debate as to whether these largest of the emerging markets of the world could translate their embryonic economic clout into larger geopolitical influence. If the answer is in the affirmative, is the rise of BRIC a prelude to a 'multipolar' – world order? In this context, multiple terminologies like 'non-polarity' (Haass, 2008), 'post-American world' (Zakaria, 2008), 'decline of the West' (Spengler et al., 1991) or the 'rise of the rest' (Hoffenberg Amsden, 2001) have become part of the global political literature (Glosny, 2009: online). 'Non-polarity' broadly implies here a system that is characterised by 'numerous centres of meaningful power'. Zakaria (2008) argues that while the US still continues to dominate in terms of political-military power, other countries such as India and China are becoming important powers in a different sense and in other sectors. The phrase 'decline of the West', coined in 1918 by Oswald Spengler, has now become common currency. The concept of 'rise of the rest' has been popularised by Alice Hoffenberg Amsden (2001). An article in *Foreign Affairs* (Hoge, 2004: 2) had noted that 'the transfer of power from West to East is gathering pace and soon will dramatically change the context for dealing with international challenges – as well as the challenges themselves'. In the context of a presumed 'multipolarisation' or 're-bipolarisation' of global politics and the People's Republic of China's (PRC) growing dynamism in multilateral bodies and associations, many have been prompted to examine whether China seeks to preserve the status quo in regional and global politics.

Historically, association with multilateral bodies or alliances has been an unpredictable variable when forecasting a power's ambition and intention or its impact on the complexity of the balance of power. Joining ad hoc multilateral bodies might allow Beijing to deflect doubts at various levels about it being an authoritarian developed country, while allowing it to continue to increase its global power ambitions and objectives smartly (Glosny, 2009: online). Working with mainstream developing countries facilitates the PRC in expanding its diplomatic clout and formulating new global rules without having to fulfil the requisites expected of developed countries (Glosny, 2009: online). China's membership of BRIC, which involves a rival power like India, confirms this global strategic design. This chapter is an effort to examine this cloaked Chinese strategy against the backdrop of BRIC.[2]

In particular, the attempt here is to locate the unseen elements of Chinese diplomatic strategy and to reveal them in the context of China's broader vision of progressing as a global power. Therefore, the chapter will address the practice and pledge of China's new advocacy of cross-continental multipolarism in the context of BRIC.[3] The plan is to highlight the extent of Chinese support for dialogue with the 'developing world' union that remains the crux of the Chinese global strategy. While the focus is on analysing the scope of BRIC in China's multilateral dialogue, the chapter will also delve into the rationale behind China's formulation and support of ad hoc bodies such as BRIC. In brief, the point here is to narrate the Chinese course of multilateralism with 'multipolarism', which is a well-constructed 'dual-mode' strategy to handle rising Western opposition and to prompt constructively a Chinese-desired future structure for global politics. This unseen combination is both Chinese and political in nature, as Beijing adapts to different practices and the global notion of multilateralism with prudent 'Chinese characteristics'.

BRIC AND CHINA: THE VARIATION

BRIC economies currently account for more than a quarter of the world's landmass and more than 40 per cent of the world population. In most prognostications, BRIC economies have a bright future. They have done consistently well, economically, in the last decade. A Goldman Sachs monthly report states that 'over the past 10 years they have contributed over a third of world GDP growth and grown from one-sixth of the world economy to almost a quarter (in purchasing power parity terms). Looking forward to the coming decade, we expect this trend to continue and become even more pronounced' (Wilson, et al., 2010: 1). Goldman Sachs estimates that by 2050 the combined BRIC economies could surpass the combined economies of those countries which are currently the richest in the world, and that their economic output and stock market values could catch up with those of the developed countries by 2039 and become the centre of the world economic growth (O'Neill and Stupnytska, 2009: 1–28).

Economists at the International Monetary Fund (IMF) similarly acknowledge that BRIC countries are no longer under pressure from the Western world (Lettieri and Raimondi, 2009).[4] Trade relations among them have their own autonomous status and they are consolidated without reliance on the US dollar (Letrieri and Raimondi, 2009). The IMF also states that BRIC economies with an annual growth of 10.7 per cent between 2006 and 2008 have emerged as major contributors to the world economy (Liu 2009). The Organisation for Economic Cooperation and Development (OECD) also emphasises optimism over the prospects of BRIC economies (Zhdannikov and Kelly, 2010).

The first BRIC summit was held on 16 June 2009 at Yekaterinburg, Russia, with Luiz Inácio Lula da Silva (Brazil), Dmitry Medvedev (Russia), Manmohan Singh (India), and Hu Jintao (China) participating. The meeting was held to tackle the global financial crisis and to explore how BRIC countries could benefit by expanding their trade and financial cooperation with each other. This summit focused on the reform of international financial institutions. The second BRIC summit was, however, more political than economic (Frolov, 2010). Its deliberations had an accent on expanding and defending the interests of developing countries (Frolov, 2010). The third BRIC summit was held in Sanya (China) in 2011 whereas the fourth BRICS summit was held in New Delhi (India) in 2012.

While Goldman Sachs emphasised the economic aspects of BRIC, its leaders are repeatedly talking about the rise of a multipolar world order led by developing countries. This has given rise to speculation whether BRIC unity will have a distinctly political angle in the future. The disparities within BRIC are of course obvious. First are the political systemic differences and cultural distinctiveness. Next, Brazil is too distant geographically from the other three.[5] Third, though China, India and Russia are located close to each other, their individual strategic contradictions may work against forming any credible alliance. Fourth, the influence of the US in individual BRIC countries' foreign policy dialogue obscures the unity of BRIC. Fifth, the potential for intra-BRIC conflict for global resources complicates the spirit of BRIC as an entity. There is also the fact that India and Brazil have set their goal for permanent membership of the UN Security Council, but China and Russia are yet to take a decisive stance on the issue.

Given China's massive economic supremacy and its rapid growth in comparison to the other BRIC members, it looks like a 'deeper shift' is taking place with the 'rise and rise of China' (Seager, 2010). The Chinese economy is in a different league to the other BRIC members: it is larger than the other three economies combined. Chinese exports and its official foreign exchange reserve holdings are more than twice as large as those of the other three BRIC economies. On paper, China is the biggest potential market and partner of the sole superpower, the US, in a G-2. It is the world's second-largest economy. It is now Brazil's top trading partner, exceeding the United States (Lopez, 2010). China's foreign exchange reserves topped $1.9 trillion by the end of 2008 (State Administration of Foreign Exchange, PRC: online). At the end of March 2010 they reached $2,447 trillion $ (ibid.). These figures and economic supremacy have to be seen within the PRC's growing global reach which is a vital tenet of China's quest for comprehensive national power (CNP).

In its foreign policy dialogue, China has always highlighted three constructive phenomena which suit its global agenda: (1) currency conversion; (2) a win-win strategy by developing multilateral diplomacy; and (3) the establishment of a democratic and multipolar world order. In effect, China's current foreign policy dialogue pivots upon five handily correlated objectives: (1) endorsing multilateral dialogue; (2) boosting links with neighbouring countries, developing countries and big powers at different levels; (3) maintaining strong economic diplomacy with energy and climate change as the main thrusts; (4) establishing a link between domestic stability and national security; and (5) promoting public diplomacy (*Wen Wei Po*, 2009). There is currently debate in China that the country should upgrade its foreign policy to keep abreast of changing world politics, that it should be 'updated to suit the dawning of the new world order' (Liu, 2010: online). China's rising economic and political muscle was, for example, clearly evident at the Copenhagen climate debate where China refused bluntly to adhere to any binding agreement to reduce its emissions (Seager, 2010). In this connection, there is a need to review the Chinese discourse on BRIC, as China prepares to emerge as one of the most powerful countries in the world.

THE CHINESE DIALOGUE WITH BRIC

There is conjecture as to whether an economically and politically 'rising China' would, with or without the BRIC alliance, try to design a new order at some point in time (Glosny, 2009). This formulation invites greater scrutiny of the structural constraints resulting from unipolarity and how they affect Chinese foreign policy objectives, its core objectives with BRIC and the degree to which both China and BRIC could imagine a multipolar world order.

Theoretically, China's association with BRIC outlines its policy perception of global conditions. Seen through a liberal prism, the PRC's increasing embrace of multilateralism through BRIC would be a move towards 'liberal internationalism'. That means Beijing has arrived at the level, seemingly against all odds, of favouring cross-regional mechanisms. In general terms, the Chinese accent on advocating multilateral alliances would seem to argue against the realist prism that nations choose flexibility in their approach by being relatively informal, with ad hoc non-binding commitments that hold little risk if intergovernmental agreements prove prejudicial to their interests (Moore, 2008). This would explain to some extent China's 'moving to take advantage' of the global system by playing safe, through various modes: in reshuffling the global economic system, security dialogues and cross-regional schemes. In a way, China is driving the process of multipolarism by inducing similar initiatives from the US, EU and other power blocs. In this context, BRIC is an apposite move. In contrast, the realist prism reads the universal Chinese invitation and its 'peaceful rise' with increasing involvement in cross-regional multilateralism as an event of 'advantage to advantage' with other major powers and alliances. Seen in this light, China is building BRIC primarily to design its own desired world order, working in a zero-sum dynamic rooted in a struggle for relative power. BRIC in this context becomes a broad gadget of 'economic' statecraft as China pursues a 'multipolar' strategy. In this context, the Chinese dialogue seems interesting.

Most Chinese literature expresses the view that it is too early to conclude that the United States of America is no longer the supreme power and to recognise the weight of 'newly emerging powers' as an essential force in global power politics. For China, besides reducing over-dependence on the US in multilateral issues, BRIC cooperation serves several other functions. The Chinese leadership's perspective is that the country benefits by creating an alliance of developing countries and stabilising the global order that would suit China's core interests (Xinhua, 2009; Glosny, 2009: online). A Chinese expert is of the view that 'the BRIC summit is not aimed at challenging the dollar. Instead, its aim is to strengthen cooperation, build consensus, and coordinate policies' (Liu, 2009: online). It is far from convincing that China is not interested in checking the dominance of the US dollar and US influence. In fact, the Chinese view is both massive and global and the leadership vision speaks about that.

Highlighting BRIC as a constructive phenomenon, Hu Jintao made a 'four-point' proposal at the first BRIC summit: (1) bring about an early recovery of the world economy; (2) push forward reform of the international financial system; (3) implement the UN Millennium

Development Goals (MDGs); and (4) ensure the security of food, energy resources, and public health (Hu, 2009). The Chinese leaders are of the view that 'China benefits from this cooperation by stabilizing the global order, helping developing countries, strengthening its developing country status and coordinating its position with other BRICs to maximize leverage on issues of mutual interests' (Xinhua, 2009). Hence, adequate emphasis is given to 'partnership' and 'collaboration'. They connect their interests with other 'developing states' pursuing similar ends (Glosny, 2009: online).

Chinese analysts understand the notion of a pole as a comfortable status or behaviour for a country or an actor which 'has the capacity to exert influence on global strategic affairs and has certain control over other world forces' (Zhao, 2004: 143). Cui Liru (2009), an influential Chinese scholar, equates a pole with a centre of force. From this perspective, states or powers having similar ends can all serve as poles in a multipolar world, exerting calculated influence over global politics. Nevertheless, the world multipolarisation process is understood in China as having a twofold scope: (1) the rise of developing countries; and (2) the interactions and readjustments of relations among major powers. '[A]n evolving international structure signifies that the rise of a group of economies with a relatively big size and immense expansion potential is reshaping the global political landscape and great powers' relations' (Cui, 2009: 2). This conforms to the post-Cold War Chinese outlook in which it sees that the structure of current world politics is of 'one superpower with several major powers'.

According to Chinese calculations, although the US is currently the most powerful state, its influence and hegemony have been curtailed somewhat (Blum, 2003; Ma, 2009/10: 28). This decline in the US's influence permits China to continuously reassess the conditions of the global order. This gives rise to optimism for the development of a multipolar dialogue and the construction of a South–South alliance. The main idea behind this design is to employ any division within the North to counter the remaining US dominance, which is the chief reason for the existing uneven global order (Clegg, 2009: 97). Broadly, this Chinese strategy matches Lenin's analysis as set out in *Imperialism, the Highest Stage of Capitalism*. The key to Lenin's approach was recognition that uneven development opened up disparities between imperialist powers. In a way, China does value the presence of America as a power factor in its emergence. At the same time, China seems to be in the lead in the transformation of the developing world into a credible counter to existing Western dominance. BRIC provides one such platform.

The parameters of this strategy are colossal. The PRC wants to achieve multiple objectives through BRIC, such as stabilising the global political and economic system; removing the suspicion at many levels that it has become a developed nation; and coordinating its position with other influential powers that matter to the USA (Glosney, 2009: online). Currency valuation is a significant objective of the Chinese – to oppose the massive US fiscal deficits and authoritarian Western monetary policies. While China is determined to keep inflation down domestically and limit appreciation of the renminbi, the real target is to achieve a modification in its favour in real exchange rates that should occur via declining US domestic prices. The plan seems to be to impose a deflationary alteration on the US, very similar to what Germany seems to be doing to Greece (Wolf, 2010). The heart of the matter is the global current account imbalances, mainly a result of the sizeable US trade deficit with China.

DEVELOPING WORLD AND THE STRUCTURAL ALLIANCE

In the post-Cold War scenario characterised by a unipolar world, China's international affairs experts tended to gravitate towards the view that unipolarity would decline gradually and new great powers would rise to shape a multipolar world order (Waltz, 1993; Glosney, 2009: online). Chinese scholars contend that there is a huge structural imbalance in today's unipolarity (Clegg, 2009: 9). There is, however, less agreement among them about the nature of the current world order, whether it is unipolar, multipolar or in a transitional phase (Pillsbury, 2000: ch. 1; Glosny, 2009: online). Amid this ferment of debate, the Chinese leadership maintains that China is still a developing country. For example, Fu Ziying, China's Vice-Commerce Minister, was quoted saying that 'China is the world's largest developing country and to strengthen relations with developing countries is a focal point of China's foreign policy' (*Renmin Ribao*, 2010).

This Chinese projection is very much in evidence in its dialogue in BRIC and other forums of developing countries. For instance, while addressing the 16th SAARC (South Asian Association of Regional Cooperation) Summit, the Chinese Vice-Foreign Minister reported saying in Xinhua that: 'China stands together with all the other developing countries including in South Asia, in firmly upholding our common interest' (Mu, 2010). The current Chinese foreign policy attaches enormous strategic importance to multilateral dialogue and affiliation to multilateral alliances (Wu and Lansdowne, 2008: 5). Chinese experts believe, and official discourse indicates, that the PRC is still learning how to build partnerships in order to exert influence over different regions.

They believe that the United States is much superior to China because of its extensive 'partnerships' and influence in most parts of the world. In cross-regional bodies like BRIC, China's presence, affiliation and policy approach is relatively new. The PRC's diplomatic affiliation with cross-regional alliances coincided with its larger interest in emerging global politics, mainly as a backdrop to a possible G2 formulation (Glosny, 2009: online). To deal with this emerging situation, China is embarking on 'partnership' and collaboration at various levels, in which the diplomatic priority is to establish multilateral linkages between the PRC and different parts of the world (Yu, 2010).[6] For the Chinese, BRIC serves to strengthen cooperation, build consensus and coordinate policies (Liu, 2009).

The evolution of BRIC suggests that in the beginning, Russia and Brazil took initiatives to push BRIC from an intangible financial concept to some sort of political grouping. In the meantime, the Chinese also seem to have taken a special interest in BRIC. Chinese officials believe that BRIC has evolved from the hypothetical (*xuni*) into a realistic platform for international cooperation. Some Chinese analysts characterise China's cooperation within BRIC as developing in a gradual manner, with no real clear point at which a decision on a 'joint BRIC' occurred. While countries like Russia, India and Brazil have taken seriously the recent rise of BRIC, the Chinese have mainly seen it as an ad hoc grouping. BRIC has been a special talking point in global politics because China is a member of the club – it being the second largest economy in the world with the largest foreign exchange reserves and a P5 member of the UN Security Council (UNSC). It is central, however, to examine where and how China will benefit by its association with BRIC.

China's approach to multilateralism has always been more regional than global (Wu and Lansdowne, 2008). Beginning with its open-door foreign policy in 1978, Chinese diplomatic effort has always been to formulate a stable regional order (Dittmer, 2008) which will favour its economy and politics. Dittmer (2008: 27) argues that 'China's interest in regional organisations coincided with the greater interest in the region that came in the wake of the collapse of the strategic triangle at the end of the Cold War, which reduced China's global leverage – isolated by the West, China launched its "good neighbour policy (*mulin zhengce*)".' In that context, both India and Russia remain a priority in the Chinese foreign policy dialogue. Historically, China has had troubled relations with both countries. The Chinese have tried different tactics at different times to keep their relationship with both Russia and India on an even course. Chinese experts argue that 'maintaining peripheral stability has been always one of the most important goals of Chinese foreign policy as well as a serious challenge' (Zhao, 2005: 67). The BRIC institution lends China some more flexibility in this regard. It has become common practice in China to advocate 'peripheral stability' by 'treating neighbours as friends and as partners' (*yulinweishan, yilinweiban*). The Chinese Premier and President have constantly used this formulation on many occasions. Also, this strategic engagement creates conditions for Russia and India not to gratuitously form or join any Western or strategic alliance.

Generally, the post-Cold War hallmark of Chinese foreign policy is to share new ideas, exchange information and take part in discussions and debates (Glosney, 2009: online). It seems that the Chinese are forthcoming in discussing some of the pressing global issues, such as food security, agriculture, energy and climate change, issues which create conditions for coordinated policy formulations in order to achieve better and preferable outcomes to those stemming from Western and European dominance. Today, as part of its 'public diplomacy' strategy which is the changing face of Chinese foreign policy, leaders and experts push hard to develop the 'soft power' image of China (Yang, 2010). For example, a recent report in *Renmin Ribao* (2010) points out that since its establishment in 1949, China has invited around 120,000 officials, technical staff and foreign dignitaries from more than 170 countries to take part in seminars, discussions, training programmes and debates in open forum. As such, developing countries are increasingly realising that exchanging ideas permits them to manage their status and make the most of their bargaining position with developed countries. That is well understood in China too. Strategists in China are of the view that if China pushes aggressively and unilaterally to reform the current international order, it would risk being singled out as being strident. A grouping like BRIC provides a good cover for this objective (Glosny, 2009: online).[7]

More than all this, contemporary Chinese foreign policy formulation emphasises regional and global multilateralism, confidence-building with countries around its periphery, the possible support within a multipolar world from like-minded countries, and developing relationships with countries in the same league (Saunders, 2006; Goldstein, 2005; Shambaugh, 2004/5). That is why the concept of 'developing country' remains important for China (Glosny, 2009). Being grouped with BRIC countries and developing its own agenda in terms of being democratic and representing the needs and interests of the developing world helps China greatly. Ambassador Zhang Yan in India once said that 'BRIC is a guardian of the interests of developing countries.'[8] To preserve its status as a developing country, China always is one step ahead when associating itself or clubbing together with developing countries (Chin, 2008).

A POSSIBLE EMERGING WORLD ORDER?

Speculation abounds, in the Western and European world in particular, as to whether the rise of BRIC will disrupt and depose the existing world order, with China taking the lead in that context. The Chinese seem to be taking a backseat at the moment and are trying to prepare the ground for when they could rise to the occasion of considering a new world order (Glosny, 2009). Chinese scholars contend that China is not equipped to rule the world together with the United States as yet, and the United States has never planned to share leadership rights or the right to formulate rules with China (Yu, 2010). They see the formation of G2 simply as a 'pseudo-thesis'; the G2 idea was originally meant for 'US–Europe' or 'US–Japan joint rule' and that in order to force China to accept more global norms and obligations, the United States has redesigned the concept of G2 and has applied it to the context of 'China–US joint rule' (Yu, 2010).

This is true to some extent. As Fareed Zakaria (2010: online) notes, 'China . . . has chosen to enter into the Western-sponsored global order, participating in the trading system and by and large maintaining cooperative relations with the West.' Therefore, it would appear at the moment that China has deepened its cooperation with BRIC and would like to live with the current order of world politics until it grows to a distinctly new and higher level. Regardless of its acknowledgement of the problems with the existing international order, China has mostly accepted to live with the current framework of world politics (Glosny, 2009: online), bringing incremental reform slowly on its own terms. Even if China has undermined the value of the US dollar and increased pressure to reform the global order these efforts do not necessarily represent a grand design for radical change in the global order, at the moment. None the less, it is possible that China's acceptance of the existing global order is a short-term strategy.

On the whole, China remains the crucial player in BRIC. Following a 'cooperative strategy' remains the key feature of Chinese diplomacy, as China steps up its calculated efforts to gain energy supplies, capture vibrant markets and counter rising powers in the process. As Shen Qiang (2009: 51) suggests, 'only by accommodating the interests of all sides, seeking common ground while shelving differences and jointly pursuing cooperation can countries properly advance and deepen the reform of the present international financial and economic system.' The Chinese demand is simple but colossal: it is advocating a global order through the expansion of its global power relations and addressing the areas of dissatisfaction in developing countries. This is a long-term strategy, looking far ahead of any short-term vision of building a new world order.

NOTES

1. Though most authors indicate that Goldman Sachs first propounded the idea of BRIC, some Russian scholars and experts say that President Vladimir Putin first suggested forming a 'cooperative coalition of developing countries' such as BRIC. This is understood following the author's discussion with various Russian scholars and diplomats. However, BRIC does not have a formal agreement, but its leaders have met both at bilateral and trilateral levels and have signed a number of documents and agreements.
2. The formal inclusion of South Africa recently has made the group popularly known as BRICS. However, this chapter was written before South Africa was formally inducted so this paper mostly discusses BRIC rather than BRICS.
3. A paper in a similar vein and with a parallel argument has been published by the Institute for Security and Development Policy (ISDP), Stockholm (2011). Though the structure and contents of this chapter are different from the paper published by the ISDP, the main premise of this chapter is constructed with the same logic and argument.
4. Mario Lettieri is a former Undersecretary for Economy in the Italian government and Paolo Raimondi is an economist from Italy.
5. The foundation of Russia–India–China (RIC) facilitated the arrangement of BRIC foreign ministers' meeting in 2006. Eventually, BRIC cooperation expanded to cover two finance ministers' meetings, leaders' summits and a separate BRIC leaders' summit in June 2009. The significance of this summit was noted in the joint communiqué issued after the summit.
6. Li Xiangyang, director of the Institute for Asia-Pacific Studies at the Chinese Academy of Social Sciences (CASS) is among those who hold this view. See Yu (2010).
7. Author's interaction with many Chinese think-tank scholars and experts.
8. 'Address at the inauguration of Pre-BRIC Summit Preparatory Meeting by H. E. Zhang Yan, Chinese Ambassador to India', 13 May 2009.

REFERENCES

Blum, Samantha (2003) 'Chinese views of US hegemony', *Journal of Contemporary China*, 12 (35): 239–64.

Chin, Gregory T. (2008) 'China's evolving G8 engagement: complex interests and multiple identity in global governance reform', in Andrew F. Cooper and A. Antkiewicz (eds), *Emerging Powers in Global Governance: Lessons from the Heiligendamm Process*. Waterloo, Ontario: Wilfrid Laurier University Press, pp. 83–114.

Clegg, Jenny (2009) 'Globalization, imperialism, and multipolarization', in *China's Global Strategy: Towards a Multipolar World*. New York: Pluto Press, p. 97.

Cui, Liru (2009) 'Globalization era vs. international order transformation', *Contemporary International Relations*, 19 (3): 2.

Dittmer, Lowell (2008) 'China's new internationalism', in Guoguang Wu and Helen Lansdowne (eds), *China Turns to Multilateralism*. London: Routledge, p. 27.

Frolov, Alexey (2010) 'The second BRIC summit: the future remains cloudy', *New Eastern Outlook*, 6 May: Online at: http://www.journal-neo.com/?q=print/451 (accessed 20 September 2010).

Glosny, Michael A. (2009) 'China and the BRICs: a real (but limited) partnership in a unipolar world', *Polity* (online), 42 (1): 100–29.

Goldstein, Avery (2005) *Rising to the Challenge: China's Grand Strategy and*

International Security. Stanford, CA: Stanford University Press.

Haass, Richard N. (2008) 'The age of nonpolarity; what will follow U.S. dominance', *Foreign Affairs*, May–June.

Hoffenberg Amsden, Alice (2001) *The Rise of 'the Rest': Challenges to the West from Late-Industrializing Economies*. New York: Oxford University Press.

Hoge (Jr), James F. (2004) 'A global power shift in the making: is the United States ready?', *Foreign Affairs*, 83 (4): 2.

Hu, Jintao (2009) Speech at the BRIC summit, in *Beijing Review*, 16 July. Online at: http://www.bjreview.com.cn/document/txt/2009-07/13/content_206952.htm (accessed 12 June 2009).

Institute for Security and Development Policy (ISDP) Stockholm (2011) 'China's "new multilateralism" and the rise of BRIC: a realist interpretation of a "multipolar" world order', *Asia Paper*. Stockholm: ISDP, pp. 1–49.

Lettieri, Mario and Raimondi, Paolo (2009) 'BRICs drive global economic recovery', *IMF Survey Magazine*, 22 July. Online at: http://www.imf.org/external/pubs/ft/survey/so/2009/rea072209a.htm (accessed 11 November 2010).

Liu, Junhong (2009) 'BRIC building road to global economic recovery', *China Daily*, 18 June. Online at: http://www. chinadaily.com. cn/thinktank/2009-06/18/content_8800032. htm (accessed 1 November 2010).

Liu, Ming (2010) 'China should update foreign policy guidelines', *Zhongguo Wang* (Official PRC portal site: China Internet Information Centre, under the China International Publishing Group and the State Council Information Group), 25 March. OSC Transcribed Text, *World News Connection* (dialog.com): 201003251477.1_401800896de0750d, accession number 296401778.

Lo, Bobo (2008) *Axis of Convenience: Moscow, Beijing and the New Geopolitics*. Washington, DC: Brookings Institution Press, pp. 43, 46, 177.

Lopez, Luciana (2010) 'BRIC Breaking: Brazil's China Syndrome', Reuters, 25 September. Online at: http://in.reuters.com/article/idINIndia-51728320100925?pageNumber=1 (accessed 11 November 2010).

Ma, Zhengang (2009/10) 'Analyses on foreign policy of the Obama Administration', in *The CHS Blue Book on International Situation and China's Foreign Affairs (2009/2010)*. Beijing: China Institute of International Studies (CMS) World Affairs Press.

Moore, T. G. (2008) 'Racing to integrate, or cooperating to compete? Liberal and realist interpretations of China's new multilateralism', in Guoguang Wu and Helen Lansdowne (eds), *China Turns to Multilateralism: Foreign Policy and Regional Security*. London: Routledge, p. 38.

Mu, Xuequan (2010) 'China Proposes Assistance to South Asia at 16th SAARC Summit', Xinhua, 28 April. Online at: http://news.xinhuanet.com/english2010/china/201004/28/c_13271448.htm (accessed 22 August 2010).

O'Neill, J. and Stupnytska, A. (2009) *The Long-Term Outlook for the BRICs and N-11 Post Crisis*, Global Economics Paper No. 192. New York and Washington, DC: Goldman Sachs, pp. 1–28.

Pillsbury, Michael (2000) *China Debates the Future Security Environment*. Honolulu, HI: University Press of the Pacific, ch. 1.

Renmin Ribao (*China Daily*) (2009) 'The weight of BRIC', 17 June. Online at: http://www.chinadaily.com.cn/china/2009sco/2009-06/17/content_8294249.htm (accessed 12 November 2009).

Renmin Ribao (*China Daily*) (2010) 'Developing countries meet in Beijing, discuss financial crisis', 20 May. OSC transcribed text, World News Connection (dialog.com) 201005201477.1_c38600645a591869, accession number 299200180.

Rothkopf, David (2009) 'The BRICs and what the BRICs would be without China', *Foreign Policy*, 15 June. Online at: http://rothkopf.foreignpolicy.eom/posts/2009/06/15/the_brics_and_what_the_brics_would_be_without_china (accessed 28 March 2010).

Saunders, Phillip (2006) *China's Global Activism: Strategy, Drivers and Tools*. Washington, DC: National Defense University Press.

Seager, Ashley (2010) 'China and the other BRICs will rebuild a new world economic order', *The Observer*, 3 January. Online at: http://www.guardian.co.uk/business/2010/jan/03/china-brics-global-economy-america-europe (accessed 16 November 2010).

Shambaugh, David (2004/5) 'China engages Asia: reshaping the regional order', *International Security*, Winter, pp. 64–99.

Shen, Qiang (2009) 'Subtle changes of major power relations: a perspective on the reform of international financial and economic system', *Global Review*, 1 (1): 51.

Spengler, Oswald, Werner, Helmut and Atkinson, Charles Francis (1991) *The Decline of the West*. Oxford: Oxford University Press.

State Administration of Foreign Exchange, People's Republic of China and the People's Bank of China (2011) *China's Foreign Exchange Reserves, 1977–2010*. Online at: http://www.chinability.com/Reserves.htm (accessed 15 November 2010).

Waltz, Kenneth (1993) 'The emerging structure of international polities', *International Security*, 18: 44–79.

Wen Wei Po (2009) 'PRC FM Yang Jiechi expounds on focus of China diplomacy in 2010', 18 December. OSC translated text at: http://www.wenweipo.com; *World News Connections* (dialog.com) 200912181477.1_17cb01f3a27aOae1, accession number 291501134.

Wilson, Dominic, Kelston, Alex L. and Ahmed, Swarnali (2010) 'Is this the BRICs decade?', *BRICs Monthly*, issue 10/03, 20 May.

Wolf, Martin (2010) 'Why America is going to win the global currency battle', *Financial Times*, 13 October, p. 11.

Wu, Guoguang and Lansdowne, Helen (2008) 'International multilateralism with Chinese characteristics: attitudes changes, policy imperatives, and regional impacts', in Guoguang Wu and Helen Lansdowne (eds), *China Turns to Multilateralism*. Routledge: London, p. 5.

Xinhua (2009) 'Chinese President Makes Proposal for Tackling Global Financial Crisis at BRIC Summit', 17 June. Online at: http://english.peopledaily.com.cn/98373/98460/98506/6770550.html (accessed 1 November 2009).

Yang, Shilong (2010) 'Open up new situation for public diplomacy', *Liaowang* (weekly general affairs journal published by Xinhua), 16 June. OSC translated text, *World News Connection* (dialog.com) 20100616477.1_4bc907de095ae746, accession number 300551241.

Yu, Lan (2010) 'An expert at the Chinese Academy of Social Sciences says "China–US joint rule" is only a pseudo-thesis for the present', *Zhongguo Xinwen She* (China's official news service for overseas Chinese). OSC transcribed text, *World News Connection* (dialog.com) 201004121477.1_df6e00753c4250d6, accession number 299200180.

Zakaria, Fareed (2008) *The Post-American World*. New York: W. W. Norton.

Zakaria, Fareed (2010) 'A "hedge" strategy towards China', *Washington Post*, 15 November. Online at: http://www.washingtonpost.com/wp-dyn/content/article/2010/11/14/AR2010111403883.html (accessed 15 November 2010).

Zhao, Gancheng (2005) 'China: periphery and strategy', in Shanghai Institute for International Studies (SMS), *China and Asia's Security*. Singapore: Marshall Cavendish, p. 67.

Zhao, Suisheng (2004) 'Beijing's perception of the international system and foreign policy adjustment after the Tiananmen incident', in Zhao Suisheng (ed.), *Chinese Foreign Policy: Pragmatism and Strategic Behaviour*. New York: M. E. Sharpe, An East Gate Book.

Zhdannikov, Dmitry and Kelly, Lidia (2010) 'OECD sees BRIC economies powering ahead in 2010–11', *International Business Times*, 26 May. Online at: http://www.ibtimes.com/articles/25056/20100526/oecd-sees-bric-economies-powering-ahead-in-2010-11.htm (accessed 10 November 2010).

Concluding remarks: China–EU relations in turbulent times: which way forward?

Jan Wouters and Matthieu Burnay

This book began with two premises. On the one hand, it recognised the formidable dynamic which is recalibrating the main institutions and instruments of global governance in the light of shifting international balances of power, and in particular the rise of China. On the other hand, it put forward the central roles played by both China and the European Union (EU) in this process. Both actors have indeed become key players in any attempts to reform the international system. The main objective of this volume was to cover the main dimensions of these global changes and to understand the incentives, constraints and prospects that shape the actions of China and the EU. The present concluding remarks aim to underline the main findings made by the contributors as well as to formulate some policy recommendations.

THE NECESSARY REFORM OF GLOBAL GOVERNANCE

Having considered very diverse bodies ranging from informal coordination fora like the G20 and the BRICS to the well-established Bretton Woods organisations, the importance of international institutions as well as the necessity of reforming them becomes very clear. Moreover, the cross-border nature of the most fundamental economic, political, security and energy challenges and the ever-increasing interdependence of states explain to a large extent why national decisions can often only provide short-term and limited solutions. As an example, the economic measures taken to boost many states' economies in the wake of the 2008 crisis did not replace the necessary systemic reforms that can only be agreed upon in policy coordination fora such as the G20 and, ultimately, within the competent international organisations.

The contributions to this book amply illustrate the current crisis of multilateralism. Both the legitimacy and efficiency of global governance mechanisms are increasingly questioned. There appear to be two main drivers that simultaneously condition and support further reforms of the international system.

Firstly, major shifts in the global balance of power put in question the legitimacy of the membership and functioning of a good number of international institutions. Most of them have indeed been created on the basis of alliances and bargaining power that have nowadays become outdated, especially for Western powers. The IMF is an obvious example in this regard. The restructuring of the international arena therefore implies pressure from rising powers, including China, to have a greater share in the decision-making processes.

Secondly, the efficiency of multilateral institutions in coping with rising global challenges is extensively questioned. The failure to seal a major deal in Copenhagen (2009) and Cancún (2010) on a new global anti-climate change regime, the difficulties in concluding the Doha Development Agenda (DDA) which has been with us since November 2001, as well as the failure to prevent the 2008 financial and economic turmoil, are evident in this regard. The causes of this lack of efficiency are numerous and include the existence of strongly diverging interests, agendas, commitments and understandings of the *res publica*.

The joint achievement of both legitimacy and efficiency proves to be very hard in multilateral institutions. An increase in the number of participants – a necessary but still insufficient step for enhanced legitimacy – indeed impedes the leverage to tackle complex concerns and agree on structural changes. In this respect, the assessment of the upgrade of the G20 at the heads of state and government level in 2008 must be nuanced. On the one hand, it is a positive development integrating more countries in the coordination of international economic development. On the other hand, the forum has still failed to clearly define and implement its post-crisis management agenda. This is mainly due to the absence of shared perspectives and converging interests among the members of the group. The DDA offers another example of stalemate caused by the presence of a large range of actors. In this context, states are often reluctant to compromise in a negotiation where the 'single undertaking' principle is still applicable.

The time when major deals were settled in the framework of small self-selected groups like the G7 and QUAD has definitely gone. The increase in the number of necessary participants around the table requires every actor to be more flexible and to be ready to make more concessions.

The legitimacy and efficiency problems inherent in multilateralism generate strong incentives for states to prioritise bilateral negotiations. The possible emergence of a G2 between the United States and China as well as the growing use of preferential and free trade agreements mirror this tendency. This can have both positive and negative consequences on multilateral negotiations. If a G2 materialises, it would have the potential to find breakthroughs between these two pivotal actors. It would nevertheless also have the side effect of decreasing the leverage of the other members of the international community. To a certain extent, the failure of the summits to address the pressing issue of climate change can be explained by the existence of trade-offs between China and the US prior to the meetings in Copenhagen and Cancún.

It is in this context that China and the EU with their strengths and shortcomings are trying to influence the agenda-setting, decision-making and reform of global governance.

CHINA'S RISE AND THE REFORM OF GLOBAL GOVERNANCE

The various contributions have emphasised the main characteristics of the Chinese re-emergence. It can be described as a gradual and cautious process, largely conditioned by domestic and international contexts, which is allowing China's power to rise in the international arena.

Concerning China's contribution to multilateralism, it appears that it generally adopted a low profile during the first years of its participation in the multilateral processes. A patient learning process has increased the Chinese ability to influence and to fully benefit from its integration into the international system. A telling example is the World Trade Organization (WTO), to which China acceded in 2001. China's evolving strategy before the WTO Dispute Settlement Body constitutes a clear example of a gradual learning process that has enabled it to gain confidence and to become an active complainant against the US and the EU.

Instrumentalism is still the main driver explaining Chinese action in multilateral institutions. These are mainly considered as tools to enhance multipolarity in the contemporary world. The degree of Chinese implication depends thus to a great extent on the interests that China has in a negotiation. The analysis of the DDA shows that when China has a weak interest in cooperating in the discussions, it is extremely reluctant to play a leadership role. Leadership can prove to be counterproductive for a country that regularly affirms its developing country status alongside its re-emergence.

It is clear that the ability of China to be a strong actor on the international stage is heavily influenced by its domestic situation. In this respect, the PRC still has many challenges ahead. These range from the fight against income inequalities, pollution and energy costs and the existence of speculative bubbles to the maintenance of social and political stability.

Accordingly, the PRC leaders are aware that Chinese 'peaceful development' heavily depends on the policy of foreign states. The mixed strategy of containing and integrating China into the international community, as endorsed by other major powers, conditions the possibilities for Chinese influence. On the one hand, the EU and the US remain highly cautious towards the Chinese rise and sometimes develop strategies not far from containment. The retention of the arms embargo is an example of such a strategy. On the other hand, at other levels strong pressure is applied to China to assume its role of a responsible international player. In this respect, the EU regularly pushes China to be a responsible negotiator in the DDA, which implies that it should assume a leadership role in the WTO.

Thanks to its membership, growing economic power and improving competence, China has become increasingly active in international institutions. This involvement has been a driving force of the Chinese re-emergence and Beijing has benefited a lot from collaboration with other states, particularly the other members of the BRICS and African countries. China is seeking a good balance between adapting to and shaping the international fora. It has appreciated the rules of most of the international institutions and is now trying to influence and reform them.

NECESSARY READJUSTMENT FOR EUROPE IN A CHANGING WORLD

China's re-emergence and the global shifts in the balance of power it entails are not without impact on the EU. The latter's member states were strongly influential at the time the multilateral system was created. Since then, the EU has struggled to become – and remain – a strong international actor. The various contributions to this volume have shown that the question whether the EU disposes of an exclusive or shared competence or not has a major impact on European ability to influence global processes and benefit from the strengths of its soft power. Unity is furthermore still very difficult to achieve and internal decision-making processes are often excessively time-consuming. The EU's preoccupation with internal dynamics and interests is sometimes very detached from the priorities and constraints of third states.

In a time when rising economies and particularly China are keen to elevate their informal and formal influence in international institutions, the fragile ability of the EU to act internationally becomes increasingly problematic. Many voices are calling for a decrease in the European representation within international organisations. The EU and its member states are criticised for having too strong but also sometimes too varied a voice when participating in international institutions.

In spite of these shortcomings, the EU is still a key actor in the international arena thanks to its combined historical influence, strong economic power and interdependence with other actors. The contributions to this volume indicate, however, that the entry into force of the Treaty of Lisbon – which aimed to strengthen the EU's ability to be an international actor through the creation of, *inter alia*, a High Representative for Foreign Affairs and Security Policy, a European External Action Service and Union Delegations around the world – has not significantly improved Europe's international influence so far. The lack of clarity surrounding this new institutional framework, as well as the difficulties for the EU to speak with one voice, explain to a large extent the shortcomings of Europe's international status.

CHINA–EU RELATIONS: WHAT CONTRIBUTION TO GLOBAL GOVERNANCE?

The unprecedented nature of China's rise explains to a large extent the dynamics underpinning China–EU relations, particularly in international organisations. Although European countries and China have interacted for centuries before the launch of official diplomatic relations between the EC and China in 1975, it is nevertheless the first time in history that the EU and China are concomitantly contributing to shape a new world order in which the former occupies a somewhat weaker position than the latter.

A combination of mutual misperceptions, competing interests in regions (especially in Africa), clashes of values and diverging interpretations of sovereignty and non-interference make bilateral interactions difficult to cope with. In this context, international fora often appear to be relevant venues to discuss common concerns. Multilateralism indeed allows third countries' interests to be integrated into the debate as well as a shared legal order. Nevertheless, the differences and competing interests of China and the EU strongly impede the strategic nature of the bilateral relationship. It makes it therefore difficult for both actors to jointly contribute to the restructuring of the institutions and instruments of global governance.

The contributions to this volume have also shown that the interactions between China and the EU in the international arena are strongly dependent on the policies undertaken by other actors, particularly the US. Many international projects require, therefore, at least the support of the three actors. This is, for instance, particularly true with regard to the struggle to restore financial stability. However, a strategic triangle between the US, China and the EU is still a long shot. The US remains the main pole of influence for both China and the EU.

Opportunities for deeper engagement leading to enhanced multilateralism do exist for the EU and China. The contributors have shown that this is possible for both non-traditional and traditional security concerns. Reference was made to possible synergies and collaboration in the context of the FOCAC and EU–Africa summits, the joint interest to revolutionise the world energy system, as well as the possible participation of the EU in the six-party talks.

To upgrade the EU–China relationship and make it achieve a major and sustainable contribution to the reform of global governance, we consider that three developments are necessary. Firstly, the EU and China should enhance their mutual knowledge and trust. Contrary to the relations with the US, the relationship between both actors is not rooted in a deep historical heritage; in spite of centuries-old relations with individual European countries, the EU remains a somewhat novel and intriguing construct for the Chinese. Mutual learning and empathy are therefore necessary to develop a stable and successful cooperation in multilateral organisations. Secondly, reflexivity in the relationship is needed to develop a mature and realistic partnership. China and the EU launched a Comprehensive Strategic Partnership back in 2003. Since then, developments have produced both hopes and disappointments. In a nutshell, the interactions have become increasingly comprehensive but have failed to become truly strategic. The bilateral dialogue covers indeed a very broad range of issues but both actors still fail to meet the great expectations attached to the cooperation. In this respect, it is necessary to pragmatically agree on a shared agenda and to set priorities. One of them should definitively be the reform of global governance. Thirdly, China and the EU should continue using multilateral institutions as an instrument to discuss their bilateral and global concerns. They should also continue their commitment to international legal norms and principles that guarantee the stability of the international order. Engaging in international institutions is the best way to ensure the viability of multilateralism.

In the end, only through sincere dialogue, thoughtful reflection and reliable engagement can the EU and China contribute to the necessary reshaping of global governance.

Index